AUTHORITARIANISM
AND
DEMOCRATIZATION

Gerardo L. Munck

AUTHORITARIANISM AND DEMOCRATIZATION

Soldiers and Workers in Argentina, 1976–1983

The Pennsylvania State University Press
University Park, Pennsylvania

Gerardo L. Munck is Associate Professor of Political Science at the University of Illinois at Urbana-Champaign.

Library of Congress Cataloging-in-Publication Data

Munck, Gerardo L. (Gerardo Luis), 1958–
  Authoritarianism and democratization : soldiers and workers in Argentina, 1976–1983 / Gerardo L. Munck.
      p.   cm.
  Includes bibliographical references (p.   ) and index.
  ISBN 0-271-01807-0 (cloth : acid-free paper)
  ISBN 0-271-01808-9 (paperback : acid-free paper)
  1. Argentina—Politics and government—1955–1983. 2. Authoritarianism—Argentina—History—20th century. 3. Civil-military relations—Argentina—History—20th century. 4. Military government—Argentina—History—20th century. 5. Argentina—Armed Forces—Political activity—History—20th century. 6. Labor movement—Political aspects—Argentina—History—20th century. 7. Democracy—Argentina—History—20th century. I. Title.
  JL2031.M78   1998
  320.982'09'047—DC21   98-7195
                                                                            CIP

Copyright © 1998 The Pennsylvania State University
All rights reserved
Printed in the United States of America
Published by The Pennsylvania State University Press,
University Park, PA 16802-1003

It is the policy of The Pennsylvania State University Press to use acid-free paper for the first printing of all clothbound books. Publications on uncoated stock satisfy the minimum requirements of American National Standard for Information Sciences—Permanence of Paper for Printed Library Materials, ANSI Z39.48-1992.

To Lisa

and to my mother and father

Contents

List of Figures　　　　　　　　　　　　　　　　　　　　　xi
Acknowledgments　　　　　　　　　　　　　　　　　　　xiii
Abbreviations　　　　　　　　　　　　　　　　　　　　　　xv
Overview　　　　　　　　　　　　　　　　　　　　　　　xvii

Part I. Introduction

1. The Political-Institutional Model: A Conceptual Framework for Regime Analysis　　　　　　　　　　　　　　　　　　3

    The Political-Institutional Model: Some Basic Principles
    The Phase of Origin: The Seizure of Power and the Challenge of Constitutional Definition
    The Phase of Evolution: The Challenge of Institutionalization
    The Phase of Transition: The Challenge of Removing the Old Governing Elites from Power
    Conclusion: The Uses of the Political-Institutional Model

2. The Political Dynamics of Bureaucratic Authoritarianism: The Problem of Representation and Conflicting Imperatives　　24

    The Concept of Bureaucratic Authoritarianism: Attributes and Cases
    The Political Dynamics of Bureaucratic Authoritarianism

    The Problem of Representation: The Achilles' Heel of Bureaucratic Authoritarianism □ The Governing Elites: Conflicting Imperatives and Military Dilemmas □ The Ruled: Labor Options and the Reconstitution of Labor as a Political Actor □ The Coalition of Support: The Functional Alliance Between Economic Elites and the Military Rulers

    Conclusion: The Uses of the Argentine Case Study

Part II. Origin

3. The Installation of Military Rulers, and the Assault on Labor in Argentina, 1976　　　　　　　　　　　　　　　49

    The Making of the Coup: Labor, Peronism, and Generalized Crisis
    The Installation of Military Rulers: Assuming the Management of the State

    The Overlap Between the Military as Institution and the Military as Government: The Military's Corporate

Pact □ The Presidency and the Cabinet: Ambiguities at the Top Level of Government □ Colonization of the State Apparatus: The "Feudalization of the State" □ Implications of the Military's Interim Institutional Arrangement

The Assault on Labor and Its Allies: Completing the Transition from the Old Regime

Conclusion

4. The Military's Project and the Reconstitution of Labor in Argentina, 1976–1979   71

The Military's Decision to Address the Challenge of Constitutional Definition: The End of War . . . The Beginning of Politics

The Reconstitution of Labor as an Actor: From Defeat to Weak Opposition

Basic Elements of a Disorganized Actor □ The Emergence of a Compliant Labor Leadership □ The Consolidation of Two Competing Labor Groupings □ The Division Between Collaborationists and Confrontationists, and the Pitfalls of Hyperautonomy

Facing Up to the Challenge of Constitutional Definition: The Military's Political Failure

Governing Elite Cohesion, Opposition Strength, and the Interim Institutional Arrangement □ The Unveiling of the Military's Proposal

Conclusion

Part III. Evolution

5. The Dynamics of a Political Situation in Argentina, 1980–1982   105

The Dynamics of a Political Situation

Ongoing Divisions Within the Governing Elites: The Issue of Presidential Succession □ Governing Elites, the Institutional Arrangement, and the Ruled: Societal Responses to the Military's Project □ The Making of a Tenuous "Political Situation": Characterizing and Explaining the Political Dynamics of Bureaucratic Authoritarianism

From a Political Situation to a Political Crisis

The Failure of Liberalization: Military Splits and Societal Opposition □ The Making of a Political Crisis: Explaining and Understanding the Significance of the Palace Coup

Conclusion

Contents ix

Part IV. Transition

6. Reform Through Rupture and Democratization in Argentina, 1982–1983   133

    From Political Crisis to the Initiation of a Transition

        Triggering the Transition: Return to the Sources, Protests, and War □ Explaining the Initiation of the Transition: The Role of Domestic and Societal Dimensions

    Reform Through Rupture as a Mode of Transition

        Military Weakness and Opposition Confrontation: The Opposition's Agenda □ Signs of Opposition Accommodation: The Military's Last Hope for Gaining Assurances □ Electoral Polarization and Antimilitary Reaction: The Defeat of the Military's Search for Assurances

    Conclusion

Part V. Conclusion

7. The Argentine Case in Comparative-Historical Perspective   165

    Bureaucratic Authoritarianism in Comparative Perspective

        The Argentine Case Summarized □ Comparative Perspective I: Chile Under General Pinochet □ Comparative Perspective II: The Brazil of the Generals

    The Political Dynamics of Bureaucratic Authoritarianism

        The Phase of Origin: The Challenge of Constitutional Definition □ The Phase of Evolution: The Challenge of Institutionalization □ The Phase of Transition: The Challenge of Removing the Old Governing Elites from Power

    Bureaucratic Authoritarianism in Historical Perspective

        Failures and Legacies □ The Argentine Case

    Conclusion: Regime Analysis and the Political-Institutional Model

Appendix A: Summary Chronology of Events   207
Appendix B: Number of Affiliates of Major Labor Unions   213
Appendix C: Basic Economic Indicators   215
Notes   217
References   283
Index   326

List of Figures

1.1	The Political-Institutional Model	8
1.2	Modes of Transition	20
2.1	The Defining Attributes of Bureaucratic Authoritarianism	29
7.1	Bureaucratic Authoritarianism in Argentina, Chile, and Brazil	172

Acknowledgments

The process of researching and writing this book has been a long one, and I have therefore incurred many personal debts. In Argentina, invaluable assistance with my research was provided by Silvio Feldman, Rosendo Fraga, and Héctor Palomino. A long list of academics and trade unionists were also generous enough to share with me their ideas and experiences. They include Elvio Ramón Agazzoni, Felipe Alberti, Carlos Anibal Azocar, José Baddouh, Marcelo Cavarozzi, Héctor Domeniconi, José Ferreri, Ricardo Gaudio, Néstor Alfredo Gómez de Saravia, Rogelio Claudio Ianella, Bernardo Kosacoff, Edgardo Lifschitz, Claudio Lozano, Eduardo Lucita, Iris Martha Roldán, Raúl E. Mathiu, Luis Mayo, José Nieva, Ofelia Pianetto de Costa, Juan Carlos Ponce, Héctor Roudil, Andrés Thompson, and Juan Carlos Torre. The generous support of the Center for Iberian and Latin American Studies (CILAS), the Office of Graduate Studies and Research, and the Department of Political Science, all at the University of California, San Diego, made this field work possible in the first place. At the University of Illinois, I had the good fortune of working in the collegial and supportive environment fostered by Pete Nardulli. Finally, working with Sandy Thatcher and Peggy Hoover of Penn State Press was a very rewarding and constructive experience.

Many people have also been generous in commenting on various parts of this book. In its first incarnation, as my dissertation, I benefited from the input from my committee, composed of Paul Drake, as chair, Ellen Comisso, Peter Smith, Carlos Waisman, and Leon Zamosc. In its current form, I owe particular thanks to two people who read and provided useful comments on the entire manuscript: James McGuire and Deborah Norden. I also benefited from comments on part of the book by Jeff Bosworth, Greg Konstantinov, Alex Kozhemiakin, and David Longenecker. These comments have made this a better book and, as usual, any errors are my responsibility. In addition, long conversations with David Longenecker helped me clarify the implications of my own thinking about political regimes beyond the Latin American context, and exchanges with David Collier helped me clarify the basic goals of this book.

Beyond this group of people, I must acknowledge some influences that either have oriented the research presented in this book or made this research possible in the first place. My brother Ronnie is a major reason why I ever became interested in the study of Latin America, and Frank McCann, my first teacher on Latin America, did much to set me on an academic path. Along this path, Richard Fagen and Wayne Cornelius have been very generous to me. Finally, much of what I have done in this book would not have been possible without the sense of direction that I drew from the work of some distinguished scholars. As the reader of this book will easily see, much of my thinking about political regimes has been greatly influenced by David Collier, Manuel Antonio Garretón, Juan Linz, Guillermo O'Donnell, and Philippe Schmitter. To them I owe an important intellectual debt.

On a more personal note, my wife and companion, Lisa, has supported me in the long years I worked on this book. Her understanding and company have made these years, and the writing of this book, a much happier experience than it would have been otherwise. My mother and father in Buenos Aires, for their part, have provided me with the support that made the intellectual journey that resulted in this book possible. My debt to them is so great that it could not possibly be repaid.

Abbreviations

AOT	Textile workers' union (Asociación Obrera Textil de la República Argentina)
ATE	State workers' union (Asociación Trabajadores del Estado)
CAL	Legislative Advisory Commission (Comisión Asesora Legislativa)
CGT	General Labor Confederation (Confederación General del Trabajo)
CGEC	Commerce workers' union (Confederación General de Empleados de Comercio de la República Argentina)
CGT	General Labor Confederation (Confederación General del Trabajo)
CGT-RA	CGT of the Argentine Republic (CGT de la República Argentina)
CGyT	Labor Action Commission (Comisión de Gestión y Trabajo)
CNT	National Labor Commission (Comisión Nacional de Trabajo)
CUTA	United Leadership of Argentine Workers (Conducción Unica de Trabajadores Argentinos)
FATLyF	Light and power workers' union (Federación Argentina de Trabajadores de Luz y Fuerza)
FATPREN	Journalists' union (Federación Argentina de Trabajadores de Prensa)
FOETRA	Telephone workers' union (Federación de Obreros y Empleados Telefónicos de la República Argentina)
ILO	International Labor Organization
Intersectorial	Intersectorial National Labor Commission–Commission of 20 (Intersectorial CNT-20)
ISI	Import substituting industrialization
MID	Movement of Integration and Development (Movimiento de Integración y Desarrollo)
MON	Movement of National Opinion (Movimiento de Opinión Nacional)
MSP	Peronist Syndical Movement (Movimiento Sindical Peronista)

MUSO	Movement of Unity, Solidarity, and Organization (Movimiento de Unidad, Solidaridad y Organización)
Obras Sociales	The union-run social service network
PDC	Christian Democratic Party (Partido Demócrata Cristiano)
PJ	Peronist Justicialist Party (Partido Justicialista)
Proceso	Process of National Reorganization (Proceso de Reorganización Nacional)
SEGBA	The state-run electrical power company, Servicios Eléctricos del Gran Buenos Aires
SMATA	Auto workers' union (Sindicato de Mecánicos y Afines del Transporte Automotor)
UCR	Radical Civic Union (Unión Cívica Radical)
UIA	Argentine Industrial Union (Unión Industrial Argentina)
UOCRA	Construction workers' union (Unión Obrera de la Construcción de la República Argentina)
UOM	Metal workers' union (Unión Obrera Metalúrgica de la República Argentina)

Overview

The analysis of political regimes and regime change—regime analysis for short—has been a central agenda in comparative politics for the past thirty years. Concerned first with the authoritarian regimes that emerged in interwar Europe, this research agenda flourished in the context of the study of Southern Europe and Latin America, as researchers focused on the changing problem of the day: first the breakdown of democracies, then the nature of the ensuing authoritarian regimes, subsequently the transitions from authoritarian rule, and finally the consolidation of new democracies. By the late 1980s, this research agenda acquired an even broader scope, as researchers responded to the sweeping move from authoritarianism by extending their comparisons to include Eastern Europe, the Soviet Union, East Asia, and parts of Africa.

The importance of this literature is shown by the fact that it has dealt with the core issues at the heart of politics, broadly conceived, in the age of the nation-state. Stated succinctly, regime analysis has been concerned with the diversity of political arrangements that determine who rules and how rulers relate to those they rule, and with the creation, consolidation, evolution, and demise of such national political arrangements. Indeed, the fundamental nature of such questions has made regime analysis one of the key sites of theory-building within comparative politics.

There is, however, one important task that regime analysts have not adequately addressed: the task of synthesis. In a sign of the vitality of this research agenda, the key contributors to this research agenda have sought to analyze the changing concerns of their time. They have not, however, engaged in a concerted effort to synthesize the various bodies of literature that have been generated along the way. This emphasis on tackling new issues over resolving old ones has not hindered the advance of regime analysis up to this point. But as regime analysis has expanded to include more and more strands of research, and as the debate on democratization in recent years has generated an explosion of contributions, the continued generation and accumulation of knowledge increasingly hinges on such an effort at synthesis. The need for an explicit characterization of regime analysis as a research program, in other words, has become more urgent.

This book seeks to contribute to the agenda of regime analysis by responding to just such a need. The current effort at synthesis, however, should be qualified. This book does not seek to provide a synthesis of all the empirical literature that fits under the label of regime analysis or to provide a sweeping analysis of the historical developments regime analysts have studied. Rather, the synthesis this book attempts is of a conceptual nature. That is, this book combines insights from a variety of bodies of literature that developed separately and that were never brought together. Then, on the basis of an exploration of the linkages, consistencies, and contradictions within the literature, a novel conceptual framework is proposed.

The usefulness of this conceptual framework is subsequently assessed through an analysis of a form of rule that was particularly significant in the recent history of South America: bureaucratic authoritarianism. First, the phenomenon of bureaucratic authoritarianism is defined and a generic challenge faced by all bureaucratic authoritarian rulers is highlighted. Next, an in-depth study of Argentina's experience with bureaucratic authoritarianism between 1976 and 1983 is provided. The driving concern is to show how the proposed conceptual framework helps to answer the key questions, which are of a comparative nature, that emerge from a consideration of Argentina's experience with bureaucratic authoritarianism: Why were Argentina's military rulers only partially successful in designing a new institutional order? Why did the military rulers thoroughly fail to provide the institutional basis for a stable form of rule? And why did the military eventually relinquish power in a particularly precipitous and uncontrolled manner? Finally, the implicitly comparative study of Argentina is turned into an explicitly comparative exercise through the addition of the comparable cases of Chile during the 1973–90 period and of Brazil during the 1964–85 period. The point of this exercise is to use the cases of Chile and Brazil to test the hypotheses that were initially formulated and preliminarily tested through the study of Argentina.

Thus, the aim of this book is not to carry out the encyclopedic task of bringing together all we have learned about political regimes in the last thirty years or so. Rather, this book makes a more modest attempt to formulate a synthesis of the contributions made by regime analysts and to show how the resulting conceptual framework, what I call a political-institutional model, can be applied to the analysis of bureaucratic authoritarianism by studying Argentina in comparative perspective.

The Political-Institutional Model: A Conceptual Framework

Seeking to contribute to the work on regime analysis, this book first provides a conceptual framework that synthesizes the broad literature that has been generated by students of political regimes and regime change. The reason for such an endeavor is that the research on political regimes and regime change that has been carried out for more than three decades has not been brought together in an encompassing manner, making it difficult to gain an appreciation of the implicit and underlying assumptions that give coherence to this body of research and that truly make it a research program. As this research program broadens its empirical scope, seeking to incorporate cases that are not part of Southern Europe and Latin America, the two regions that were originally at the center of this research agenda, the need for an explicit characterization of regime analysis as a research program has become more imperative. Otherwise, there is a real danger that there will be a tendency to reinvent the wheel and, even more serious, that the very ability to accumulate knowledge will be impeded.

If the value of such an endeavor is apparent, the formulation of such a synthesis is anything but a simple matter. There can be no doubt that different authors would conceptualize this agenda in distinct manners, placing more or less emphasis on different issues. Such divergences are probably inevitable, and a discussion of these divergences is certainly needed if the agenda of regime analysis is to be refined and advanced. Thus, no claim to definitiveness or unanimity is made here. The point, rather, is that such a debate concerning the appropriate manner of synthesizing the literature on regime analysis has not been carried out until now and that the current effort seeks to contribute to such a debate.

The present attempt to synthesize the literature on regime analysis and to elaborate what can be called a political-institutional model of regime change and regime functioning starts with what is the most fundamental point made in this literature: the distinction between fluid and structured moments in politics. This is a most basic distinction because it provides the basis for distinguishing variable patterns of interaction between actors and institutional rules, thus providing the rationale for distinguishing between three phases in the life cycle of an attempt at regime founding, each one characterized by a distinct actors-to-institution relationship: an initial phase of origin, during which actors seek to design institutions; a subsequent phase of evolution, during which the newly created institutional arrangement potentially provides the framework for the actions of actors as well as for the interaction among actors; and, finally, a phase of transition, during which actors reject established institutions and displace the elites that have supported these institutional rules. These three phases, in turn, provide a way to characterize the changing dynamic of political regimes and to analytically distinguish and connect the central explanatory challenges in regime analysis.

A full presentation and justification of this political-institutional model is offered in Chapter 1. In this Overview, therefore, only a brief discussion of the model is provided, in order to introduce the key concepts used throughout this book and the core questions addressed in regime analysis. (For a summary presentation of the overall model, the reader can turn to Figure 1.1 in Chapter 1.) Regime analysis begins, logically, with the study of the phase of origin, the moment when a new actor displaces the rulers of the old regime and attempts to define an institutional framework that embodies its vision of a new political order. The explanatory challenge, thus, is to account for the ability of the new governing elites to design institutions that would provide the framework for a new political regime, or, in other words, to account for the ability of the new governing elites to respond to the challenge of constitutional definition.

Because of the very plastic nature of politics during the phase of origin, attempts at explanation have highlighted, on the one hand, the creative power of actors by drawing attention to the new governing elites that aspire to found a new political regime and, in particular, to the degree of cohesion of the new governing elites as they go about consolidating their newly acquired power. On the other hand, explanations have also stressed that the new governing elites do not operate in a vacuum. Most important, they are likely to be affected by the degree of opposition offered by the displaced forces, and the interim institutional arrangement that they may have devised as a way of dealing with the short-term imperative of managing the state. It is the interplay among these three factors, in effect, that explains the new governing elites' success or failure in meeting the challenge of constitutional definition and that determines whether the process of regime formation enters a second phase, of evolution; whether the new governing elite must confront the challenge of constitutional definition anew, with even fewer prospects of success; or whether this elite must directly acknowledge the aborted nature of their attempt at regime foundation.

In the following phase, of evolution, the dynamics of politics is affected by a new element that was not present in the previous phase. This is so because the opening of this phase presupposes at least a partially successful response to the challenge of constitutional definition, which results in the introduction of a new set of institutional rules. While actors continue to have great analytical importance, then, what is distinctive about this phase is that the institutional rules that the governing elites themselves created in the previous phase begin to have an independent impact on the political process. This crucial point can easily be missed, because the challenge at the center of the phase of evolution is the challenge of institutionalization—the transformation of the newly created institutional rules into rules that are accepted and routinely used by all major political forces. In one sense, therefore, the importance of institutions is the outcome that must be explained. Nonetheless, these very institutional rules can be properly used as an explanatory factor.

The governing elites' success in tackling the challenge of institutionalization, indeed, comes from the interaction among the governing elites, those they rule over, and the institutional arrangement they have designed. As in the previous phase, the degree of cohesion of the governing elites continues to be a key factor, now through its effect on the ability of the governing elites to pattern their own behavior according to the very rules they have created, as well as to enforce these rules on those they govern and to sanction those who seek to bypass them. But the process of institutionalization is a result of a more complex interplay of factors. On the one hand, it is affected by the institutional arrangement the governing elites seek to institutionalize, partly because the new institutions affect the cohesiveness of the governing elite and partly because they affect the orientation of societal actors as a result of their differential capacity to process conflict and accommodate change. On the other hand, it is also affected by a complex process of actor formation within society, a process that depends on society's organizational efforts and on the actions of governing elites, and that determines, in turn, the strength of societal actors and their ability to constitute a threat or impediment to the process of institutionalization.

As in the previous phase of origin, the possible outcomes to the challenge of institutionalization are quite varied and have significant consequences for the dynamics of politics. At one extreme, if the governing elites are successful in tackling the challenge of institutionalization, the process of regime formation will have been completed, making the stable persistence of the newly founded political order or national political regime quite likely in the near future. At the other extreme, if none of the significant political actors accepts the proposed institutional rules, the failed response to the challenge of institutionalization generates a political crisis, making the displacement of the governing elite—that is, a transition—increasingly likely. Finally, in between these two outcomes, a partially successful response to the challenge of institutionalization gives rise to what could be labeled a political situation—characterized by the coexistence of dominant actors who accept the proposed institutional rules alongside other, relevant actors who do not accept these rules—which makes the unstable persistence of the proposed political order the likely outcome in the near future. In sum, the different outcomes to the challenge of institutionalization determine the extent to which politics becomes truly structured by institutional rules or, to put it differently, the extent to which a new political order is actually shaped.

In the final phase, the transition stage, as in the phase of origin, politics once again takes on a plastic quality. Rather than hinging on the creative power of actors, as in the phase of origin, however, the politics of this phase depends more on the destructive power of actors. Indeed, the distinct challenge actors in the phase of transition face is the challenge of removing the old governing elites from power and establishing themselves as the new power holders—that is, the new governing elites. The distinctiveness of transition processes notwithstanding, a transition can be linked to the dynamics during the preceding phase of evolution, given that it represents but the most extreme failure of the effort of a governing elite to institutionalize a political order, and it can be explained thus in terms that draw on but extend the analysis of the phases of evolution. What is at stake, in short, is whether the interaction between the governing elites, those they rule over, and the institutional arrangements—the same three factors considered in the analysis of the phase of evolution—leads not just to resistance toward, or disregard of, the proposed institutional framework, but, more important, to the development of an actor that is sufficiently powerful to challenge the governing elites and to contend for power.

The occurrence of transitions, then, is explained largely in terms of the rise of actors that are in principled opposition to the prevailing institutional order and that are strong enough to displace the elites that stand for the status quo—that is, in terms of the orientation and strength of the old governing elites and societal actors. But a full explanation of the range of possible modes of transition demands not only an accounting of the identity of the actors that carry out a transition, but also an accounting of the distinct question concerning the strategy whereby the agent or agents of change bring about a transition—that is, whether the emerging elites must accommodate some of the conditions the outgoing elites attempt to impose on them, or whether they can actually succeed in displacing the old elites through a direct confrontation that allows them to set the agenda more fully. Nonetheless, these alternative strategies can be explained in terms of same process of interaction between the governing elites, those they rule over, and institutional arrangements that explains the very occurrence of transitions. Indeed, because strategies used in transitions are determined by the relative power of the antichange sectors within the governing elites vis-à-vis the agent or agents of change, which is but another way of thinking of the orientation and strength of the old governing elites and societal actors, whether a transition occurs or not, and how a transition occurs, can be explained in terms of the same factors.

The political-institutional model, in sum, highlights the specifically political nature of the challenge involved in the various phases of the entire life cycle of a regime-founding attempt and pinpoints the key explanatory variables, and the possible outcomes, during each specific phase. It must be stressed, however, that this conceptual framework is only a general framework and does not tell us anything about empirical cases. The elaboration of substantive arguments about particular attempts at regime founding, indeed, constitutes a second step in regime analysis, a step that draws on the analysis of empirical cases and that, by spelling out substantive arguments in the general terms provided above, shows the usefulness of the conceptual framework introduced in this section. To this step we turn next.

Bureaucratic Authoritarianism: The Substantive Argument

The Concept of Bureaucratic Authoritarianism and the Problem of Representation

The formulation of this book's substantive argument starts in Chapter 2, with an analysis of the concept of bureaucratic authoritarianism— that is, the concept that is used to anchor the empirical analysis. The choice of which political phenomenon one studies, of course, is always somewhat arbitrary. Nonetheless, the choice of focusing on bureaucratic authoritarianism, a subtype of authoritarianism, is quite appropriate in light of the broader aim of this book, which is to provide a sense of regime analysis as a research program. First, it was through the study of authoritarianism that regime analysis originally developed, and it was in the context of authoritarianism that regime analysts debated the issues pertaining to the entire life cycle of a regime-founding attempt. Second, given the existence of cases of authoritarianism that have gone through all the phases highlighted by regime analysis, the study of authoritarianism provides an opportunity for testing the entire political-institutional model this book proposes.

Having selected the concept of bureaucratic authoritarianism as a substantive focus, then, this book first proceeds to clarify the concept's key attributes and the range of empirical cases encompassed by it. As a result, bureaucratic authoritarianism is defined as a subtype of authoritarianism that is characterized by the limited pluralism that characterizes the governing elite, and the lack of extensive and intensive mobilization of the population—two general attributes that bureaucratic authoritarianism shares with other authoritarian forms of rule and that distinguish such authoritarian forms of rule from democratic and totalitarian forms of rule—and by the particular manifestation of these two general attributes, which serve to distinguish bureaucratic authoritarianism from other subtypes of authoritarianism: the rulership by a bureaucratized military institution, in alliance with business elites, and the exclusion of a previously mobilized labor movement. Using this conceptualization, then, examples of bureaucratic authoritarianism include Brazil (1964–85), Argentina (1966–73, 1976–83), Chile (1973–90), and Uruguay (1973–85), as well as Greece (1967–74).

But the purpose of analyzing the concept of bureaucratic authoritarianism is also to identify a generic aspect of the political dynamics of this form of rule and to thus provide a first approximation to the study of this political phenomenon. In this regard, Chapter 2 also highlights a distinctive challenge that is as inescapable as it is unresolvable from the perspective of the bureaucratic authoritarian rulers seeking to found a new political regime. The core of this challenge is that bureaucratic authoritarianism, as a political formula, allows for the existence of preexisting societal interests, and even the growth of societal interests, but is unable to provide a suitable mechanism for interest intermediation. Because these excluded interests, moreover, are not minor but represent instead the interests of labor, an actor that expresses a main cleavage in the societies where bureaucratic authoritarian rule has been established, this challenge is inescapable, in the sense that it must be confronted if a stable form of rule is to be instituted. Bureaucratic authoritarian rulers face, in short, a problem of representation.

To make matters worse, this challenge is unresolvable in that it gives rise to a fatal dilemma from the perspective of bureaucratic authoritarian rulers. Seeking to lay the foundation of a new political order, bureaucratic authoritarian rulers are drawn, on the one hand, to acknowledge the problem of representation. But this exposes these rulers to the danger of a loss of cohesion and/or the threat of opposition from society. Thus, in order to avoid threats to its cohesion or the expression of societal opposition, bureaucratic authoritarian rulers are pushed to ignore the problem of representation, implicitly rejecting any attempt to consolidate their power. The problem of representation, in short, is a challenge that is distinctive of bureaucratic authoritarianism and that, inasmuch as it gives rise to a conflicting imperative that prevents these bureaucratic authoritarian rulers from successfully laying the basis of a new political order or political regime, constitutes the Achilles' heel of bureaucratic authoritarianism. The best bureaucratic authoritarian rulers can aspire to is to shape a "political situation."

Such an analysis, it bears emphasizing, provides no more than a first approximation to the study of bureaucratic authoritarianism, offering no more than an argument concerning the distinctive challenge faced by all bureaucratic authoritarian rulers as opposed to those faced, for example, by democratic or totalitarian rulers, without thereby indicating why different bureaucratic authoritarian rulers may respond to this shared challenge in different ways. In other words, it does not say anything about the different responses bureaucratic authoritarian rulers may give to the shared challenge they all confront or about the varying impact these different responses have on the evolution of bureaucratic authoritarianism. An answer to these questions, indeed, hinges on the more complicated analytical task of integrating the political-institutional model presented in Chapter 1 and the conceptual analysis of the notion of bureaucratic authoritarianism presented in Chapter 2.

Applying the Political-Institutional Model to the Study of Bureaucratic Authoritarianism: The Case of Argentina, 1976–1983

The task of applying the political-institutional model to the analysis of bureaucratic authoritarian rule is first confronted in Chapters 3 through 6, in the context of an in-depth case study of Argentina's 1976–83 experience with bureaucratic authoritarianism. That case study shows how the proposed conceptual framework—the political-institutional model—can be operationalized in the context of the study of bureaucratic authoritarianism. To this end, the investigation about Argentina is organized around three key questions, each linked to one of the three phases posited by the political-institutional model. The orienting question concerning the phase of origin is: Why were Argentina's military rulers only partially successful in designing a new institutional order? Concerning the phase of evolution: Why did the military rulers thoroughly fail to provide the institutional basis for a stable form of rule? Finally, concerning the phase of transition: Why did the military eventually relinquish power in a particularly precipitous and uncontrolled manner?

Although these three questions are phrased in comparative terms, as a single case study, the analysis of Argentina can be only implicitly comparative. The point of this case study, then, is not to show the generalizability of a particular hypothesis, but rather to advance the preliminary but crucial task of showing how the political-institutional model helps to answer these questions, how the causal mechanisms highlighted by this model actually operate as posited, and what constitutes plausible testable hypotheses concerning the different responses bureaucratic authoritarian rulers can give to the shared challenge they all confront and the varying impact on the evolution of bureaucratic authoritarianism of these different responses.

Having generated some testable hypotheses on the basis of the Argentine case, this book turns to the question of the generalizability of the substantive arguments elaborated through the study of Argentina. Indeed, after completing the study of the Argentine case, the hypotheses that were initially formulated and preliminarily tested on the basis of this case are further tested, in Chapter 7, by means of a small-n comparative study that seeks to extend the findings of the Argentine case to two new cases of bureaucratic authoritarianism: Chile during the 1973–90 period and Brazil during the period 1964–85.

The comparison between Argentina, Chile, and Brazil is one of the main contributions of this book. But this explicitly comparative analysis makes sense only in terms of the earlier attempt to connect the political-institutional model to the study of bureaucratic authoritarianism that is carried out in the context of the Argentine case study. Thus, to give the reader an initial sense of how the political-institutional model can be applied to the analysis of bureaucratic authoritarian rule, and how it can be used to explain the variable response that bureaucratic authoritarian rulers offer to the common challenge they face, it is convenient at this point to focus on the argument developed on the basis of the Argentine case. (For the comparative analysis, the reader can directly turn to the final chapter.) The remainder of this section, therefore, provides a quick glance at how the variables highlighted by the political-institutional model help to explain the particular way in which bureaucratic authoritarianism developed in Argentina and, more specifically, how these variables help to answer the three key questions—linked to the three phases, or origin, evolution, and transition—that organize the discussion of the Argentine case.

The Phase of Origin

The phase of origin of bureaucratic authoritarianism in Argentina, discussed in Chapters 3 and 4, starts with the seizure of power, a process that was initiated with a military coup d'état in March 1976 and that was essentially completed by late 1976. Thereafter, the rulers of the Process of National Reorganization (Proceso de Reorganización Nacional, hereafter Proceso), the label the military rulers themselves used to characterize their attempt to found a new political order, turned their attention to the challenge of constitutional definition.

As the new governing elite sought to tackle this essentially political problem of establishing a basis for a new political order, an essential aspect of the dynamic of this process was the interaction between two factors emphasized by the political-institutional model: the degree of cohesion displayed by the new governing elite and the degree of opposition offered by the displaced forces. Argentina's military rulers initially acted in a cohesive manner, seeking to control an opposition force that was perceived as being quite strong with a large dose of repression. But already by the end of 1976, while a rapprochement with society was still rejected by significant sectors of the military rulers, other sectors of the military started to view important societal actors as quite malleable and initiated an opening to society with the purpose of gaining support for the new order the military sought to inaugurate. Thus, the Argentine military responded to the problem of representation that all bureaucratic authoritarian rulers face by partially acknowledging the need to incorporate those actors that represented important interests in society, in such a way that a split was introduced between hard-line elements within the military, who saw no role for compromise with societal forces, and a soft-line wing, which sought to foster "responsible" allies within the labor arena. In short, the decisions made by the military, in response to an opposition that was deemed a target of repression but also partly malleable, resulted in the erosion of the military rulers' cohesion, which in turn, prevented them from tackling the challenge of constitutional definition with any great degree of resolve.

The military's problems were further exacerbated by the third factor highlighted by the political-institutional model—the interim institutional arrangement the military had adopted immediately upon taking power in 1976, in response to the need to assume the management of the state. Indeed, it is important to not overlook the problematic implications of two key aspects of the military's interim institutional arrangement: the temporary nature of the arrangement whereby the Commander-in-Chief of the Army would serve both as a member of the Junta and as president of the country, on the one hand, and the full-scale "colonization" of the state apparatus, an arrangement whereby the three branches of the military participated directly in the management of the state, on the other hand. Time and again, these two features introduced points of contention that would be the focus of a series of heated negotiations, while also generating an incentive that favored factious power struggles rather than unified action. In effect, the military's own choice of interim institutions reinforced the military rulers' lack of cohesiveness and forced them to focus increasingly on their internal problems. The ability of the military to agree on the nature of a political project they could all back was thus severely hampered.

It is not surprising, then, that the military's response to the challenge of constitutional definition was a hesitant and partial one. Indeed, there were severe deficiencies in two documents approved by the military in late 1979, which were offered to the public as the basis for a new political order. On the one hand, the "Political Foundation of the Armed Forces" was an extremely vague and noncommittal document lacking concrete proposals concerning the institutional changes that would undergird the restricted democracy the military rulers ostensibly sought to introduce. On the other hand, the Law of Professional Associations, which aimed at revamping the union structure and setting the basis for a new model of industrial relations, was clear about the concrete institutional changes it envisioned. Nonetheless, because the new labor code worked at cross-purposes with the extensive preparatory efforts by key sectors of the military to foster responsible allies in the labor arena, it too was politically deficient. At best, Argentina's military rulers had been only partially successful in designing a new institutional order.

Why were Argentina's military rulers only partially successful in designing a new institutional order? In a nutshell, the military rulers acknowledged, early on, the need to provide an institutional foundation for the new political order they sought to introduce in Argentina. But in doing so, the military rulers began to fall prey to the conflicting imperative generated by the problem of representation: the need to open channels for the representation of excluded forces in order to provide the basis for a new political order, along with the equally strong imperative to resist any such opening, given its negative impact on the cohesiveness of the military rulers and the opportunities such openings provide for opposition groups in society. Indeed, by attempting to seek allies in society, a course of action that appeared viable in light of the moderate strength of the displaced forces, the military had split. These divisions, moreover, were exacerbated by the interim institutional arrangement. As a result, the military rulers could not agree on a specific political proposal and, after repeated vacillation, finally opted for a technocratic response to the challenge of constitutional definition that essentially refused to acknowledge the political nature of such a challenge. Having sought allies and seen the consequences of such overtures on their cohesiveness, the military rulers in effect decided to retrace their steps and ignore, once more, the need to open channels for the representation of excluded forces. But, remaining divided, the military rulers simply lacked the resolve to design a new institutional order.

The Phase of Evolution

As halfhearted as the response of the military rulers to the challenge of constitutional definition was, it did open a new phase, the phase of evolution of the Proceso, centered around the challenge of institutionalization—the challenge of transforming the set of institutional rules designed in the preceding phase into the horizon within which all relevant actors strategized. One of the most obvious determinants of the military's ability to succeed in tackling this challenge, as Chapter 5 elaborates, was the orientation of societal actors, a factor that was, in turn, partly affected by the perceived appropriateness of the proposed institutional arrangement. Indeed, in the Argentine case, as in all cases of bureaucratic authoritarianism, the attempt to institutionalize the project of the governing elite was hampered because some key societal actors rejected the institutional arrangement proposed by the military rulers. Thus, the very institutional arrangement envisioned by the military's two foundational documents was not accepted by significant societal actors, who rejected them as illegitimate and opposed them in a principled fashion. Coming from actors that were strong enough to be relevant to the institutionalization of bureaucratic authoritarianism, such a principled refusal to accept the proposed constitutional order was sufficient to disrupt and block the process of institutionalization.

But in the Argentine case, the problem facing the military rulers also had its roots in another factor highlighted by the political-institutional model: the ongoing degree of cohesion of the military rulers. In this regard, the ongoing lack of cohesiveness among Argentina's military rulers was quite patent. Indeed, continuing the pattern that was evident during the preceding phase, the military remained divided over just how to deal with society, injecting intramilitary struggles during much of 1980 into key issues, such as the presidential succession. This was very consequential. For one, societal actors began to organize and strengthen, taking advantage of the military's internal problems. Moreover, just as before, when the military's divisiveness had prevented them from agreeing to a specific institutional proposal, now the military's divisiveness prevented them from implementing their somewhat vaguely conceived project with resolve. Thus, the military not only failed to establish a broadly legitimate and thus firmly institutionalized political order, but also fell short even of the more modest goal of enforcing an institutional order that would organize relations between rulers and ruled along legal lines.

Why did Argentina's military rulers thoroughly fail to provide the institutional basis for a stable form of rule? Continuing the pattern set during the phase of origin, the military rulers were undecided about what would be the appropriate response to the problem of representation, vacillating between the option of recognizing key actors, such as trade unions and political parties, and fearing that such a policy would foster activation of opposition, ignoring or even repressing these societal actors. Consequently, they ended up with the worst of both worlds. On the one hand, the military's divisions over the issue of how to respond to societal groups prevented them from backing a legal framework with any convincing degree of resolve. On the other hand, the disunity among the military provided an opportunity for opposition forces to organize. The political dynamics during the phase of evolution was thus shaped in large part by the dialectic and institutionally unmediated relationship between rulers and the ruled. To be sure, this was a relationship in which the military were clearly the dominant actor. But if the military rulers were clearly still in control, as a result of their failures vis-à-vis the challenge of institutionalization, they had not been able to consolidate their power by founding a new political regime, generating instead what could be characterized as a tenuous "political situation."

The Phase of Transition

With the failure of the military rulers to adequately handle the challenge of institutionalization, the possibility of a very different process began to emerge in 1981. As the military's failure to consolidate power became apparent, their removal from power increasingly became a realistic possibility. Indeed, as Chapter 6 shows, the link between the dynamics that began to unfold during the phase of evolution and the unleashing of a transition was quite direct.

The primary impetus for the transition came from society, as the process of actor formation that had begun barely one year after the military rulers assumed power in 1976 continued, and particularly as those forces that expressed a principled opposition to military rule increasingly coordinated their activities throughout 1981. The gradual strengthening of societal opposition forces had a clearly detrimental effect on the military rulers. First, because increased opposition activities led hard-line elements to battle and eventually prevail over those sectors of the military that sought to explore the idea of a political opening with a still very accommodationist societal opposition, the military missed its key opportunity to cut their loses and retreat to the barracks while they had sufficient power to condition a transition. Second, because the opposition spurred the military's hard-line elements to adopt an increasingly erratic pattern of behavior, which culminated in the fatal decision to invade the Falkland/Malvinas Islands in April 1982, the military rulers were quickly faced with the unenviable position of not only being unable to block a transition but, even more dramatic, of not being able to even set the terms of a transition. Indeed, because the self-inflicted defeat at the hands of the British in June 1982 not only pushed the Argentine military to reassess the costs and benefits associated with supporting the existing political order and to abandon their resistance to a transition, but also had weakened the military as a whole vis-à-vis society, they had indirectly strengthened the hands of the opposition and removed the incentive for opposition accommodation. Therefore, Argentina would undergo a "reform through rupture" and, as is characteristic in such a mode of transition, the transition process itself would be relatively uncomplicated, as the agenda of the transition process was basically dictated by the opposition. When the military transferred power to the new civilian rulers in December 1983, a fairly clean break with military rule was established.

The key question concerning the phase of transition, why the military eventually relinquished power and, more precisely, why they did so in a particularly precipitous and uncontrolled manner, can thus be answered as follows. During the phase of evolution, the full consequence of the conflicting imperative to which the military rulers were subjected, as a result of the problem of representation, worked itself out. The weakness of the military rulers was already evident in their failed attempt to tackle the challenge of institutionalization. Indeed, the military rulers' response to the problem of representation had both prevented them from establishing even a legal institutional order that would serve to channel and mediate the relationship between rulers and ruled, and provided the conditions for the formation and strengthening of an actor that sought an end to military rule. From this situation, then, it was but a small step for the societal opposition to become not merely an actor that resisted military rule, but also one that could be an effective force for change. In effect, as the societal opposition gained strength, it essentially pushed the military rulers on a course of action that would force them to change their orientation, in response to the short-term dynamics of political events, and allow an unconditioned transition that brought an end to the cycle that began with the seizure of power by the military.

Organization of the Book

In sum, this book has two key aims. At a conceptual level, it seeks to combine various bodies of literature that developed separately to explain different phases in the development of political regimes. This exercise highlights linkages, consistencies, and contradictions within the literature that have not been adequately examined, and leads to the proposal of a general framework for the study of political regimes. At an empirical level, this book seeks to demonstrate the usefulness of the proposed conceptual framework through the study of Argentina's 1976–83 experience with bureaucratic authoritarianism and through a comparative exercise that tests the hypotheses that initially were formulated and preliminarily tested through the study of Argentina by considering the comparable cases of Chile and Brazil.

To advance this agenda, this book has been organized along the following lines. In Chapter 1, the research program of regime analysis is characterized and the political-institutional model is presented. The reader more concerned with the substantive problem of authoritarianism can turn directly to Chapter 2, where the concept of bureaucratic authoritarianism is discussed and where the generic argument about the problem of representation all bureaucratic authoritarian rulers face is analyzed. Thereafter, Chapters 3, 4, 5, and 6 present the Argentine case, showing how the political-institutional model helps to explain the way in which bureaucratic authoritarianism evolved in Argentina. Chapters 3 and 4 focus on the phase of origin, Chapter 5 on the phase of evolution, and Chapter 6 on the phase of transition. Finally, Chapter 7 recapitulates the argument about the Argentine case, while placing it in a comparative context. In that final chapter, the cases of Chile and Brazil are discussed for the purpose of ascertaining the generalizability of the arguments presented in the study on Argentina. That chapter also goes beyond the discussion offered in the body of this book by placing bureaucratic authoritarianism as a form of rule in a broad historical perspective and by analyzing the legacies of bureaucratic authoritarianism rule in Argentina after the military stepped down in 1983.

Part I
Introduction

Chapter 1

The Political-Institutional Model
A Conceptual Framework for Regime Analysis

Regime analysis—a central concern within comparative politics over the past thirty years—has contributed to our understanding of a series of extremely pressing political concerns. Indeed, starting with an interest in the experience of fascism in Western Europe, this research agenda has advanced in response to the turn of events affecting a wide range of political regimes found in numerous regions of the world. In the 1970s, the focus was on the breakdown of democracy and the nature of the subsequent authoritarian regimes in Southern Europe and Latin America. In the 1980s, the problem of transitions from authoritarian rule in the same two regions gained attention. By the 1990s, interest in the problem of transitions remained strong, now as it affected Eastern Europe, the Soviet Union, East Asia, and Africa; and a new concern, with the consolidation of the democratic governments that emerged throughout the world, moved to the fore. Throughout, the rise of democracy in Western Europe was a constant point of reference. Driven by a concern with this broad-ranging set of substantive concerns, indeed, the work on regime analysis has been one of the most active and vital areas of research in comparative politics over the last twenty-five years.[1]

At the same time, starting with the publication of, and subsequent debate on Guillermo O'Donnell's *Modernization and Bureaucratic Authoritarianism* (1973), a book that in many ways constitutes one of the founding moments of regime analysis as a research program, there has been an important degree of coherence to the inquiries pursued by practitioners of regime analysis. The questions that have been asked about a broad variety of forms of rule—democracy, authoritarianism, bureaucratic authoritarianism, totalitarian, neopatrimonial, and so on—have basically been the same: How do they originate? How are they to be characterized? How do they function? How do they change? This quite remarkable thematic unity has enabled regime analysis to become one of the key sites of theory-building within political science.

Despite the well-acknowledged contributions made by this literature, however, regime analysts have not been very adept at synthesizing the findings of this evolving body of literature. As the field of studies has moved on, keeping up with rapidly changing events in a very fertile manner, no one has pulled together the various strands of research. Interesting linkages have gone unexplored, key contradictions have gone unresolved, important gaps have gone unnoticed, and the overall coherence of regime analysis has never been clearly formulated.

These shortcomings have not hindered its advance up to this point. But, as the research program has expanded to include more and more strands of analysis, and as the debate on democratization in recent years has generated an explosion of collective contributions, which are increasingly global both in terms of the countries they focus on and in terms of the national origin of the contributors, the need for an explicit characterization of regime analysis as a research program has become more urgent. What is at stake is, in a negative sense, that we might forget what we have learned from three decades of research, or, in a positive sense, the very possibility of accumulating knowledge. To avoid the tendency to reinvent the wheel and to continue contributing to theory-building, what is needed is an exercise in retrieval with the intent of providing a theoretical synthesis that could serve both to organize what we have already learned and to orient future research.

The goal of this chapter, then, is to pull together and synthesize this fairly large body of literature and to show how it constitutes a coherent body of research—indeed, a research program—that provides a systematic way of addressing the most important questions that arise in the study of politics.[2] The nature of this synthesis, however, requires clarification. Rather than attempting to synthesize all the empirical literature that fits under the label of regime analysis, and to provide a sweeping analysis of the historical developments regime analysts have studied, this chapter offers a very general conceptual framework by drawing on a variety of bodies of literature that developed separately and have never been brought together with the aim of elaborating a general framework for the study of political regimes and regime change. Subsequent chapters assess the usefulness of this framework by applying it to the study of a specific political phenomenon: bureaucratic authoritarianism. For now, however, the focus is on elaborating a novel conceptual framework—what I call a political-institutional model—that explores the linkages between numerous theoretical debates, resolves apparently contradictory theoretical arguments, fills some important gaps, and makes explicit the coherence of regime analysis as a research agenda.

The Political-Institutional Model: Some Basic Principles

In order to clarify the sense in which regime analysis constitutes a research program, it is crucial to start out by considering the most basic and encompassing concepts around which the literature has been built.[3] In this regard, the most central notion in regime analysis concerns the role of agents in the life cycle of an attempt at regime founding. The point is made most clearly and forcefully by Philippe Schmitter, who argues that the problems of transition and consolidation can be distinguished in terms of how political actors behave. Very succinctly, while in transitional periods, "an exaggerated form of 'political causality' tends to predominate," making outcomes depend on the choices of actors; in consolidated polities, actors are "conditioned" and constrained by "routine" aspects that make "the behavior of actors . . . more predictable."[4] There is thus an "epistemological" divide rooted in the very nature of political action, which serves to distinguish the distinct fields of inquiry Schmitter labels as "transitology" and "consolidology."[5]

If a core insight of regime analysis is that the very nature of politics changes over time, it is imperative that an encompassing regime analysis agenda must acknowledge and conceptualize the changing role of agents and avoid one-sided views that portray actors' behavior as either fully constrained, or not at all constrained, by contextual factors. Short of this, it would be conceptually impossible to synthesize the agenda of regime analysis in a coherent manner. But such an acknowledgment does not take us very far. Indeed, it is necessary to build on the notion that actors can both shape and be shaped by their context of action, a key foundation of regime analysis as an encompassing research program, by spelling out the implications of such a notion. This is what I shall do in outlining the three key and closely connected basic principles of what I will call a political-institutional model.

The first basic principle of a political-institutional model that must be emphasized is the manner in which it conceives of actors and institutions. Seeing politics as fundamentally about the power of actors to make decisions, such a model highlights the role of actors. At the same time, recognizing the insight offered by institutional analysis that much of politics takes place within the limits of preestablished institutional rules, this model emphasizes the complex connection between actors and institutions. The recognition of the importance of institutions as a key contextual factor shaping and constraining the action of actors does not mean that the point at which it makes sense to talk of an actorless process, as institutionalists sometimes do, is ever reached. Rather, institutions are never seen as literally having a life of their own. In the first place, and most obvious, actors must build the institutional frameworks that eventually shape their behavior. Thereafter, actors must decide to pattern their choices and interactions according to institutional rules. And, finally, even once the institutionalization of political life has been completed, the reproduction of institutions remains dependent on the action of actors. Over time, actors may follow institutional rules increasingly less so as a result of a conscious choice and more out of habit. But it remains the case that institutions remain alive only inasmuch as they are used by actors. In other words, actors and their choices never disappear from the picture.

The second basic principle of a political-institutional model, one that follows directly from the first, is that the dynamic relationship between actors and institutions can be spelled out properly only by means of a diachronic model that distinguished among phases, each characterized by a distinct connection between actors and institutions. At the most basic level, the changing relationship between actors and institutions can be captured through a definition of three distinct phases: an initial phase, or phase of origin, during which actors design institutions; a subsequent phase, of evolution, during which actors interact with and through preselected institutions; and finally, a phase of transition, during which actors abandon established institutions.[6] Simple as it is, this distinction between three phases, which is spelled out in greater detail below, plays a fundamental role in organizing the agenda of regime analysis, providing the analytical underpinnings for an effort aimed at distinguishing the various strands of research carried out within regime analysis. As with the phases of birth, adulthood, and death, in a person's life cycle, the phases of origin, evolution, and transition define the distinct processes and crucial turning points in all necessarily tentative attempts of regime founding. By stressing the specific problems pertaining to each particular phase, therefore, this schema provides a lens through which the key explanatory challenges in regime analysis can be identified and located within the overall problematic of regime analysis.

The third basic principle of a political-institutional model, again spelling out the implications of the previous point, is that while regime analysis may focus on one or another analytically distinct phase, its ultimate goal is to fit such phase-specific explanations into a broader analysis that encompasses the entire life cycle of a regime-founding attempt. The point of the distinction between different phases is not only to organize the research agenda into manageable questions, but also to consider the possibility of a synthesis that brings together the research carried out separately on the origin, evolution, and transition of various attempts at regime founding into an integrated research program on regime analysis.

Such a task of synthesis is not easy to advance. On the one hand, there are various bodies of literature on regime analysis that have never been integrated, and, on the other hand, there have been heated debates and serious disagreements over many issues among regime analysts. In what follows, however, I will attempt to build on the basic principles of a political-institutional model and to show that in many instances it is possible to link theoretical debates in a coherent manner and to harmonize apparently contradictory positions, and that in other instances it is necessary to fill gaps in the literature. I proceed by conceptualizing the nature of the problem or challenge at the center of the three distinct phases identified above. Thereafter, I assess how well the factors emphasized in the literature can explain the different ways in which these challenges are tackled. Because the goal of this exercise, it bears emphasizing, is to develop a general model—a model that could be applied to all cases—this search for explanatory factors necessarily moves at a high level of generalization. Much of this chapter, thus, is an effort to draw on a literature focused on specific regimes and on cases, and to conceptualize problems and explanatory factors in such a way that they are applicable across all regimes and cases. We turn now to the presentation of the political-institutional model (summarized in Figure 1.1), focusing on one phase at a time.

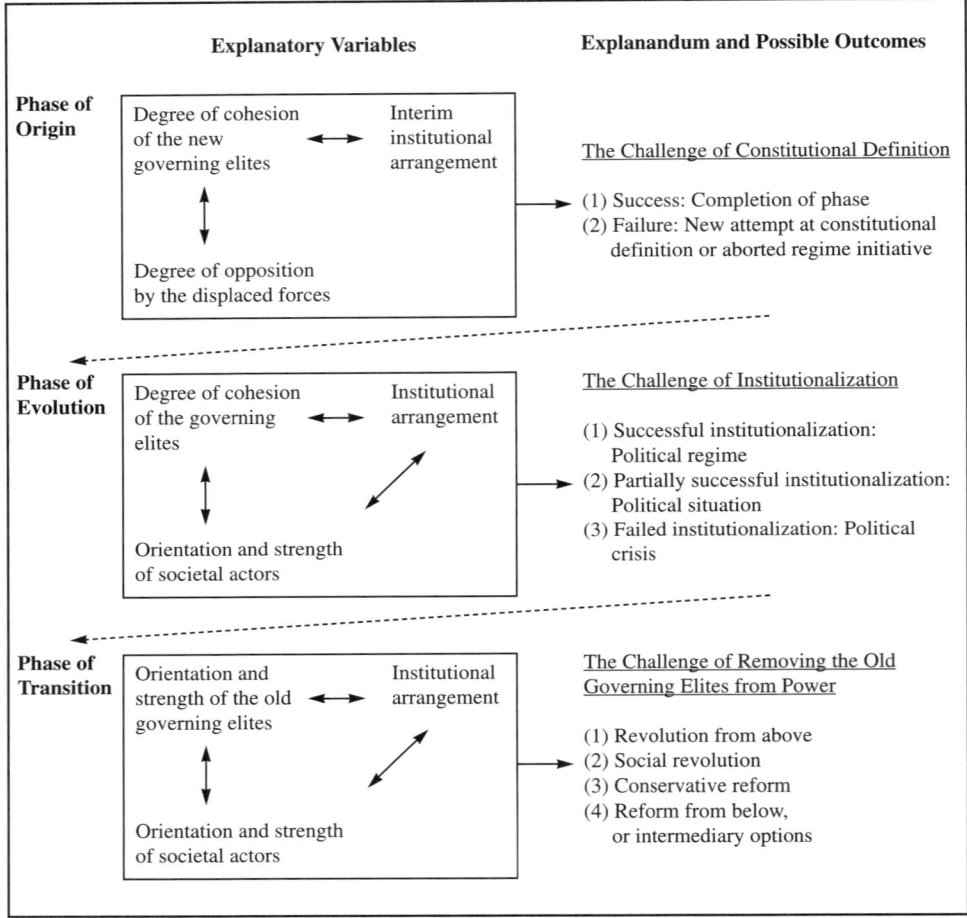

Figure 1.1. The Political-Institutional Model

The Phase of Origin: The Seizure of Power and the Challenge of Constitutional Definition

The attempt to conceptualize the phase of origin of regimes, a moment when the old and the new touch, must start by disentangling the double process whereby regimes are born: the seizure of power by a new elite, and the initiation of an attempt by the new governing elite to consolidate their newly gained hold on power.[7]

The seizure of power or the displacement of the old governing elite by a new elite entails the assumption of the management of the state by, and the formal installation in power of, a new governing elite. As such, this process can affect the shape and prospects of any new regime. But, over and beyond this role, the conceptual significance of the seizure of power for the analysis of regimes is that it brings the transition *from* the previous regime to an end, thus raising the possibility of founding a new order and opening the phase of origin.[8] Indeed, because it does not make sense even to pose the question of regime formation until it is clear that a new elite has seized power, the seizure of power serves as a precondition for any attempt to create a new political order.[9]

If the seizure of power is, thus, merely the point of departure in the analysis of new regimes, the key concern in the study of the phase of origin is the process whereby the new governing elites *initiate* an attempt to consolidate power, a process that involves the defining and institutionalizing of a new political order.[10] The consolidation of power, it is crucial to highlight, can be seen as consisting of two distinct challenges involving rather different processes, which deserve to be analyzed separately. A first challenge, the challenge of constitutional definition, hinges on the design of new institutions. This is an important moment in the attempt of the new elites to consolidate power, because it represents their opportunity to define the outlines of the political order they seek to shape and embed it within an institutional framework. Inasmuch as the new elites are successful in tackling this challenge, however, they are immediately forced to face a new challenge: the challenge of institutionalization. Indeed, as soon as new institutional rules are defined and made public, governing elites must face a second and very different challenge: transform the newly created institutional rules into rules that are accepted and routinely used by all major political forces—the clearest sign of consolidation of the governing elites' power.

For analytical purposes, it is important to study these two distinct processes separately and to focus first on the design of institutions.[11] The first explanatory task that regime analysts face, thus, is to account for the relative success of the new governing elites in meeting the challenge of constitutional definition, whereby the new governing elites attempt to define an institutional framework that embodies their vision of a new political order.[12]

It is surprising that, in tackling this explanatory task, the literature on regime analysis has been relatively silent. Compared with other areas of regime analysis, the literature is underdeveloped with regard to this question.[13] Nonetheless, some important factors that help to account for the ability of the new governing elites to respond to the challenge of constitutional definition have been highlighted in the literature.

Probably the key insight that can be drawn from the literature is that, because of the plastic nature of politics during the phase of origin, it is necessary to highlight the creative power of actors by drawing attention to the new governing elites that aspire to found a new political regime and, in particular, to the degree of cohesion of the new governing elites as they go about consolidating their newly acquired power.[14] That is, even though introducing a new order necessarily entails a visionary or programmatic element that by its very nature is nonpredictable and difficult to study in a systematic manner, the ability of the new governing elite to put forward a vision of a new political order and to design the institutions that would embody this vision hinges quite directly on their ability to act in a unified and concerted manner. Quite simply, if the new governing elite is unable to agree about the nature of the political order they seek to found, they will have defeated their own political aspirations.

The new governing elites, however, do not confront the challenge of constitutional definition in a vacuum. In this regard, there are two types of sequential effects, associated with the very way in which power was seized by the new governing elite, that condition the new governing elites and that have been the subject of some attention.[15] The most commonly studied sequential effect concerns the degree of opposition offered by the displaced forces to the new governing elites, a factor that captures the extent to which the new governing elites are constrained or bound by the old power holders and their supporters as they go about defining a new constitutional structure.[16]

In addition to this factor, which draws attention to the relative power of the outgoing and incoming power holders, there is a less frequently studied sequential effect that is of a more institutional nature, which plays an important role in those cases where the new governing elites assume power *before* the challenge of constitutional definition has been completed.[17] In this scenario, the installation of new governing elites is accompanied by the creation of an interim institutional arrangement that responds to the short-term imperative of managing the state. That is, the seizure of power by a new elite leads to the creation of certain institutional rules that have a clearly temporary or provisional status. This interim arrangement is important, nonetheless, because it provides an institutional constraint on the new governing elite during the very period in which they are attempting to define an institutional framework that embodies their vision of a new political order.[18]

In sum, although regime analysts have paid less attention to the challenge of constitutional definition than to the challenges that affect subsequent phases in the life cycle of an attempt at regime founding, it is possible to begin addressing this gap in the literature by drawing attention to the manner in which the ability of the new governing elites to successfully confront the challenge of constitutional definition is shaped by the interaction among these three factors. A general hypothesis concerning the phase of origin can be advanced in the following terms: The ability of the new governing elites to succeed or fail in meeting the challenge of constitutional definition—the first challenge they must meet in their attempt to consolidate their power—is determined primarily by the degree of cohesion of the new governing elites, as well as two factors that condition and constrain the new governing elite. The two factors are the degree of opposition offered by the displaced forces to the new governing elites, and the interim institutional arrangement that the new governing elites may set up in response to the short-term imperative of managing the state.

In explaining the outcome of the phase of origin, these three factors determine the nature of the challenge that will dominate a country's politics. On the one hand, an elite's success in tackling the challenge of constitutional definition changes the nature of the political process by putting a new challenge, the challenge of institutionalization, on the agenda. In this case, then, the new governing elite's attempt to consolidate power moves ahead and the process of regime formation enters a second phase, the phase of evolution. On the other hand, a failure of the elite to respond to the challenge of constitutional definition makes the issue of institutionalization moot, for the opening of the second phase in the life cycle of a regime-founding attempt is contingent on at least a partially successful response to the challenge of constitutional definition.[19] In that case, then, failure to respond to the challenge of constitutional definition represents a serious setback for the new governing elite's attempt to consolidate power and raises some grim options. Indeed, in this scenario, the new governing elite faces the difficult option of confronting the challenge of constitutional definition anew, under even more adverse conditions as a result of their prior failure, or the plainly dramatic option of acknowledging the aborted nature of their attempt at regime foundation—something that could well provide the opportunity for a new elite to seize power. In sum, the success or failure of the new governing elites in meeting the challenge

12   Introduction

of constitutional definition is a key determinant of the overall development of an attempt at regime founding and the type of issues that will dominate the political agenda.

The Phase of Evolution: The Challenge of Institutionalization

The opening of the second phase in the life cycle of an attempt at regime founding, which starts if and when the new governing elites respond successfully to the challenge of constitutional definition, puts a new issue at the top of the political agenda: the challenge of institutionalization. As soon as the new governing elites manage to define an institutional framework that embodies their vision of a new political order, they are driven by the attempt to transform the newly created institutional rules into rules that are accepted and routinely used by all major political forces. In many ways, this second challenge is linked to the first challenge that governing elites face, constituting a challenge that these elites must face if they are to complete the process of consolidation of power begun during the phase of origin, as well as complete the process of regime formation.[20] But the challenge of institutionalization, the dominant political concern during the phase of evolution, is a distinct challenge. Thus, while an explanation of the ability of the governing elites to meet this new challenge is likely to draw on factors discussed in the analysis of the phase of origin, the phase of evolution must be analyzed in its own right.

In tackling this second explanatory task, we can turn to a wealth of literature. Indeed, in contrast to the situation faced in analyzing the phase of origin, there is no paucity of literature on the issue at the heart of the phase of evolution, and no gap to be filled. There is a problem with this literature, however, related to the apparently contradictory nature of the arguments regime analysts have advanced concerning the impact of force and legitimacy, and of governing elites and non-elites, on the governing elites' hold on power. A brief review of this debate is therefore justified.

One position in this debate, associated with a statist perspective, is that the key factor affecting the ability of governing elites to hold on to power is their ability to coerce or repress, which is seen as a function of their unity or cohesion. This is a position put forth quite forcefully by Theda Skocpol (1979:32), who simply dismisses the problem of legitimacy, stating: "What matters most is always the support and acquiescence not of the popular majority of society but of the politically powerful and mobilized groups, invariably including the regime's own cadres. . . . Even after a great loss of legitimacy has occurred, a state can remain quite stable . . . , especially if its coercive organizations remain coherent and effective." This quite persuasive argument draws attention to the unity or cohesion of the governing elites and the uses of repression, issues that regime analysts ignore at their own peril. But in arguing that the governing elites' hold on power is determined by the governing elites' willing to repress, which hinges in turn on their degree of cohesiveness, and that the legitimacy or lack of legitimacy the government has in the eyes of the population is unimportant, this formulation of the problem articulates a contrast between coercion and legitimacy, and between governing elites and non-elites, that is not very productive.

That formulation ignores, first, how the problem of legitimacy directly affects the cohesion of the governing elites, and hence their capacity to repress. As Juan Linz (1973b:240) states, "questions of legitimacy will inevitably be asked [by the governing elites themselves]. . . . Only praetorian guards or the lowest ranks of a police force do not ask such questions. Anyone in a position of responsibility, one who must kill or die to defend a regime, must ultimately ask questions about why he should do so and whether he should obey in a crisis situation." The legitimacy of the political order that elites seek to uphold, in other words, sheds light on the cohesion of elites and their ability to control the population.[21]

Skocpol's formulation also ignores how the problem of legitimacy affects non-elites in a way that is directly relevant to the governing elites. As institutionalists have argued, political institutions have different degrees of legitimacy, which have clear political consequences. Indeed, the lack of legitimacy of particular institutional arrangements is likely to serve as an impetus not merely for the spread of diffuse feelings of opposition within the general population but, more important, for the formation of actors seeking solutions outside of the existing institutional arrangement.[22] The problem of legitimacy, therefore, affects the very need of the governing elite to repress and the scale of opposition that elites must confront.

In seeking to explain the ability of governing elites to confront the challenge of institutionalization, the key explanatory task in the analysis of the phase of evolution, it is thus crucial to be guided by a formulation of the problem that sees the ability of governing elites to consolidate their power as a function of both coercion and legitimacy and of the governing elites' cohesiveness and the scale of opposition these elites must confront.[23] Moving beyond a statist perspective, this formulation of the problem allows us to resolve arguments usually presented as contradictory. Indeed, it allows us to pursue the highly desirable goal of developing an explanation that combines the different insights regime analysts offer about the interaction between the governing elites, those they rule over, and institutional arrangements.

Proceeding in this fashion, the first insight that should be highlighted is the manner in which the actions of the governing elites are directly relevant to the challenge of institutionalization. First it is incumbent on the governing elites to believe in the institutions they designed in the phase of origin and to pattern their behavior according to the new rules, something that is likely to be directly affected by their ability to remain a cohesive force. But if the governing elites are to successfully meet the challenge of institutionalization, they must not only follow their own rules but also take steps to enforce these rules on those they govern, and sanction those who seek to bypass them, something that will again hinge on their ability to act cohesively. In short, just as the ability of the governing elites to meet the challenge of constitutional definition during the phase of origin is strongly determined by their cohesiveness, so too is their ability to confront the challenge of institutionalization partially a function of the degree of cohesion of the governing elites.

If cohesiveness of the governing elite remains a central explanatory factor, just as it was in the analysis of the previous phase, the analysis of the evolution as opposed to the origin of regimes must also take into consideration a new factor: the institutional arrangement that the governing elites designed during the phase of origin and that they seek to transform into the basis of a new political order in the phase of evolution. As indicated above, the perceived legitimacy of these institutions affects, on the one hand, the cohesiveness of the governing elite, much as the interim institutional arrangement conditions the governing elites during the phase of origin. But the impact of these institutions and their perceived legitimacy goes far beyond the governing elites. Inasmuch as the process of institutionalization depends not only on the governing elites but also on every major actor within society framing their actions within the new institutional arrangement,[24] the linkage between these actors and the proposed institutional arrangement must be considered.

This can be done by focusing on two distinct but connected issues. One issue is the effect that the institutional arrangement has on the orientation of societal actors, the very actors that will be subjected to the caging force of the institutions proposed by the governing elites. It is important to recognize that inasmuch as institutional arrangements have a differential capacity to process conflict and accommodate change, they exercise a pull effect on actors—that is, as a result of their predicted impact, generating different orientations within these actors or different types of opposition that affect the process of institutionalization.[25] Thus, if a particular institutional arrangement does not allow societal actors to express their conflicting demands, it is likely to foster an orientation of *principled opposition* to the proposed institutional order that is not conducive to institutionalization. Alternatively, if an institutional arrangement does allow societal actors to express their conflicting demands, it is likely to foster an orientation of *pragmatic opposition* to the proposed institutional order, which is conducive to institutionalization.[26]

If the perceived legitimacy of the institutional arrangement thus sheds some light on the reason that governing elites may face resistance in their attempt to institutionalize a new political order, it is only in conjunction with a second issue—the strength of societal actors—that we can gain a real sense of the impact societal actors have on the process of institutionalization. Governing elites have little to worry about if the orientation of principled opposition is nothing but a diffuse feeling within the general population. Indeed, it is crucial to clarify that the prospects of institutionalization are inversely related to the strength of principled opposition actors, and that it is only inasmuch as this orientation of principled opposition is held by powerful societal actors that the attempt of the governing elite to institutionalize a new political order is threatened "from below."[27]

To fully grasp the impact of societal opposition on the process of institutionalization, in other words, it is necessary to consider not only the effect that the institutional arrangement has on the orientation of societal actors, but also the complex process of actor formation within society. That is the process—which depends on society's organizational efforts as well as on the actions of governing elites, and which can start as soon as a new governing elite comes to power—that determines the strength of societal actors and their ability to constitute a threat or impediment to the process of institutionalization, or, in other words, their relevance to the process of institutionalization.[28]

In sum, the political dynamics of the phase of evolution is shaped by the interaction between the governing elites, those they rule over, and institutional arrangements. The interaction among these three factors, as the discussion has sought to show, is complex and cannot be easily captured in a succinct statement. The gist of the analysis, however, can be boiled down to a general hypothesis: the ability of the governing elites to succeed or fail in meeting the challenge of institutionalization—the second challenge they must meet in their attempt to consolidate their power—is jointly determined by the degree of cohesion of the governing elites, the effects of the institutional arrangement on both the governing elites and societal actors, and the orientation and strength of societal actors.

As in the analysis of the phase of origin, one can see that this argument sheds light on the variable response by the governing elites to the challenge of institutionalization, a matter that is significant in and of itself. In addition, the possible outcomes to the challenge of institutionalization have important ramifications and are themselves an important determinant of a country's political dynamics in the near future. This point can be spelled out briefly.

If the governing elites are successful in tackling the challenge of institutionalization, the process of regime formation will have been completed. Indeed, only through this outcome can we properly speak of the successful foundation of a new political order or national political regime and the emergence of a new challenge, hinging on the reproduction of institutions—that is, the continued use of already accepted institutions. Success in this task is by no means guaranteed. The path of evolution could therefore involve either stable persistence—that is, the maintenance of a consolidated regime[29]—or deinstitutionalization of the regime.[30] But the likelihood of stable persistence in the near future is greater when the governing elites have responded successfully to the challenge of institutionalization than when they have not.[31]

When the governing elites fail to respond adequately to the challenge of institutionalization, the options they face are much more ominous. If the governing elites are only partially successful at institutionalizing their hold on power—that is, where they are able to ensure that the orientation of dominant actors is one of acceptance of the institutional rules they designed, but where some relevant actors nonetheless display an orientation of principled opposition—the process of regime formation will remain incomplete. In the face of this distinctive outcome, which could be called, following Linz (1973b:235), a political situation,[32] the governing elites may still have a chance at completing the unfinished process of regime formation. A more likely path of evolution in the near future is a pattern of unstable persistence, which could last for some time but which also could devolve into a political crisis characterized by a lack of acceptance of the proposed institutional rules by the dominant actors.[33] Indeed, a political crisis, which can be either the direct outcome of a failed response to the challenge of institutionalization, or the result of the gradual strengthening of actors that display an orientation of principled opposition, is something that is always quite possible in the context of "political situations."[34]

The Phase of Transition: The Challenge of Removing the Old Governing Elites from Power

The first two explanatory tasks that regime analysts face in building a comprehensive framework for the analysis of regimes, as discussed above, hinge on the challenges faced by the governing elites whose seizure of power raises the possibility that a new political order or regime will be founded. As argued, the success of these elites is anything but guaranteed. Nonetheless, because these elites control the government, the very questions that drive the analysis are framed from the perspective of the governing elites. That is, regime analysts ask themselves whether the governing elites will succeed in designing a new institutional framework and whether this framework will be accepted by all major political forces and thus pattern political interaction. This formulation makes sense because the very seizure of power by an elite means that they have established themselves as the main political force in a country and that the country's political dynamics is driven primarily by their initiatives and reactions or resistance to their initiatives.

As analysis moves beyond the phase of origin and evolution and starts to address the issue of regime transition, however, it is crucial to acknowledge that the nature of the challenge that lies at the heart of transition processes is very different from the challenges that frame the analysis of the phases of origin and evolution. Rather than centering around either the design of an institutional framework or the allegiance toward this framework by relevant political forces, transitional processes are all about the raw political confrontation between actors and the power politics through which political initiative changes hands, from the "old" or established elites—those who hold power at a certain point in time—to the contending or emerging elites. The key explanatory task that students of transitions face is therefore best framed from the perspective of the contending elites, as the need to account for the success or failure of emerging elites to meet the challenge of removing the old governing elites from power and establishing themselves as the new power holders—that is, as the new governing elites.³⁵

In tackling this explanatory task, as is the case with the analysis of the phase of evolution, we can turn to a wealth of literature, much of which takes as its point of departure the seminal work of O'Donnell and Schmitter (1986), *Transitions from Authoritarian Rule: Tentative Conclusions About Uncertain Democracies*.³⁶ In developing an explanation of transitions, however, it is crucial to see both how positions advanced as contradictory in the literature do not need to be seen as such, and how some gaps in the literature can be easily filled by linking the discussion about the phase of evolution to the phase of transition better than has been done until now.

While acknowledging the distinctive challenge at the heart of transitions, one of the key concerns of regime analysts has rightly been to identify the actors that could potentially mount a challenge to the old elites. This literature, however, has suffered from two important problems. The first problem concerns the sterile debate that has pitted scholars who see change as coming "from above," due to decisions that sectors of the governing elites themselves make when they realize the need to introduce changes, against scholars who see change as coming "from below"—more as a result of the role of societal actors and popular sector actors in particular than of initiatives coming from sectors of the governing elites.³⁷ There is no reason to present these approaches as contradictory, for these two positions do no more than point to two extreme possible sources of change, which, along with a series of intermediary options, represent the full range of actors that could initiate a transition.³⁸

If this first problem with the literature can therefore be resolved quite easily by conceptualizing the possibility of transitions being initiated by a sector of the governing elites that turns against the status quo, by an actor that emerges within society, or by some combination of both of these actors, a second and more severe problem with the literature on transitions has to do with its ability to go beyond an identification of the actors that could mount a challenge to the old elites and actually explain the source of change. Indeed, there is an important gap in the literature in this regard, in that most of the literature on transitions takes actors as givens and simply focuses on spelling out the implications of their actions.³⁹ A full explanation of the process of actor formation involves issues that are too complex to be adequately addressed here. But it is possible to begin to understand the process of actor formation by homing in on a simply and consequential point:

that an explanation of the rise of agents of change must be rooted in an understanding of the dynamics of the regime from which a transition would represent a departure, and that the study of transitions must not begin at the point when a transition begins to occur, but rather must be linked to, and draw on, an analysis of the phase of regime evolution.[40]

The basis for linking the analyses of the phases of evolution and transition is that a transition represents but the most extreme failure of a governing elites' effort to institutionalize a political order, the challenge at the heart of the phase of evolution. Thus, what explains a transition is in many ways simply the accentuation of trends that account for the failure of governing elites to meet the challenge of institutionalization. What is at stake is whether the interaction between the governing elites, those they rule over, and institutional arrangements—the same three factors considered in the analysis of the phase of evolution—leads not just to resistance toward, or disregard of, the proposed institutional framework, but also to the development of an actor that is sufficiently powerful to challenge the governing elites and contend for power.

This could occur, on the one hand, if a societal force holding an orientation of principled opposition developed during the phase of evolution and gained strength to the point that it would not only be a relevant actor—that is, one capable of effectively resisting the institutionalization of a political order—but actually became a dominant actor, an actor able to advance its own initiative rather than just reacting to the agenda of the governing elites.[41] On the other hand, the impetus for a transition could originate within the governing elites if the political dynamics of the phase of evolution created an incentive for a fundamental split within the governing elites, whereby one sector of these elites, strong enough to dominate the agenda, not only ceased to support the institutional framework of government but went a step further and adopted an orientation of principled opposition that led it to support the adoption of a new institutional framework.[42] Finally, a transition could occur as a combination of both these processes, with actors both from society and from within the governing elite pushing for change.

In sum, the occurrence of transitions, as processes that hinge on pure power politics, basically can be explained in terms of the orientation and strength of the old governing elites and societal actors—that is, in terms of the rise of actors that hold an orientation of principled opposition to the prevailing institutional order and that are strong enough to displace the elites that stand for the status quo. These fac-

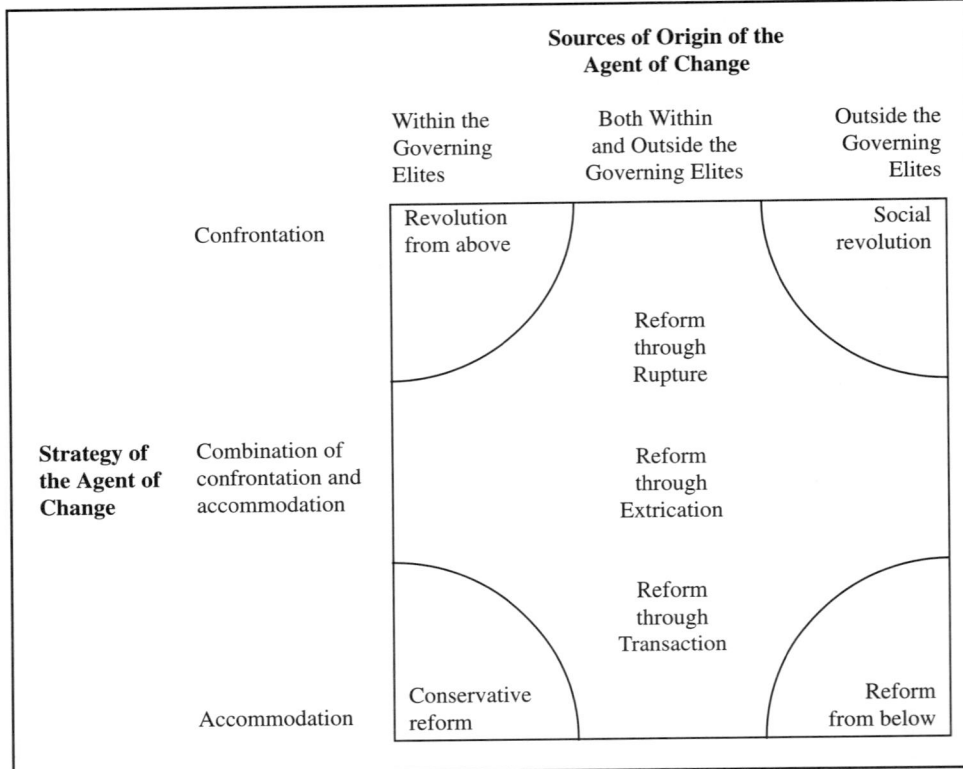

Figure 1.2. Modes of Transition

tors, however, only partially explain the full range of possible modes of transition, a concept widely used in the transitions literature to distinguish the manner in which the old governing elites are removed from their position as dominant authorities (see Figure 1.2).

By explaining *whether* a transition occurs, one does answer in part *how* a transition occurs, because an explanation of the very occurrence of a transition necessarily accounts for the identity or source of origin of the agent or agents of change, which is a dimension of the mode of transition that distinguishes transitions according to whether the transition was advanced by actors constituted either within the governing elite or outside the governing elite—that is, in society—or by both types of actors simultaneously. But an account of who carries out a transition must still address the question concerning the strategy that the agent or agents of change use to bring about a transition, a second and widely stressed dimension that distinguishes transitions according to whether the agent or agents of change bring about a transition by relying on a strategy that puts emphasis either on confrontation or accommodation vis-à-vis the governing elites or sectors of the governing elites opposed to a transition, or that combines elements of confrontation and accommodation.[43]

It is ironic that a clear answer to this question is never given in the strategic choice literature on transitions. For all the talk about strategic choices in this literature, it is more concerned with analyzing the consequences of actors' strategic choices than with explaining why actors choose particular strategies. To be sure, some of the key contributors to a strategic choice model of transitions operate with an implicit theory of why actors pick the strategies they do,[44] but it is possible to go beyond such implicit formulations by drawing on other bodies of literature that have studied political change.

In order to explain the strategic choices that actors make, it is crucial to grasp an essential feature of transitions. As argued above, transitions necessarily hinge on the inability or unwillingness of the old elite to block a transition. Nonetheless, inasmuch as there are sectors of the old elites that remain opposed to a transition, they will affect the process of transition through their relative capacity to resist change, much as a defeated army may nonetheless be able to condition the terms of its surrender. In other words, a transition represents a defeat for old elites who continue to support the old order, but a defeat in which the extent or abruptness of the break with the past is determined by the relative power of the antichange sectors within the governing elites vis-à-vis the agents or agents of change.[45] This is a crucial argument from which two implications can be derived.

First, this argument suggests a fairly clear hypothesis about the strategies used in transitions. The suggestion, on the one hand, is that when the antichange elites are relatively powerful they provide an incentive for emerging elites to seek change through a strategy of compromise, which is likely to involve important concessions to the outgoing rulers and generate a fairly smooth break with the past. On the other hand, the suggestion is that when the antichange elites are relatively weak they provide an incentive for emerging elites to seek change through a strategy of confrontation, which is likely to involve few concessions to the outgoing rulers and to generate a quite abrupt break with the past.

But, even more important, this argument suggests that while the question about the strategy the agent or agents of change might use to bring about a transition may be distinct from the question about the identity of the agent or agents of change, an explanation of the strategies used in transitions draws on the same analysis that accounts for the identity of the agent or agents of change. That is, because the relative power of the antichange sectors within the governing elites vis-à-vis the agents or agents of change is but another way of thinking about the orientation and strength of the old governing elites and societal actors, this argument suggests that both whether a transition occurs and how a transition occurs can be explained in terms of the interaction between the governing elites, those they rule over, and the institutional arrangements. In sum, this analysis of the strategies used in transitions reinforces the very basic point that emerges in the analysis of the identity of the actors that choose these strategies: that the study of transitions must not begin at the point when a transition starts to occur, but rather must be linked to, and draw on, an analysis of the phase of regime evolution.

Conclusion: The Uses of the Political-Institutional Model

This chapter has provided a general conceptual framework for the analysis of political regimes and regime changes, both conceptualizing the specifically political nature of the challenge involved in the various phases in the entire life cycle of a regime-founding attempt, and identifying the key explanatory variables that account for the variable responses to these distinct political challenges. This task has been advanced through an effort at synthesis, an effort that has sought to highlight some important gaps in the literature and to propose ways to remedy these gaps, to resolve apparently contradictory views advanced in the literature, and to establish links between bodies of literature that have until now been unconnected, especially by showing how the resolution of challenges the governing elites face in one phase affect, in a path-dependent manner, subsequent political developments.

The resulting synthesis—what has been called a political-institutional model—provides an encompassing framework for regime analysis that makes explicit the coherence of regime analysis as a research agenda. As a general framework, moreover, it can be used to study whatever regime type a researcher may be interested in. A key concern in building this model, indeed, has been to provide a shared language that could be applied to the study of the various regimes that have been influential in modern history, allowing us to connect the study of various regimes that have until now been carried out in isolation from each other and to compare and assess the findings of quite distinct bodies of literature.

The encyclopedic task of organizing the knowledge about political regimes that has been accumulated in the last thirty years or so, however, is not the goal of this book. Rather, having outlined the basic characteristics of regime analysis as a research program, the next task for this book is to show how this conceptual framework could be put to work by applying it to the study of one specific political phenomenon: bureaucratic authoritarianism. This task is first addressed, in the next chapter, through the development of a substantive but still generic argument concerning bureaucratic authoritarianism. Thereafter, this task is carried to completion, in the remaining chapters of this book, by mean of a case study of Argentina's experience with bureaucratic authoritarianism during the 1976–83 period, and a comparative exercise that includes the comparable cases of Chile during the 1973–90 period and Brazil during the 1964–85 period. The basic idea is to use the Argentine case to formulate and preliminarily test several hypotheses concerning the dynamics of bureaucratic authoritarianism in terms of the explanatory factors highlighted by the political-institutional model, and to subsequently test the generalizability of these hypotheses by comparing Argentina with the cases of Chile and Brazil.

Chapter 2

The Political Dynamics of Bureaucratic Authoritarianism
The Problem of Representation and Conflicting Imperatives

While regime analysis can be characterized as a research program at an abstract level, as in the previous chapter, regime analysis is always concerned with the study of some specific form of rule. This study is no exception, focusing on the phenomenon of bureaucratic authoritarianism, a term coined by Guillermo O'Donnell to capture the distinctiveness of a new form of authoritarian rule that emerged in South America in the 1960s and 1970s. This choice of subject matter is somewhat arbitrary, but there are some sound reasons for this choice in light of the goal of this book, which is to provide a comprehensive overview of the regime analysis research program. First, there is the real-world significance of this phenomenon, a factor that is somewhat obscured by the focus on democratic and totalitarian systems of government in much of the post–World War II period, because of the significance of these two regime types as alternatives in the Cold War struggle between the United States and the Soviet Union. Indeed, one of the most frequently found forms of government was actually authoritarianism, a third common alternative conceptualized by Juan Linz. Given the somewhat paradigmatic status of bureaucratic authoritarianism within the broader class of authoritarianism, thus, the study of bureaucratic authoritarianism is central to our understanding of authoritarianism, a significant twentieth-century political phenomenon.

Second, the study of authoritarianism has played a significant role in the development of the agenda of regime analysis. Partly because the distinctiveness of authoritarianism was less apparent to students of politics in the context of the Cold War, students of this phenomenon were forced to be more explicit in their conceptualization and in their attempts to explain the dynamics of this phenomenon. It was through the study of authoritarianism that the research agenda of regime analysis first developed. And it is in the context of authoritarianism that students of regime analysis have debated the issues pertaining to the entire life cycle of a regime-founding attempt. It is therefore crucial to rescue the contributions to regime analysis made in the course of the study of authoritarianism—an effort that Chapter 1 has already begun, in order to avoid the tendency to reinvent the wheel. Finally, given that we have empirical cases of authoritarianism that have gone through the entire life cycle of a regime-founding attempt, the study of authoritarianism provides an opportunity to test the usefulness of the entire conceptual framework outlined in the preceding chapter that the study of recently established democracies does not afford us.[1]

Having selected bureaucratic authoritarianism as this study's substantive focus, this book develops an argument about bureaucratic authoritarianism through a two-step process. The first step, and the task of this chapter, consists of an analysis of the very notion of bureaucratic authoritarianism. This analysis of the concept that is used to anchor the empirical analysis serves two purposes: it helps to clarify the precise attributes of the specific form of rule in question and the range of empirical cases encompassed by the concept, and it serves to identify a generic aspect of the political dynamics of this form of rule and therefore to provide a first approximation to the study of this political phenomenon.

The key argument that follows from this discussion is that the very defining attributes of bureaucratic authoritarianism give rise to a common challenge that is associated with the political exclusion of labor and its political allies and that all bureaucratic authoritarian rulers must face in their attempt to found a new political order. The significance of this challenge is that it gives rise to a conflicting imperative that prevents bureaucratic authoritarian rulers from successfully laying the basis of a new political order. In brief, inasmuch as the bureaucratic authoritarian rulers acknowledge the need to gain labor support, they tend to split among competing factions and/or allow for the concerted action of opposition forces; and inasmuch as they refuse to politically acknowledge the interests of labor, given that labor is an actor that expresses a main cleavage in the societies where bureaucratic authoritarian rule has been established, they implicitly abandon the pretense to found a new political order.

Such an argument does not mean that all bureaucratic authoritarian rulers will respond in the same manner to the conflicting imperatives they face, or that such different responses do not have consequences for the development of bureaucratic authoritarianism. Thus, once the conceptual analysis provided by this chapter is completed, and on the basis of this analysis, the second task is to address the question of what accounts for the different responses bureaucratic authoritarian rulers provide to the shared challenge they confront, and for the political consequences of these different responses on the evolution of bureaucratic authoritarianism. This task, which hinges on the integration of the political-institutional model outlined in Chapter 1 and the conceptual analysis provided in this chapter, and which completes the movement from a general framework to a substantive argument, is taken up starting in the next chapter and is the focus of the rest of this book.

The Concept of Bureaucratic Authoritarianism: Attributes and Cases

The concept of bureaucratic authoritarianism originated in O'Donnell's (1973:95) work on the military governments that came to power in Brazil and Argentina in the mid-1960s. These military governments were perceived by O'Donnell to be a new and distinctive political phenomenon within the Latin American region, which was related to the phenomenon Linz had begun to conceptualize on the basis of the experience of Spain under Franco.[2] Indeed, from the outset, bureaucratic authoritarianism was conceptualized as a subtype of authoritarianism, explicitly drawing on Linz's previous effort to define the distinctive nature of authoritarianism as a regime type. In O'Donnell's original conceptualization, therefore, bureaucratic authoritarianism was a form of government that emerged in Brazil and Argentina following their respective military coups in 1964 and 1966 and that entailed a number of attributes, such as rule by the military as an institution, an alliance between the military and both domestic and foreign capitalists, and the exclusion of an already activated urban popular sector.[3]

Over time the meaning of the concept of bureaucratic authoritarianism underwent some significant changes. On the one hand, O'Donnell's work on bureaucratic authoritarianism was used to consider a range of cases beyond the initial two that served as the basis for his original conceptualization. Thus, starting first with the geographically proximate cases of Chile and Uruguay following their military coups in 1973, and the case of Argentina once more, following its 1976 coup, the concept of bureaucratic authoritarianism was invoked in studies on Mexico, South Korea, the Philippines, Poland, Hungary, Greece, and

China, among other cases.⁴ On the other hand, as David Collier (1993:97) points out, because many of the attributes originally associated with the term were not necessarily present in these new cases, the concept of bureaucratic authoritarianism underwent a reformulation, serving "more generically to refer to modern (rather than traditional) authoritarianism that has a major bureaucratic dimension."⁵ In seeking to use the concept of bureaucratic authoritarianism to study Argentina, thus, we start out with an analysis of the concept of bureaucratic authoritarianism that aims at clarifying the way in which it will be used in this book. We begin by considering the attributes that bureaucratic authoritarianism shares with all subtypes of authoritarianism, and then proceed to discuss the attributes that define the distinctiveness of bureaucratic authoritarianism vis-à-vis other subtypes and to define the cases to which the concept refers.⁶

There is no better place to begin the discussion of authoritarianism than Linz's effort to define the attributes of authoritarianism in the context of his broader attempt to develop a typology of political regimes in the twentieth century. To this end, Linz stresses two dimensions: one pertaining to the rulers or governing elites, which are distinguished in terms of the extent of pluralism that characterizes the governing elite; the other pertaining to the ruled populations, which are distinguished in terms of the pattern of participation or exclusion they display. With regard to the first dimension, Linz distinguished between a democracy, in which a plurality of political forces representing social forces have access to power; a totalitarianism system, in which the governing elites form a single body that does not represent social forces but is instead an expression of state interests; and an authoritarianism system, in which there is one primary governing elite but in which "there remain groups not created by nor dependent on the state which influence the political process" (Linz 1964:298). With regard to the second dimension, Linz distinguishes between a democratic system, which is characterized by the autonomous and voluntary participation of the population through multiple channels; a totalitarianism system, characterized by the nonautonomous and obligatory mobilization of the population through one single channel for participation; and an authoritarianism system, characterized by the lack of extensive and intensive mobilization of the population.⁷

Following Linz's pioneering efforts, the concept of authoritarianism is defined in terms of two necessary attributes—limited pluralism and the lack of extensive and intensive mobilization of the population—which serve to distinguish authoritarianism from other types of regime in terms of the two attributes of the overarching concept of political regime: the extent of pluralism that characterizes the governing elite, and the pattern of participation allowed, or exclusion imposed, on the ruled population.[8]

Starting from this definition of authoritarianism, the next task in conceptualizing bureaucratic authoritarianism is to show how bureaucratic authoritarianism is generated as a subtype from the concept of authoritarianism. This is a far from simple task, and regime analysts have derived the concept of bureaucratic authoritarianism from that of authoritarianism in different ways. Again following Linz, this study distinguishes among subtypes of authoritarianism in terms of the same attributes used to define authoritarianism—that is, by specifying the "particular" forms through which a "general" defining attribute may manifest itself.[9] Thus, as Figure 2.1 shows, bureaucratic authoritarianism is conceptualized as a subtype of authoritarianism defined in terms of the particular form in which the two attributes of authoritarianism are expressed in bureaucratic authoritarianism: the rulership of a bureaucratized military institution, in alliance with business elites, and the exclusion of a previously mobilized labor movement.[10]

Regarding the first general attribute, pertaining to the governing elite, bureaucratic authoritarianism was from the outset conceived as a form of military rule. What was distinctive about bureaucratic authoritarianism, moreover, was that it involved the "military as an institution." This meant that the military had been bureaucratized and that the military as a whole becomes institutionally involved in the process of governing.[11] If the military as an institution constituted the governing elite in bureaucratic authoritarianism, it did not constitute the only actor with access to key governmental positions. Indeed, as discussions on the coalition of support for bureaucratic authoritarianism have stressed, bureaucratic authoritarianism does have a civilian component inasmuch as business elites have access to decision-making, particularly in the economic sphere, both formally, through appointments in the ministries of economy or finance, and informally, through "bureaucratic rings."[12] But, although bureaucratic authoritarianism is characterized by limited pluralism, it remains the case that the military as an institution constitutes, for all practical purposes, the governing elite in bureaucratic authoritarianism that determines "which groups [will be allowed] to exist and under what conditions" (Linz 1975:266; see also Kaufman 1986:89; Touraine 1989:371–72).

Regarding the second general attribute, pertaining to the ruled population, bureaucratic authoritarianism was also conceived from the outset as a form of military rule that was exclusionary of previously mobilized and incorporated labor movements. Indeed, efforts at char-

Regime Types/Subtypes \ Defining Attributes	Governing Elites: Extent of Pluralism	Ruled Population: Pattern of Participation/ Exclusion
Democratic	Almost unlimited pluralism	Voluntary participation
Authoritarian	Limited pluralism	Lack of extensive and intensive mobilization
• Bureaucratic authoritarianism	• Bureaucratized military institution in alliance with business elites	• Exclusion of premobilized labor movement
Totalitarianism	Monism	Channeled obligatory participation

Figure 2.1. The Defining Attributes of Bureaucratic Authoritarianism

acterizing bureaucratic authoritarianism have stressed not only its specificity as a postpopulist phenomenon—that is, one that emerges following a period during which labor had been activated and mobilized as a political force—but also as a response to the immediate prior polarization along the capital-labor cleavage.[13]

On the basis of this conceptualization of bureaucratic authoritarianism as defined by two particular attributes—the rulership of a bureaucratized military institution, in alliance with business elites, and the exclusion of a previously mobilized labor movement—the empirical referents of the concept can be defined. On the one hand, this definition justifies the exclusion of cases that are more properly seen as examples of other types of regime or other subtypes of authoritarianism (O'Donnell 1988:33). Thus, the common Latin American experience during the nineteenth century with *caudillo,* or "chieftain," rule, as well as more recent experiences with personalistic rule in cases such as Cuba and Nicaragua, can be clearly differentiated from cases of bureaucratic authoritarianism in that the former were not ruled by a bureaucratized military institution and emerged before the working class had been activated and mobilized as a political force. They are better understood as examples of a distinct and essentially premodern or traditional regime type.[14] Other cases are more properly seen as examples of other subtypes of authoritarianism. Such is the case with

Mexico, due to the civilian nature of its governing elites and the lack of exclusion of a previously mobilized labor movement, and with Peru during the 1968–80 period of military rule, due to the considerable scope of popular mobilization.[15] That is also the case for Spain under Franco and Portugal under Salazar, cases of authoritarianism that emerged before the working class had been activated and mobilized as a political force (Diamandorous 1986:154–55), and for China under Deng Xiaoping, due to the civilianized leadership that continues to rule through a single party and the absence of the kind of social pluralism that is a precondition for the type of exclusionary thrust that is so central to bureaucratic authoritarianism.[16] The case of South Korea, which resembled bureaucratic authoritarianism to a large extent particularly during the 1972–87 period, also diverges from our concept of bureaucratic authoritarianism in that the state had always been exclusionary and no inclusion of labor comparable to that associated with Latin America's import-substituting industrialization had occurred (Cumings 1989:11). And the case of the Philippines under Marcos, characterized by its highly personalistic tendencies and the absence of the military as an institution running the government, is probably best seen as a case of sultanism (Thompson 1995:2–5).

Besides singling out cases that are not referents of the concept, such a conceptualization of bureaucratic authoritarianism helps, on the other hand, to justify the extension of the concept of bureaucratic authoritarianism to those cases that are clearly referents of the concept. Specifically, this conceptualization justifies the extension of the concept of bureaucratic authoritarianism to the cases of Chile (1973–90), Uruguay (1973–85), Argentina (1976–83), and Greece (1967–74). Hector Schamis (1991) is certainly correct in distinguishing between the economic policies pursued by the military rulers that came to power in Brazil and Argentina in the 1960s and the military rulers that came to power in Chile, Uruguay, and Argentina in the 1970s. This distinction, nonetheless, does not override the similarities of these cases in terms of the explicitly political attributes stressed in my conceptualization of bureaucratic authoritarianism.[17] Similarly, while Nancy Bermeo (1995) points to some significant differences between the Greek and the South American cases, Greece still does deserve to be classified as a case of bureaucratic authoritarianism on account of some basic political similarities (Diamandorous 1986:154–55).

In sum, the concept of bureaucratic authoritarianism is defined in terms of two attributes—rulership by a bureaucratized military institution, in alliance with business elites, and exclusion of a previously mobilized labor movement—and is seen as clearly referring to six cases: the original two cases for which the term was coined, Brazil (1964–85) and Argentina (1966–73); the three regionally proximate cases that originated in the 1970s, Chile (1973–90), Uruguay (1973–85), and Argentina (1976–83), and the case of Greece (1967–74).[18] That is a fairly small number of cases. But this fact does not in itself undermine the utility of the concept of bureaucratic authoritarianism. For if bureaucratic authoritarianism is but one of a large number of subtypes of authoritarianism, the significance of bureaucratic authoritarianism goes beyond the sheer number of cases that can be labeled as such. Indeed, as the subtype of authoritarianism that is "furthest removed from any similarity to democratic political systems but also from modern totalitarianism," it has somewhat of a "paradigmatic" status.[19] In other words, within the broad family of authoritarianisms, cases of bureaucratic authoritarianism are probably more basic or typical examples and, as such, play a crucial role in theorizing about authoritarianism as a whole.[20] The argument that I develop about bureaucratic authoritarianism, thus, is of significance beyond the small set of bureaucratic authoritarianism cases identified here.

The Political Dynamics of Bureaucratic Authoritarianism

While this conceptualization of bureaucratic authoritarianism establishes the attributes of bureaucratic authoritarianism as a subtype of authoritarianism, and clarifies the extension of the concept or the cases to which it refers, it also serves as the basis for theorizing about bureaucratic authoritarianism. Indeed, an initial argument about bureaucratic authoritarianism is spelled out precisely in terms of the defining attributes highlighted in the conceptual analysis presented above. Put very schematically, these defining attributes constitute the basic outlines of the political project that the military seeks to advance and shape the political dynamics of bureaucratic authoritarianism by giving rise to conflicting imperatives that define the key dilemma faced by the elite that seeks to establish a bureaucratic authoritarian regime.[21] The argument thus elaborated, it bears stressing, is but a first approximation to the study of bureaucratic authoritarianism. It constitutes an argument about the shared challenge faced by bureaucratic authoritarian rulers as they seek to consolidate their power, a type of challenge that helps to distinguish the attempt at regime-founding by democratic and totalitarian rulers from that led by bureaucratic authoritarian rulers. As the analysis in subsequent chapters seeks to show, however, it is only on the basis of the application of the political-institutional model elaborated in Chapter 1 that the particular and variable response to this common challenge, along with the consequences of such variable responses, can be spelled out and accounted for.

The Problem of Representation: The Achilles' Heel of Bureaucratic Authoritarianism

The defining attributes of bureaucratic authoritarianism are important from the perspective of the political dynamics of this form of rule, because they constitute the features that define a distinctive challenge that is as inescapable as it is unresolvable from the perspective of the bureaucratic authoritarian rulers seeking to found a new political regime. Therein lies the reason that bureaucratic authoritarianism is an inherently unstable form of rule. The core of this challenge can be spelled out by contrasting the situation bureaucratic authoritarian rulers face to that faced by democratic and totalitarian rulers in light of the fact that bureaucratic authoritarianism, as a political formula, allows for the existence of preexisting societal interests, and even the growth of societal interests, but is unable to provide a suitable mechanism for interest intermediation.

These characteristics set bureaucratic authoritarianism apart from democratic forms of rule. For democracy, unlike bureaucratic authoritarianism, allows for participation from below and political pluralism at the top, in such a way that conflicting interests are not only permitted or allowed to exist but also incorporated as a legitimate part of the political process in the form of a "loyal opposition" (Linz 1978:16, 36–37). Unlike democracy, then, bureaucratic authoritarianism does not seek to channel or manage the societal interests it allows through the system-strengthening role of a pragmatic or loyal opposition, but adopts, instead, the awkward formula of confining societal interests to nonpolitical activities. While not sharing in the strength of democracy, bureaucratic authoritarianism, moreover, does not share in the strength of totalitarianism for the simple reason that under bureaucratic authoritarianism, unlike in the case of totalitarianism, the line between state and society is not blurred and societal groups are allowed a degree of independence. Bureaucratic authoritarian rulers, thus, lack the option that totalitarian rulers have to ensure order by eliminating the very problem of interest intermediation through the suppression of society as an autonomous realm and the full incorporation of politics within the state.

In sum, bureaucratic authoritarianism can be seen as a distinct political formula that, unlike democracy or totalitarianism, has an inbuilt destabilizing tendency due to the problem of representation of excluded societal interests that bureaucratic authoritarian rulers face.[22] Because these excluded interests are not minor, but instead represent the interests of labor—an actor that expresses a main cleavage in the societies where bureaucratic authoritarian rule is established—this challenge is inescapable, in the sense that it must be confronted if a stable form of rule is to be instituted. Such a challenge is equally unresolvable in that it gives rise to a fatal dilemma from the perspective of the bureaucratic authoritarian rulers. Seeking to lay the foundation for a new political order, the bureaucratic authoritarian rulers are drawn to acknowledge the problem of representation of excluded forces. But this exposes bureaucratic authoritarian rulers to the danger of a loss of cohesion and/or the threat of opposition from society, for instead of the stabilizing role that loyal oppositions play within the functioning of democratic systems, bureaucratic authoritarianism has a tendency to generate a principled or antisystem opposition that will seek political expressions that destabilize bureaucratic authoritarianism as a form of government. To counter such a tendency, and to avoid threats to their cohesion or the expression of societal opposition, bureaucratic authoritarian rulers are pushed to ignore the problem of representation, implicitly abandoning any attempt to consolidate their power. The problem of representation, in short, is a challenge that is distinctive of bureaucratic authoritarianism and that, inasmuch as it gives rise to a conflicting imperative that prevents these bureaucratic authoritarian rulers from successfully laying the foundation for a new political order or political regime, constitutes the Achilles' heel of bureaucratic authoritarianism.[23] As the central argument concerning bureaucratic authoritarian rule in this book, this conflicting imperative and the inescapable and fatal dilemma it gives rise to deserve to be spelled out.

The Governing Elites: Conflicting Imperatives and Military Dilemmas

The conflicting imperatives that the problem of representation gives rise to affects all key actors that play a part in bureaucratic authoritarianism. Its most direct impact on the political dynamics of bureaucratic authoritarianism, however, is through the impact it has on the choices the military, constituted as a governing elite, faces. The problem of representation, indeed, has a particularly powerful impact on the political dynamics of bureaucratic authoritarianism because it draws the military elites in two mutually exclusive directions and exposes them to a conflicting imperative that constitutes a dilemma that the military rulers can neither elude nor resolve.[24] Indeed, herein lies the key weakness of bureaucratic authoritarianism as a political formula and the main reason that it cannot constitute a stable form of government.

A first option military rulers face in light of the problem of representation is to simply ignore it—that is, the military rulers can allow social pluralism to flourish but repress its political expression. Such an approach, which is generally prevalent in the initial period of military rule, does not, however, constitute a solution, for it entails important costs from the perspective of the governing elites. As O'Donnell (1988:164) has pointed out in his analysis of bureaucratic authoritarianism, "the government and its allies suppress the channels of popular representation at the cost of losing information about the excluded sectors and the tendencies emerging within them," thus falling prey to the "solitude of power."[25] Such a situation is not directly threatening to the military rulers' hold on power, but the repression of excluded sectors does make bureaucratic authoritarianism illegitimate in the eyes of relevant actors, and this illegitimacy does undermine the ability of military rulers to consolidate their power and lay the foundation for a new political order. If through the strategy of passive withdrawal of consent, probably the only viable strategy at the disposal of an actor that is excluded and repressed, a relevant actor can express its principled opposition to bureaucratic authoritarianism, and such a form of opposition is sufficient to call into question the stability of the proposed new order.

Because of the lack of legitimacy that hinders the ability of the military to consolidate power when they pursue this first option, the military rulers may attempt another option they face in light of the problem of representation: to confront rather than ignore it. The costs of this choice, however, are even greater than with the first option. Indeed, in addition to the greater risks this option entails, the likely result is actually counterproductive, diminishing rather than increasing the prospects of consolidation of power. For inasmuch as military rulers seek to tackle and overcome the problem of representation, they expose themselves to a situation that directly threatens the military rulers' hold on power either from within or from the outside.

The military rulers are threatened from within because, inasmuch as they address the problem of representation, they are forced to deal with essentially political problems that cannot be managed according to the bureaucratic-technocratic and apolitical orientation that ensures the cohesiveness of the military rulers. In other words, by seeking to legalize the role of the excluded social forces, the military will be drawn into a debate about the future of state-society relations that will politicize the military. Politicization may result from the process of intramilitary debate with regard to how the legalization of excluded social forces should be carried out, or in response to actions of excluded social forces after they have been legalized. Alternatively, politicization may lead to calls for a return to the repressive policies around which the military's cohesiveness was cemented at the time of the coup, or to calls for the withdrawal from power as a means for the military to retain their corporate cohesiveness. This does not matter, for the consequence is basically the same: an acknowledgment of the problem of representation is likely to undermine the military's ability to rule by generating splits within the governing elite.[26]

In addition to exposing the military rulers to threats from within, their decision to confront the problem of representation also generates threats from the outside. The reason for this is that, even when the military does seek to address the problem of representation, given the bureaucratic-technocratic orientation of the military institution, the military rulers can at best offer only the unworkable formula of "negative integration," whereby "a political system permits a hostile mass movement to exist legally, but prevents it from gaining access to the centers of power" (Roth 1963:8–10, 305–22). Such an integration of a labor movement, in a strictly subordinate fashion, into a national community was pursued in Imperial Germany and did ensure stability through the moderating influence that the "controlled expression" of conflict generated (Roth 1963:8, 315; Mann 1993:671–78, 683).[27] But negative integration is not feasible under bureaucratic authoritarianism. Inasmuch as it seeks to perpetuate if not the direct exclusion of labor at least the controlled subordination of labor, it does not generate real support for bureaucratic authoritarianism or modify in any significant respect labor's principled opposition to bureaucratic authoritarianism. Yet, inasmuch as it does allow labor leaders some mechanism to represent labor interests, it provides an opportunity for labor leaders to express their opposition to the continuation of military rule. Again, whether the excluded forces take advantage of the informal spaces that are generated as a consequence of the process of intramilitary debate on the problem of representation or, alternatively, whether they take advantage of the legal spaces that the rulers' acknowledgment of the problem of representation affords them, the consequence is basically the same: the weakening of the military rulers' hold on power as a result of both the strengthening of opposition forces and the deepening or even the generation of military splits. Negative integration, in short, represents an unworkable formula that, from the perspective of the military rulers seeking to provide a foundation for a stable political order, creates more problems than it is intended to solve.[28]

In sum, the problem of representation associated with the societal interests that are allowed to exist but that are not provided with a suitable mechanism for interest intermediation lies at the heart of the political dynamics of bureaucratic authoritarianism and constitutes the central and most insurmountable obstacle to the establishment of bureaucratic authoritarianism as a stable form of rule. The problem of representation is particularly damaging, from the perspective of the military rulers, because it gives rise to a conflicting imperative that pulls the military in two mutually exclusive directions and impedes the military from consolidating their power. As discussed, to avoid threats to its cohesion and/or the threat of opposition from society, the military is drawn to ignore the problem of representation, acting solely around destructive goals and implicitly rejecting an attempt to consolidate their power. But, seeking to lay the basis of a new political order, the military is simultaneously drawn to acknowledge the problem of representation, exposing itself in the process to the dangers of losing its cohesion as well as facilitating the growth of societal opposition. This conflicting imperative presents an unresolvable dilemma for the military rulers, because either choice entails an unavoidable trade-off that undermines the military's ability to consolidate their power. The military's dilemma revolves around the contradictory need to confront the problem of representation, in order to legalize the role of all relevant actors and thus in turn consolidate their power, but also to shun the problem of representation, to avoid threats to their internal cohesion and/or the threat of opposition from society.

The problem of representation is, indeed, a problem that the military can address only by ceasing to function as a military institution, and the reason that, as Alain Rouquié (1986:110–11) puts it, "the army cannot govern directly and durably without ceasing to be an army."[29] To solve this problem, the military rulers would have to generate an ideology that would legitimate bureaucratic authoritarianism as a form of rule. However, given that the military qua military institution is not capable of doing this, and that the military as an institution is *the* central political actor within bureaucratic authoritarianism, this is a problem that cannot be resolved within the limits of bureaucratic authoritarian rule. The military rulers that preside over bureaucratic authoritarianism base their incursion into politics on a discourse, commonly referred to as a "doctrine of national security," that identifies a set of enemies and political practices that are to be repressed and supplanted by technocratic practices, and that ensures the military's cohesion but not the legitimacy of the form of rule they seek to establish.[30] Then, inasmuch as they seek to address the problem of representation, as a requisite of stable rule, the military is torn between two orientations that lead them to practice "dictatorship and repression in the present while promising democracy and freedom in the future." The result is an "ideological schizophrenia" that fails to generate legitimacy and that is not capable of solving the problem of antisystem opposition by relevant actors (O'Donnell and Schmitter 1986:15).[31] In sum, because the lack of allegiance of relevant actors is both the key reason that bureaucratic authoritarianism is an unstable form of rule, and the reason that the military rulers that seek to advance bureaucratic authoritarianism as a political formula eventually cede power, the problem of representation constitutes the Achilles' heel of bureaucratic authoritarianism.[32]

The Ruled: Labor Options and the Reconstitution of Labor as a Political Actor

If the conflicting imperatives the problem of representation gives rise to affects the military rulers, pulling them in two mutually exclusive directions that impede the military from consolidating their power, the conflicting imperatives that the military are subjected to also affect labor, as already hinted, inasmuch as the two options the military face have a direct impact on the fate of labor and on the potential role of labor under bureaucratic authoritarianism.[33] The variable impact on labor of the military's choice between their two main options is quite stark. There is little labor can do when the military chooses to repress all political expressions of societal pluralism. Inasmuch as the military follows the first option outlined above—the technocratic orientation that leads to the repression of excluded sectors, as is common during the initial period of military rule—labor is most likely to be placed in a plainly reactive and defensive role in the face of a military offensive aimed at disorganizing labor as a political actor. Thus, it is really only inasmuch as the military tilt toward their second option—that is, when they seek to expand their basis of support by dealing with the problem of representation—that labor starts to have some positive choices that determine how labor is reconstituted as an actor, a process that has a fundamental impact on the political dynamics of bureaucratic authoritarianism.[34]

The military's second option has a huge importance for labor because it confronts labor leaders with certain important choices concerning the military rulers' project that are not relevant when the military pursue their first repressive option. That is, if repression places labor on the defensive and focuses labor's concern on mere survival, inasmuch as the military recognizes the need for political dialogue as a way to deal with the problem of representation, labor leaders begin to face the realistic need to define their position with regard to the options that the military present them with. The military's second option is fundamental for labor because it provides the context for an internal debate through which labor is reconstituted as a political actor.

The dynamic through which labor is reconstituted as a political actor is fairly complex, reflecting the two central options that labor has in the face of the military's recognition of the need for political dialogue. The first option that labor leaders face is to collaborate—that is, to advance their goals by supporting the military rulers and their project. Particularly when repression seems to be the only viable option, there is always a strong temptation for labor labors to seek advancement by allowing themselves to be co-opted. This option, however, is not a stable option, from the perspective of both the military and labor leaders.

From the perspective of the military rulers, this option is not viable because although co-optation may be positive in that it reduces the need for repression by dividing and weakening labor, it cannot fulfill the function of representation and deliver the support of workers that labor leaders supposedly represent. As Linz (1973a:203–4) states, "The co-optation offer is often made to the leaders as individuals rather than as leaders in a formal sense." Indeed, "since there are no open mechanisms like fair and open elections . . . [these leaders] can neither claim support nor commit their constituents."[35] The detachment of these leaders from the bases of trade unions, the reason that makes these leaders readily co-optable, is the same reason that renders their support useless. The co-optation of labor leaders, thus, does not solve this tension and does not represent a solution to the dilemma faced by the military in light of the problem of representation.

From the perspective of the labor leaders, this option is unstable for the same reason that makes it a less-than-full response to the problem of representation from the perspective of the rulers. The problem is that the leaders that pursue the collaborationist option and are coopted immediately expose themselves to challenges from other labor leaders that claim to better represent, and have closer links with, the rank and file within their unions, and that can use the semi-freedom that the military must allow for the first collaborationist labor option to flourish in order to advance a second and more clearly oppositionist or combative labor option. The emergence of labor leaders that espouse an oppositionist option, thus, has far-reaching consequences, because the internal politics of labor under bureaucratic authoritarianism quickly exposes the illusions of negative integration in a way that affects the posture of those co-opted leaders. The fact that the military rulers provide no real spaces for labor leaders to advance the interest of the rank and file exposes these collaborationist leaders to competition from leaders that speak more clearly for labor interests. Thus, while the military's search for labor support is likely to lead to the clustering of labor leaders around two positions, this leadership competition for the allegiance of rank-and-file members not only weakens the credibility of the collaborationist leaders but also drives them to echo the demands of the rank and file of labor and to adopt a less collaborationist and more oppositionist posture.[36]

If the military's option to open to labor is thus unlikely to succeed, it does nonetheless provide an important opportunity for labor. The challenge labor faces can be stated quite succinctly: to take advantage of any and every overture that the military make in their direction to advance labor's interests. This is not a straightforward process, hinging rather on the reconstitution of labor through the competition between two wings, which reflect the two central options labor has in the face of the military's disposition to expand their basis of support. The process of labor reconstitution is likely to be complex and somewhat obscure, because there is a tendency for the distinct issues of goals and strategies to be confused. There is a fine line between one issue and the other, and that makes it hard, for example, to distinguish clearly between the opportunism regarding goals that is at the heart of the collaborationist option, and the strategic use of all opportunities to advance the oppositionist option (Unger 1990:104–9). Such difficulties are likely to lead to endless and difficult to resolve claims and counterclaims among labor leaders. Nonetheless, these debates remain significant, because it is through this internal politics that labor's reconstitution as a political actor takes place, and through what seems at times like little more than symbolic politics, that, in the absence of any cut-and-dried way to decide on the representativeness of leaders under nondemocratic conditions, labor leaders reestablish their links with the rank-and-file elements within their union and advance their claims of representativeness.

To recapitulate, then, while the military's decision to address the problem of representation is unlikely to lead to a broadening of the basis of support for the military rulers, for all that the rulers can offer is the co-optation of labor leaders that are unable to function as representative leaders, such a decision is likely to unleash a process of internal competition that leads to the formation of labor as a political actor and provide the avenue for the rise of a real opposition force. The policy of co-optation is still partially useful, from the perspective of the military rulers, for if it does not expand the basis of support for their rule, it does at least divide labor, reducing the costly use of repression as a means of control. But the problem is that, from the perspective of the rulers, such a policy of co-optation does not really work and never constitutes more than an unstable option. While the military rulers can offer collaborationist leaders only the role of "semi-opposition"—a term Linz uses to refer to "those groups that are not dominant or represented in the governing group but that are willing to participate in power without fundamentally challenging the regime"—because of the competition among labor leaders such a policy unleashes, this semi-opposition tends to become either a "pseudo-opposition" that ceases to provide even the moderate function of dividing labor or, more ominous, a real or principled opposition, such as Linz's "alegal" and "illegal" oppositions (Linz 1973a:191–92; italics in original omitted).

The crux of the problem always remains that if labor leaders are allowed to function as truly representative agents, they will voice their opposition to the military's project of negative integration. Thus, the attempt to broaden the basis of support for the military rulers by seeking to address the problem of representation is bound to fail. The military rulers remain unable to encourage the formation of an opposition force that would adopt a pragmatic attitude—that is, an opposition that would accept the projects of the military rulers and play by the rules of the game they set down. Because of the illegitimacy of the rulers' project of negative integration, if labor is given the option to express its voice, it results not in loyalty to the rulers but rather in the exercise of an exit option.[37] The outcome is an impossible game that confronts the military rulers with the increasingly dangerous option of using greater repression or embarking on difficult-to-control experiments at liberalization that are likely to lead to important schisms within the governing elite. While the military rulers may be able to set up a bureaucratic authoritarian form of government, this fundamental problem, linked as it is with the illegitimacy of bureaucratic authoritarianism, undermines the military's ability to consolidate their power and turn bureaucratic authoritarianism into a stable form of rule.[38]

The Coalition of Support: The Functional Alliance Between Economic Elites and the Military Rulers

The emphasis this book places on the ruled and on labor as explanatory factors in the political dynamics of bureaucratic authoritarianism does not contradict the importance of the economic elites that constitute the military rulers' allies, which is stressed repeatedly in the bureaucratic authoritarianism literature. Indeed, while there may be reasons to question the strong version of these arguments, which link the rise and fall of bureaucratic authoritarianism to the offering and withdrawal of support by economic elites for the military, it would be foolish to argue against the position that the offering and the withdrawal of support of economic elites to the military has an impact on the political dynamics of bureaucratic authoritarianism.[39] But there are two points concerning this argument that should be emphasized.

First, the political dynamics of bureaucratic authoritarianism cannot be fully accounted for in terms of the relationship between the military rulers and their elite allies. This is shown most clearly in the Chilean example of bureaucratic authoritarianism, where the transition was triggered without a break in the alliance between the military and business.[40] Thus, the political dynamics of bureaucratic authoritarianism must be understood in terms that go beyond the support or lack of support that the military rulers receive from their elite allies. Second, because the relationship between the military and their elite allies raises the question about how preexisting societal interests are able to voice their interests, the problem underlying the issue of elite support is similar in nature to the problem of representation that is raised by labor's exclusion. This point deserves to be spelled out.

The difference between the economic elites and labor is that while the economic elites generally support the military and are part of the coalition of support for bureaucratic authoritarianism, labor is a target of the policies of bureaucratic authoritarian rulers and generally one of the actors to first express opposition to bureaucratic authoritarianism. But the reason for support of the military on the part of the economic elites is not that the military is able to provide a suitable mechanism for interest intermediation when it comes to elite interests but not to labor interests. The support of the military by economic elites is, rather, less a function of the extent to which mechanisms for the representation of elite interests are provided by the military than of the performance of the military's policies. This can be best described as an alliance in support of bureaucratic authoritarianism based on the functional convergence of the interests of the military and the economic elites.

Thus, while this functional convergence of the interests accounts for the formation of the coup coalition that brings the military to power, the relationship between economic elites and the military rulers is quite peculiar (O'Donnell 1973:79–89).[41] While the economic elites do have some say in decisions after the military come to power, it is important to see that the mechanisms of access to power never really allow for a true representation of interests (Faucher 1981:12–18; Touraine 1989:371–75; Acuña 1995:241–43). The access to governmental posts by these economic elites is carried out both through formal appointments in the ministries of economy or finance and through the more informal mechanisms of access to power that are afforded by what Fernando Cardoso (1993: chap. 5, 168–74) called "bureaucratic rings"—that is, by the informal mechanisms that business leaders used to voice their concerns to governmental officers holding strategic posts (see also Oszlak 1984:14–19; 1987:35, 39–40). In contrast to the formal channels, which constitute more the seat of technocratic logic than of representation of economic organized interests, these informal channels did allow for some input into economic policy-making. But it is crucial to stress that rather than providing representatives of business elites with a firmly institutionalized role in the formulation of policy, all these bureaucratic rings did was add a particularistic thrust on top of the technocratic thrust afforded by the appointments to the ministries of economy or finance (Linz 1973a:193, 199, 202–4; Faucher 1981:16–17).

The inclusion of business within the coalition of support for bureaucratic authoritarianism does not therefore represent in any manner a solution to the problem of representation discussed above. Just as in the case of labor, business elites lack an adequate mechanism for interest representation, making their support hinge primarily on the vagaries of economic performance. If and when business elites withdraw their support for bureaucratic authoritarianism, they expose the same basic weakness of bureaucratic authoritarianism that labor does: its inability to provide a suitable mechanism for interest intermediation. The significance of the withdrawal of business support for military rule, then, comes not from the fact that it raises qualitatively new issues concerning bureaucratic authoritarian rule but from the fact that economic elites represent a significant actor that can add weight to opposition forces. Indeed, because economic elites are originally part of the coalition of support for bureaucratic authoritarianism, business is not likely to be at the forefront of change. Their subsequent move into opposition to bureaucratic authoritarianism is, no doubt, significant, affecting the ability of military rulers to control the timing of a transition and the terms under which the military rulers retreat from power. As Stephen Haggard and Robert Kaufman (1995:74, 28–32, 37–45, 64–66) argue, however, all it does is help to deepen "preexisting divisions within the ruling elite," rather than explain the more crucial emergence of divisions within the military rulers.[42]

So it is a central argument of this book that if we are to understand the source of these divisions it is necessary to consider the challenges that military rulers face, even before business elites consider the possibility of defection, and also that the relationship between bureaucratic authoritarian rulers and labor provides the best clues as to the source of the loss of military cohesion. This focus is justified because labor has a crucial role in the functioning of bureaucratic authoritarianism. Indeed, because labor is a mass actor within the societies in which bureaucratic authoritarian rule emerges, and because modern forms of government necessarily involve a mass base, labor holds the key to the prospects that bureaucratic authoritarian rulers would be able to successfully found a new political order (Mouzelis 1986:179–83; Diamandorous 1986:145–55). Moreover, labor's role is fundamental because labor, as the target of bureaucratic authoritarianism, is likely to become an opposition actor before business elites consider moving into an opposition role and thereby force the problem of representation onto the agenda. It is a useful perspective, then, to focus on labor and the predicament bureaucratic authoritarian rulers face in light of military-labor relations, while considering the role of business elites only inasmuch as they contribute to the same predicaments.

Conclusion: The Uses of the Argentine Case Study

The defining attributes of bureaucratic authoritarianism associate it with a specific dynamic of state-society relations that undermines the ability of the military rulers to govern and consolidate bureaucratic authoritarianism as a political regime. This does not make bureaucratic authoritarianism politically irrelevant or less theoretically interesting from the perspective of regime analysis, for if bureaucratic authoritarianism lacks a political formula for stable rule, bureaucratic authoritarianism originates and gives rise to something more than a merely transitional or caretaker form of government. Bureaucratic authoritarian rule is neither a fleeting nor an enduring political phenomenon. Instead of being geared toward a caretaker role, as was the case in previous military incursions into politics, the military rulers in bureaucratic authoritarianism use their awesome despotic power to destroy a mobilized labor actor. But the other side of this primarily reactive thrust to a perceived threat from below is that the military rulers operate with a truncated time horizon, defining themselves in terms of a future return to democracy. In fact, implicitly acknowledging that "a permanent system of military rule is almost a contradiction in terms" (Rouquié 1986:111),[43] these military rulers make solemn announcements, from the very start of their assumption of power, regarding the temporariness of military rule (Bobbio 1989:161–63). Bureaucratic authoritarianism thus represents a form of rule that is effective in many ways but that remains unable to become a fully functioning system. It is best thought of, to use Linz's (1973b:235) term, as an authoritarian "political situation."

This characterization is significant because such unstable forms of rule, which are more than short-term arrangements but which are nonetheless unable to become fully legitimate, are extremely common. In that bureaucratic authoritarianism illuminates the distinctive problem of a "political situation," the study of bureaucratic authoritarianism is theoretically fruitful from the broader perspective of regime analysis. In the following chapters, we therefore turn to the task of integrating the general model for the study of political regimes and regime dynamics presented in Chapter 1—the political-institutional model—with the analysis of the substantive problems associated with bureaucratic authoritarianism provided in this chapter. That task is carried out by means of a case study of Argentina's 1976–83 experience with bureaucratic authoritarianism.

The reason for focusing on a single case is that case studies lend themselves to a more in-depth analysis than studies based on a large number of cases. The detailed analysis of the complex processes underlying regime dynamics that such a case study would permit is in turn best suited to the crucial task of this book: to show that the causal mechanisms highlighted by the political-institutional model actually operate as posited and to generate testable hypotheses about the dynamics of bureaucratic authoritarianism.

While the study of Argentina is therefore, strictly speaking, a case study, it is likewise important to underline the two ways in which this book puts the Argentina case in comparative perspective. First, this case study is implicitly comparative, as is evident from the key questions about the three key phases in the life cycle of Argentina's bureaucratic authoritarianism experience: Why were Argentina's military rulers only partially successful in designing a new institutional order? Why did the military rulers thoroughly fail to provide the institutional basis for a stable form of rule? And why did the military eventually relinquish power in a particularly precipitous and uncontrolled manner? That is, the very questions that drive the research are actually formulated in comparative terms. After seeking to answer these questions by focusing on the Argentine case, this book concludes with an attempt to consider Argentina from an explicitly comparative perspective. By comparing Argentina's experience with bureaucratic authoritarianism with the experiences of Chile and Brazil, the generalizability of the findings based on the Argentina case will be explicitly tested. The remainder of the book, then, shows how the political-institutional model outlined in Chapter 1 can be applied to the analysis of bureaucratic authoritarianism by studying Argentina in comparative perspective.

Part II
Origin

Chapter 3

The Installation of Military Rulers, and the Assault on Labor in Argentina, 1976

The entry point proposed by this book into the study of Argentina from 1976 to 1983, as a case of bureaucratic authoritarianism, is the very particular and fluid political process whereby the attempt at regime foundation originates. This is a moment when the old and the new touch, as the new governing elite seeks both to displace the old governing elite and to consolidate its newly gained hold on power. The process of consolidation of power by a new governing elite, as discussed in the framework presented in Chapter 1, can be broken down into two distinct challenges: the challenge of constitutional definition, which entails the definition of an institutional framework that embodies the new governing elite's vision of political order, and the challenge of institutionalization, which entails the transformation of the newly created institutional rules into rules that are accepted and routinely used by all major political forces. Given the distinct processes entailed in meeting the challenges of constitutional definition and institutionalization, these two challenges are at the heart of two distinct phases in the life cycle of a regime-founding attempt. Thus, as argued, constitutional definition is seen as the key challenge faced by the new governing elite during the phase of origin, and the challenge of institutionalization is seen as the challenge at the heart of the phase of evolution. But if the challenge of constitutional definition is the first central issue that must be addressed in the study of an attempt to set up a bureaucratic authoritarian form of government, such a challenge presupposes, first, the clear seizure of power—that is, the fairly pointed process whereby a new set of rulers is installed in power and completes the transition from the previous form of rule.

The analysis of the Argentine case therefore starts with the seizure of power that opens the phase of origin and that constitutes the basic precondition and immediate background for undertaking constitutional definition, a challenge that will be addressed in the next chapter. The seizure of power entails two distinct dimensions: the installation of the new governing elites in power, a move that forces the new governing elites to devise an institutional arrangement as a way of managing, at least provisionally, the tasks of governing; and the completion of the transition from the previous form of rule by doing away with the elements of the old system that has just been replaced, which in cases of bureaucratic authoritarianism is carried out primarily through an assault on labor and its allies. These two dimensions are worth exploring in some depth because the resolution of these tasks shapes the context within which the challenge of constitutional definition is subsequently undertaken. To set the scene for this discussion, a few words must be said about the process leading up to the seizure of power by military rulers, emphasizing the labor-capital cleavage and the inability of political actors to manage the conflicts generated around this cleavage.

The Making of the Coup: Labor, Peronism, and Generalized Crisis

As in the case of most coups, the military coup of March 24, 1976, was an event in the making for some months. What makes this case distinctive, however, is the small element of surprise associated with the coup. Its eventual occurrence was suspected, in some strange and fateful way, since the day Juan Domingo Perón died on July 1, 1974. It had been expected with a good degree of certainty at least since the spiraling of inflation in June 1975 and the crisis in civil-military relations in August 1975. The last doubts about its imminent occurrence were erased in mid-December 1975 with the uprising of Air Force Brigadier Jesús O. Capellini, and even its precise date was mentioned three months in advance, in a Christmas Eve speech in which Army Commander-in-Chief Jorge Rafael Videla gave a warning about the need to make decisions to solve the country's problems.[1] The immediate cause or causes of the coup, then, should be sought in the period of Peronist government following a transition from military rule in 1973, for the military coup was the culmination of the failure of the civilian politicians to consolidate democracy.

The Installation of Military Rulers, and the Assault on Labor 51

But the military coup can be fully understood only in terms of longer-term factors, such as the role of labor in Argentine society and the intimate association between the workers' movement and Peronism.[2] In broader historical terms, the coup was but the last in a series of attempts by the military to deal with Peronism. One key difference, compared with the previous attempts, launched in 1955, 1962, and 1966, was that this was the first military takeover of power since the Peronist movement had become leaderless due to the death of the chief, Juan Perón. But still, as in case of these previous coups, the 1976 coup was what Samuel Huntington (1968:219–37) calls a "veto" coup—that is, a coup against a politically activated and mobilized labor, which in the Argentine context meant that the coup was a response to Peronism and an attempt to move Argentina into post-Peronist age. An analysis of Peronism is therefore necessary to the understanding of the making of the 1976 coup.

The foundation of Peronism as a result of the incorporation of labor in the 1943–55 period was particularly significant for Argentine history because of the political dynamics to which it gave rise (Collier and Collier 1991:331–50; Torre 1990).[3] Post-1955 Argentina was defined, as Guillermo O'Donnell put it, as an "impossible game" whereby the anti-Peronists, feeling threatened by a Peronist movement that constituted a majority of the electorate, sought to ban Peronist candidates from running for key political offices, while never being able to constitute a stable governing coalition on their own accord.[4] It can also be said that, starting in 1955, Argentina had suffered the characteristic ungovernability of a divided society (Cavarozzi 1989; Collier and Collier 1991:349–50). Inasmuch as an open competitive politics was allowed, the Peronists could count on winning—a move that would call forth a military coup, but inasmuch as the Peronists were proscribed from running in elections or were excluded from power as a result of military rule, the Peronist unions, which had become the organizational backbone of the Peronist movement both because of the personalistic style of Peron's leadership during the 1943–55 period and because of electoral proscription thereafter,[5] could destabilize any government it faced.

The country was essentially divided between Peronists and anti-Peronists. And if the anti-Peronists could maintain an electoral ban on the Peronists or resort to outright military intervention, to ensure that the Peronists would not take over the presidency, the Peronists were strong enough to make the country ungovernable. In this situation, which O'Donnell refers to as an "impossible game," each side could veto the other's project but not advance their own. And as a manifestation of this dilemma, Argentina's history began to display an increasingly vicious and dangerous pendular move, as a succession of weak civilian and increasingly bold military governments followed.

The destabilizing power of the Peronist movement was most clearly demonstrated through the 1969 Cordobazo, a semi-insurrectionary uprising in the city of Córdoba that shook the military government led by General Juan C. Onganía since 1966 and that forced the military to negotiate with Perón and accept his return to the country after a forced exile of eighteen years.[6] For a variety of reasons, however, the lifting of the electoral ban on Peronism, along with Perón's return to the country and his assumption of the presidency in October 1973, did not solve Argentina's ungovernability problem.[7] As a result of the policies that Perón himself had pursued in order to avoid any potential challenges to his leadership while he was in exile, the Peronist trade union structure had divided between a conservative trade union "bureaucracy" and more leftist union leaders, while radicalized middle-sector youths had formed a guerrilla organization called the Montoneros.[8] Now that Perón sought to govern, the forces he had unleashed could not be easily controlled. Indeed, the tone of politics for the next years was set by the armed confrontation between these two wings of the Peronist movement, as they awaited Perón's return from exile at the Ezeiza airport (Verbitsky 1985a).

Upon assuming power and seeking to control the movement he had created, Perón quickly reversed his previous strategy, drawing the trade union bureaucracy close to the government while turning his back on the Montonero guerrillas. The results were anything but social peace. On the one hand, the top trade union leadership used their newly found power, as set out in the new legal guidelines of the recently approved Law of Professional Associations, to move against the most visible heads of the radicalized labor movement, such as Agustín Tosco and René Salamanca, by displacing them from their union posts.[9] On the other hand, the immediate response by the sectors against which Perón was now turning was defiance, as the left wing of the Peronist movement did not accept Perón's mandate to turn away from armed struggle. They therefore continued a campaign against their opponents within Peronism, which had previously targeted powerful labor leaders, such as Augusto Vandor and José Alonso, as traitors to the working class, now assassinating the head of the General Labor Confederation (Confederación General del Trabajo [CGT]), labor's single peak organization, José Rucci. Whether Perón would eventually be able to harmonize the heterogeneous groups he had fostered at one time or another during his exile became a moot point, as Perón had only a few more months of life.

The struggle between the different elements of Peronism that Perón had manipulated so skillfully throughout his exile would continue and deepen, and ultimately those centrifugal forces would not be contained by Perón's widow—María Estela Martínez de Perón, or simply Isabel Perón—who as vice-president at the time of Perón's death assumed the presidency in July 1974. Indeed, under Isabel Perón, who proved to be a very inept president, Argentina witnessed growing polarization, which resulted in the widespread use of violence by state and nonstate actors and unprecedented economic instability.

The inability of Isabel Perón to manage the economy became increasingly apparent (Torre 1983a; Di Tella 1983). In response to the austerity measures advanced by Minister of Economy Celestino Rodrigo in June 1975—the so-called Rodrigazo—workers reacted with a wave of wildcat strikes that forced the CGT to call a general strike in July 1975, the first such measure taken against a Peronist government. In the wake of this general strike, the government of Isabel continued to be battered by the actions of trade union leaders, who now engaged in a process of mutual outbidding, whereby the substantial wage increases gained by key unions such as the metal workers' union (Unión Obrera Metalúrgica de la República Argentina [UOM]) provided the standard that other unions then sought to emulate. In short, worker demands were fueling a process of hyperinflation, which reached an annual rate of 335 percent in 1975 and discredited Isabel Perón's government.

The economic crisis was not the only problem affecting Isabel Perón's government. The spread of violence increasingly threatened the state's ability to secure a basic modicum of political order. In November 1974, the Peronist government, supported by the trade union bureaucracy, declared a state of siege, giving the army and the police greater powers to deal with the left. Later the government passed decrees allowing the military to extend their fight to exterminate guerrillas, first in the mountainous area of Tucumán and then increasingly throughout the entire national territory.[10] Furthermore, the Argentine Anti-Communist Alliance (Alianza Argentina Anticomunista [AAA]), organized by José López Rega, minister of social welfare and close associate of Isabel Perón, was engaged in the task of decimating activists at the rank-and-file level. As the guerrillas responded to this offensive with their own actions, violence became a common weapon in the struggle between opposed forces, and the government of Isabel was weakened by the growing impression that it was unable to secure political order.

This combination of factors—whereby the government proved itself unable both to rein in the wave of violence and to manage the economy—produced a generalized crisis. If the banning of the Peronists from government had made the country ungovernable from 1955 to 1973, the return of the Peronists to power in 1973 not only left the problem of governability unresolved but generated the conditions for an even greater threat. If the bureaucratic authoritarian experiment of 1966–73 had failed to manage the divide between Peronists and anti-Peronists, and its leaders had turned to Perón in the hope that he could control the Peronist movement, the 1973–76 experience with a Peronist government had proved that such a hope was misguided. If Argentine workers had not fully broken with their Peronist leaders, these leaders had begun to lose control over sections of the working class (Munck with Falcón and Gallitelli 1987:199, 202–3, 253). The redistributive conflicts of the past began to pale in comparison with the greater threat posed now by labor, in the form of a possible alliance between radicalized workers close to the rank and file of the trade union structure acting in conjunction with guerrilla forces. The threat to the capitalist order represented by this increasingly autonomous force based in the working class and drawing on disenchanted middle-class elements cannot be underestimated.[11] Indeed, it is in response to the generalized crisis that began to develop since 1973, and the new options this crisis was opening, that a cohesive coup coalition, which included the military institution, the more transnationalized sectors of business, and sections of the middle class, began to take shape.

The unraveling of the Peronist government led to some desperate moves to avert a coup.[12] A last-ditch attempt to bring the armed forces into the government, in order to gain its support, was the appointment of Colonel Vicente Damasco, an active military officer, as minister of the interior. But this move turned out to be a grave miscalculation, representing a crucial factor in alienating the army. Most military officers disapproved of the appointment, and that caused a crisis in civil-military relations in August 1975. In the crisis, the main supporters of Isabel Perón, orthodox Peronists and the "62 Organizations" (62 Organizaciones)—the labor wing of the Peronist Justicialist Party (Partido Justicialista [PJ])—sided with Lieutenant General Alberto Laplane and General Alberto Cáceres against General Videla and General Roberto Viola. The episode led to the breaking off of any relationship between the army group that would carry out the coup and Lorenzo Miguel, the leader of both the powerful metal workers' union and the

62 Organizations, and the appointment of Videla as head of the army (Fraga 1988:211–15, 217). Thereafter, some internal sectors of the army posited the inevitability of a coup.

By December, the fate of Isabel Perón's government was cast. A desperate move, whereby the Peronist government would submit to Congress a series of bills that would have given the military almost unlimited powers to pursue their "war against subversion,"[13] had no effect. The decision to take power had already been made, in a unanimous manner, by the armed forces, and it therefore came as no surprise when the military staged a coup on March 24, 1976. The day before the coup had been ripe with rumors of imminent changes and with newspaper reports reminding Argentines that precisely ninety days had elapsed since a public speech by Army Commander-in-Chief Videla gave a ninety-day ultimatum to the government, asserting that "if the house was not in order" by then the military would have to take power in "the interests of the nation." The end was indeed near. After a series of long and tense meetings, and as the first minutes of the 24th were ticking away, President Isabel Perón's helicopter flew from the roof of the Government House—the Casa Rosada—en route to the presidential residence in Olivos. But unbeknownst to Isabel, the helicopter was on its way to the airport of the city of Buenos Aires, where she was detained and informed that she was president no longer. Back in downtown Buenos Aires, labor boss Lorenzo Miguel and Minister of Labor Miguel Unamuno had left the Casa Rosada and walked across the Plaza de Mayo to the labor ministry nearby. There, several dozen labor leaders waited to meet with them. On learning the fate of Isabel, however, everyone left the government building, promptly and in a disorderly fashion. At 10:40 in the morning a new government was formed, headed by a military junta made up of the three commanders-in-chief of the armed forces: Army General Videla, Navy Admiral Eduardo Emilio Massera, and Air Force Brigadier General Orlando Ramón Agosti. Two days later, Videla was named president, and on the March 29 his cabinet was sworn in. Thus began what the military rulers themselves called the Process of National Reorganization (Proceso de Reorganización Nacional, hereafter Proceso).[14]

As a clearly preannounced coup, the March 24 coup was somewhat anticlimactic. If a battle to defend the constitutional government was lost, it was lost not on March 24 but during the previous twenty-one months. No great show of military force was necessary, as little resistance was expected and offered. The turning point for labor had really come with Juan Perón's death on the gray day of July 1, 1974, twenty-two years after Evita had gone to the grave. No one had so dominated

Argentine politics since an unforgettable October 17, 1945, when the people had marched to the Plaza de Mayo demanding that their protector be released from prison. Suddenly the centripetal force at the center of an amply majoritarian movement had vanished. And although Perón's wife, Isabel, attempted to play the part of charismatic leader, she was not able to prevent the movement from falling to pieces.

Going further back in time, however, the March 24, 1976, coup can be seen as the end point of a process that was initiated on the legendary October 17, 1945, when the working class was born to Perón. That was the beginning of a Golden Age for workers. Even when the tide turned against them with the 1955 coup that ousted Perón, workers were able to launch what was known as the "heroic resistance." In 1976, however, there was nothing to look forward to, only social gains to be defended and better days to be remembered. In both cases there was a foretaste, a two-year preparation for the big day. But the contrast between the response on both occasions was stark. The challenging attitude of 1945 had turned into the resignation of 1976. As the Peronist government's Minister of Labor Miguel Unamuno (1982:102–3) asserted quite bluntly during the last days of Isabel's government: "At this point there was no organized labor movement, there were sectors, internal lines or whatever you may want to call them. . . . The labor movement was divided." Given the lack of organized resistance, the coup itself was carried out amid an atmosphere of tranquillity.

But it was an eerie tranquillity. It was clear that the March 24 coup would initiate a period of vast changes. As time would show, the overthrow of the labor-based Peronist government and the democratic system was the opening bout of what was to be the darkest period in Argentine history, as the military sought to launch an all-out attack on what they perceived to be the root causes of the instability that had afflicted Argentina since labor's incorporation and the rise of Peronism.

The Installation of Military Rulers: Assuming the Management of the State

Upon coming to power through the March coup, the immediate task the military faced was to complete the seizure of power. There were two distinct aspects of that task: the new military rulers had to complete their formal installation in power by assuming the management of the state, and the new military rulers had to complete the transition from the previous form of rule by undermining the actors that had been central to the functioning of the system they had just replaced. Given that the resolution of this immediate task shapes the context within which the challenge of constitutional definition was subsequently undertaken, this chapter presents a fairly detailed discussion of the issues involved, beginning with a discussion of the first aspect of the seizure of power.

With regard to the first aspect of this task—the installation proper of military rulers in power—it is important to note that its achievement can overlap, timewise, to a greater or lesser extent with the fulfillment of the challenge of constitutional definition. That is, the installation of a new governing elite can lead, simultaneously, to the setting up of institutions that are intended to provide the basis for a future political order. In the case of military coups, which effect a transition through violent displacement of the previous governing elites, however, it is more likely that the new governing elites will define a set of institutional rules that will allow them to assume the management of the state, a challenge that must be handled immediately and without delay, before they are able to address with any degree of seriousness the long-term issues raised by the challenge of constitutional definition. The need to assume the management of the state, in short, is likely to force military rulers to set up some sort of interim institutional arrangement.

The significance of such an interim institutional arrangement, as discussed in Chapter 1, goes beyond the problem of the administration of government. Indeed, such an interim institutional arrangement has an impact, through a short-term sequential effect, on the manner in which the military subsequently handle the more enduring issues raised by the challenge of constitutional definition. This section will therefore discuss the interim institutional arrangement that the military devised, as a way to manage the affairs of the state, as soon as it took power in March 1976.[15]

The Overlap Between the Military as Institution and the Military as Government: The Military's Corporate Pact

The primary thrust of the institutional rules whereby the military would administer the government was given by an explicit agreement of the armed forces—a "corporate pact"—to participate directly and equally in the exercise of power. This pact had its origins in the military's reaction to previous experiences of military rule, and in particular to the presidency of General Onganía (1966–70), when "the army as an institution did not retain power" (Rouquié 1982a:269).[16] This time around the leadership role traditionally assumed by the army was not accepted by the air force, and even less so by the navy. In an attempt to avoid the problems that hampered the military's previous experience in government, then, power was firmly placed in the hands of the military corporation.

This pact was enshrined in a series of legal documents signed by the military junta immediately after the military came to power.[17] These documents defined the powers of, as well as the relationship among, the military junta, the president, and the armed forces. Also defined in these documents were the functions of the Legislative Advisory Commission (Comisión Asesora Legislativa [CAL]) and the procedures by which laws were to be written and approved. These documents, outlined, in short, the rules the military set for themselves in order to administer the government in a predictable fashion, or what was commonly referred to as the "power arrangement."

The military junta, which was to be integrated by the commanders-in-chief of the army, navy, and air force, was designed as the "supreme organ of the nation."[18] Specifically, the role of the junta was not to be overshadowed by the president, as was the case when the military had taken power in 1955 and 1966. Therefore, the faculties accorded to the junta included ones assigned by the constitution to the president and Congress, and which under previous military governments usually belonged to the executive. The attributes of the junta included the power to name and replace the president and members of the supreme court,[19] the power to declare war and a state of siege, and an arbitrating power in cases of disagreement between the executive and the CAL. Furthermore, the junta was to impart general directives for the government as well as constitute the body to which all officers of the military government, including the president, were accountable.[20]

The president had to be a high officer of the armed forces designated by the junta. If the powers of the president were diminished, compared with those held by the president under previous military governments, the office of the president retained great powers, including the legislative powers that the constitution previously delegated to Congress. Nonetheless, the legislative powers of the president were curtailed by the presence of the CAL. The same article that conferred these powers on the president goes on to say that the CAL is to participate in the "formation and ratification of laws." As a body, the CAL was to be made up of nine active-duty superior officers designated, three apiece, by each branch of the armed forces. Its role and function were to provide advice on legislative matters "in representation of the armed forces," thereby putting the executive power in touch with the military institution's interpretation on a whole range of matters. The CAL was to serve, in short, as a mechanism to involve the armed forces as a whole in the tasks of government.[21]

Thus, the key aspects of this institutional setup placed power firmly in the hands of the military corporation and ensured that its exercise was to be a joint responsibility of all three branches of the armed forces, represented at the peak of power—the junta—by their respective commanders-in-chief. The institutional involvement of the military within the junta was further ensured, in a fashion similar to that of the CAL, through a complex decision-making process involving lengthy consultations within each branch as well as across branches. Any issue to be considered by the junta was first to be remitted to the secretaries-general of the three branches; the matter was then considered by consultative teams that acted as a kind of advisory cabinet within each service branch, and later by teams of interservice compatibilization (Equipos de Compatibilización Interfuerzas), and finally by the secretaries-general again.[22] Only then did the junta make a decision, which technically required only a simple majority but which usually resulted from unanimous approval.

In sum, the legal norms guiding the administration of government, and particularly the junta and the CAL, involved the three commanders-in-chief and the military high command in the tasks of government and ensured the full overlap of the military as an institution and the military as the government. The implications of this tight overlap were of great importance. It could result in a government that drew on the power of the military institution and thus have great strength, or it could give rise to a situation in which tensions within the military institution were rapidly and quite directly transferred to the government, resulting in incoherent policies and actions. For this reason, it is important to discuss two additional aspects of the interim institutional arrangement devised by the Argentine military, for these two aspects clearly presaged problems, particularly with regard to the military's ability to face up to the challenge of constitutional definition.

The Presidency and the Cabinet: Ambiguities at the Top Level of Government

The first potentially detrimental aspect of the military's interim institutional arrangement pertained to the issue of the "distribution of power" among the three services. As a reaction to previous experiences of the armed forces in government, when the military as an institution did not retain power and when the army had also clearly dominated the other services, the military had assumed power on the basis of a corporate pact among the three branches of the armed forces whereby the notions of direct and equal participation in government of the three services and the subordination of the presidency to the junta were to be basic principles in the military's power arrangement. These principles were demanded by the leaders of the air force and even more strongly by leaders of the navy, who made it clear that this time they were not going to compliantly accept the leadership role traditionally assumed by the army. Even though the institutional formula discussed above did, in principle, provide for the co-equal participation of all the services in the government, this formula did not resolve all issues. The filling of the presidency and the makeup of the cabinet, in particular, still had to be resolved, and those issues proved to be important points of contention.

The key dispute over the presidency centered on whether the person holding the office could remain active as commander-in-chief or whether he should be a retired officer. It would be difficult to sustain the argument that all three forces participated equally in the government if the commander-in-chief of one branch was the president. That issue was bitterly disputed both within the army and between the army and the navy. The army would not allow the president to be chosen from the navy, in part because of the traditional rivalry between the two services, a rivalry that was exacerbated by the ongoing disputes between Videla, commander-in-chief of the army, and Massera, who as commander-in-chief of the navy held high personal ambitions and favored a distinct political project (Fontana 1987:47–48, 57–58). The army thus pushed its claim that because of the perceived threat of social conflict, power needed to be concentrated in the presidency. Furthermore, it argued that the office should be occupied by the army commander-in-chief because the army had a greater role in the fight against the guerrillas. In the end, the army prevailed and Videla became president, but the issue was not clearly resolved and continued to be a source of internal debate.

Videla's appointment was the result of an unstable agreement. The army had persuaded the other two services to go along with a declaration of a temporary "state of exception" *(situación de excepcionalidad)*, whereby the president could be an active army officer. But such an acknowledgment of the temporary and abnormal situation did little to fix the problem. Not only had the army's demand been met at the cost of violating, right away, the formula on which the support for the government of the full armed forces was premised—that is, the principles of equal participation by the army, navy, and air force in government and subordination of the presidency to the junta. In addition, the ambiguity in the institutional setup of the government had introduced a point of contention that would be the focus of a series of heated negotiations within the armed forces. Perforce, this served as a distraction from long-term unitary goals.[23]

A second item central to the institutional involvement of the military in government, again potentially divisive, concerned the formation of the cabinet. After a protracted and complicated process of decision-making, the allocation of ministries was announced on March 29, 1976. The eight cabinet positions were divided among the three services, two apiece, with the remaining two going to civilians.[24] The army took control over the ministries of the interior and labor. It wanted the ministry of the interior because that ministry had direct control over the federal police as well as other areas touching on the "war against subversion." And the army sought the ministry of labor because it viewed labor conflicts in reaction to the government's future economic policies as a very real possibility and thus requiring serious attention.[25] The remaining ministries were divided among the navy, which got foreign relations and social welfare; the air force, which received defense and justice; and civilians, who were put at the head of the ministry of economics and the ministry of culture and education. With the exception of the retired officer at the head of the ministry of defense, all cabinet officers were on active duty in the military.

Two obvious patterns emerge from this cabinet lineup. Once again, as in the case of the office of president, and in spite of the formal equality of participation, the army had prevailed. It had taken control over the two ministries that clearly had a greater possibility of shaping the future course of the military government. The only other ministry that could claim to rival the ministries of the interior and labor in importance, in terms of potential impact, was the ministry of economics, and this ministry was to be headed by a civilian, José Martínez de Hoz.[26]

Thus, from the moment the armed forces took over the state apparatus in March, ambiguities with regard to the military's corporate pact, centered on the co-equal participation of all the services in the government, made the issue of the distribution of power among the three services a constant concern and subject of debate within the military institution. Rather than providing a mechanism to cement the cohesion of the military rulers, this institutional arrangement actually had the potential to undermine military cohesion and hinder the ability of the military to rule.

Colonization of the State Apparatus: The "Feudalization of the State"

A different sort of problem was created in the areas where the military's corporate pact was not abridged but actually applied. The presence of the military institution in government had few limits. Indeed, to a greater extent than in the previous successful coups of 1930, 1943, 1955, 1962, and 1966, the 1976 coup led to nothing short of a full-scale "colonization" of the state apparatus (Rouquié 1987a:295). Not only did the military take over the commanding heights of the state, they also spread throughout all its different levels and bureaucracies. In this area, the explicit corporate pact among the three branches to participate directly and equally in the exercise of power, and thus share in the responsibility of government, was more fully respected. Except for the provincial governorships, where the division of posts again favored the army, the majority of important public posts were occupied by thirds by the army, the navy, and the air force.[27] The three service branches were present in government through a real tripartite institutional apparatus.

The resulting situation is best captured by the notion of "feudalization of the state" (Fontana 1987:32; Oszlak 1987:39). Instead of fostering a shared responsibility in government by all three branches, the involvement of the military in the tasks of government through this tripartite division of posts led to a phenomenon whereby power was compartmentalized and exercised individually by each service branch. From the cabinet down, the state apparatus was for all practical purposes segmented under the control of individual services, and this created a distinct problem for the military.

Rather than undermine the cohesion of the military by creating a fertile topic for ongoing internal debate, as was the case with the ambiguities introduced in the corporate pact at the top level of government, the feudalization of the state affected the cohesion of the military rulers by introducing a mechanism whereby it became more difficult to create and maintain cohesion. Because this arrangement created fiefdoms, where the particular interests of the different branches would be protected, it did away with any institutional incentive to resolve differences. Moreover, because of the manner in which this arrangement ensured that the overlap between the military as an institution and the military as government would be replicated throughout the state apparatus, this arrangement meant that ongoing military disputes were transferred to every site the state apparatus reached. Indeed, the full-scale colonization of the state apparatus by the military institution reduced the capacity for concerted action and created a strong tendency toward incoherence and indecision. Rather than induce clear coordination among the three services, this mechanism was more conducive to chaotic and sometimes contradictory policies carried out by superior officers who were distrustful of other branches and protective of their sphere of influence.[28]

Implications of the Military's Interim Institutional Arrangement

To recapitulate, according to the legal documents that provided the foundation for military rule, the administration of government was to be a joint responsibility of all three branches of the armed forces, represented at the peak of power, in the junta, by their respective commanders-in-chief. A special Legislative Advisory Commission (CAL) involved the military high command in the tasks of government. The mechanisms of access to decision-making circles, and the way in which policy was implemented, ensured that the heads of all three services, as well as the high commands *(altos mandos militares)*, which are decision-making bodies within each service branch and which include division generals in the army, vice-admirals in the navy, and major brigadiers in the air force, were given a key role in deciding crucial political issues faced by the military. The full overlap of the military as institution and the military as government was firmly institutionalized.

This full entrenchment of the military in the tasks of government had important implications for the ability of the military to rule and consolidate their power. The arrangement had the potential to give the government great strength, because it could bring the full force of the military organization to bear on its actions. But this institutional arrangement also had some potential pitfalls that would become apparent as the military began to face the challenge of constitutional definition. Such was the case with the abridgment of the principle of co-equal participation of all services in the government, introduced by the peculiar settlement of the dispute over the presidency, given that it introduced ambiguity at the top level of government. This was also the case with the full-scale colonization of the state apparatus, which, if carried out in compliance with the military's corporate pact, introduced nonetheless a tendency toward feudalization of the state. This institutional arrangement therefore had the potential to harm the military's ability to act cohesively with regard to long-term issues, as will be discussed in the next chapter.

In the short run, however, these features created no significant problems for the military. Given the military's perception that they were facing a comparatively greater threat than they had in the past, and given that the coup had been carefully prepared and launched with the backing of the entire military structure, the military rulers displayed greater internal cohesion than they had in previous episodes of military rule, such as following the 1966 coup.[29] Accordingly, and despite the potential difficulties the interim institutional arrangement could produce once they sought to tackle the challenge of constitutional definition, the military rulers were able to effectively unleash sweeping actions, aimed at destroying the actors they opposed.

The awesome power of the military rulers was seen and felt especially in terms of their ability to engage in destructive action. The particular methodology used in the "war against subversion" was one of "decentralized authoritarianism" (Groisman 1987a:63). Directives in the form of very explicit and detailed orders were handed down by the commanders-in-chief that formed the military junta, but the Work Groups (Grupos de Tarea) that were organized to carry out these orders operated in fairly autonomous ways. The issue of responsibility was thus diluted and could be assigned to excesses of the overly zealous officers who headed the Work Groups. Complicating matters even more, the organization of repression obeyed the same principle of tripartite division of the state apparatus that led to the feudalization of the state. Thus, while the activities of repression were directed by the commander-in-chief of each force, there was little coordination at the top.[30]

The result was a truly terrifying force, for as the purposeful lack of coordination of vertically organized terror combined with the not uncommon competition between branches, state terror spread through the compartmentalized actions of the three service branches, each of which had their own operations, with their own intelligence services, their own clandestine detention centers, and their own Work Groups.[31] If lacking precision, these security forces constituted a deadly weapon. With a scatter-gun approach, they exterminated the intended target, the guerrillas, along with pretty much anything that stood in the way. Even though the institutional arrangement was not conducive to coordinated action by the military as an institution, the military clearly had the capacity to carry out devastating acts, unleashing a campaign of terror that was unprecedented in Argentine history.

The Assault on Labor and Its Allies: Completing the Transition from the Old Regime

If the installation proper of military rulers in power was a crucial aspect of their seizure of power, a second and equally important aspect was the completion of the transition from the previous form of rule by doing away with the legacies of the old regime. That process occurred in part through the very installation in power of the military. As part of the process of installation, the Argentine military had restructured lines of authority through a series of negative measures that directly cut off the old governing elites from the power they had held. Thus, labor and its political allies were clearly affected by the very measures that the military's interim institutional arrangement necessitated or implied, such as the closing of Congress, the banning of political parties, the prohibition of political activities, and the removal of provincial governors.[32] But there was more to the military's policy toward labor. Going beyond these measures, which merely prohibited labor's political manifestations, the military launched an all-out attack that aimed at destroying both the legal and extralegal basis of power of labor (Thompson 1985:87–89).

One way in which labor was transformed was through a barrage of legal measures that altered the basic organization and function of trade unions.[33] The outright "intervention" *(intervención)* of a union, a process whereby military officers were appointed as trustees, to administer the affairs of unions in the place of elected union officials, was one such measure.[34] Immediately following the March 1976 coup, several union offices were put under military control, as the leadership of several unions was replaced by government-appointed trustees. The pace of such a rollback of union rights was quite swift. The very day of the coup, the highest level of organized labor was directly affected by Law No. 21270, which put the CGT under military control. Simultaneously, the powerful 62 Organizations—the labor branch of the Peronist Party—was dissolved, and any future organization that might take on the role of the 62 Organizations was prohibiting by Decree No. 10/76.[35] One day later, military personnel occupied the Buenos Aires headquarters of a series of important unions, including those organizing metal workers, textile workers (Asociación Obrera Textil de la República Argentina [AOT]), auto workers (Sindicato de Mecánicos y Afines del Transporte Automotor [SMATA]), telephone workers (Federación de Obreros y Empleados Telefónicos de la República Argentina

[FOETRA]), construction workers (Unión Obrera de la Construcción de la República Argentina [UOCRA]), and journalists (Federación Argentina de Trabajadores de Prensa [FATPREN]). In the province of Córdoba a similar fate befell several locals of national unions.[36] The move against unions continued, as the labor minister ordered the "intervention" of a dozen unions on March 31, and eighteen more "interventions" throughout the month of April. By the end of May, the number of worker organizations with government-appointed trustees rose to forty-five.[37]

The overall impact of these "interventions" was considerable. All in all, the number of unions under military control was small. But they were the unions with the greatest political clout and the greatest number of affiliates, including almost every union with more than 100,000 affiliates (see Appendix B).[38] In one fell swoop the top leadership level of unions, representing 80 to 90 percent of Argentine workers covered by collective bargaining agreements, was displaced. Furthermore, the unions under military control included a series of unions in the public sector considered to be decisive, such as the railroad workers' union (Unión Ferroviaria), the light and power workers' federation (Federación Argentina de Trabajadores de Luz y Fuerza [FATLyF]), and the already mentioned telephone workers' unions. In a very short time, the union movement that had the power to select ministers only a few months before had been partially decapitated and quite firmly muzzled.

The impact of these actions went beyond the actual interventions by reminding labor leaders of nonintervened unions of the constant threat represented by the possible interventions of nonintervened unions. This threat hung over the heads of union leaders like a Damoclean sword and served to moderate their views and stifle possible actions that would be adverse to the government's goals. This "comply or else" logic was not to be taken lightly either, as new "interventions "did indeed occur, while subservient union leaders were rewarded through the extension of their mandates as elected union leaders.[39] Indeed, the military adopted a pattern of selective "intervention" of individual unions. First of all, only some union heads were replaced by military leaders, while others were not. Furthermore, those removed were treated differently: some went to prison, while others were free to walk the streets.[40] Indirectly, some leaders lost power, while others increased theirs.

The effectiveness of such a divide-and-rule strategy, however, was weakened by the general restrictions put on trade union activities. Even unions that were not put under military control were severely restricted. A blanket measure (Decree No. 9/76) declared that all union activities, with the exception of those pertaining to the internal administration of unions and the unions' social service network (Obras Sociales),[41] were to be temporarily suspended. The suspension of union activities and the powers of the labor ministry were further delineated in Law No. 21356, which both banned union elections and banned unions from calling assemblies and congresses.[42] If this decree and supplementary law did not make it clear enough, Laws No. 21261 and No. 21262 suspended the right to strike. With regard to collective bargaining, a similar restriction held.[43] In effect, these measures added up to the abolition of the Law of Professional Associations, the most comprehensive piece of labor legislation, which had previously provided the legal framework that regulated the constitution and functioning of unions.[44]

Beyond these measures, which drastically reshaped the legal context within which labor acted in the first few months after the March 1976 coup, the military affected labor in other crucial ways. The use of terror by the state was certainly the most brutally effective instrument the military employed to eradicate the problems they perceived labor to be creating. It is important, however, to note the differential impact that repression had for elements in the rank and file of the labor movement and the leadership level.

A goal of state terrorism was to bring an end to labor activism, particularly at the rank-and-file level of the labor movement, where guerrilla organizations were seen as having their greatest chance of infiltration. Decisive action was therefore seen as an acute necessity, and it is not surprising that the bulk of the workers who disappeared came from this level.[45] Those were workers who had been active in political parties and in workers' committees within the workplace *(comisiones internas)*, and workers who protested against management prerogatives.[46] While certain geographic areas were particularly hard hit, such as Córdoba and Rosario, where there had been an important resurgence of labor militancy in the late 1960s and early 1970s, the targets of repression were, more broadly, unions or locals of unions and certain factories know to "harbor troublemakers."

It is worth pointing out that the "war against subversion" within the factories, where the linking up of workers and guerrillas was seen as potentially explosive, was carried out jointly by business and the armed forces. The armed forces and business clearly shared a complementary interest, if for different reasons. Business, which had always opposed the advances unionists made under the Peronist government of 1973–76, wanted to regain control over the production process, to avoid slowdowns and other disruptive tactics. The military were concerned with blocking any advances by the guerrillas within the workplace. Business leaders were thus instructed by the military rulers to isolate troublemakers and to pass on lists of such people to the army and the other services. As a result, it became common for workers to be dragged away from assembly lines or out of offices, in plain daylight and in the presence of their co-workers—a method with clear intimating effects that created a culture of fear.[47]

Although state terror was used as a weapon against the rank and file of the trade union structure, direct and physical repression was rarely used against the leadership level. As discussed above, imprisonment of union leaders whose unions had been put under government control was a common option. But the reasons for such measures were not a labor leader's past radical actions but his position at the head of a union that had some independent weight within the union movement. At the leadership level, cases of imprisonment of radical leaders, such as Julio Guillán, were rare. Most of the purging of left and radical union leaders had been accomplished by the time of the 1976 coup. Already in mid-1974, national unions had "intervened" locals with dissenting leadership, as was the case with the auto workers' union in Córdoba and the metal workers' union in Villa Constitución. Meanwhile, other left or "anti-bureaucratic" leaders, such as Tosco and Salamanca, had been killed or had disappeared. Thus, the majority of unionists imprisoned after the coup, such as Lorenzo Miguel and Jorge Triaca, were fairly conservative Peronists whose distinction was that they had led their unions during the 1973–76 years or, as "verticalists" *(verticalistas)*, supported Isabel Perón. They were imprisoned even though they shared the goals of the "war against subversion" and had fought against the left within their own unions.

Along with the use of state terror, the military rulers sought to eliminate what they perceived as the labor problem through a series of measures aimed at restructuring the Argentine economy and undermining the structural basis of trade union power. Such a transformation was sought, in part, through the government's own role as an employer. To this end, the military embarked on an ambitious policy of trimming the public sector, enacting Law No. 21274, the Law of Redundancy *(de prescindibilidad)*, at the end of March 1976. This law gave the military ample discretion to fire employees in the public administration and other state dependencies, and its impact was quite widespread. The number of employees in the national administration, as well as in state enterprises and public banks, which had grown by more than 23 percent between 1970 and 1975, now declined by more than 16 percent between 1975 and 1980.[48]

Moving beyond these policies aimed at cutting back employment in the public sector, the military had a much broader impact through the neoconservative economic program put in place by the military's minister of economy, Martínez de Hoz.[49] This economic program not only served as an "instrument of social control," as Adolfo Canitrot (1983) put it, but also began to introduce such sweeping changes in Argentina's economy that the very conditions that had allowed for the creation and eventual reproduction of labor, along with other actors that had been part of the Peronist coalition, would eventually be undermined.[50]

Conclusion

During the first six months or so after the March 1976 coup, the new military rulers successfully seized power. The new governing elites defined an institutional arrangement that would organize their management of power on an interim basis. Moreover, the military rulers moved swiftly and decisively to complete the transition from the old system. In the first few months after taking power, the military rulers had drastically reshaped the legal context within which labor acted; they had also launched a brutal and effective war against society; and they had begun an economic program that would eventually undermine the structural basis of trade union power. The ability of the military government to engage in destructive action gave the new rulers the appearance of being endowed with awesome powers. In the short run, indeed, the Proceso did not appear to suffer any grave weakness.

The big question, however, was whether the powers of the military were suited to the next task that the military would face as they took the first key step in consolidating their power by addressing the challenge of constitutional definition. Such a challenge would force the military to design institutions that not only dealt with intragovernmental issues, as had been the case until then, but also addressed the problem of state-society relations. It would force the military to cease treating society solely as a target, whether of repression or some other negative measure, and to confront the problem of representation that was described, in Chapter 2, as the Achilles' heel of bureaucratic authoritarianism. This task would entail a very different type of challenge, compared with the one the military had successfully handled in the first six months after they had come to power in March 1976. If the military had, until then, been well served by the strong degree of internal consensus and cohesion they had generated around purely reactive objectives, there was no guarantee that they would be equally successful in tackling the more complex and essentially political problem of institutionalizing excluded social forces.

The key significance of the problem of representation, as would become clear shortly, was that it did not involve the type of issues that had allowed the military to develop a purely reactive, short-term, and militaristic sense of purpose for bringing about the coup and for seizing power. Instead, it would force the military rulers to face a fundamental dilemma that ultimately could not be resolved and that would subject the military to conflicting imperatives that could directly threaten their sense of cohesion. The ability of the military rulers to respond to the challenge of constitutional definition, moreover, would be affected by the interim institutional arrangement they had set up in the wake of the coup. As this chapter has sought to show, the interim institutional arrangement appeared to present no obstacle to the military in the short run. But the institutional arrangement clearly had some potential pitfalls, particularly inasmuch as it introduced an abridgment of the principle of co-equal participation of all the services in the government, which lay at the very heart of the military's corporate pact, while also generating a tendency toward the feudalization of the state.

If in late 1976 there could be no question about the extent to which the military rulers had dealt a defeat to labor and its allies, there was nothing that ensured that success in the task of seizing power would ensure success in the next challenge, that of constitutional definition. For all the power the military had displayed up to that moment, the lingering questions were how the military rulers would go about addressing the problem of representation, how labor would be affected by any military initiatives in that regard, and how the relationship between the military rulers and labor would affect the military's ability to confront the challenge of constitutional definition. To these questions we turn in the next chapter.

Chapter 4

The Military's Project and the Reconstitution of Labor in Argentina, 1976–1979

As the military rulers' attempt to seize power—by assuming management of the state and completing the transition from the previous form of rule—the priority of these rulers turned to the central challenge of the phase of origin of any regime-founding attempt: the challenge of constitutional definition. This shift was highly significant because the challenge of constitutional definition was of a different nature, compared with the challenge involved in the seizure of power, and had important implications from the perspective of the cohesion of the military rulers. While the cohesion that enabled the military to seize power successfully was cemented both before the military staged their coup—indeed, as a condition for the staging of the coup—and around purely reactive, short-term, and militaristic objectives, the cohesion that would enable the military to tackle the challenge of constitutional definition successfully was, for the most part, something that had to be fashioned once the military was installed in power and with regard to the forward-looking and essentially political problem of establishing a basis for a new political order. This challenge thus brought the military face to face with the need to incorporate actors that represented important interests in society and the problem of representation, which, as discussed in Chapter 2, both lies at the heart of the military's decisions concerning a future political order and constitutes the Achilles' heel of bureaucratic authoritarianism as a political project.

The significance of the problem of representation is that it gives rise to a conflicting imperative that constitutes a fundamental and ultimately unresolvable dilemma for the military rulers. The military is drawn, on the one hand, to lay the foundation of a new political order by acknowledging the problem of representation. But because of the way in which such a choice exposes the military rulers to the danger of a loss of cohesion, as well as the threat of principled opposition by a relevant actor, the military is also drawn to simply ignore the problem of representation. In other words, because the military's cohesion with regard to such a proactive and political objective is much more difficult to craft and maintain than the cohesion that enables the military to stage a coup and seize power, success with regard to the seizure of power is no indication or guarantee that the military will be as successful in subsequently tackling the challenge of constitutional definition.

This chapter considers how the Argentine military rulers, having successfully seized power, responded to the challenge of constitutional definition. The discussion focuses first on the military's formal and public acknowledgment of the need to address the challenge of constitutional definition by shaping new institutions, in early 1977, and on their decision to search for allies in the labor arena. Then the impact of the military's opening to labor on the reconstitution of labor as an actor is addressed. Finally, the military's decision concerning the challenge of constitutional definition, embodied in two key documents released in late 1979, the "Political Foundation of the Armed Forces for the Process of National Reorganization" and the Law of Professional Associations, is assessed. Seeking to explain this response, moreover, the key question concerning the phase of origin of military rule in Argentina—why the military rulers were only partially successful in designing a new institutional order—is answered in terms of the interplay between three factors highlighted by the political-institutional model outlined in Chapter 1: the degree of cohesion of the new governing elites, the degree of opposition offered by the displaced forces, and the interim institutional arrangement.

The Military's Decision to Address the Challenge of Constitutional Definition: The End of War . . . the Beginning of Politics

The first few months of the Process of National Reorganization (Proceso de Reorganización Nacional), covered in the preceding chapter, were centered on the task of assuming power and the elimination of those elements of the system they had just replaced that were considered as threatening. As the military settled into power, and as the perception that such threatening elements had been contained took root toward the end of 1976,[1] however, a new issue emerged on the military rulers' agenda: the definition of a constitutional basis for a new political order. Once it became clear that most of the radical changes of a reactive nature that the military set out to make had been accomplished by the time they celebrated their first year in power, in March 1977, the need for a political proposal was acknowledged by President General Jorge R. Videla. He emphasized: "If we do not give this 'Proceso' a political direction, a political proposal, we run the risk that it could end up like other military processes, with a compromised opening, as a consequence of not having found a political motivation and from having sterilized itself in a rigid attitude" (quoted in Troncoso 1985: 36).[2] In other words, as the worst of the old had been removed or at least suppressed, the state's political relationship to society regained importance.

The indication that the military rulers perceived a need for a political proposal did not represent, in any shape or form, a broad and unequivocal invitation to excluded actors to participate in the shaping of future political institutions. Rather, most of the debate concerning the political proposal was to be carried out behind the scenes, among military officers. In this sense, political power still resided firmly in the hands of the military institution.[3] But it would be a mistake to see the challenge of constitutional definition only in terms of an intramilitary debate, for as a central part of the effort to undertake this challenge of constitutional definition, the military sought to foster "responsible" allies that were courted by means of a dialogue. The expectation was that, at an appropriate time, they could become participants in a project that, as President Videla asserted, envisioned civilian participation.[4] In short, while societal and civilian actors did not have a hand in shaping the military's political proposal, to the point that even the topic of such a proposal almost disappeared from the public eye over the next two years,[5] what the military did seek to do, through both official and informal encounters between the military and civilians, was foster "responsible" allies that could subsequently lend support for the project that the military had devised.

This search for allies, which aimed at expanding the basis of support for the military rulers' project, quite naturally led the military into the labor arena. Whatever shape the military's political proposal eventually took, the potential opposition by an actor that expressed a key cleavage in Argentine society was something the military had to take into account. Indeed, because the role of Peronism, which during this period of military rule was more than ever dominated and organizationally based within labor, was at the source of the problem of governability in Argentina, what to do about labor was the key question to be confronted by those advancing a project of refoundation of the political system (González Bombal 1991:52).[6] Thus, even as the military were forcefully moving to silence labor and forestall any resistance, and even before the guerrillas had been fully defeated, the military began a series of contacts with select labor leaders.[7]

The first military-labor contacts responded to a clearly opportunistic move by some union leaders, who saw the change in government as a chance to gain from the new conjuncture of events. Because many of their rivals—the strongest elements in the labor movement—had been imprisoned or weakened and were out of favor with the new government, they believed the time was propitious for them to improve their standing. Thus, amid the turmoil and uncertainty of the very first days of the new government, these unionists made their move and approached the government with conciliatory talk.[8] But, moving beyond these first extremely opportunistic initiatives, there was a more-or-less continuous dialogue, carried out both formally and informally between high military officers and labor leaders, at the initiative of both sets of actors. Official contacts took place in the labor ministry and in the General Labor Confederation (CGT)—until it was abolished in late 1979—between the labor minister, the undersecretary of labor, or the CGT's military overseer *(interventor)*,[9] on the one hand, and union heads or general secretaries of union locals, on the other hand.[10] Unofficial contacts took the form of personal and secret conversations between top military officers and only a handful of unionists with privileged access to the circles of power.

As soon as the military rulers believed that they faced a malleable actor, the military sought to combine the destructive force of their antilabor policies with a more constructive attitude, which aimed at transforming labor as an actor in a more positive manner by affecting the manner in which labor was reconstituted as an actor. The goal of the military was to replace the old political unionism by a type of unionism that would be supportive of their project. Whether such a goal was ultimately attainable or not—that is, whether the "negative incorporation" the military could offer labor was a workable formula—was an essentially political question. What mattered was that such an opening to labor had important political consequences both for the military and for labor, and that the very political dynamic that was unleashed by the military's decision to reach out to society would determine whether the military's goal of seeking labor's support for their project was viable.

The military's decision to seek labor allies was quite important, from the perspective of the military, because it raised the possibility of important risks. The most important internal risk entailed by such an endeavor was that it put a great strain on the cohesion of the military. As discussed in Chapter 3, the military came to power with a strong sense of cohesion built around purely reactive objectives, such as the "war against subversion" and the containment of labor militancy. These reactive objectives were codified in the form of a Doctrine of National Security, a discourse that provided the armed forces with a sense of internal cohesion or corporate unity. The problem with such a discourse was that it was directed only at the military and not at society (Rouquié 1986:111; Fontana 1985:96–98). Thus, as the credibility of the threat posed by the guerrillas receded, and as the political issue of the state's relationship to society regained importance toward the end of 1976—that is, as the transition from the previous form of rule was completed and the challenge of constitutional definition came to the fore—a fundamental weakness of bureaucratic authoritarianism, which was not apparent during the period when the military could focus on purely reactive goals, began to be exposed. The military simply lacked a discourse for society.[11]

In seeking allies within society—a challenge the military had to confront if they were to continue to prove themselves as effective rulers—the discourse of the Doctrine of National Security, which had provided a basis for military cohesion, was simply useless. The military's cohesion would have to be recast in relation to the challenge of developing a political project and seeking support for such a project.[12] That was a tougher challenge than bringing about the coup and seizing power, and the military's difficulties in tackling it would put a severe strain on the military's cohesion. Indeed, as the argument in Chapter 2 predicts, important splits within the military began to emerge as soon as the need for a political proposal and the appropriateness of a dialogue with civilians was raised by President Videla.[13]

If the strain on the cohesion of the military that the challenge of constitutional definition generated had fundamental implications for the political dynamics of bureaucratic authoritarianism, so did a second risk associated with the military's decision to seek labor allies. This is so because the decision to address the political issue of the state's relation to society unleashed a process whereby labor was gradually reconstituted as an actor and in such a manner that it was likely to adopt an orientation of principled opposition rather than pragmatic support for the military's project. The military's decision to seek labor allies had significant consequences from the perspective of labor, because it was really only inasmuch as the military tilted toward this option that labor started to have some positive choices that would enable it to reestablish itself as a political actor.

As discussed in Chapter 3, the old labor actor had been clearly defeated through the series of measures enacted in the wake of the 1976 coup. As a result of the initial measures of the military government, labor had been thoroughly disorganized and lost almost all capacity for collective action. The military had moved rapidly to muzzle and decapitate what had been, until then, a powerful labor movement, and now labor lacked the capacity to offer any effective resistance. Indeed, it was quite clear that inasmuch as the military sought to repress the excluded sectors, there was little that labor could do. There were only a few isolated instances of resistance, and the hopes and expectations of a labor plan to fight back rapidly disappeared as it became clear that a general strike would have little chance of success.[14] The norm was therefore a moderation based on fear and apprehension on the part of labor leaders who knew that they could well follow in the path of the leaders who were displaced from their unions, or of those who were now in prison. Unionists knew that the new government meant business when it prohibited all forms of labor action.[15]

From the perspective of labor, therefore, the military's decision to reach out to society in search of "responsible" allies among labor leaders provided a new context, which was marked in particular by the uninterrupted if difficult dialogue that the armed forces opened with selected labor leaders. The overwhelmingly negative thrust of the military's labor policy would be supplemented with a more positive orientation, which provided labor leaders with certain spaces within which they could act with a degree of autonomy and which opened up important new possibilities. The beginning of such a dialogue, in short, signaled a new phase in post-1976 state-labor relations, one that would be characterized by the reconstitution of labor as an actor. To be sure, this process of reconstitution would be a long and complex one, shaped by the interaction between a diverse set of labor leaders and their military interlocutors, and by the interaction between these labor leaders and the workers they sought to represent. But, as a process that would allow labor to regain its capacity for collective action, it would have a fundamental impact on the political dynamics of bureaucratic authoritarianism. It is a process that deserves detailed consideration.

The Reconstitution of Labor as an Actor: From Defeat to Weak Opposition

The process whereby labor was reconstituted as an actor was critical to the political dynamics of bureaucratic authoritarianism because the outcome of this process affected the military's long-term prospects of gaining support for their project, through its impact on the manner in which the military went about the challenge of constitutional definition and on the subsequent evolution of the new political order that the military sought to establish.[16] This section looks at the manner in which labor was reconstituted as an actor and regained its capacity for collective action. The focus here is on the period that extends from labor's defeat in March 1976 through its first major action, the general strike of April 1979. Building on this analysis, the impact of the labor-military relations on the military's decision concerning the challenge of constitutional definition will be considered in the next section.

Basic Elements of a Disorganized Actor

To advance the analysis, it is necessary to begin by briefly considering the basic elements that served as the building blocks in the process of labor's reconstitution as an actor. If labor had been thoroughly disorganized as a result of the assault on labor carried out by the military rulers, as discussed in Chapter 3, it is possible to isolate within this field of destruction three different types of labor leaders that would play a role in the reconstitution of labor: (1) former leaders displaced by military overseers; (2) leaders of union locals or branches *(seccionales)* "intervened" at the national level and leaders of local unions belonging to "intervened" federations *(filiales del interior)*; and (3) leaders of unions still under labor control.[17]

One common measure the military used was the "intervention" *(intervención)* of a union—that is, the appointment of a trustee in the place of labor leaders. Thus, in a matter of a few months most of the visible heads of the union movement during the period 1973–76 were removed from their positions in labor unions. Even though the number of intervened unions was relatively small, intervened unions were usually large and politically important unions, accounting for approximately two-thirds of the entire union structure. But if all displaced leaders lost their legal mandate as labor leaders, there were nonetheless significant differences in terms of how the government dealt with displaced leaders. While some displaced leaders, usually those with great political weight, such as Lorenzo Miguel, were imprisoned for up to four years, others, such as José Rodríguez of the auto workers' union (SMATA) and Leslio Romero of the metal workers' union (UOM), were not imprisoned and were able to reenter the labor scene as soon as 1977, if handicapped by their lack of a legal mandate. Former leaders displaced by the military thus represented a first category of labor leaders that would play a role in reconstituting labor as an actor.[18]

The flip side of the process of "intervention," which displaced well-established leaders, was that second-line leaders were thrust into positions of greater importance as representatives of workers' views.[19] In the situation after the 1976 coup, military overseers could not and did not want to run big union organizations alone. Thus, they were eager to find old hands to fill the role of collaborators. Indeed, much of the nonelected personnel who ran labor organizations before they fell under military control stayed on. But more important, military overseers needed to deal with a world of workers that was, for the most part, unfamiliar to them. Military contacts with workers were thus mediated by second-line unionists, who became the main spokespersons for the workers vis-à-vis the military overseers.[20] Therefore, previously obscure and little-heard-of general secretaries of locals *(secretarios generales de seccionales)*, in the case of unions and associations, and general secretaries of unions, in the case of federations, were thrust into the limelight for the first time—becoming, for all practical purposes, the formal heads of their organizations. These leaders were handicapped because they had never been elected to lead their unions, as had been the case with the established leaders that were removed from office, and because they lacked experience as leaders at the national level.[21] Nevertheless, these leaders of union locals or branches "intervened" at the national level, and leaders of local unions belonging to intervened federations constituted a second category of labor leaders that would shape the reemergence of labor in the post-1976 years.

Finally, there were the leaders of generally small unions, which had not been particularly prominent during the 1973–76 period and had not been "intervened" after the coup. Their position was quite unique. Unlike the situation of the established leaders that had been displaced by the military, these leaders retained their positions legally. Unlike the situation of second-line leaders discussed above, the leaders of these unions had both been elected and headed their unions for some time. This element of legality and legitimacy translated into an increase in power and visibility on the national scene and made these leaders of unions still under labor control, our third category of labor leaders, particularly important players in the labor field in the years immediately after the 1976 coup.[22]

The Emergence of a Compliant Labor Leadership

If these were the basic elements that could play a role in the reconstitution of labor, the road to recovery was long and difficult. There were few developments that really justify talking about the beginning of the reconstitution of labor as an actor during the nine months following the coup, given that the military were still primarily occupied with dismantling the old pattern of industrial relations. The government did begin a regular dialogue with union leaders in May 1976, but this dialogue was circumscribed to the very limited and regulated locus of the General Labor Confederation (CGT), now under the control of the CGT's military overseer, Commodore Julio César Porcile.[23] Not satisfied with such a constrained setting, labor leaders pushed, through the end of the year, for the holding of a plenary meeting. Such a meeting, to be held independent of governmental directives, would allow labor leaders to discuss their position toward the new government and provide an appropriate avenue for the national union structure, which had become thoroughly disorganized and disoriented by the 1976 coup, to regroup. To this end, labor leaders formed multiple commissions, all of which were constituted primarily of leaders that retained control of their unions and more or less overlapped in terms of leadership, and politely requested meetings with the government's labor authorities.[24] But such initiatives bore no real fruit. Government authorities, who had little to worry about in the face of the requests by these labor leaders, simply insisted that the ban on union activities contained no exceptions and denied labor's petition to hold a plenary meeting. In response, labor leaders, well aware of the costs that might be associated with oppositional activity, adopted a wait-and-see attitude that translated into a fairly compliant and nonantagonistic relationship toward the government.[25]

The limited role of this compliant labor leadership contrasted with the activities of workers at the rank-and-file level of the union movement. In relation to workers, who reacted to the deterioration of their situation, after six months of relative tranquillity, with a number of strikes, these union leaders did not function either as agents of representation, from the perspective of the workers involved in conflicts, or as agents of control, from the perspective of the government.[26] This was particularly clear in the first important strike since the coup, in which auto workers in several plants went on strike, demanding better wages, during the first three weeks of September 1976. In this strike, as in most other major conflicts that occurred soon thereafter, a key feature was that the striking workers belonged to unions that had been "intervened" and whose cause was not taken up by the labor leaders who were unwilling to jeopardize the few liberties they still enjoyed. Thus, in the absence of union coordination and solidarity, strikers remained isolated, offering at best "a vigorous though defensive and dispersed resistance" to the government's policies (Munck with Falcón and Gallitelli 1987:214; Falcón 1982:130–31).[27]

While these wildcat strikes showed how far the delinking of the rank and file and activists at this level, and the union leadership, had gone, it also showed that the government's policy of union intervention was a double-edged sword. Because the auto workers' union was "intervened," and no visible leaders headed these protest actions, there was a lack of a clearly identifiable actor to bargain with. Labor conflicts thus took on an anarchic character that compounded the government's problems in exercising social control. The government was forced to respond with repressive measures. Thus, it sanctioned the Law of Industrial Security, No. 21400, which, in prohibiting concerted measures of direct action such as strikes, expanded and further defined Law No. 21262, which had suspended the right to strike immediately after the coup, by establishing penalties of one to six years of prison for those participating in any "measure of force," and one to ten years for those that publicly instigated others to go along with these measures.[28] It also sent troops to occupy the interior and the perimeter of factories, an extreme measure that the military themselves would have preferred to avoid because the army sensed that sending troops to guard and occupy plants in cases of labor disputes would eventually lead to an erosion *(desgaste)* of the authority of the military. The military thus acknowledged that the control of labor conflicts in the absence of an established labor leadership created its own problems for the government.

At this point in time, however, the problems associated with labor anarchy and the use of repression were less important, from the perspective of the government, than the possibility of labor conflicts spearheaded by militant labor leaders. This became very evident in the case of the leadership organizing workers in SEGBA (Servicios Eléctricos del Gran Buenos Aires), a state-run electrical power company. The electrical power workers first went on strike for sixteen days in October 1976, on the heel of the auto strike, in protest over the firing of more than two hundred workers, including the general secretary of the Federal Capital local of the light and power workers' federation (Sindicato de Luz y Fuerza-Capital Federal), Oscar Smith,[29] under the Law of Redundancy.[30] Subsequently, the same workers went on strike again from January 21 to February 9, 1977, over the application of Law No. 21476, which modified the "special regimes" *(regímenes especiales)* that regulated the activities of workers in the state sector (Pozzi 1988a:42–45; Pion-Berlin 1989:112–14).[31] In this case, which was particularly important from the government's perspective, given that it put to a test the government's ability to control labor conflicts among its own workers,[32] the military acted with unyielding determination. For the first time, government authorities applied some of the sanctions envisioned in the Law of Industrial Security; but more important, as an agreement seemed to have been reached and workers returned to their tasks, having bowed to most of the changes introduced by Law No. 21476, the recently fired general secretary, Oscar Smith, was kidnapped in February 1977 and never reappeared, dead or alive.

While it remains unclear who was responsible for Smith's kidnapping, and exactly why he was kidnapped,[33] the implications for other union leaders willing to head protest movements was all too clear. News of Smith's abduction sent shock waves within the union structure. Particularly for leaders who remained at the head of their unions, the stakes in taking the lead in conflicts were not only loss of control over the union apparatus but also apparently their very lives. Thus, even though such incidents were fairly rare, the Smith case in particular served as a warning of what might happen if union leaders did challenge the government. Just as the threat of "intervention" hung over the head of union leaders and served to moderate their views, the ripple effect of Smith's disappearance would temper the militant passion of labor leaders in all sorts of situations, regardless of whether or not they retained an official role within a particular labor union.

In sum, the first important labor conflicts after the 1976 coup brought into sharp relief some of the key trends in state-labor relations. The actions of labor leaders had consisted of fairly timid attempts to regroup and plan their strategy toward the government. The push for a plenary meeting was the most consistent demand, given that it was seen as the clearest way for a national union structure that had been battered by the 1976 coup and that continued to be disorganized and disoriented to regroup. Lacking a forum in which to meet and jointly debate their position vis-à-vis the government, the actions of the unionists were perforce diluted in their mutual isolation. But more important than this trend was what the pattern of labor conflicts revealed: that these labor leaders remained extremely disconnected from the rank and file and activists at this level, unwilling to jeopardize the few spaces the government still allowed.

Having effectively beheaded the more established and politically oriented union leaders, government authorities did not have to worry much about the potentially disruptive actions of this compliant labor leadership. But the very weakness of these labor leaders left the military rulers with no option but to deal with labor problems through pervasive fear and draconian actions. Thus, even though labor peace was an important priority for the military,[34] the military rulers were unwilling to allow for any serious reconstitution of labor as an actor, for fear that such a trend would rebound against them. The government was, as yet, less preoccupied with the spread of anarchic conflict than with the emergence of militant labor leaders and still saw the crippling of labor's organizational power as the most important objective at this stage, regardless of the negative effects it could have in terms of managing industrial relations. As the military sought a more lasting solution to the management of industrial relations, however, the government would have to give labor leaders more freedom to reconstitute themselves as representative actors, for such a development was a necessary precondition for labor to function effectively as a responsible ally.

The Consolidation of Two Competing Labor Groupings

If until early 1977 the leadership level of labor was characterized by its extremely tentative and cautionary proceeding and its isolation from workers, over the next two and a half years labor would gradually reconstitute itself in such a manner that it crystallized as an actor divided between two quite distinct and opposed wings. Thus, by mid-1979, as the military entered the final phase of decision-making with regard to constitutional definition, labor had been reconstituted so that one wing had adopted a clearly collaborationist orientation toward the military, while the other wing defined itself in terms of a more clearly oppositionist stance.

Signs of change within the labor leadership began to emerge as 1977 got off to a start. Their obsession with constituting and reconstituting commissions, which did little more than politely request meetings with the government's labor authorities and reiterate time and again their desire to hold a plenary meeting, began to give way to less compliant attitudes. Now labor leaders were busily discussing the preparation of a document that would be critical of the military government. There was disagreement between those who wanted to publish the document as a statement of their position on the government's labor policy, and those who believed that publication of the document would harm their chances of continuing a dialogue with the government—closing, in effect, what was seen as an important channel for influencing the government. But in the end, despite this disagreement, leaders of nonintervened unions resolved to publicize the document.[35] The text of the document, entitled "To the National Government" (Al Gobierno Nacional) and signed by representatives of seventy-eight unions, was made public on January 4 and printed in its entirety by the daily *La Opinión* two days later (Grupo de los 25 1977; Abós 1984:117–25). In it, labor leaders demanded a wage increase, a lifting of the ban on union activity, an end to the "intervention" of the CGT as well as of individual unions, the repealing of Law No. 21476, which modified the "special regimes" that regulated the activities of workers in the state sector, the release of unionists held without cause, and clarification of the status of all detained unionists.

This first sign of courage on the part of union leaders presented the government, for the first time, with a fait accompli. Tentative as it still was, it was a risky move that circumvented the carefully controlled channels of interaction between the state and labor. Moreover, the initiative eventually led to an important development: the formation of the Group of 25 or Commission of 25 (Grupo de los 25, or Comisión de los 25) in March 1977. The Group of 25 was distinct from the previous commissions formed by labor leaders, not only because the existence of the latter had been extremely ephemeral. More crucial was that while previous commissions had all grown out of the CGT—an intervened body that the military authorities had arbitrarily divided into seven subgroups, the Group of 25 was the first site for debate among the top labor leadership level constituted *outside* a government-sanctioned framework.[36]

The publication of the critical document in January, and the Group of 25's subsequent rebuff of the government's invitation to form part of a delegation to the annual International Labor Organization (ILO) conference in Geneva,[37] led the government to freeze the dialogue between unionists and the government and to turn to other labor leaders in its pursuit of "responsible" labor leaders. To this end, the initiative to form a series of consultative commissions was the government's most comprehensive effort. These consultations were organized within the locus of the CGT and under the supervision of its military overseer, who appointed unionists to various advisory committees *(comisiones de consulta)*, whose assignments were to discuss key issues pertaining to the normalization of union life.[38]

What this signified was a fairly dramatic reconfiguration of the dialogue between government authorities and labor leaders, which both expanded the scope of the government-union dialogue and at the same time circumvented the leaders that until then had been the government's key interlocutors. If, until then, the only leaders that participated in conversations with government authorities had been the heads of approximately one hundred nonintervened labor organizations, now the government focused its attention on leaders of locals of unions or associations who had retained their positions even while their organizations had been "intervened" at the national level, on leaders of unions belonging to "intervened" federations, and on unionists from the provinces of the interior of the country. In short, by shifting the dialogue to the controlled arena of the CGT, the government gave greater importance to second-line unionists while circumventing the labor leaders, who, if belonging to the small unions that had not been "intervened," were relatively more established than the second-line unionists the government now turned to.[39]

But while the government demonstrated the ample discretion it had in determining the form of any dialogue between labor and government authorities, along with an ability to sanction leaders who acted with some independence, if nothing else than by refusing to dialogue with them, the limits of such a strategy were rapidly revealed. Thus, by the end of the year, the government made an about-face in its strategy. The trigger for this rapid change was the resumption of labor conflicts after a lull in strike activity following the strike by electrical power workers in January and February 1977. The renewal of labor conflicts started with strikes by auto, railroad, and subway workers in October 1977, a series of strikes that was only the beginning of a wave of conflicts that erupted in November and December.[40] These labor conflicts gave evidence of the creativity of the rank and file, which engaged in diverse forms of resistance, including Sicilian strikes, consisting of slowdowns in the production process without the actual calling of a strike *(trabajo a tristeza, huelga de brazos caídos)*, work-to-rule *(trabajo a reglamento, quite de colaboración)*, and sabotage. Such forms of protest had the characteristic of avoiding direct and potentially more harmful confrontation with the authorities, which, given the current legislation, would have heightened the threat of retaliation with no clear extra gain (Falcón 1982:114–17; Pozzi 1988a:81). Just as important, these conflicts were all organized outside the formal union leadership structure.

As had been the case with the strikes in late 1976, the strike wave during the last trimester of 1977 revealed the problems associated with the prohibitions placed on the normal functioning of trade unions. Moreover, for the first time since the coup, business people began to express their worries about spontaneous shop-floor activity and began calling for labor representatives or legitimate interlocutors *(interlocutores válidos)*. This rediscovery of the virtues of trade union functions provided an opportunity for established labor leaders to argue that the current restrictions on traditional union activities were part of the reason for their occurrence. Unionists not only made statements about the role they could play in bringing order to the field of industrial relations,[41] but also showed the continued legitimacy of unions in the eyes of workers when the government demanded that all union members submit a written declaration of their intent to remain affiliated with their unions. The positive response by more than 90 percent of union members was a clear indication of the continued vitality of unions and of the difficulties the military would face in circumventing the established leadership (Pozzi 1988a:152–53).[42]

The government was keenly aware of the significance of these trends. Signaling a shift in the government's understanding of industrial relations, the labor minister, General Horacio Tomás Liendo, met with a group of ten general secretaries of nonintervened unions, including the five leaders of the "Commission of 5" (Comisión de los 5), which functioned as the executive committee of the Group of 25, toward the end of 1977. After attempting to weaken the power of the more established labor leaders congregated in the Group of 25 earlier in the year, the labor minister was treating the leaders of the Group of 25 as virtual representatives of the labor movement.

The establishment of the Group of 25 throughout 1977 as the first real labor grouping *(nucleamiento sindical)* to emerge since the 1976 coup, important as it was, did not bring the process of reconstitution of labor as an actor to an end. Because of its quite heterogeneous composition, the Group of 25 was fraught with internal divisions and far from being a stable entity.[43] Indeed, the tension between more moderate and more confrontationist sectors within the Group of 25 soon led to a fundamental development within the labor arena: the emergence of a new labor grouping called the Labor Action Commission (Comisión de Gestión y Trabajo [CGyT]), in April 1978. The importance of the formation of this second labor grouping, which aimed at providing a clear alternative to the more confrontationist stance adopted by the Group of 25, cannot be overstated. The emergence of the CGyT, characterized as it was by a professionalist orientation and by the inclusion of big unions, would clarify the profile of labor precisely as the military moved toward the critical decisions concerning the challenge of constitutional definition.

Regarding its orientation, the CGyT was very explicit in distinguishing between a political and a "professional" orientation, and in advocating the latter. While the heterogeneous composition of the Group of 25 had prevented it from adopting a clear orientation, the top leaders of the CGyT, in contrast, made it clear from the beginning that they did not intend to participate in political debates and that they sought to restrict their sphere of action, in a professional manner, to narrowly defined trade union matters. This labor grouping represented, in short, the rise of a group of labor leaders that was very much open to reaching a compromise with the military rulers and to acting as their allies.

The other significant feature about the CGyT was that it signaled the return of big unions.[44] The move to form the CGyT was initiated by union leaders representing metal workers (UOM), textile workers (AOT), construction workers (UOCRA), light and power workers (FATLyF), commerce workers (Confederación General de Empleados de Comercio de la República Argentina [CGEC]), and plastics workers (Unión Obreros y Empleados Plásticos).[45] The fact that these unions were large and important unions introduced a complication: because most of these unions had been intervened and were led by labor leaders who were no longer officially at the head of their unions,[46] the nonofficial status of these leaders was a problem in establishing an easy relationship between the new labor grouping and the government.

But the government quickly got beyond this formalistic issue and began to have an open dialogue with the leaders of the CGyT.[47] Given that some CGyT key leaders, such as Armando Cavalieri and Jorge Triaca, had close contacts with President Videla and Division General Roberto Eduardo Viola,[48] and that the military rulers knew these labor leaders were basically supportive of the military rulers, it came as no surprise that the formation of the CGyT was well received in government circles (Pozzi 1988a:119–22; 1998b:120–22). The formation of the CGyT provided the military rulers with their most serious prospects so far of actually finding responsible allies in the labor arena.

Besides presenting the military rulers with a potential ally, the formation of the CGyT had a big impact on the Group of 25. Because of the very heterogeneous set of unions that coexisted in the Group of 25, a debate over the wisdom of adopting a political or professional orientation had been carried out by labor leaders within this labor grouping.[49] Now, the emergence of a clear professional alternative to the Group of 25 added fuel to the already heated internal debate. The heterogeneous Group of 25 was shaken up, as the newly formed CGyT served as a pole that attracted those within Group of 25 who were not content with the more oppositionist and polemical stance of some of its leaders. Problems arose at the Group of 25's very first meeting after the announced formation of the CGyT, as tensions already present between the "independent," "participationist," and Group of 8 sectors, on the one hand, and the "verticalist" and "orthodox" sectors, on the other, erupted in an overt manner. Thereafter, when the politically oriented "verticalist" and "orthodox" sectors allied to create the Peronist Syndical Movement (Movimiento Sindical Peronista [MSP]), which was basically a new version of the outlawed "62 Organizations" and which openly identified with Peronism and adopted a confrontationist position toward the government, an important reshuffling of union alignments began to take place.[50]

As a result, both the Group of 25 and the CGyT were reconfigured. The dissatisfied sectors and individual leaders within the Group of 25 defected from that group[51] and, along with other unionists who had remained at the margins of the Group of 25's activities, gravitated toward the CGyT. And to accommodate this expanded basis of support, a new labor grouping known as the National Labor Commission (Comisión Nacional de Trabajo [CNT]) and consisting of some seventy-one labor unions was formed in August 1978.[52] Following the lead of its most powerful internal sector, the CGyT, the CNT espoused a professional orientation. For its part, the Group of 25 was weakened numerically by the multiple defections, but, because of the relative greater dominance of the MSP within the labor grouping, it had also clarified its political orientation. Since the formation of the CGyT, it had become a more cohesive gathering of unions, and, in contrast to the CNT, which coalesced around the CGyT leaders and their professional orientation, was distinguished by the MSP and the political orientation of this sector (Senén Gonzalez 1984:93–94, 98–101). In sum, by August 1978 the profile of labor had become both more complex and better defined, as two labor groupings with alternate orientations had become consolidated.

Thereafter, and despite much talk of the possibility of cementing the unity of the leadership level of unionism through an agreement between the two labor groupings, the division at the top level of labor only deepened. In the very context of a series of formal "unity meetings" that begun in late March 1979,[53] the Group of 25 decided to alter the pace of events and up the ante, unilaterally calling for a "day of national protest" *(jornada de protesta nacional)* to be held on April 27. The form of protest would be a work stoppage for a full day as a means of backing demands that included restoration of workers' buying power, the return of the collective bargaining law, opposition to changes in the Law of Professional Associations and of Obras Sociales (the union-run social service network), the normalization of union life, and the release of detained unionists.

This call for a general strike, clearly the boldest move on the part of the union leadership in three years of military rule, did much to distinguish the Group of 25 from the CNT. Leaders of the CNT met immediately and decided to not support the strike. The government, too, reacted negatively.[54] The ministry of labor put out a communiqué calling the decision of the Group of 25 "irresponsible" and stating that it was subject to sanction under the Law of Industrial Security, Law No. 21400, which established severe penalties for those who organized and participated in strikes. The government immediately arrested the top leaders of the Group of 25 and continued its intimidatory tactics, seeking to weaken the resolve of some unionists and to splinter the leadership of the Group of 25 by releasing unionists who signed a document stating that they did not support the protest, while at the same time arresting more unionists who came out in support of the strike. Despite the CNT's lack of solidarity and the government's threats, however, the Group of 25 pushed ahead with their plans, forming a provisional decision-making body and confirming that the protest measure was still planned. Thus, on April 27, the first general strike against the military rulers was carried out.[55]

The Division Between Collaborationists and Confrontationists, and the Pitfalls of Hyperautonomy

Because the April 1979 general strike was the culmination of a process whereby the profile of labor as an actor was defined, it is useful to interrupt the chronology of events at this point in time in order to take stock of the outcome of the process discussed so far. If it made more sense three years earlier to talk about the disorganization of labor and about the basic elements that could play a role in the reconstitution of labor, by mid-1979 it was clear that labor had made considerable advances in reconstituting itself. This was significant, from the perspective of the analysis of bureaucratic authoritarianism, because the new profile labor had acquired affected the role labor could play in the context of the military rulers' decisions concerning the challenge of constitutional definition.

One of the most important and most visible characteristics of Argentine labor in mid-1979 was the fact that it had coalesced into two labor groupings: the CNT and the Group of 25. At its core, the split was over the orientations that labor leaders thought they should adopt. Thus, while the CNT espoused what was commonly referred to at the time as a collaborationist *(colaboracionista)* position, or what I have referred to as a professional orientation, the Group of 25 championed a confrontationist *(confrontacionista)* position, or what I have referred to as a political orientation. This was a crucial distinction that had important ramifications for the political dynamics of bureaucratic authoritarianism.

The rise of the CNT was, from the perspective of the government's desire to find responsible labor allies, the most significant positive development since the coup. Initially, as a result of the critical actions by the Group of 25 in 1977, the military rulers sought to shape the way labor was reconstituted by privileging the role of second-line unionists. These unionists had been important beneficiaries of the military's decision to foster responsible labor allies, being allowed a degree of freedom to act, while at the same time depending on the military overseers with whom they collaborated. These second-line leaders were being prepared as a new and reliable leadership that would provide the basis for the projected normalization of unions. These efforts by the labor ministry notwithstanding, the military rulers had good reasons to welcome the rise of the CNT.

Of most immediate importance was the CNT's espousal of a clearly professional orientation, which meant that CNT leaders were willing to focus on narrowly defined union issues and to seek to make gains and advance their position while accepting the de facto power of the military rulers. The CNT's demands were actually of a fairly moderate nature, revolving around a call for the normalization or legalization of union life, for better wages, and for the release of imprisoned unionists. It is significant that references to the Law of Professional Associations, which provided the legal framework for regulating the constitution and functioning of unions and which the military were in the process of revising, were avoided, as were frontal attacks on the government's economic program (Fraga 1980:26–29).[56] If the CNT's professional orientation was thus amenable to the military, the CNT also had something the second-line unionists did not have. Unlike the obscure and inexperienced second-line unionists, CNT leaders had a proven capacity to exercise control over the workers belonging to big unions. If not recognized early, this fact began to weigh more heavily with the spread of labor conflicts organized outside the formal union leadership structure, as with the strike wave during the last trimester of 1977. Thus, by mid-1979 the CNT had emerged as the most likely supporters within the labor arena of the military's goal of establishing a new political order.

In contrast to the CNT, the Group of 25 favored a political orientation that saw the advancement of workers' interests as intimately tied with the nature of the political regime. The possibility of advancing workers' interests within the framework that the military might offer was rejected, and worker gains were seen as linked with the defeat of the military's attempt to install a new political order. Thus, in contrast to the CNT's collaborationist orientation, which was based on the acceptance of the de facto powers of the military rulers and the search for gains within the parameters set by the military, the Group of 25 was characterized by a confrontationist orientation vis-à-vis the military rulers. This orientation was evident in the demands and actions of the leaders of this labor grouping. Under the dominance of the MSP, the Group of 25 had by mid-1979 become the core of labor opposition to the military rulers, not only criticizing the government's economic program but also stating their clear opposition to any changes in the Law of Professional Associations.[57] In particular, the call for the general strike in April had been the key move in strengthening the oppositionist credentials of the Group of 25 and in reestablishing the links between national labor leaders and rank-and-file elements of the workers' movement.

The efforts of the Group of 25 to reestablish the connection between the rank and file and labor leaders notwithstanding, a central characteristic of Argentine labor in mid-1979, along with the division of labor between two labor groupings espousing different orientations, was the hyperautonomy of labor leaders vis-à-vis the rank-and-file level of the labor movement (Thompson 1985:91–92). In part, the detachment of the leadership from the rank and file of the union structure was a consequence of the freezing of traditional union activities, such as the negotiation of wages and the organization of strikes, as well as the suspension of union elections and the forceful removal of leaders through the "intervention" of their unions.[58] But there was also the military's offensive against the rank-and-file level of the union movement. Historically the link between union leaders and the workers within the workplace, based on the shop stewards *(delegados)* and the factory committees *(comisiones internas)*, had been particularly strong, and as such a source of the vitality of Argentine labor.[59] All this changed, however, with the 1976 coup. As discussed in Chapter 3, one target of state terrorism was workers active at the rank-and-file level of the labor movement, where guerrilla organizations were seen as having their greatest chance of infiltration. As a result, the role of the shop stewards and the factory committees tended to languish.[60] Those that were not killed or fired, or those that voluntarily retired, held on to their posts. But even they faced opposition from business managers, the chiefs of different military zones and the regional delegations of the labor ministry, to the point that in some cases they were simply prevented from entering their workplaces. Furthermore, given that such union activities as assemblies and elections were prohibited, no new leaders emerged at the firm level.

The combined effect of these measures on the manner in which labor was reconstituted in the aftermath of the 1976 coup was quite powerful. They prevented the left and the guerrillas from joining forces with labor.[61] But these measures also ensured that labor was reconstituted in such a manner that the two labor groupings emerged through a process that was not directly affected by the decisions of workers within the workplace. That is, while the two labor groupings differentiated themselves in terms of their alternative orientations, the reconstitution of labor took place primarily through a competition among national leaders that was constrained more by the capacity of the state than of the workers to sanction leaders.[62]

It is not surprising that the clearest symptom of the hyperautonomy of union leaders was the continuous debate they held with regard to the representativeness of individual labor leaders. The most common situation involved the disputes between leaders who had lost legal control over their union, as a result of government action, and leaders who retained legal control over their union. In this case, there was a tendency for some of the "legal leaders" to question leaders who not did retain a legal mandate to lead their unions. But the legitimacy of such claims was clearly in doubt, because the displaced leaders still saw themselves as legitimate leaders, given that they had been illegitimately displaced, while the claims of those who retained their posts were less than unassailable, given that they not only had ceased to carry out the traditional tasks that linked them to the rank and file in more open periods but also given that their own legal mandate had not been reconfirmed through elections in a while.[63] At the root of this complex situation, therefore, was the thorny relationship between legality and legitimacy in an authoritarian context, which gave rise to counterposed yet, due to the lack of an electoral process, ultimately unresolvable claims that fostered incessant and somewhat fruitless disputes among leaders. The reconstitution of labor as an actor took place, thus, primarily through a leadership game of cupolas, in which labor leaders were like free-floating actors who could seek to establish a dialogue with their followers through symbolic acts, but who could never really settle the issue of the representativeness of individual labor leaders.[64]

In sum, if by mid-1979 it was clear that labor had moved beyond a state of disorganization and had made considerable advances in reconstituting itself, the most significant characteristics that defined labor as an actor—the division of labor into two competing labor groupings, and the weakness of the links between labor leaders and workers— gave an indication of the role labor was capable of playing. The military had clearly been successful in reshaping labor inasmuch as they had managed to divide labor and co-opt a significant segment of the labor leadership that appeared quite willing to support the military. But the limits of the military's achievements were also glaring.

Although labor protests had been contained to a large extent, there were also signs of a revival of opposition in the labor arena. In this regard, the April 1979 general strike is very indicative. In a sign of labor's weakness as an opposition actor, there was no escalation of protest in the aftermath of the general strike. Unlike what had happened with the 1969 Cordobazo, when national labor leaders gave coherence to and amplified the effect of the actions of radicalized workers at the rank-and-file level of the union movement, in 1979 the actions of workers were not only tempered by the effects of repression, but also muffled because of the distance between union leaders and workers, who were thus isolated from each other.[65] Following the general strike, indeed, most labor leaders returned to their routine discussions with the government. But if the weakness of labor opposition to the military, especially when compared with the military's previous experience in government between 1966 and 1973, was very evident, the general strike was clearly an important act of defiance on the part of the confrontationist Group of 25. Even though adherence to the general strike was low and spotty, its symbolic effectiveness and impact should not be underestimated. By calling for a general strike, the Group of 25 had not only managed to give voice to economically battered and politically excluded workers, but also reestablished, if only symbolically, the links between labor leaders and workers. And through its confrontation with the government, the Group of 25 had also helped to break with a culture of fear that had led to a paralysis of action in people of all walks of life.[66]

In addition, although the government appeared still very much in command of the situation on the labor front in mid-1979, there were reasons to doubt the military's ability to succeed in gaining labor support in any meaningful way. The success of the military in containing labor opposition and finding potential allies in the labor field had been accomplished by generating the conditions that were conducive to the hyperautonomy of labor leaders. That is, the military had engaged in only an extremely tentative opening to labor, which weakened the capacity of labor to act as an opposition force to military rule but which also prevented the collaborationist wing of the labor union structure from adequately fulfilling the function of representation needed to deliver the support of workers. Yet, as the revival of labor opposition suggested, it was clear that a broader opening would serve as a double-edged sword. The ability of labor's collaborationist wing to provide a mass basis for the military's project was contingent on such an opening, inasmuch as unionists could deliver labor support only to the extent that they became representative actors. But such an opening could also turn labor into a stronger opposition actor. Thus, as the military rulers entered a crucial period of deliberation concerning the challenge of constitutional definition in 1979, this thorny issue was never far from their minds.

Facing Up to the Challenge of Constitutional Definition: The Military's Political Failure

After much deliberation about the precise shape of the political order, and equally extensive efforts to foster allies that would lend support for such a project, the moment of truth appeared to be arriving for the military rulers. During the last half of 1979, the military rulers made their final decisions concerning the challenge of constitutional definition, and in late 1979 the military made public two foundational documents that embodied their attempt to shape a new institutional order. This critical moment represented the culmination of a long process whereby the military had sought to affect the reconstitution of labor, and that would have a great influence on the future dynamics of military rule. It is now time to draw together the various elements of the analysis in this chapter and the previous one and to show how the outcome of the military's effort to confront the challenge of constitutional definition can be well accounted for in terms of the interplay between the three factors highlighted by the political-institutional model outlined in Chapter 1: the degree of cohesion of the new governing elites, the degree of opposition offered by the displaced forces, and the interim institutional arrangement.

Governing Elite Cohesion, Opposition Strength, and the Interim Institutional Arrangement

The critical interaction is that between governing elite cohesion and opposition strength. If the ability of the military rulers to respond to the challenge of constitutional definition is primarily affected by the cohesion displayed by the military, inasmuch as an actor's capacity to act is always linked to its sense of unity, the military's ability to remain a cohesive actor, as it moved beyond the purely reactive, short-term, and militaristic objectives associated with the seizure of power, is itself affected by the degree of opposition it faced in society. This is a critical variable, indeed, because it affects how the military respond to the problem of representation—the problem that lies at the heart of all attempts by bureaucratic authoritarian rulers to institutionalize their power.

In this regard, Argentina's rulers provided probably the worst possible response to the excruciating choice between acknowledging the need to politically incorporate the actors that represented important interests, such as labor, or simply to continue to repress these actors. Facing an opposition that was only moderately strong, Argentina's military rulers navigated a middle course, both by responding with a high degree of repression and technocratic logic and by opening a dialogue with society fairly early on, even as repression continued. Argentina's military rulers could not decide whether the support they might be able to gain by opening to society outweighed the risks such an opening might invite, and thus they simply split over the appropriate course of action.

This split was evident, almost from the beginning of military rule, over the economic policies of José Martínez de Hoz, which touched in part on what was the appropriate role for unions to have.[67] Moreover, as soon as President Videla announced the need for a political proposal and the appropriateness of a dialogue with civilians, barely a year after the coup, important splits within the military began to emerge over the wisdom of engaging in the political process geared to expand the basis of support for the military, as opposed to the continued use and possible extension of repression as a means of control.[68] During the first three years of the Proceso, the military was torn between hard-line elements, which saw no role for compromise with societal forces, concerning either economic or political matters, and a soft-line wing, which was responsible for promoting and conducting a dialogue aimed at broadening the support for the military.

In short, the cohesiveness the military had built around reactive ob-

The Military's Project and the Reconstitution of Labor 95

jectives was rapidly lost, as important sectors of the military began to become concerned with the issue of institutionalization and the forward-looking and political objectives that entailed. Argentina's military rulers were divided over the very desirability of confronting the challenge of constitutional definition, and that would prevent them from tackling the challenge at hand in a concerned and determined manner.

If the decisions made by the military, in response to an opposition that was partly deemed as a target for repression but also partly malleable, resulted in a loss of cohesion on the part of the Argentine military rulers, another factor—the interim institutional arrangement whereby the rulers tackled the tasks of government while they elaborated a response to the challenge of constitutional definition—also played an important role. As intimated in Chapter 3, the interim institutional arrangement adopted by the Argentine military when they took power in 1976 had the potential to harm the military's ability to act cohesively.

One pointed problem introduced by the interim institutional arrangement had to do with the unstable agreement whereby the military decided to abridge the corporate pact, which was based on the principles of co-equal participation by the army, navy, and air force in government and the subordination of the presidency to the junta, by allowing General Videla, an active army officer, to be the president. The problem was that while the declaration of a temporary "state of exception" *(situación de excepcionalidad)*, whereby the commander-in-chief of the army would serve temporarily both as a member of the junta and as president of the country, allowed the army to focus effectively on the fight against guerrillas and the perceived threat of social conflict, it also introduced a point of contention that would be the focus of a series of heated negotiations within the armed forces (Fontana 1987:63–72, 75–76, 110; Jordán 1993:128–29). The unstable arrangement provided the context for internal divisions to fester, forcing the military to engage in intramilitary negotiations on this issue, starting in early 1977 and continuing until mid-1978, when the issue was finally resolved. Under the new agreement, General Videla was redesignated as president from August 1978 through March 1981, but now as a retired officer of the army. This prevented the previous overlap between the presidency and the military junta, while the military junta would undergo a full renewal.[69]

Another problem introduced by the interim institutional arrangement concerned the full-scale "colonization" of the state apparatus, whereby the three branches of the military participated directly in the management of the state. Here again, the military's interim institutional arrangement provided an incentive for each service to focus on its own particular interests. As discussed in Chapter 3, rather than ensuring the unified backing of all services for the government's policies, this arrangement resulted in the feudalization of the state, which generated a tendency for factious power struggles rather than for unified action.

This interim arrangement provided, in short, a context for tensions within the military to arise, and forced the military to focus increasingly on their internal problems. In the short run, this turn inward quite simply forced the military to postpone consideration of the political proposal through which they sought to respond to the challenge of constitutional definition. Thus, while debate on this political proposal had begun within the military junta and the high commands in December 1977, it was put on the back burner while intramilitary negotiations focused on the problem introduced by the temporary "state of exception." Of more lasting importance, however, this turn inward reflected a more profound inability of the military to deal with political questions (Fontana 1987:90–94). Once the military did get down to debating their political proposal, starting gradually in late 1978 and then with full force throughout 1979, this significant weakness would be clearly exposed.

In sum, the process whereby the military confronted the challenge of constitutional definition was affected by the interplay between three factors: the degree of cohesion of the new governing elite, the degree of opposition offered by the displaced forces, and the interim institutional arrangement. It was not the case that, as a result of the sustained dialogue that had occurred starting as early as May 1976, a strong labor actor had reemerged that could directly topple the military. In fact, labor had split, giving rise to a collaborationist wing, and was able to offer, just as was the case with other actors in society, only weak resistance to the military rulers. But the activities of this weak opposition were enough to cause serious friction and divisions within the military, divisions that were then reinforced by the interim institutional arrangement the military had adopted in 1976. While President Videla ably mediated these internal differences within the military and avoided having them break out into open policy conflicts (Fontana 1987:131, 153), these divisions did represent a problem, in that they led the government to pursue policies in an ambiguous and sometimes partly contradictory manner.[70] More critically, this serious lack of cohesion as the military rulers approached the final and decisive phase in their deliberations would severely hinder the ability of the military to respond resolutely to the political challenge at hand.[71]

The Unveiling of the Military's Proposal

In the end, the military did formulate its "political proposal" and make it public toward the end of 1979, but the two basic documents that constituted the military's response to the challenge of constitutional definition represented, if in slightly different ways, huge political failures. The first and broadest document elaborated by the military, which formally embodied the political proposal that President Videla had alluded to in June 1977 and represented the military's proposal for society as a whole, was the "Political Foundation of the Armed Forces for the Process of National Reorganization" (Bases Políticas de las Fuerzas Armadas para el Proceso de Reorganización Nacional), made public on December 19, 1979.[72] Despite the heightened expectation created by a document that was the product of much deliberation within the military and touted as the culminating statement of the Proceso, the flaws of this document were readily apparent. Although it had been presented as a document that drew on and further defined the goals outlined in a series of legal documents—such as the "Proclamation of the Process of National Reorganization," the "Act for the Process of National Reorganization," the "Purpose and Basic Objectives of the Process of National Reorganization," and the "Statute for the Process of National Reorganization"—as well as in countless other written and oral statements, it was extremely vague and noncommittal.

No positive source of legitimacy was offered, as the military continued to justify their hold on power in the same schizophrenic terms used to justify the original usurpation of power through the 1976 coup—that is, in terms of a future return to democracy.[73] Even more important, the document did not provide a sense of the concrete institutional changes the military envisioned. No timetable for lifting the prohibition on political activities and for normalization of political parties was given. No specific reform of the constitution, aimed at defining the military's political role in future constitutional government, was included. Moreover, instead of a concrete reference to the formation of a much rumored official party—the Movement of National Opinion (Movimiento de Opinión Nacional [MON])—which would embody the military's permanent political legacy, only the need for a civilian-military convergence was alluded to (González Bombal 1991:16–20). But even this more modest goal was not clearly developed, as the instrumentation of the so-called "political dialogue" to be carried out with political parties, a key means of achieving this civilian-military convergence, was left undefined. The "Political Foundation of the Armed Forces," in short, was a document that stood out for its lack of content.

In order to satisfy the divided opinions within an armed forces that was simply unable to agree about anything substantive, a number of key issues were simply left unresolved.[74] What was offered, then, was a document that responded to the challenge of constitutional definition only in form. All the military really offered in the "Political Foundation of the Armed Forces" was a document stating a vague hope for some kind of restricted democracy that was less prone to Argentina's longstanding problems. Not only had the military failed to overcome their illegitimate and ultimately contradictory formula for exercising political power, but they had not even been able to provide a legal basis for the changes they sought to introduce (Fontana 1987:88, 93; González Bombal 1991:14–16).

A second and narrower document, which had been in the process of consideration by the military since April 1976 and which responded to the military's view that any future political order had to rest on a revamped union structure and a new model of industrial relations, was Law No. 22105, a new Law of Professional Associations (Ley de Asociaciones Gremiales de Trabajadores), sanctioned in mid-November 1979.[75] This document, unlike the "Political Foundation of the Armed Forces," was not vague and was not noncommittal. The new Law of Professional Associations aimed at decentralizing power within the union structure by eliminating third-level entities and therefore disbanding the "intervened" CGT; by weakening the power of the common second-level entities with national jurisdiction, previously the locus of collective bargaining, through the forced provincialization of collective bargaining; and by banning any union activities of a political nature, while also seeking to purge the union movement of its better-known leaders through a provision that prohibited unionists with a criminal record to run for office.[76]

With the clear aim of reducing the economic power of trade unions, the new law also envisioned a measure, to be expanded on by a subsequent law, that withdrew the Obras Sociales from control by the unions.[77] Furthermore, the new law tightened the grip of the labor ministry in matters relating to the granting of legal recognition or "legal personality" *(personería gremial)* and the holding of assemblies, while making the labor ministry's "intervention" of unions unappealable. Finally, the number of workers' representatives in the workplace *(delegados del personal)* per firm was drastically reduced, while the job stability of the remaining workers' representatives was eliminated. In short, the new Law of Professional Associations pointed toward a radical restructuring of the union structure that had its origins in the early Peronist governments (1946–55), going further than any of the attempts made to curtail the power of unions following the toppling of Juan Perón in 1955.[78]

But if the new Law of Professional Associations, unlike the "Political Foundation of the Armed Forces," was clear about the concrete institutional changes it envisioned and laid out a legal basis for a new model of industrial relations, it still represented a political failure. The key problem was that the new law worked at cross-purposes with the extensive and preparatory work that had been conducted by key sectors of the military, led by Generals Roberto Eduardo Viola and Horacio T. Liendo, who had sought to foster "responsible" allies in the labor arena. Thus, while this more political approach had led the military to favor the emergence and strengthening of the CNT, a labor grouping that had adopted a clearly collaborationist position vis-à-vis the military rulers, now the military offered labor as a whole a document that was technocratic both in conception, in that its elaboration had bypassed any serious dialogue with labor leaders and was being imposed unilaterally by the military,[79] and in substance, in that it aimed above all to eliminate politics from the labor arena and reduce the political power of the Peronist-dominated unions. Torn between a position that recognized a need for political dialogue and sought to cultivate "responsible" allies, and a position that was technocratic in orientation and saw little positive role even for the collaborationist labor leadership that had emerged in the wake of the 1976 coup, the military had finally opted for a technocratic response that stood little realistic chance of gaining labor support.

In sum, toward the end of 1979 the military rulers did pronounce themselves on the challenge of constitutional definition they had acknowledged as relevant in March 1977, but in a way that immediately raised serious doubts about the possibility of their moving into a new phase, in which they would have to consolidate their power by institutionalizing the arrangement they had laid out, with any sustained momentum. Their problems were to a large extent prefigured in the very response the military had given to the challenge of constitutional definition. As emphasized, the "Political Foundation of the Armed Forces" was a document that was noncommittal and that lacked content. Because the arrangement through which the military sought to consolidate their power was, in this case, so unclear and ad hoc, there was a real question concerning what institutional rules were at stake in the process of institutionalization.

The problem with the new Law of Professional Associations was slightly different, though not unrelated. In this case, the legal framework was clearly laid out. But, if in the case of the "Political Foundation of the Armed Forces" the divisions within the military had not allowed for a precise definition of a set of institutional rules, a lingering question surrounding the new labor code concerned the military's resolve to fully implement the new law. Given that parts of the military had quite clearly shown a disposition toward dialogue with established labor leaders, and that even the labor leaders the military had courted as potential allies would now be severely hampered by the new legislation, it was unclear just how committed the military as a whole would be to the institutionalization of the proposed model of industrial relations.

Conclusion

Already at the end of 1976, and then even more clearly once the military had celebrated the first anniversary of the coup through which they came to power, the military rulers acknowledged the need to provide an institutional foundation for the new political order they sought to introduce in Argentina. As part of the process whereby the military sought to establish a basis for a new political order, and even though most of the debate concerning the two key foundational documents was carried out only among military officers, the military rulers sought to foster "responsible" allies within the labor arena that could, at an appropriate time, become participants in the military's project. This opening to society, while clearly restricted and while carried out at the same time that repression continued to be used, was initiated fairly early on because labor was seen as a potentially malleable actor. That is, important sectors of the military believed that, through a combination of inducements and constraints, they could shape the manner in which labor was reconstituted as an actor. This opening to society, then, was seen as a preparation phase in the military's effort to establish a new order.

The decision to seek allies within the labor arena had important consequences. From the perspective of labor, this decision opened a new phase in the post-1976 state-labor relations. If in the first six months or so after the March 1976 coup the military's all-out repressive campaign had thoroughly weakened labor, in this new context labor was reconstituted as an actor and partially regained its capacity for collective action. The outcome of this process was mixed. On the one hand, the military had clearly been successful in reshaping labor, inasmuch as they had managed to divide labor and co-opt a significant segment of the labor leadership that appeared quite willing to support the military. On the other hand, the military had so restricted activities of labor leaders that their link with the rank-and-file level of the labor movement had been cut off almost totally. The representativeness of labor leaders, a characteristic that is key to their capacity both to mobilize and to control union members, had been strongly curtailed. The boldest move on the part of labor, the April 1979 general strike called by the Group of 25, thus did not lead to an escalation of protest action against the military rulers.

From the perspective of the military rulers, despite their relative success in containing labor protests and in fostering the emergence of a collaborationist labor grouping, the CNT, the opening to society created serious problems. The military split over the very decision to court labor and over how to respond to the actions of a newly reconstituted actor that they could not fully control. Even though societal actors had been excluded from the debate over the future of the country, the behind-the-scenes discussions were affected by the politicization of the military organization that occurred as they sought to respond to the problem of representation.

The problems the military faced as a result of their relationship with society were only compounded by the interim institutional arrangement devised by the military, immediately after the 1976 coup, to respond to the pressing need to assume the management of the state. The interim institutional arrangement through which the military ruled after 1976 provided a context for internal divisions to fester while reinforcing the tendency for each service to focus on their particular interests. It forced the military, in short, to focus increasingly on their internal problems, and it further undermined the military's ability to remain unified and to act in concert in the pursuit of the forward-looking and essentially political goal of shaping a new order.

Thus, while the military rulers had acted with a high degree of consensus both in staging the 1976 coup and during the first year they were in power, thereafter the consensus was increasingly shattered. The military had proven quite capable of acting around purely reactive, short-term, and militaristic objectives, but as soon as the task of sweeping the old aside had been completed and the military started to focus on a new challenge that was very different in nature, the original consensus began to vanish. Indeed, as soon as the military began to acknowledge the need to provide an institutional foundation for the new political order and to address the challenge of constitutional definition, as opposed to the more pointed task of seizing power, some of the weaknesses of the Argentina's military rulers became evident.

The loss of cohesion of the military rulers would have far-reaching consequences for the political dynamics of the Proceso, affecting from the outset the military's ability to design and back a legal framework that would provide the foundation for a new order. The military's response to the challenge of constitutional definition was both a hesitant and an ultimately partial one, because the military had not been able to agree on an institutional model that could be supported by all branches of the military. This was, from the perspective of the military rulers, a serious political failure that would affect the future of the Proceso. This political failure would not directly undermine the military's ability to remain in power. But because the military moved into the next phase, the phase of evolution, with very little momentum, it became apparent not only that it would be virtually impossible for the military to consolidate their power through the institutionalization of a new political order, but also that quite likely the military would find it increasingly difficult simply to rule effectively. As the account of the subsequent political dynamics of the Proceso provided in the next chapter seeks to show, the lack of a clearly defined legal framework backed by the military rulers in a unified manner spelled trouble for the military rulers.

Part III
Evolution

Chapter 5

The Dynamics of a Political Situation in Argentina, 1980–1982

Following the publication of two key foundational documents—the "Political Foundation of the Armed Forces for the Process of National Reorganization" and the new Law of Professional Associations in late 1979—the military-led "Process of National Reorganization" (Proceso de Reorganización Nacional) entered a new phase. As argued in Chapter 1, although new governing elites begin to consolidate their power by designing an institutional order, once such constitutional issues have been addressed the challenge of institutionalizing the proposed political order comes to the forefront. In other words, once the challenge of constitutional definition has been confronted, rulers must face a new challenge, that of institutionalization, which hinges on transforming the newly created institutional rules into rules that are accepted and routinely used by all relevant actors.

In facing this new challenge, Argentina's military rulers were impaired by a number of serious difficulties. This chapter starts out by analyzing the obstacles that hindered a process of institutionalization of the military's project during the period from late 1979 through the inauguration of General Roberto Eduardo Viola as president in March 1981. Then the key question concerning the phase of evolution of military rule in Argentina—why the military rulers totally failed to provide the institutional basis for a stable form of rule—is answered in terms of the factors outlined in the political-institutional model. Thereafter, the focus is on the deepening problems that developed during the Viola administration and that led to Viola's displacement from power by means of a palace coup and his replacement by General Leopoldo Fortunato Galtieri in December 1981. Finally, the causes as well as the significance of this palace coup for the evolution of the Proceso are discussed.

The Dynamics of a Political Situation

As the military moved on to the challenge of institutionalization, having confronted the challenge of constitutional definition, in late 1979, by means of two foundational documents—the "Political Foundation of the Armed Forces for the Process of National Reorganization" and the new Law of Professional Associations—a number of obstacles that cast serious doubts on the military's ability to successfully manage the challenge at hand emerged almost immediately. Some of these problems concerned the internal divisions within the military rulers themselves, while others concerned the response to the military's project on the part of key actors within society. In this section, the evolution of the Proceso is considered in terms of the interaction among the key factors that the political-institutional model outlined in Chapter 1 highlights as affecting the resolution of the challenge of institutionalization: the degree of cohesion of the governing elites, the orientation and strength of societal actors, and the institutional arrangement the governing elites seek to institutionalize. This leads to a characterization and explanation of the political dynamics of bureaucratic authoritarianism in Argentina as corresponding to an authoritarian "political situation" and not an authoritarian "political regime."

Ongoing Divisions Within the Governing Elites: The Issue of Presidential Succession

Part of the problem facing the military rulers had to do with the ongoing tensions within the military. Those tensions had made the response to the challenge of constitutional definition very tentative in the first place, and now they slowed the momentum with which the governing elites moved to consolidate their power by institutionalizing the project that they had sought to outline in late 1979. Actually, following the military's pronouncement on the matter of constitutional definition, military divisiveness not only continued but became worse, as the focus of debate turned, starting in April 1980, to the issue of presidential succession.[1]

The problem of presidential succession was divisive, just as the debate over the military's foundational documents had been, because it forced the military to discuss the future, a topic on which different sectors within the military had quite diverging opinions. The debate centered, in particular, around General Roberto Viola, who had retired in

December 1979 and quickly became the most likely candidate to succeed General Jorge R. Videla as the next president. Viola had significant support within the army as well as the air force. Because of the views he held, however, Viola also faced strong opposition within the navy, and most of all within the army itself, by a sector led by General Galtieri, who had replaced Viola as commander-in-chief of the army and had thus assumed the army's seat on the junta.[2] Besides Galtieri's well-known personal ambitions to accumulate power, there was a clear political divide separating those who supported Viola and those who opposed him. Thus, while Viola had developed close links with trade union leaders over several years, opposed José Martínez de Hoz's economic program, and now adopted the soft-liner position of favoring a political opening,[3] the hard-line sectors led by Galtieri argued for the continuity of Martínez de Hoz's economic program and were steadfastly against a political opening.[4]

Complicating the debate over the presidential succession issue was the fact that the beginning of the unraveling of Martínez de Hoz's economic plan, marked by the April 1980 financial crisis (Peralta-Ramos 1987:50–57; Damill and Frenkel 1992:13–17),[5] made the outcome of the military's internal debate a matter of particular concern for significant elements that constituted part of the military's coup coalition. With the first signs of an impending economic crisis, important sectors of business, which had begun to drift away from their position in support of the military already in late 1978, started to question the logic of Martínez de Hoz's economic program and to pressure the military for a change in economic policy.[6]

There was also increased skepticism among business sectors with regard to the military's labor policy. Beginning in October 1979, an explosion in the number of labor conflicts pointed to the resurgence of anarchic forms of labor conflicts.[7] This raised the same issue that had already been brought up by the strike wave during the last trimester of 1977. What was different this time around and gave greater urgency to the problem was the scale of labor protests[8] and the fact that now the strikes involved less of an overt confrontation with the government's policy in the labor arena, as had been partly the case with the strikes in late 1976 and early 1977, and more of a direct response to issues of an economic nature, such as layoffs and suspensions, the closing of industrial plants, and problems with back pay.[9] In the context of growing economic problems, important sectors of the business community were not only questioning the government's economic policies but also insisting once more on the need to reestablish the old union leadership.[10] In effect, the economic situation and the labor problems

108 Evolution

pushed erstwhile military supporters among national industrialists—sectors that had supported the coup and that constituted part of the military's support coalition—to question the government's policies and to support the types of policies Viola stood for.

Even though, in the end, Viola did prevail in the intramilitary struggle over the issue of presidential succession and was nominated on October 2, 1980, to succeed Videla as president for the 1981–84 period, this decision did not put an end to the problem of military divisiveness.[11] In a sign of the troubles that lay ahead, divisions continued and actually became more deeply rooted in the military's structure of government, as Viola, who had already been in retirement for close to ten months before his nomination as president, was forced to wait another six months until assuming the presidency on March 29, 1981—at the very time that his opponent, Galtieri, continued to seek support for his views, both as commander-in-chief of the army and as a member of the military junta. But what was immediately important about the debate over the issue of presidential succession was that as soon as the military rulers had responded to the challenge of constitutional definition through two foundational documents, the military become engrossed with internal issues that were highly divisive. The ongoing lack of cohesion of the military rulers was to have a crucial impact on the military's ability to move with any momentum toward the institutionalization of a new political order (Portantiero 1987:267–69).

Governing Elites, the Institutional Arrangement, and the Ruled: Societal Responses to the Military's Project

The impact of the lack of cohesion among the governing elites was apparent in the lack of decisiveness with which the military rulers went about building support for their project, a factor that, along with the very institutional arrangement envisioned in the military's project, shaped the response of key actors in society. As discussed in Chapter 4, there were some significant distinctions between the extent to which the "Political Foundation of the Armed Forces for the Process of National Reorganization" and the new Law of Professional Associations actually defined an institutional or legal framework. As the ensuing analysis seeks to show, however, there was nonetheless a single logic underlying the response of societal actors to the military's political project, as embodied in their two foundational documents.

Responses to the "Political Foundation of the Armed Forces"

Although the "Political Foundation of the Armed Forces" was a document that pointed toward the need for some kind of restricted democracy, it did not envision concrete institutional changes. All that came out of this document was the initiative to conduct an official "political dialogue" that was put in motion by President Jorge R. Videla and that began in late March 1980, when the minister of the interior, General Albano Eduardo Harguindeguy, met with leaders of the Progressive Democratic Party (Partido Demócrata Progresista).[12] Thereafter, the "political dialogue" continued at an uneven pace during the ensuing months, through a series of meetings the minister of the interior held with Ricardo Balbín, the head of the Radical Civic Union (Unión Cívica Radical [UCR]), in early May; with five representatives of the Peronist Justicialist Party (PJ), including Raúl Matera, and with labor leaders of the CNT in late August;[13] and with Arturo Frondizi, a former Argentine president and leader of the Movement of Integration and Development (Movimiento de Integración y Desarrollo [MID]), in late September. Although these talks had attracted representatives of Argentina's two major parties, including the leadership of the UCR but only relatively minor figures within the Peronist party, such talks did not have a realistic chance of leading to the institutionalization of a new political order. The problem was that the military rulers were more immediately concerned with the issue of presidential succession and that, because they remained divided, they were unwilling to pursue such a dialogue with any clear sense of purpose. And because the military was not able even to define clearly just what their project legally entailed—that is, just what concrete institutional outlines the military's project would have—the relevance of these preparatory talks was diminished. There was never anything more concrete behind these talks than the vaguely stated purpose of cementing a "civilian-military convergence" that would embody the military's permanent political legacy in an as yet unspecified manner (González Bombal 1991: 31–35).[14]

If there was little that the military gained from these talks, there were, on the other hand, some loses. Even though the "political dialogue" was intended as a forum for the interaction between government officials and select "personalities" of society, who could have belonged to political or social organizations but who now were supposed to interact with the government on a personal basis and not as representatives of this or that party or organization (Sigal and Santi 1985:

160–63), it did provide the basis for the reactivation of political parties as organizations. The slight liberalization that had accompanied the call to a "political dialogue" unintentionally provided party leaders with somewhat of an excuse to engage in internal debate, as well as an opportunity to raise the issue of democracy.[15] Thus, even though the military came out with clear statements that the "political dialogue" was not intended as a vehicle for political parties and not aimed at the initiation of a transition to democracy, the holding of these talks did provide party leaders with an opportune juncture to express their opposition to the military's project as illegitimate and to place the topic of a transition on the agenda.[16]

Responses to the Law of Professional Associations

If the obstacles facing the military rulers in their attempt to institutionalize a new order were readily apparent in the context of their attempt to implement the "Political Foundation of the Armed Forces," the difficulties that lay in the path of the military rulers were even clearer with regard to the new Law of Professional Associations. Because the military had gone further both in seeking allies within the labor arena and in outlining a legal-institutional framework that would embody the military's project vis-à-vis labor than it had with regard to the civilian political allies that were to provide the basis of the restricted democracy envisioned by the "Political Foundation of the Armed Forces," the contradictory tendencies confronting the military rulers as they sought to institutionalize their power were both more forcefully and more completely expressed in the context of the military's attempt to implement the 1979 labor code.

Labor's initial reaction to the new labor code was to form the United Leadership of Argentine Workers (Conducción Unica de Trabajadores Argentinos [CUTA]), a labor grouping that unified the conduction of Argentine labor in September 1979 by bringing together the CNT and the Group of 25 and that sought to oppose the increasingly imminent approval of the Law of Professional Associations.[17] The military had accomplished what labor had not been able to do on its own by providing a target, the new labor code, that brought together the two main labor groupings that had emerged following the 1976 coup under one umbrella organization encompassing approximately 90 percent of the total number of union affiliates. It is important not to overemphasize the extent to which the CUTA represented the unity of Argentine labor. There were clear limitations to this new initiative on the part of labor, given that the CUTA was based on an extremely formalistic agreement among the CNT and the Group of 25. Essentially, the CNT and the Group of 25 remained distinct entities within the CUTA, which continued to engage in internal disputes, to the point that the CUTA never accomplished much and became defunct by April 1980.[18]

But still, the formation of the CUTA had significant consequences, for it pointed to the military's failure to gain support for their labor code from any significant elements within the labor arena, and particularly because it gave an indication that the military rulers had even alienated the generally complacent CNT labor leaders. The problem was that, although the military had tolerated and even encouraged the formation of the CNT labor grouping, now the military rulers had enacted a law about which they had not really been consulted[19] and that sought to break up the unions of national scope—that is, the very level to which the established trade unionists that led the CNT belonged to. Feeling threatened by the new labor code, therefore, even the CNT leadership opposed it.[20]

Despite sharing this opposition to the new labor law with the Group of 25, however, the CNT split with the Group of 25 over the best strategy to confront the labor code. The CNT's strategy was to bet on the internal divisions within the military as a way to subvert the military's project as outlined in the Law of Professional Associations. To be more precise, the CNT speculated that the splits within the military would delay the process of union normalization and that, in the likely case that General Viola would be nominated to the presidency, the new president would both water down the aspects of the law they opposed and reward them, relative to the Group of 25, in exchange for their displays of moderation.[21] Having developed a close bond with General Viola and his advisers, the CNT's expectations were not baseless; moreover, their assessment of the military's determination to push ahead with the normalization of unions under the new Law of Professional Associations proved to be quite accurate.

The CNT's wait-and-see attitude appeared to work, as progress toward the normalization of unions can be described, at best, as slow. Most unions presented their requests for new jurisdictions to the labor ministry within the time frame of an extended deadline, in late March 1980.[22] But thereafter the process of normalization was stalled due to the government's inaction.[23] In May, the labor ministry announced that new jurisdictions had been approved for twenty-three unions of the approximately 2,100 applications by registered unions, but the majority of cases the labor ministry acted on affected only small unions, generally from the interior of the country. Even as the end of 1980 approached, the cases of all major unions, such as the metal workers' union (UOM), the construction workers' union (UOCRA), the bank workers' union (Asociación Bancaria), the commerce workers' union (CGEC), the state workers' union (Asociación Trabajadores del Estado [ATE]), the textile workers' union (AOT), the municipal workers' union (Union Obreros y Empleados Municipales), the auto workers' union (SMATA), the food service workers' union (Unión de Trabajadores Gastronómicos de la República Argentina), the transport workers' union (Unión Tranviarios Automotor [UTA]), and the public administration workers' union (Unión del Personal Civil de la Nación), remained unresolved.[24] Thus, the labor minister's announcement in late January 1981 that union elections would be held later that year seemed to be wishful thinking. For if elections were held within two minor unions for the first time since 1976 in the last week of March 1981, this goal still appeared quite distant. Only a mere 688 new jurisdictions from the total of close to 2,100 petitions presented in March 1980 had been approved a year later, in March 1981. Moreover, after settling the problem of jurisdictions, the time-consuming process of adjusting the union's internal statutes to fit the new jurisdiction and the new regulations of the Law of Professional Associations, and then the granting of official approval of these statutes, had to be completed before elections could be held. The military rulers were far behind schedule.[25]

From the perspective of the CNT labor leadership, their strategy of circumventing without confronting the new labor code appeared well grounded. Throughout 1980, the military rulers, divided and engrossed with the issue of presidential succession, simply lacked the resolve to move with determination to implement the new Law of Professional Associations. Their hope that a more labor-friendly president would be selected was also realized. Viola's selection as the next president was crucial for the CNT. From their dialogues with Viola, CNT leaders had built the expectation that, as president, Viola would not push for the radical transformation of the union structure envisioned in the Law of Professional Associations and that he would water down the law by rolling back some of the more drastic changes it envisioned. Having cultivated a close relationship with General Viola and his advisers, the CNT also expected to receive an important payoff for their opportunistic strategy, through measures that would strengthen the hand of the CNT leaders relative to the more militant Group of 25 leaders.[26]

The Group of 25's strategy to confront the new Law of Professional Associations was quite different. During the brief period during which the Group of 25 coexisted with the CNT within the CUTA, the Group of 25, and, within it, the Peronist Syndical Movement (MSP), had opposed the CNT's collaborationist strategy and proposed a more confrontationist one that would not simply rely on the divisions within the military with the hope of making some gains relative to other labor leaders, but rather take advantage of the slight liberalization of the political context in 1980, to increasingly coordinate action at the leadership level and to reconstitute the linkage between leaders and the rank and file of the labor union structure. The point was to strengthen the organizational basis of labor in order to improve the prospects of successfully opposing the military's entire project.

The Group of 25's first efforts at leadership coordination took place in the context of the CUTA. Initially, these efforts consisted of meetings with representatives of political parties, meetings that were part of a widely successful drive to drum up opposition to the new labor code[27] and were carried out jointly with the CNT leaders within the CUTA. But the differences between the more confrontationist Group of 25 leaders, who sought to mobilize increasingly broader sectors of the population against the military rulers, and the more collaborationist CNT leaders, who were more concerned with the prospects of immediate relative gains than with the end of military rule, rapidly complicated matters. The tensions between the CNT and Group of 25 leaders became evident, first of all, when the Group of 25 members within the CUTA pushed unsuccessfully for a multisectoral meeting *(multisectorial)*, with the purpose of making a pronouncement on the impact of the economic and social policies of the military government.[28] After repeated clashes between the CNT and Group of 25 leaders, these tensions reached the breaking point when the CNT leaders responded positively to the government's invitation to participate in the official "political dialogue" that the military had put in motion within the framework of the "Political Foundation of the Armed Forces."[29]

Rather than enter into this dialogue with the government, Group of 25 leaders focused their energies on coordinating their actions with their political allies within the Peronist party so as to better oppose the military. Thus, as the "political dialogue" got off to a start, the MSP core of the Group of 25 coordinated its positions with the top leadership of the Peronist party and spoke out against the proposed dialogue.[30] In other words, the Group of 25 sought to take advantage of whatever spaces, or opportunities, the military had allowed, as part of their admittedly tentative effort to reach out to society, to reactivate the traditional links between the Peronist party and trade unions, and to thus assist in the reorganization of societal forces opposed to military rule. While the CNT did little more than wait, expectantly, for the change of government, the Group of 25 was, in contrast, engaged in a flurry of activities. Going against an important provision of the new labor law, the Group of 25 leaders, along with other union leaders, reconstituted the CGT in late November 1980.[31] Moreover, in a display of growing boldness that met with clear government resistance, they sought to build up labor's strength by setting up regional organizations and establishing contacts with political leaders of the Peronist party as well as of other parties, and to articulate the demand not only for a change in the military's labor policy but also for a transition from military rule itself.[32] In sum, together with parallel efforts throughout 1980 by political parties and human rights organizations, the Group of 25 was contributing to the development of antiauthoritarian forces.[33]

The Making of a Tenuous "Political Situation": Characterizing and Explaining the Political Dynamics of Bureaucratic Authoritarianism

If by late 1980 some trends concerning the prospects of institutionalization of the military's project of a new political order were becoming apparent, during the following year, especially after General Viola became president in March 1981, the course of events began raising a different, if related, issue: the origins of a political crisis. It is therefore convenient to pause here to sum up the ongoing analysis by considering how the three factors that the political-institutional model stresses as affecting the resolution of the challenge of institutionalization—the degree of cohesion of the governing elites, the orientation and strength of societal actors, and the institutional arrangement the governing elites seek to institutionalize—help to explain the political dynamics in Argentina following the military's pronouncement on basic constitutional issues.

The impact of the cohesiveness of the governing elites on the process of institutionalization was both direct and fundamental. As discussed earlier, the splits within the military rulers had already accounted for a hesitant and ultimately a partial response to the challenge of constitutional definition through the two key foundational documents made public in late 1979. Thereafter, throughout 1980, the ongoing lack of military cohesion accounted for the rulers' failure to implement the envisioned new order with determination. In the case of the "Political Foundation of the Armed Forces," the military rulers' lack of cohesion prevented them from clarifying the institutional-legal outlines of a political project that had been defined only in vague, noninstitutional, terms, and from resolutely conducting the "political dialogue" envisioned by this document as a way of gaining the support of civilian allies.

In the case of the Law of Professional Associations, although the problem was slightly different, the logic behind the military's failure was similar. In this case, the military had successfully outlined a project in clear legal and institutional terms. But a lack of consensus with regard to its implementation remained, a lack of consensus that had already been evident in the very definition of a labor code that advanced goals that clearly diverged from those that animated the extensive preparatory work conducted by key sectors of the military. Given that this lack of consensus within the military lasted throughout 1980, the military rulers were simply unable to back the full implementation of the new Law of Professional Associations in a unified manner.

From the perspective of society, the military's project, in the form of both the vaguely defined "Political Foundation of the Armed Forces" and the clearly defined Law of Professional Associations, was seen as illegitimate and rejected as such. In other words, the very institutional arrangement envisioned by these foundational documents—a restricted democracy and a new model of industrial relations that eliminated politics from the labor arena and reduced the political power of the Peronist-dominated unions—was not accepted by the relevant actors, who responded by opposing them in a principled fashion. While the head of the UCR had participated in the "political dialogue," the formal leadership of the Peronist party, as well as a number of other parties, had rejected the "Political Foundation of the Armed Forces," and all labor groupings, including the leaders of the CNT, had rejected the legitimacy of new Law of Professional Associations.

But the failure of the military rulers to handle the political challenges they had sought to tackle throughout 1980 went beyond a failure to set up a legal framework that would be considered legitimate by key actors in Argentine society and that therefore stood a chance of becoming institutionalized. Because the military rulers had so obviously worked at cross-purposes and continued to be overtly divided, they would even have trouble making their proposals stick as a legal, if illegitimate, framework. In the case of the "Political Foundation of the Armed Forces," this issue was not really relevant, because the document did not spell out any legal rules that societal actors had to decide whether to accept or reject. Indeed, because the military rulers were never unified enough to define the legal institutional aspects entailed in their vision of a restricted democracy, societal actors were never offered anything more concrete than the invitation to become the "responsible" allies that would form the basis of a friendly transition government organized along the lines of some sort of restricted form of democracy. In the case of the Law of Professional Associations, however, labor did face such a choice.

The military's failure to channel labor's actions into legal avenues is instructive. In the case of the confrontationist Group of 25, and its successor labor grouping, the CGT, the matter was pretty cut and dried. The legality of the new labor code was questioned simply because it was viewed as illegitimate. More telling was the case of the more collaborationist CNT leaders, who were more opportunistic in their dealings with the military but who nonetheless did not fully accept the legality of the new labor code. Knowing full well that parts of the military had shown a disposition toward dialogue with established labor leaders, a disposition that had allowed for the reconstitution of labor and the organization of the very labor groupings that now rejected the new labor code, CNT leaders had well-founded doubts about the likelihood that the military would resolutely push for the full implementation of the Law of Professional Associations. What they sought to do, therefore, was ostensibly comply with the text of the law while actually playing on the divisions within the military to circumvent and eventually subvert the aims of the new legal framework.[34]

Thus, if in the case of the "Political Foundation of the Armed Forces" the military rulers' lack of cohesion directly accounted for their failure to even present a clear legal proposal that would spell out their vision of a new political order, the impact of the ongoing lack of cohesion of the military rulers in the case of the labor code was more convoluted. In this case, the ongoing lack of cohesion of the military rulers accounted for their failure to establish a legal foundation for a new political order in a more indirect manner, by enabling the CNT leadership to subvert the new labor code from within.

To recapitulate, the explanatory argument is as follows. The degree of cohesion of the governing elites directly affected their ability to push for implementation of their project, hindering the momentum needed to institutionalize a new political order. But the process of institutionalization depended on other factors as well. First, the response of societal actors to the proposed institutional arrangement played an important role. The institutional arrangements proposed by the military were deemed as illegitimate or inappropriate and rejected as a matter of principle. The principled refusal to accept the proposed constitutional order on the part of actors that were strong enough and central enough to the functioning of society to be relevant to the institutional-

The Dynamics of a Political Situation in Argentina 117

ization of bureaucratic authoritarianism was sufficient to disrupt and block the process of institutionalization.

But in the Argentine case, the problem went beyond the illegitimacy of the proposed institutional arrangement. There was also a failure to establish even a political order that was legally based. The problem, from the perspective of the military rulers, was that precisely because their attempts to reach out to gain support within society led to the emergence and deepening of military divisiveness, they turned inward, concerning themselves with more purely military questions, and never developed a unified position with regard to more basically political questions. The mixed signals the military were emitting, in turn, affected societal actors, who based their decision even to accept the legality of the military's project on the expectation that the military rulers themselves were unlikely to firmly back a legal order. In other words, with the governing elites lacking sufficient cohesion to back the legal foundations for a new political order, through their failures to either design or fully support a new institutional framework, societal actors that would be negatively affected by such a new order had no incentive to accept its legitimacy, or even the legality of the new arrangement the military was proposing.

The outcome of the process of institutionalization in Argentina around late 1980 can therefore be characterized first of all as an authoritarian "political situation." As discussed in Chapter 1, what is peculiar about a political situation is that the governing elites are strong enough to retain firm control of the government, thus avoiding a political crisis, but not strong enough to consolidate their power through an institutionalized order, as in the case of a political regime. That is, while the military's control over the government was not in doubt, their failure to shape institutional mechanisms that were accepted as permanent mechanisms for the management of conflict by all major actors in the political system, the true sign of a successful attempt at regime founding, was also clear. Thus, while there was one procedure regulating the exercise of political power that was clearly dominant, significant actors oriented themselves with reference to an alternative institutional order.

It is also appropriate to emphasize the extent to which this was, at best, a tenuous political situation. That is, the Argentine case was characterized not only by the lack of legitimacy of the project advanced by the military rulers, a characteristic shared by all cases of bureaucratic authoritarianism, but also by the debilitating feature of the military project's lack of legality. This feature, which was primarily due to the rulers' lack of cohesion and hence a lack of determination to design and then enforce an institutional order that would organize relations between rulers and ruled along legal lines, had significant consequences. Above all, it gave rise to a political dynamic shaped in large part by the dialectical and institutionally unmediated relationship between rulers and ruled, a dynamic that was particularly dangerous from the perspective of the governing elites.

This dialectical relation between rulers and ruled had, in the first place, led to the splits within the military that had hindered the Argentine rulers' attempt to institutionalize their power, starting with the very design of institutional rules. Subsequently, as an unintended consequence, these splits had allowed for the gradual reorganization of forces in society that sought to replace military rule by an entirely different system of rule. Therein lay, from the military rulers' perspective, a very destabilizing dynamic. If in 1980 this principled opposition was strong enough only to block the military's aspiration to institutionalize their power, this opposition would be increasingly difficult to control, and as it grew in strength its actions would put even greater strain on the military's cohesion.

The destabilizing consequences of such a dynamic were clear. Until then, the military's failure had forced them to abandon their attempt to organize relations between rulers and ruled along legal lines and to continue to rule, by default, on the basis of the interim institutional arrangement set up in 1976 and partly modified in 1978. But increasingly, even such a basis could be threatened. There was a very real prospect that the deepening rifts within the military that were likely to emerge in the context of a growing principled opposition would threaten the military's ability to continue abiding by the very interim institutional arrangement that constituted the main reason for characterizing Argentina in 1980 as a political situation.

In sum, if in late 1980 Argentina's military rulers were still able to provide the government with a sense of direction, the continued growth of the opposition, made possible in part by the splits within the military, appeared to be leading to a deepening of these splits, which in turn increased the likelihood that the military would even break with the rules that ensured their involvement in, and backing of, military rule. The Argentine case, along with other cases of bureaucratic authoritarianism at comparable phases in their development, should therefore be characterized as an authoritarian political situation. Furthermore, it is also appropriate to stress the extent to which there was a clear tendency, not far beneath the surface, that pointed to a potential political crisis and that made Argentina's political situation a tenuous one at best.

From a Political Situation to a Political Crisis

As Argentina's military rulers struggled with the challenge of institutionalization, an important event, which would prove to be a turning point in the phase of evolution of the Proceso, was the assumption of the presidency by General Viola in March 1981. Until then, the key challenge facing the military was the challenge of institutionalization, a challenge that had come to the fore once they had responded to the challenge of constitutional definition in late 1979. The military had not been very successful in meeting this challenge, giving rise to what was just characterized, in an effort to underline the extent to which the military had failed to institutionalize a new political order, as a tenuous political situation. But after March 1981, the destabilizing dynamic that resulted from the dialectical relationship between rulers and ruled began to be unleashed with full force and devastating consequences not only for the military's ability to advance the institutionalization of their project, something that had already appeared unlikely throughout 1980, but also, and more important, for their capacity to simply retain control over the government and govern effectively.

As military splits deepened and societal opposition grew, in a process whereby these two trends fed on each other, the Proceso moved toward a political crisis. The increasing inability of the military to conduct their business according to the rules envisioned in the institutional arrangement they had agreed to in 1976 was a clear sign of impending crisis. And the growth of a principled opposition force that appeared to be capable not only of blocking the process of institutionalization but also of raising the more ominous issue of a transition, spelled trouble for the military. Focusing on this dual process, this section analyzes the deterioration of what was already a tenuous political situation throughout 1981.

The Failure of Liberalization: Military Splits and Societal Opposition

General Viola's accession to the presidency on March 29, 1981, was particularly significant in that it captured both the strengths and the weaknesses of Argentina's military rulers. The transfer of power from Videla to Viola was an important accomplishment in that it was effected peacefully and according to the rules the military had set down upon assuming power. The problem of presidential succession is always a thorny issue for rulers in the context of bureaucratic authoritarianism (Huneeus 1986), and it had never been successfully managed by the Argentine military rulers that led the country in their previous experience with bureaucratic authoritarianism during the 1966–73 period. Thus, on the positive side, Viola's selection and assumption of power was the first time that the problem of presidential succession had been managed according to the rules the military had previously agreed to.[35] But, as the intramilitary debate concerning Viola's election discussed at the beginning of this chapter showed, even if the military had managed to legally select and install Viola in power the divisions that erupted in the process pointed to a crucial weakness of Argentina's military rulers. Indeed, the military's infighting would reach such a level in the course of only a few months that the selection of Viola would become the last key decision that the military rulers managed to make within the rules set down in 1976.

As expected, Viola's presidency represented an important departure from Videla's tenure.[36] Viola rapidly appointed a cabinet that represented a shift away from the neoconservative economics of the first five years of military rule[37] and began a rapprochement with political parties and trade unions that was part of a strategy of liberalization that sought to "redefine the alliances" on which military rule was based and recover "civilian support for the military government" (Fontana 1987:130–31, 134).[38] As became clear early on, however, such a strategy was unlikely to succeed. The problem Viola faced was that while liberalization was unlikely to satisfy the demands of parties and labor leaders, even minor moves in the direction of a political opening were sufficient to antagonize the hard-line sectors within the military that had already opposed Viola's nomination as president and that remained well entrenched within the military hierarchy. Rather than solve the problems afflicting Argentina's military rulers, Viola's liberalization strategy actually accentuated the destabilizing dynamic that had been developing ever since soft-liner elements within the military had reached out to society.

The link between Viola's government and political parties was rapidly established with the initiation of a round of consultations between party leaders and the new minister of the interior, General Horacio Tomás Liendo, hinging on the elaboration of a Statute of Political Parties (Estatuto de los Partidos Políticos) that would provide the basis for the relegalization of political parties. If this dialogue was thus formally linked with the "Political Foundation of the Armed Forces," the military's foundational document of late 1979, in that this document had stated that such a statute would be promulgated sometime after the second half of 1980, the dialogue Viola initiated was very different from the "political dialogue" carried out during 1980. As discussed above, in 1980 the military rulers had engaged in a dialogue explicitly intended as a forum for the interaction between government officials and selected "personalities" of society, who interacted with the government on a personal basis and not as representatives of this or that party or organization. The aim, moreover, was to cement some sort of a "civilian-military convergence" that would lead to the formation of an official party, presumably on the basis of the small conservative provincial political parties, that would embody the military's permanent political legacy in an as yet unspecified manner. By contrast, the dialogue spearheaded by the Viola government was carried out without these strictures, as the government recognized the old political party leaders as such, even explicitly treating the Peronist party as a valid interlocutor. The aim of the dialogue was to gain the support from established and traditional political forces rather than to fashion a new political force.[39]

This distinctive approach had significant consequences, because it allowed an autonomous force that could not be controlled by the military rulers to be reorganized, and triggered a strong reaction from the hard-line elements within the military. As soon as the political opening afforded by the government's disposition toward dialogue started, parties began to reorganize and discuss an issue that was not on Viola's agenda but that was central to their own agenda—the transition to a democratic form of government. And as soon as these old parties resurrected and voiced their demand for democracy, the hard-line elements within the military responded forcefully. To show their displeasure, these sectors issued a warning to President Viola through a document called "Orientations No. 2," which was sent to Viola by the military junta and cautioned him against a political opening. Moreover, in the military junta's new "Guidelines" for the president, Viola was urged to postpone the sanctioning of a Statute of Political Parties until the end of 1982 and to promote, as the "political dialogue" carried out during 1980 had, the formation of the Movement of National Opinion (MON) as a vehicle for the advancement of the military's project (Fontana 1987:128–29; González Bombal 1991:88).[40] The hard-line elements, in short, sought a freezing of the process that had allowed the old parties to be resurrected and continued to press for a full-blown recomposition of the political elites through a process that was to be controlled by the military and that would lead to the formation of a new political force untainted by previous political practices. The dissension between the soft-liners and the hard-liners was such that barely two months after Viola became president rumors of a coup d'état began to circulate.

The political parties responded quite strategically to the mixed messages emanating from the state. Because they recognized that Viola had only a tenuous grip on power, they initially adopted a fairly accommodationist strategy and sought to avoid widespread mobilization against the military. Party leaders not only feared that such actions would jeopardize the greater spaces the government was conceding by triggering a backlash from the hard-line sectors. They also fearing that a radicalized opposition would emerge and, as in the Argentine transition of 1972–73, escape control of the party leaders, with negative long-term consequences from the perspective of the established party leaders (Fontana 1987:133–36). However, party leaders were unwilling simply to back off from their demand for a transition and, when faced with signs of intransigence from the government, they increasingly responded with more vigorous and confrontational action.

The first sign that political party leaders were going to abandon the tentative approach they originally displayed came as a result of a declaration in early June by President Viola, who, under pressure from the hard-liners, stated that there was a great likelihood that a new military government would succeed him in 1984—that is, when Viola was scheduled to end his term. This statement was immediately followed by a reply from Balbín, head of the UCR, who referred to Viola's declaration as constituting "an aggression to civility" (quoted in Sáenz Quesada 1993:143), and by calls by the UCR for all political parties to elaborate a joint strategy for bringing democracy back. Thus emerged, in the most significant move taken by party leaders since the 1976 coup and as a direct challenge to the ban on political activities, a multiparty alliance called the Multipartidaria. This loose body, which had as a precedent the Hour of the People (Hora del Pueblo) agreement signed by Juan D. Perón and Balbín himself in 1972, moved rapidly, in its first meeting on July 14, to form a joint leadership with political leaders representing five of Argentina's main parties: the UCR, the Peronist party, the MID, the Christian Democratic Party (Partido Demócrata Cristiano [PDC]), and the Intransigent Party (Partido Intransigente [PI]) (Cavarozzi 1986:151–52, 168; González Bombal 1991:90–95). Then, without giving up on their attempts to reach some form of accommodation with the government, the Multipartidaria responded to the military's statements that power would not be handed over to civilians in 1984, by breaking off the dialogue with the government and turning to pressure tactics. Political parties, which had lagged behind labor in terms of sheer forcefulness of presence, had reentered the political arena in a unified and deliberate manner.[41]

The situation with trade unionists was slightly different, compared with that of the party leaders, given that labor was not unified around the goal of opposing military rule. But even so, just as the government's oscillation between political opening and intransigence provided the context for political parties to organize, while making it virtually impossible for them to reach any sort of compromise with the government, labor responded to the same contradictory signals emanating from the state. The peculiarity of state-labor as opposed to state-party relations had to do with the different nature assumed by the issue of compromise. With the collaborationist CNT wing of labor, which had formed an alliance with the Commission of 20 (Comisión de los 20) to form the Intersectorial CNT-20 (hereafter, the Intersectorial) in April 1981,[42] the issue of compromise was not about how to seek a controlled transition from military rule but about how to reach a compromise that would allow the CNT to become part of the new alliance of supporters that Viola was seeking to fashion. Because of their pragmatic orientation, as opposed to the principled opposition expressed by parties, therefore, with regard to the Intersectorial the military soft-liners had an opportunity to gain support for their reformulated vision of what the military's project should be.

Notwithstanding the Intersectorial's positive predisposition with regard to Viola, however, the soft-liners were simply unable to offer the kinds of concessions that would make a collaborationist orientation viable. Building on the frequent contacts that CNT leaders had had with Viola during 1979 and 1980, these collaborationist labor leaders had the expectation that Viola would reform the new labor code in such a way that its anticentralizing and antibureaucratic aspects would be watered down, but also, as a even more urgent issue, that changes in the economic program would alleviate the pressure labor leaders were feeling from a rank and file battered by a deepening economic crisis (see Appendix C). The viability of the Intersectorial's strategy hinged, in short, on the ability of these leaders to show that improvements in workers' conditions could be obtained without jettisoning the military rulers. But this basic condition was simply not met. Although the leaders of the Intersectorial adopted an open position toward the government and the business leaders Viola was courting, the Intersectorial found out early, through meetings with the labor minister, Brigadier Julio César Porcile, and the business representatives of the Argentine Industrial Union (Unión Industrial Argentina [UIA]), concerning a possible agreement on wage levels, that the tangible benefits they depended on were not forthcoming.

Thus, although Viola's access to power was the moment the CNT, now a part of the Intersectorial, had been waiting for since early 1980, things did not turn out as expected. When the promise of improvement through a compromise with the government led by Viola did not appear likely, therefore, the labor leaders of the Intersectorial were essentially forced to harden their position and criticize the government. Even if the rank and file did not have the immediate capability to sanction them, it was imperative for these labor leaders to gain legitimacy in the eyes of the rank and file, by either delivering some tangible results or criticizing the system that was responsible for the harsh conditions workers were enduring. President Viola's problem with regard to the Intersectorial was that he was unable to gain their support, despite the political opening he had initiated.

With regard to the CGT, the labor grouping that had been reconstituted in November 1980 around the confrontationist Group of 25, Viola's problem was different, in that the leaders of this labor wing simply took advantage of the political opening to continue their push to bring an end to military rule. Starting in June in a parallel development to the formation of the Multipartidaria, the CGT began to plan a second general strike against the Proceso—a general strike or day of protest *(jornada de protesta)* that was eventually carried out on July 22. This time around the strike was more successful in gaining workers' support than in 1979, and, more significant, this time the CGT was able to count on the backing from many political parties.[43] Building on developments in 1980, the CGT was able to synchronize its actions with its Peronist political allies, as well as other parties opposed to military rule, and carry out a protest action that reflected the growing reorganization of civil society.

The Viola government still did not face a fully unified opposition, as the Intersectorial continued to find a way to work with Viola. Thus, just as the CNT had rejected supporting the Group of 25's call to a general strike in 1979, now the Intersectorial did not adhere to the general strike called for by the CGT. Moreover, as was the case in 1979, the Intersectorial attempted to take advantage of the circumstances in order to gain favor among government authorities. Thus, as part of a new drive toward conciliation, the Intersectorial held several meetings, with Labor Minister Brigadier Porcile, Minister of Economy and Finance Lorenzo Sigaut, and the business sectors represented by the UIA, with the aim of exploring the possibility, as they had done earlier in the year, of reaching an agreement on wage levels and the reactivation of the economy. But again the Intersectorial's overtures were rebuffed, and in a sign of Viola's failure to garner the support of the very leaders that were willing to side with him, the Intersectorial was pushed to assume a critical stance. The business sector was accused of not fully understanding the current situation and the acuteness of the problems faced by workers, and the government was criticized for putting the leadership of the Intersectorial in an increasingly untenable position.[44]

Less than half a year into his presidential term, in sum, Viola's position had been seriously weakened, as his problems were compounding. By this point, not only was his failure to cement a new coalition of support becoming quite evident,[45] but his inability to exercise control over an increasingly coordinated movement opposed to military rule was also very apparent. By September, the problem with the opposition was reaching a critical dimension. The trigger, which opened this critical phase in the relationship between Viola and the opposition, was the failure of a new government overture toward political parties. The government had attempted to reopen the process of political dialogue through a meeting between Minister of the Interior Liendo and a delegation of representatives of the UCR party in late August. But once again this overture was followed a few weeks later by the announcement that there would be no transition to civilian rule in 1984, an announcement that in effect rejected once more the Multipartidaria's demand that a Statute of Political Parties to relegalize parties be approved quickly and that elections for president be set for 1984.[46] Occurring, furthermore, at the time of the death of Ricardo Balbín, the top leader of the UCR and a figure that had been extremely willing to entertain the military's concerns, this announcement forced party leaders to reevaluate their accommodationist strategy toward the military government.[47] Faced with the government's intransigence, then, the Multipartidaria shifted gears, as the last vestiges of moderation were replaced by a confrontationist stance. As the Multipartidaria led a mass mobilization against the military at the end of September, it was clear that a turning point in the opposition's evolution had been reached.

The Multipartidaria's decision to mobilize was crucial for the opposition to military rule, because it was the step that initiated a massive wave of protest by a broad movement, encompassing the confrontationist wing of labor and human rights organizations, as well as every major political party in the country (Dabat and Lorenzano 1984:73–76). The CGT continued to show that unionists remained certainly the most massive militant force if not the main opposition force—not ready to cede its role as mass convenors to the newly emerged party alliance. In this role, the CGT pressured the government once more, with a 10,000-strong demonstration called the March of Work (Marcha del Trabajo), on November 7. This protest measure counted among its participants some human rights activists and was backed, as in the case of the CGT's general strike in July, by a series of individual political parties, including the Peronists, the Christian Democrats, the center-left Intransigent Party, the Communists, and the Socialists. Only the still hesitant attitude within the UCR held the Multipartidaria back from throwing its support behind the measure. But if labor, as represented by the CGT, was now part of an increasingly strong societal opposition force that escaped the control of the military government, the emergence of a broad protest movement did not move the country directly toward democracy. Rather, the protests in society provided the context within which the embattled President Viola was displaced by his internal foes through a palace coup and replaced by General Leopoldo Galtieri on December 22.[48]

The Making of a Political Crisis: Explaining and Understanding the Significance of the Palace Coup

The palace coup that displaced Viola from the presidency was a highly significant landmark in the history of the Proceso that showed just how quickly the military were losing power. The coup was nothing less than a prelude to an unfolding political crisis that would trigger a transition from bureaucratic authoritarianism. The irony of the palace coup of December 1981 was that, although it was a response by the hard-line elements within the military to the perceived weakening of the military's power that resulted from Viola's pursuit of a strategy of liberalization, it actually accentuated the weakness of the military's power and set the Proceso on a course that not only did nothing to hold back the growing momentum of societal forces demanding a transition but also exposed the military to a fate far more ominous from the perspective of the very power of the military as an institution.

The reasons for Viola's displacement were quite clear. Viola's attempt to recover civilian support for the military government through a redefinition of the alliances on which military rule was based was a total failure. His attempt at liberalization had no chance to gain the support of political parties and the CGT, given that these actors were interested in using the openness provided by liberalization only as a stepping-stone on the way to democracy. What happened to Viola, therefore, is what transition theorists argue is a common pattern with all liberalizers: the attempt to liberalize, so as to strengthen rulers, escaping the control of the liberalizer and leading to the strengthening of antiauthoritarian forces that come to life as part of a "resurrection of civil society" (O'Donnell and Schmitter 1986:48–56). But Viola's liberalization strategy was also a failure in that it did not succeed in cementing an alliance of support on the basis of the groups, such as national industrialists and the collaborationist wing of labor, that were predisposed to supporting Viola. As the relationship between the government and the Intersectorial shows, even the groups that were not opposed to military rule were unable to deliver the kind of support for Viola that would have strengthened his position and provided a counterbalance to the power of the hard-liners.

As a consequence of this failed attempt at controlled liberalization, President Viola had not only failed to gain support but also allowed for the accelerated reorganization of the forces that took advantage of the political opening to advance their goal of opposing military rule, a development that antagonized the hard-liners in a manner that increasingly paralyzed the government.[49] In effect, President Viola had managed to antagonize the hard-line elements, which reacted negatively to the growing and concerted action by opposition forces pushing for an end to military rule, without gaining the support of any allies that would strengthen his hand relative to the hard-line elements that sought a "return to the sources"—that is, to the military's project as originally envisioned at the time of the 1976 coup. In the end, the political dynamics of state-society relations in the context of Viola's liberalization attempt accentuated an intramilitary division that had already been festering since 1977 (Fontana 1987:138, 137) and that was "resolved" when the hard-line military officers reacted by displacing the weakening soft-liners from power.[50]

With General Galtieri's assumption of the presidency, however, the political problems Argentina's military rulers had been facing since the initiation of Viola's attempted liberalization were only exacerbated. Not only did the palace coup do nothing to control the despised consequences of Viola's liberalization policies—that is, the rise of a broad-based movement in opposition to military rule—but the manner in which Galtieri had become president and set out to rule obliterated the last thing that had given Argentina the semblance of a "political situation," if a tenuous one at that: the fact that until March 1981 the military rulers had at least respected the rules they had selected for managing the state. Galtieri's assumption of the presidency led to the breakdown of the military's own rules for the management of the state, first by abridging Viola's presidential term in violation of the formal process of presidential succession, and second by allowing Galtieri to become president without relinquishing his position as commander-in-chief of the army and member of the military junta, in direct conflict with the arrangement the military had agreed to in mid-1978, whereby the president would be a retired officer. Thus, the December 1981 palace coup was not only the culmination of the struggle between soft-liners and hard-liners but also the most finished and damaging expression of the erratic manner in which the military had been governing as a result of this struggle. Instead of ending the political turmoil that had characterized the Viola presidency, now an even greater uncertainty over the ability of the military rules to govern was introduced, as it became increasingly apparent that the military rulers had become little more than managers of recurring crises.[51] Political turmoil, in sum, gave way to an open political crisis.

Conclusion

Once the military rulers had addressed the basic constitutional issues in late 1979, there are two stages in the evolution of the Proceso that can be distinguished. The first stage ran from late 1979 until March 1981 and was characterized by the difficulties that the military rulers faced in terms of institutionalizing their vision of a restricted democracy. The governing elites had failed to implement their project with determination because the military rulers lacked cohesiveness and because of the principled refusal to accept the proposed constitutional order on the part of societal actors that rejected the military's project as illegitimate and that were strong enough to be relevant to the institutionalization of bureaucratic authoritarianism. This failure, however, was only a partial failure. If the military rulers had not managed to define a project that would gain the support of key actors, they still did manage to maintain order by keeping a fairly tight lid on the opposition, and they also managed what is one of the more delicate issues faced by military rulers under bureaucratic authoritarianism, the issue of presidential succession, within the rules that the military had set down for themselves. In sum, while failing to institutionalize a new political order, the culmination of a regime-founding attempt, they had at least succeeded in creating an authoritarian "political situation."

But even this mild success began to vanish during the second stage in the evolution of the Proceso, which began in March 1981 with Viola's assumption of the presidency. Viola's rise to power was significant in that it represented the rise of soft-liners and the beginning of an explicit liberalization policy. As is usually the case, Viola's liberalization, intended to strengthen the governing elites' position, had the unintended consequence of leading to increased organization of the opposition. The reaction to Viola's liberalization from within the military was rapid and strong, but in the face of the failure of his liberalization policy Viola hesitated, occasionally giving in to pressures from the hard-liners without fully abandoning his attempt at liberalization, thus continuing to antagonize the hard-liners while shying away from the only thing that would allow him to counter the hard-liners' pressure: his conversion from a liberalizer to a reformer or democratizer. In the end, the hard-liners simply displaced the weakened soft-liner president. But, as argued, this only increased the military's problems, plunging the military rulers into a political crisis that increasingly raised the prospects of a transition.

The military rulers were gradually succumbing to the increasingly destabilizing dynamic that had begun to develop with the first attempts by soft-liner elements within the military to reach out to society back in 1977. The divisions this had introduced within the military had originally prevented the military from clearly defining their project and institutionalizing their hold on power. It had also allowed for the gradual reconstitution of labor, as seen in the previous chapter, starting in 1977–78, and the opposition of labor to the military's project. Viola's liberalization strategy was significant, then, not in terms of introducing a new factor but in terms of accentuating the already extant destabilizing dynamic of state-society relations that grew out of the response the military rulers had given to the problem of representation. That response oscillated between the options of recognizing key actors, such as trade unions and political parties, and then, fearing the opposition such a policy seemed to foster, ignoring or even repressing these societal actors. During 1981, as Viola pursued his policy of liberalization, the military's internal schisms became increasingly menacing, and the reconstitution of actors in society accelerated as political parties emerged and the confrontational labor grouping joined forces with these parties. It is significant that the palace coup that displaced Viola and installed Galtieri was not only the result of this dynamic but also deepened it, making the likelihood of a transition even greater. Thus, even though the developments during Galtieri's brief presidency are properly seen as part of the phase of evolution, given that they pertain quite directly to the transition that began in June 1982, they will be discussed in the next chapter.

Part IV
Transition

Chapter 6

Reform Through Rupture and Democratization in Argentina, 1982–1983

Argentina's transition from authoritarian rule was triggered by the deepening of the political crisis that opened when General Leopoldo Fortunato Galtieri became president through the palace coup of December 1981. Although Galtieri's intent was to bring about a "return to the sources"—that is, to the military's project as originally envisioned at the time of the 1976 coup—the course of events rapidly escaped his control. Facing increased societal pressure, and in line with an increasingly erratic manner of governing, the military launched a surprise invasion of the Falkland/Malvinas Islands in April 1982. The outcome of the war with Britain that ensued proved to be a turning point, in that a transition was initiated as soon as Argentine forces surrendered in June 1982. Thereafter, events moved swiftly, as political parties were relegalized and elections were rapidly scheduled. By December 1983, elected authorities had assumed power and the military had stepped down.

Focusing on this series of events, this chapter addresses two fundamental questions that are at the heart of regime analysis. First, there is the question of why the transition was initiated. This question has given rise to much polemic, centering on the relative explanatory role of external and state-centered factors as opposed to the role of domestic and societal forces. After providing an account of the developments that led to the initiation of the transition, an attempt to assess the various positions in this debate is advanced and an explanation is provided in terms of the factors outlined in the political-institutional model presented in Chapter 1: the orientation and strength of the old governing elites and societal actors, which shape who the potential source of change is likely to be; and the relative power of the antichange sectors within the governing elites vis-à-vis the agent or agents of change, which determines the strategies used in transitions.

The second key question this chapter focuses on concerns the process of transition itself and why the military eventually relinquished power in a particularly precipitous and uncontrolled manner. This aspect of Argentina's transition has not been debated as much as the preceding question. Indeed, compared with the polemic surrounding the problem of why a transition was initiated in Argentina, little attention has been given to the problem of characterizing and explaining the process of transition itself. The aim of this chapter is to fill this gap by applying the conceptual framework elaborated in Chapter 1 and by attempting to account for Argentina's mode of transition: a "reform through rupture."

From Political Crisis to the Initiation of a Transition

The palace coup that brought General Galtieri to the presidency, as argued in Chapter 5, not only did not solve the political problems Argentina's military rulers were facing since the initiation of General Roberto Viola's attempted liberalization, but actually accentuated them, plunging the military rulers into a political crisis. Not only did Galtieri's project of returning to the sources have no chance of institutionalizing military rule, something that had eluded the military even before Viola's presidency, but, as the destabilizing dynamics that began to develop during the Viola administration continued, and as the tendency for the military rulers to react in an increasingly erratic manner to the advance of the opposition persisted, the possibility of a transition emerged as an increasingly realistic option. This section describes, first, how the military rulers increasingly moved toward disaster and triggered the beginning of a transition. Then it faces the challenge of accounting for why the transition was triggered both when and how it did.

Triggering the Transition: Return to the Sources, Protests, and War

As had been the case with the Viola administration, the weakness of the Galtieri administration was evident from the very beginning.

While the palace coup "resolved" the division between soft-liners and hard-liners that lay at the root of the political turmoil characterizing the Viola presidency, by reestablishing the dominance of the hard-liners, this move did not solve the military rulers' predicament. Instead, it simply created new and worse problems, because Galtieri's strategy had even less chance to succeed than Viola's strategy of liberalization. Galtieri sought a return to the sources of the Proceso, sources that entailed, on the economic side, a return to the type of neoconservative economic program advanced by José Martínez de Hoz, and on the political side, a resurrection of the project of creating an official party, which had been discussed by the military since 1978.[1] But the conditions under which this attempted return to the sources was to be carried out differed from those under which the military had attempted to consolidate power in the early years of the Proceso, in such a way that the obstacles Galtieri faced in seeking to institutionalize the military's original project were even greater than those the military rulers had faced in their first and failed attempt at institutionalization.

The conditions under which the military would be carrying out this attempt were extremely adverse. On the internal front, as stated in Chapter 5, the military rulers' hold on power had been severely weakened due to their own failure to abide by the rules they had set down so as to manage the tasks of governing in an orderly fashion. Indeed, Galtieri's assumption of the presidency had led to the breakdown of the military's own rules for the management of the state. The societal front, moreover, had also become more inauspicious for the implementation of the kind of project Galtieri was spearheading. Rather than face an atomized and demoralized society, now the military faced a society that had taken important steps toward reorganizing itself and that steadfastly opposed the military's political and economic plans. At the very core, therefore, the problem with the Galtieri government was that it seemed unlikely that it could reverse the despised consequences of Viola's liberalization policies and the problem that had triggered the palace coup—the rise of a broad-based movement in opposition to military rule. In effect, the destabilizing dynamic that resulted from the rise and strengthening of an autonomous political force would continue, if in a slightly modified manner, after Galtieri became president.

The inability of the military rulers to control the surging protest movement was the first sign of the rapidly deteriorating power of the military rulers. Building on developments during Viola's tenure in office, society kept pressuring the military rulers through increased and better-coordinated activities on various fronts. On the party front, the political parties that had come back to life throughout 1981, and that were now gathered in the multiparty alliance called the Multipartidaria, demanded with increasing resolve a quick return to democracy. To this end, the Multipartidaria issued its boldest and most comprehensive critique of the Proceso in mid-December, just a few days after General Viola was forced to resign as president, in a document entitled "Before It Is Too Late" (Antes que sea tarde) (Multipartidaria 1982a:161–84). In this document the Multipartidaria castigated the military for their poor record in government and called for an immediate return to civilian rule. Soon afterward these parties began organizing a campaign of mobilization, which was launched on March 28, 1982, with a political act gathering some 5,000 people in Paraná (Fontana 1987:144).

Opposition was also growing on the labor front. There was strong resistance to the anti-inflationary program put into effect by Minister of Economy Roberto Alemann, a program that included a wage freeze for an undetermined period of time (Smith 1989:244–46). The resistance this economic program faced was greater than when Martínez de Hoz had initiated his economic program. Trade union leaders had recovered from the defeat of 1976, and pressures from a rank and file that had mobilized in response to the economic crisis starting in 1980 forced both wings of Argentina's labor movement to oppose Alemann's economic program (Munck with Falcón and Gallitelli 1987:217–20). For the Intersectorial CNT-20, the weakening and subsequent displacement of Viola was a blow to their strategy. After having slowly and painstakingly built a relationship of confidence with Viola throughout 1979 and 1980, and just when payoff time seemed to have arrived, Viola was unable to deliver. With Viola's displacement from power, the dialogue between the government and the Intersectorial was, for all purposes, cut off. Despite contacts with Labor Minister Brigadier Julio César Porcile in February 1982, the new government appeared unyielding. Thus, in mid-February, the labor ministry announced that the government did not intend to reintroduce collective bargaining during 1982, and early in March the labor minister himself rejected any possibility of the government lifting its wage freeze. Having criticized Alemann's economic policies from the outset, by March the Intersectorial was turning its attention toward a plan of mobilization. In the absence of government concessions of tangible benefits to an increasingly impatient rank and file, the Intersectorial's collaborationist strategy was becoming almost untenable.

The oppositionist General Labor Confederation, for its part, continued to push for broadly coordinated protest measures aimed against Alemann's economic policies as well as military rule per se.[2] Concrete steps to advance these aims were discussed among the CGT's top leaders starting in January, but the discussions were progressively broadened to include the "62 Organizations," the traditional labor branch of the Peronist movement that labor boss Lorenzo Miguel had resuscitated in October 1981, the Peronist party, and the regional branches of the CGT. Moreover, once the idea of a mobilization that would end with a massive gathering in the center of Buenos Aires, and not a general strike, was agreed on within the CGT sphere, contacts were made with the Multipartidaria to ensure support across the political spectrum for the protest action. Only the Intersectorial, which was still careful not to engage in any global critique of the government and which distinguished their attacks on the economic policies of the government from an attack on military rule as a form of government, did not back the demonstration. But the Intersectorial was becoming increasingly isolated, as the government's intransigent response to societal demands strengthened the hand of leaders that adopted the kind of confrontationist stance that the Intersectorial leadership refused to adopt.

The mass demonstration organized by the CGT and held on March 30 was a landmark event. This event represented a culmination of efforts to coordinate the actions of multiple opposition groups; it was the first time since the 1976 coup that all major opposition groups, including the Multipartidaria, had backed a protest measure demanding a return to democracy. It was also by far the largest demonstration against the military government since the 1976 coup, drawing an estimated turnout of 30,000 to 50,000 people. If the military could still display its intimidatory powers, as it did by repressing the march and arresting more than 1,000 demonstrators, the very confrontation between the military and an opposition movement that was now taking to the streets showed the extent to which the opposition had taken the offensive. The surge of this emboldened opposition was a clear sign of how the military's power had deteriorated, indicating that Galtieri's attempt to return to the sources and to institutionalize the original project that the military had envisioned had less of a chance of succeeding than Viola's own failed attempt at liberalization.

It was in this context that the military made a decisive choice: to invade the Falkland/Malvinas Islands, a set of small islands in the South Atlantic under British control but long claimed by Argentina, on April 2. This military action would turn out to be decisive for the evolution of military rule, because it exposed the military rulers to the dangers of foreign war with a superior power, Great Britain. Indeed, following various failed attempts to find a peaceful resolution, actions on the battlefield showed that Argentina's poorly prepared and poorly equipped forces were not much of a match for the Task Force sent from Britain to regain control of the Falkland/Malvinas Islands. Despite the brave actions of Argentine Air Force pilots, which inflicted heavy losses on the British fleet, Argentina was bound to be defeated in the "little war" with Britain. And a mere ten weeks after the invasion began, President Galtieri announced to the Argentine population that the military had surrendered to the British forces on June 14.

The fallout of defeat was swift in coming and hit the military rulers to the bone. The day after Galtieri acknowledged defeat, all the cabinet ministers presented their resignations, while Galtieri himself resigned as commander-in-chief of the army and president and was replaced by General Cristino Nicolaides, who became commander-in-chief of the army, and by General Alfredo Saint Jean, the minister of the interior, who became the interim president on June 18. A few days later, even more dramatic events occurred, as General Nicolaides unilaterally and without consultation designated Retired Army General Reynaldo Bignone as president, to assume power on July 1. This move triggered an immediate reaction by the navy and the air force, which withdrew from the military junta, arguing that such a move violated a basic rule of the Proceso, that the president be designated through a joint and unanimous decision of the military junta. At this point, the key mechanism for incorporating the armed forces as a whole into the tasks of governing, a central feature of the Proceso from its very origin, was thus done away with, and the army became the sole basis of the government. The military rulers were simply too divided to continue backing the institutional rules set up in 1976, and the military junta in effect collapsed. The profound disarray within the armed forces was such that they considered the Proceso to be essentially over. The only thing they could agree on was to start a process of transition immediately (Fontana 1987:161, 167–68; Melo 1989:31–35). A political crisis had given way to a transition.

The beginning of a transition did not in itself ensure that the transition would be successfully completed. Indeed, the process of transition raised distinct issues that are considered later in this chapter. But before moving on to an analysis of the process of transition itself, it is necessary to tackle the challenge of how to explain the initiation of the transition—that is, why Argentina's transition from bureaucratic authoritarianism began on June 14, 1982. In part because of the catalytic role that the defeat in war against a foreign power played, Argentina's transition has led to a fair amount of polemic in the literature concerning the causal power of societal opposition movements. Given that this issue goes to the heart of the argument in this book, we turn now to this question.

Explaining the Initiation of the Transition: The Role of Domestic and Societal Dimensions

The turn of events that triggered the transition in Argentina raises some complex issues of interpretation. The standard view, advanced by some of the best-known analysts of Argentine politics, is that the transition in Argentina was "brought about by the intramilitary crisis that follow[ed] the defeat in the South Atlantic" and that "the military regime [fell] apart under its own weight, without pressure from civil society being a major factor in that destruction" (Fontana 1987:161, 187). The causes of the transition are thus considered to be external—in that military defeat at the hands of a foreign power is seen to have played an important role—and state- or ruler-centered, in that decisions made by the military rulers in abstraction from the actions of societal actors are seen as having a key impact.[3] Such an interpretation addresses an important aspect of the Argentine transition. But in playing down the role societal forces had in triggering the transition, it overlooks the extent to which the transition can be fully explained only through a consideration of domestic and societal factors—or, more precisely, through the political dynamics of state-society relations that this book has been emphasizing.[4]

An interpretation of the events leading up to the initiation of the transition depends a good deal on how the critical decision to invade the Falkland/Malvinas Islands is viewed, and, more precisely, on what role societal pressure played in making that decision. In this regard, it appears to be quite clear that neither the idea of the invasion itself nor the timing of the invasion was directly related to the March 30 mass demonstration. The idea of the invasion itself was one that the navy had considered for quite some time. Plans for a possible invasion had been drawn up during 1977, when Admiral Eduardo Emilio Massera headed the navy, and later, during 1980, when the navy had pushed for the idea in the context of the debate on the issue of presidential succession.[5] With regard to the timing of the invasion, not only had the planning for the operation begun several months earlier, but the decision to invade on April 2 appears to have been precipitated less by the need to react immediately to the March 30 demonstration than by the process that was precipitated by the arrival of an Argentine scrap merchant on the South Georgia Islands to dismantle an old whaling station on March 19.[6] Acknowledging that the March 30 mass demonstration did not lead to the idea of an invasion or determine the actual timing of the invasion, it is plausible, nonetheless, that the actual decision to invade was driven by the predicament the military rulers faced in light of the destabilizing dynamics of state-society relations that was manifested by the March 30 protest but that had begun to develop earlier, when Viola became president in March 1981.

The key reason for considering the causal impact of societal forces on the decision to invade is that the army's decision to support an invasion makes most sense in light of the dynamics of state-society relations. The importance of the army's position is not a complicated issue. Quite simply, the army's support for the idea of an invasion was a critical element, because without the backing of the army the invasion would simply not take place. Thus, while the idea of an invasion had been seriously pursued by the navy, as during 1980, it did not become the government's policy until December 1981, when the idea received backing within the army. The problem, then, is to explain why the army decided to support the navy's plan to invade the Falkland/Malvinas Islands when it did, a decision that points to two crucial and interrelated considerations that were strongly affected by societal forces.

The first consideration pertains to Army Commander-in-Chief Galtieri's response to Viola's liberalization strategy. As discussed in Chapter 5, Galtieri led the hard-liner elements within the military, which first reacted negatively to the growth of opposition to military rule taking place during the Viola administration, and then displaced Viola through a palace coup. But Galtieri could not act against Viola on his own. As a payoff for the navy's support of Galtieri's move to displace Viola, Galtieri had to commit to support the navy's long-hatched plans to intervene militarily in the Falkland/Malvinas Islands.[7] The decision to invade was thus set in motion as a result of the reaction by hard-line elements within the army to the dynamics of state-society relations that had developed during the Viola administration and that entailed the growth of an opposition force that was seen as increasingly threatening to the military's ability to remain in power.

The second consideration involves the strategy that Galtieri sought to advance in place of Viola's strategy of liberalization. It is important to note that Galtieri not only sought to resurrect the notion of creating an official party to embody the military's permanent political legacy, an idea that had been abandoned by Viola, but also, in contrast to the idea of a civilian-headed pro-military party that had circulated in 1980, now expected that he himself would lead this new party.[8] In face of an increasingly concerted opposition, however, it was unlikely that Galtieri could successfully postulate himself as a pro-regime candidate unless something dramatic occurred to shift opposition away from the military rulers and provide Galtieri with a broad basis of support. Because the decision to invade the Falkland/Malvinas Islands, in allowing Galtieri to drum up a sense of national pride, was seen as just such a dramatic occurrence, the link between the difficulty the military increasingly faced in their attempt to control society through 1981 and the decision to go to war is again quite direct.[9] Thus, the destabilizing political dynamics that began to characterize state-society relations in the wake of Viola's assumption of the presidency, a dynamics that was clearly manifested in the March 30, 1982, demonstration but that had originated at least a year earlier, appears to explain quite well why the policy decision to invade the Falkland/Malvinas Islands was made when it was.[10]

It is certainly correct to argue that in the end it was the military rulers who had to make the decision, and that the internal debates within the military should therefore be considered. But that is not the issue raised here. What is at stake is the always thorny question of whether the military rulers—the only actors that could make the decision to invade or not to invade—"jumped or were pushed." In this regard, the argument here seeks to reassess the usually ignored role of societal forces and to argue that society did push the military rulers to make the decision to invade in a fairly direct manner, not as a result of the March 30, 1982, demonstration, which came too late to have much impact on the military's decision-making process, but as a result of the way in which societal forces had increasingly undermined the ability of the military to rule. The significance of this argument deserves stressing. Not only should the invasion of the Falkland/Malvinas Islands be properly seen as a case of a set of rulers "projecting their internal problems outward" (O'Donnell 1992:24; O'Donnell and Schmitter 1986:18), but the very causes of the transition that was initiated once the Argentine forces surrendered to the British should also be seen in terms that capture the dynamics of state-society relations rather than in the state- or ruler-centered terms advanced by the standard view about the origins of Argentina's transition.

If the causes of the transition are best seen, therefore, in terms of the political dynamics of state-society relations rather than in state- or ruler-centered terms, there is also the issue of assessing up to what point the transition can be accounted for in terms of domestic versus external factors, an issue that is clearly relevant in light of the determinative power that events on the battlefield had on the timing of the beginning of the transition. The obvious importance of military defeat to the triggering of the transition notwithstanding, it is important to place the importance of external factors on Argentina's transition in perspective.

There is, first of all, the very real sense in which the military's defeat at the hands of the British was "self-inflicted." What this means is that while military defeat played a role in initiating the transition, the deeper cause of the transition was the decision to launch an invasion that had little chances of success. Indeed, the Falkland/Malvinas war was "an absurd war which was lost before it ever started" and which was launched in the first place because Argentina's rulers responded to the challenges of ruling under increasingly adverse conditions in an erratic and self-defeating manner (Borón 1988:141).[11] The key strategic error was the belief by the Argentine military that the British would not fight and that the April 2 occupation of the Falkland/Malvinas Islands could only help them, giving them the upper hand in negotiations. This strategic calculation, based on the belief that the United States would not oppose the invasion, and that U.S. President Ronald Reagan would prevail over and restrain British Prime Minister Margaret Thatcher, as a result of the assistance the Argentine military were offering Reagan in his effort to "combat communism" in Central America, was a fundamental misreading of the realities of the North Atlantic Treaty Organization (NATO) military alliance, as well as of the desire and willingness on the part of Thatcher, who was just as belligerent and in need of stirring up jingoistic feelings at home as they, to take Britain into war.[12] Once the prospects of a negotiated settlement disappeared and the war began, things hinged on the ability of the Argentine military to win on the battlefield, a contest that was predictably shaped by the Argentines' lack of military readiness in the face of a superior military power.[13] While the transition to democracy was triggered, then, as a result of military defeat by a foreign power, the deeper causes must be sought in the internal or domestic problems that pushed the military to make a gamble they had no realistic chance of winning, either by forcing the British into negotiations or through a victory on the battlefield.

While this assessment of the impact of external factors on the triggering of Argentina's transition is primarily supported by the truly reckless nature of the Argentine military's gamble, it also is upheld when considering the counterfactual situation of a victorious outcome for the Argentine forces. The evidence appears to suggest that even though such a scenario would probably have given new life to the military rulers, extending the durability of military rule, it would not have altered the basic dynamics to which the military were reacting in launching the Falkland/Malvinas invasion and that served as the underlining cause of the transition. Even though an Argentine victory would have allowed the military to ride a wave of nationalistic feeling, it is clear that the popular reaction to the news that Argentine forces had invaded a territory that Argentina had long claimed as its own was not one of uncritical support for the military (Dabat and Lorenzano 1984: chap. 1).

From the perspective of society's growing oppositionist movement, the invasion of the Falkland/Malvinas Islands, at precisely the moment when repudiations were cast against the government on account of the repressive response the March 30 union-sponsored demonstration met with, did introduce all kinds of uncertainties and dilemmas. In an effort to solidify the sense of national unity and to show the world that the country stood firmly behind the war effort, unionists not only called off measures that were planned to protest the government's response to the March 30 demonstration, but even began devoting their energies to diplomatic overtures on behalf of the military rulers.[14] The pressures to unite behind the national flag's colors, however, did not entirely subsume the antimilitary banners of the opposition. This was evident in the notion that "the Malvinas are Argentine" but that support for the invasion did not mean support for Galtieri and the military rulers, a notion expressed in the slogans chanted and the posters carried by the jubilant and massive crowds gathered in the Plaza de Mayo in front of the Casa Rosada—the Government House.[15] Further signs of the ability of social forces to criticize the military nature of the government while supporting a nationalistic cause came when CGT representatives, on their trips abroad as well as through their communiqués, made the point that their backing of the military junta's actions in the South Atlantic did not alter their criticisms of the government's labor policies,[16] and when some party leaders issued calls for an immediate transition to democracy to be led by a civilian government.[17] While the war certainly affected the plans of opposition leaders, the nationalistic euphoria had not altered the political problem from which the military sought to divert attention by means of a foreign adventure and had not fully drowned out demands for a change in government (Makin 1985:164–66).

In sum, there are a variety of reasons for arguing that military defeat at the hands of a foreign power had only a marginal independent impact on the triggering of the Argentine transition. First, the domestic roots of the decision to invade made the war a cause of the transition only in a derivative manner. Second, while in some cases war can produce uncertain outcomes that can greatly affect the course of domestic events, in the case of the Falkland/Malvinas war Argentina had no realistic chance of success.[18] The consequences of what is best seen as a self-inflicted defeat should therefore be attributed not as much to the role of the victorious foreign power as to the domestic policy-making process that generated the decision to invade in the first place. Third, as the argument based on the counterfactual situation of an Argentine victory shows, even such an outcome would probably have only delayed rather than erased the forces that were working to cause the triggering of a transition.[19] In the end, while the outcome of the war led directly and quite dramatically to a transition, this was the case only because of the combination of military defeat and domestic problems. Although the transition took place through war, the war and its outcome were less the cause than the last straw that merely accelerated the likely course of events, based on developments concerning domestic actors and the political dynamics that had characterized the polity before the invasion and military defeat in the South Atlantic.[20]

The causes of the initiation of the transition can be summarized, in line with the political-institutional model's emphasis on the orientation and strength of the old governing elites and societal actors, in the following terms. The driving force behind the initiation of the transition was the formation and progressive strengthening of a societal actor oriented toward displacing the military rulers from power. The formation of this opposition actor was a gradual process that began, as seen in Chapter 4, barely one year after the military rulers assumed power in 1976 and that advanced considerably throughout 1981, in the context of General Viola's presidency. By late 1981, the military rulers faced a principled opposition that increasingly coordinated its activities and that had become a contending elite the military could not afford to ignore.

The impact of the gradual strengthening of societal opposition forces on the political dynamics of state-society relations was both quite swift and direct. First, the opposition drive during the Viola presidency contributed to a destabilizing dynamics, as the opposition's actions reinforced and exacerbated the long-standing splits within the military rulers to the point that hard-liner elements within the military reacted against the government of Viola by staging a palace coup in December 1981. The irony of the palace coup was that, while it was a response by the hard-line elements within the military to the perceived weakening of the military's power that resulted from Viola's pursuit of a strategy of liberalization, which had aimed at rebuilding support for the military rulers but had unintentionally unleashed a force it could not harness or control, it actually accentuated the weakness of the military rulers. For even as the coup had ostensibly restored some degree of cohesion to the military rulers, it had led the military to break their own rules for the management of the state, while doing nothing to hold back the growing momentum of societal forces demanding a transition. A tenuous political situation had evolved into a political crisis.

After Galtieri assumed the presidency, the opposition's drive continued to affect the political dynamics of state-society relations. The opposition's actions prevented the unified hard-line government from containing the degenerative dynamics that increasingly characterized the evolution of military rule and that accentuated the prospects of change. Thus, rather than moving resolutely in their attempt to return to the sources, the military rulers continued to display the erratic type of behavior that they had already demonstrated in reacting to the consequences of Viola's liberalization policy, and were actually driven to pursue a strategy that was riskier than anything that might have resulted from the strategy of liberalization pursued by Viola. Soon enough the military rulers were pushed to invade the Falkland/Malvinas Islands, a decision that put the military on course to a self-inflicted defeat. In the end, as a result of military defeat at the hands of the British, the military rulers were further weakened and, assessing the risks of continued involvement in the management of the state, changed their orientation, abandoning their commitment to military rule and accepting the opposition's basic demand to start a transition.

It is important to stress, in sum, that the decision to invade the Falkland/Malvinas Islands, and the impact of the outcome of the war, make sense only within the context of the choices of domestic actors and the political dynamics of state-society relations. The Falkland/Malvinas fiasco was quite literally the result of the attempt by the hard-line sector within the military first to contain the consequences of the soft-liners' attempt to gain support for military rule, and then to gain support from a society that clearly opposed them. As the military rulers were increasingly exposed to the pressure of a societal opposition it could not control, the hard-liners adopted decisions that were increasingly risky and self-defeating. Reacting to the consequences of Viola's liberalization strategy through the palace coup of December 1981, the military had undermined their power by breaking the very rules they had set down for the management of the state. Reacting to the growing mobilization of society in late 1981 and early 1982, the military undermined their power by making an unwinnable make-or-break gamble that forced them to abandon even the slightest pretense to rule. Thus, although military defeat at hands of a foreign power was the event that most immediately triggered the transition, by bringing about a change in the orientation of the military rulers, the deeper causes of the transition lay in the gradual strengthening of societal opposition groups that called for an end to military rule, and in the impact that this factor had—via their exacerbation of a destabilizing dynamics—on the very orientation of the military rulers. The initiation of the transition was, in effect, but the final consequence of the conflicting imperative to which the military rulers were subjected as a result of the problem of representation, which led them to acknowledge the need to open channels for the representation of excluded forces, in order to provide the basis for a new political order, but also to resist any such opening, given its negative impact on the cohesiveness of the military rulers and the opportunities such openings provide opposition groups in society.

Reform Through Rupture as a Mode of Transition

The very manner in which the transition was triggered, important in itself, also affected the process of transition by determining the mode of transition. Thus, the process of transition would be shaped, on the one hand, by the fact that the transition was supported both by societal forces and by the military rulers who had abandoned their antichange posture. On the other hand, the process of transition was very much affected by the particular strategy that dominated the transition. In this regard, it is important to emphasize how things could have been different in Argentina and how the military's own blunders ended up hurting them. Indeed, during most of 1981, the societal opposition had adopted a very accommodationist strategy vis-à-vis the military rulers, in recognition of the clear power the military had at that point in time. Because of the actions of the hard-line elements, which battled and eventually prevailed over the sector of the military that sought to explore the idea of a political opening, however, the military missed the opportunity to cut their loses and retreat to the barracks, while still retaining sufficient power to condition a transition. By mid-1982, the same options were not available. By then, the military as a whole had been weakened vis-à-vis society, as a result of their defeat at the hands of the British. And by indirectly strengthening the hands of the opposition, they had removed the incentive for opposition accommodation. Thus, when Argentina initiated its transition from bureaucratic authoritarianism on June 14, 1982, it would undergo a reform through rupture (see Figure 1.2 in Chapter 1).

The impact of this mode of transition on the political dynamics during the process of transition itself was quite clear. The military's relative weakness meant that an openly confrontational strategy toward the outgoing rulers would prevail and that the agenda of the transition process would basically be dictated by the opposition. In addition, the support for a transition both within society and within the governing elites, and in particular the virtual disappearance of an antichange disposition within the governing elites, meant that the transition would be marked by little uncertainty concerning the successful completion of the transition. Jointly, these two factors would shape a transition in which a previously unified opposition, not needing to worry about the threat of an authoritarian regression, became more concerned with the competition for access to power than with the need to secure a successful transition,[21] and in which the very dynamics of the democratic transition would undermine any attempt by the outgoing military to seek an accommodation with societal actors and ensure that any accord between the outgoing rulers and potentially conciliatory opposition elements would be swept away. To this process of transition we now turn.

Military Weakness and Opposition Confrontation: The Opposition's Agenda

Once the transition was triggered by the defeat of Argentine forces at the hands of the British in the South Atlantic, the process of transition proceeded quite rapidly, as the weakened military rulers could do little to force the opposition into an accommodationist strategy. While the transition itself was overseen by the incumbent caretaker government of Retired General Bignone, which was set up on July 1, 1982[22]—an interim arrangement usually associated with a relatively high degree of control by the outgoing rulers, the societal opposition in effect confronted the military rulers with their own agenda for the transition and forced this agenda on the government.[23]

The military's lack of control of the agenda was evident, first of all, in the pace at which the transition advanced and the content of the rules under which the transition was carried out. Very rapidly, in mid-July, the president signed Law No. 22617, which repealed the law, No. 21323, that had prohibited political activities.[24] This was followed, in August, by the approval of a Statute of Political Parties, which set the guidelines for relegalization of political parties and thus triggered a surge of party activity. With the sanctioning of this statute, parties began a frantic process of reorganization centered around a recruitment drive that led in a matter of months to the combined affiliation of a phenomenal 31 percent of the electorate (Melo 1989:41–43). If the military appeared to exercise some control over the pace of events by delaying the announcement of an official election date until February 1983 and the approval of the Electoral Law (Ley Electoral) until June 1993, the setting of elections for October 30, 1993, a mere sixteen months after the initiation of the transition, and the setting of the transfer of power for January 30, 1984, did little to alter what was a fast-paced transition process.[25]

Aside from the inability of the military rulers to control the pace of political activities, the content of legal documents that regulated the transition also demonstrated the rulers' lack of control over the transition process. Basically, these legal documents did nothing to ensure the emergence of political forces favorable to the military,[26] and, not surprisingly, they led to the reactivation of the traditional political parties that had dominated the political scene before the 1976 coup and that the military had blamed for the country's problems. Because the military rulers had failed to institutionalize their project through a legal framework during the preceding phase of military rule, it was unlikely that the military rulers, weakened as they were, would be able to control the political process through legal means during the process of transition itself. In fact, recognizing their limited abilities, the outgoing military rulers never made a serious effort to advance their interests by means of the political party statute and the electoral law. And having failed earlier to confront the challenge of constitutional definition with any real success, the possibility of amending the constitution was not even discussed, and the old 1853 presidential constitution was simply reintroduced (McGuire 1995:190, 199–202).

In addition to their failure to tailor the rules under which the transition would be carried out, the military's lack of control of the agenda was evident in their attempt to gain assurances from the emergent political forces concerning one of the most worrisome problems the military faced: their dismal record of human rights abuses.[27] As soon as the military junta was reconstituted, after a three-month hiatus, on September 21, the military rulers began to seek assurances that no future government would prosecute them for having a record of human rights violations, or even conduct inquiries into their human rights record. To this end, they issued a fifteen-point document on November 11, 1982.[28]

But this attempt to safeguard the military's position in the post-transitional setting was soundly rejected by society and by party elites. There was a broad societal repudiation of the military's attempt to condition any post-transition government that was manifested through the "March of Resistance" (Marcha de la Resistencia) led by human rights groups over a twenty-four-hour period starting on December 10, and the "March of the People for Democracy and National Reconstruction" (Marcha del Pueblo por la Democracia y la Reconstrucción Nacional), which was organized by the Multipartidaria and backed by both wings of labor, and which drew about 100,000 supporters on December 16 (Multipartidaria 1982c).[29] In sum, the military rulers not only appeared to have little real input into the process whereby a new set of rulers would be installed in power, but also seemed to have little ability to condition the future government's policies. The agenda of the transition was being dictated in a fairly one-sided manner by an opposition that refused to compromise with the outgoing military rulers.[30]

Signs of Opposition Accommodation: The Military's Last Hope for Gaining Assurances

If it appeared quite improbable that the military rulers would gain the assurances they were seeking by appealing in an open manner to all sectors of society, the military did not desist from trying. Rather than abandon the attempt to gain assurances by means of an agreement with all political forces, the military began to pursue another option late in 1982: an agreement with the Peronists.[31] The rationale for approaching the Peronists was quite straightforward. The Peronists had won every free election since 1946 and were assumed to be the favorites to win the 1983 election. Hence, an agreement with the Peronists would grant the military the security they sought.

While such a partial, as opposed to general, agreement was easier to conclude, due to the relative balance of forces among internal sectors within the Peronist party at the time the transition began, the process of accommodation between the Peronists and the military rulers was nonetheless bound to be convoluted. Essentially, in mid-1982, the Peronist party was composed of three sectors represented by political leaders that were closely associated with different labor groupings.[32] There were the right-wing "moderates" *(moderados)*, led by Angel Robledo and Raúl Matera and supported by the General Labor Confederation-Azopardo (Confederación General del Trabajo—Azopardo [CGT-Azopardo]), the new name given to the collaborationist Intersectorial.[33] The centrist "hard-liners" *(duros)*, for their part, gathered the top "verticalist" leaders, such as Deolindo Bittel and Antonio Cafiero, and were supported by Lorenzo Miguel's 62 Organizations and the Movement of Unity, Solidarity, and Organization (Movimiento de Unidad, Solidaridad y Organización [MUSO]), a loose gathering of unions coming mainly from the Group of 25, the most confrontationist labor grouping within the CGT-Brasil, the new name given to the CGT.[34] Finally, there was the Intransigence and Mobilization (Intransigencia y Movilización) faction, organized around Vicente Leonides Saadi and backed by left-wing trade unionists Andrés Framini and Sebastián Borro.[35]

The problem, from the military's perspective, was quite simple: if they had little to worry about as a result of the marginal role played by the Intransigence and Mobilization faction, the relative balance of power among sectors clearly favored the hard-liners over the moderates. The hard-liners were in control of the party apparatus[36] and had established strong links going back to 1980 with the CGT-Brasil and its precursors and subsequently with the 62 Organizations of Miguel—two labor groupings that by now accounted for a majority of the trade union movement.[37] Thus, it appeared unlikely that the moderates, which had had a close relationship with the military rulers and which had consistently shown a predisposition toward compromise, would gain control over the crucial process of naming candidates for the upcoming national elections. The prospects of a rapprochement between the Peronists and the military rulers would have to be based, therefore, on the dominant hard-liner sector and would have to involve a reversal of the policy of favoring the CGT-Azopardo and its various forerunners, a policy that had been sustained throughout the entire period of military rule and that continued immediately after the beginning of the transition.

If such a rapprochement was likely to involve a complicated rearrangement in military-labor relations, it was not an unrealistic goal for the military to pursue. For one, the dividing line between the two groupings was being partly erased, as the CGT-Azopardo leadership, responding to pressure from below, took bolder actions than in the past. Thus, after some initial hesitance and after seeking some form of accommodation with the government over the issue of wages, the CGT-Azopardo called for a general strike at the end of November.[38] This general strike, the third since the 1976 coup, was held as planned on December 6 and was highly successful. It is significant that, given the

CGT-Brasil's backing of the measure, this was the first general strike since 1976 to be supported by both wings of labor.[39] But it also was the first general strike to be called by the until then clearly collaborationist wing of the labor movement. Indeed, while the CGT-Azopardo continued to be open to compromise with the government, and the CGT-Brasil continued to be relatively confrontationist,[40] the initiative appeared to have moved to the camp of the longtime moderates, or collaborationists. In effect, responding to new governmental delays in attending to their demands for higher wages, the CGT-Azopardo soon organized a new general strike, which was again supported by the CGT-Brasil, on March 28, 1983 (Centro de Investigaciones sobre el Estado y la Administración 1984a:101).[41]

The differences between the two wings of labor were also being erased as a result of the actions of a single person, Lorenzo Miguel, who was a powerful labor leader within the hard-line wing of labor but who displayed a clear disposition toward accommodation with the military rulers.[42] In this regard, Miguel's critique of the left wing of the Peronist party on the occasion of the celebration of the traditional Peronist October 17 celebration, in 1982, was quite telling. In what was a clearly conciliatory overture to the military, Miguel stated that some people "have tried to separate the people from its armed forces, but this is going to come to an end" (quoted in Sáenz Quesada 1993:190–91). Miguel showed, in short, that he shared the military's view of the legitimacy of the "war against subversion."[43] The significance of such overtures was that, on the basis of the 62 Organizations, which he had reconstituted, Miguel provided a counterbalance to the more confrontational Group of 25 within the CGT-Brasil, as well as within the Peronist party's hard-liner sector, where Miguel's 62 Organizations coexisted side by side with the Movement of Unity, Solidarity, and Organization, the Group of 25's vehicle with the Peronist party. Indeed, Miguel's influence was in large part responsible for the change in the roles played by the CGT-Brasil and the CGT-Azopardo, a change captured in Framini's comment to the effect that "the 'moderates' [have] harden[ed] up, while the 'hard-liners' dialogue" (Cordeu, Mercado, and Sosa 1985:77).[44] While remaining clearly opposed to military rule, Miguel's strong moderating influence on the CGT-Brasil wing of labor and the hard-liner sector of the Peronist party made the possibility of accommodation between the military rulers and the dominant sectors of Peronism less far-fetched than it would have appeared before the beginning of the transition.

There was, actually, a clear basis for a rapprochement between the hard-liners that had control of the Peronist party, and the military rulers. For if the military wanted assurances they believed Miguel could offer, Miguel also wanted something that the military could help him get. After regaining his freedom in April 1980, Lorenzo Miguel, who had led the metal workers' union until the 1976 coup and who had been one of the country's most powerful figures during the Isabel Perón government, had slowly reentered the labor scene. He had worked within the hard-liner wing, partly because his competitors within the UOM were aligned with the collaborationist CNT and later the CGT-Azopardo, and he had moved to consolidate his position within the union movement by reconstituting the Peronist labor grouping called 62 Organizations in mid-October 1981.[45] But Miguel had still not been able to fully reassert his control over the UOM.[46] This was a crucial step, because it provided the core organizational base from which Miguel could move on to consolidate his power. Thus, there was something that the government could offer Miguel in return for his promise to steer the Peronists in the direction that the military wanted.

This was the quid pro quo that served as the basis for the new relationship between Miguel and the military rulers. From Miguel's perspective, such a rapprochement with the military rulers offered him the possibility of reasserting his preeminence within the labor movement as well within the Peronist party. From the military's perspective, Miguel was correctly perceived as a crucial player that probably had the best chance of becoming the dominant figure within Peronism. Given that the Peronists were believed to be the likely winners of the upcoming election, Miguel seemed to be the person that could deliver the guarantees the military were seeking in the human rights arena. Some kind of deal with the Peronists appeared to be the military's last hope of conditioning the transition.

Whether a formal agreement or pact between Miguel and the military was ever reached, as the press reported in November 1982, is somewhat besides the point. While Miguel and General Nicolaides, the central figures in this alleged pact,[47] denied these rumors, the denunciation of the CGT-Azopardo that such a pact would give Miguel and his allies an unfair advantage in the union normalization process seems to be partially supported by the evidence.[48] There was a quite noticeable reversal of the military's policy of favoring the CGT-Azopardo, and a decided push to help Miguel, who consolidated his power to such an extent that by mid-1983 he was the most dominant labor and political figure within Peronism.

A significant landmark in Miguel's rise was his important victory over the CGT-Azopardo in early 1983. As the CGT-Azopardo formed its own 62 Organizations in January and February 1983,[49] seeking to challenge Miguel's claim that the 62 Organizations he controlled was the legitimate labor wing of the Peronist party, Miguel was able to engineer the reincorporation of a number of unions that had split from the CGT-Brasil in May 1982 back into the CGT-Brasil. This move, which led to the partial reorganization of the CGT-Brasil and its renaming as the CGT of the Argentine Republic (CGT de la República Argentina [CGT-RA]), allowed Miguel not only to gain strength vis-à-vis the CGT-Azopardo but also to increase his leverage within the CGT-RA relative to the more confrontationist Group of 25 members.[50] To culminate this process of consolidation of power, Miguel also recovered control of the metal workers' union, seven years and four months after having been displaced from the union and imprisoned, when the military rulers returned the union to the workers on August 9, 1983 (Aznárez and Calistro 1993:139–40, 145; Carpena and Jacquelin 1994: 196–200).

Miguel had steered himself into a position whereby he could dominate the nomination process of the Peronist party. While enabled to play a direct political role in the upcoming elections when the military junta ended the restrictions imposed on Miguel by the Act of Institutional Responsibility (Acta de Responsabilidad Institucional) of 1976 (Aznárez and Calistro 1993:130–31),[51] Miguel rejected the possibility of himself being the vice-presidential candidate. He preferred, rather, to play the role of éminence grise, influencing the process behind the scenes. Indeed, after a fairly long and convoluted process, Miguel's decision to support Italo Luder against Cafiero was crucial in forming a ticket, in late August, that had Luder as presidential candidate and Deolindo Bittel as vice-presidential candidate.[52]

In sum, as Miguel had reestablished himself as the dominant figure within the labor movement and, because of labor's central position within Peronism, as the kingmaker within the Peronist party, the military rulers appeared to have found a backdoor way of getting assurances that the military had been unable to secure in an open dialogue with all political forces. Given that the military were clearly unable to control the transition process by openly and directly appealing to society and party elites, the less public and more restricted option they eventually pursued was the military's last hope of gaining the assurances they were seeking. It remained to be seen, however, whether such a pact or mere understanding between the Peronists and the military rulers was viable in the context of the political dynamics that characterized Argentina's transition.

Electoral Polarization and Antimilitary Reaction: The Defeat of the Military's Search for Assurances

The viability of such a pact would be tested in the electoral contest between Argentina's two traditional parties—the Peronist party and the Radical Civic Union (UCR)—a contest that, on the basis of the previous electoral record, appeared to favor the Peronists quite overwhelmingly. On the surface, moreover, as the electoral campaign began, the Peronists appeared to be overcoming some of the problems that had surfaced in the precampaign phase.[53] Setting aside the image of a divided Peronist party that had emerged during the nomination process, labor made its best effort to display its unified support for the Peronist candidates. Soon after the Luder-Bittel formula was proclaimed, support for the Peronist duo came not only from Miguel's 62 Organizations and the CGT-RA but also implicitly from the CGT-Azopardo, which joined forces with the CGT-RA in a call for a new general strike, to be held on October 4 (Centro de Investigaciones sobre el Estado y la Administración 1984a:398–99, 404), and in a proclamation of the "monolithic and total unity of the Argentine labor movement" in mid-October.[54] In addition, government concessions leading to a substantial increase in workers' wages during 1983 helped to legitimize the Peronist union leadership (Damill and Frenkel 1992:26, 64). Not only did government leaders believe the Peronists would win the election, but public opinion polls—geared to ask not who respondents were going to vote for but who they thought would win the election—registered the feeling among the population that the Peronists would win.[55] Despite the military rulers' weakness and inability to extract guarantees in an open manner from a broad spectrum of representative political forces, it looked as though they might still manage to condition the transition through their secret and partial pact with the Peronists.

Such a judgment about the Peronists' invincibility, however, was based on a misperception of the electorate, which considered it in static historical terms and failed to perceive how the shape of the electorate was being changed under the influence of the political dynamics of the transition. What was actually happening was somewhat akin to the usual pattern of polarization between electoral forces supporting pro–old-regime candidates and antiauthoritarian candidates that characterizes "foundational elections" in democratic transitions (O'Donnell and Schmitter 1986:61; Scully 1992: 192). The peculiarity of the Argentine case was that because the military had failed to generate a pro-military political force, there was no officialist candidate and the division between the old regime and the antiauthoritarian candidates was cast on the two main parties that had jointly opposed military rule within the Multipartidaria.

This dynamic began to be evident late in April 1983, as the military rulers attempted, for a second time, to obtain assurances that they would not be prosecuted for human rights violations, by publicizing the "Final Document of the Military Junta on the War Against Subversion and Terrorism" (Junta Militar 1984).[56] As when the military had published their fifteen-point document in November 1982, the reaction by human rights organizations was decisive and unambiguous. To reject the government's "Final Document," these organizations staged a protest march on May 20.[57] But such an unequivocal response was not forthcoming from all political sectors. Indeed, with the recent setting of a definitive timetable for national elections, the main political forces, which until then had operated together in opposition to the military within the Multipartidaria, began to confront each other as electoral opponents and to differentiate their messages.[58]

Thus, while Luder, who was at that time a likely Peronist presidential candidate, ventured only cautious and uncompromising statements,[59] Raúl Alfonsín, still battling for the UCR presidential nomination, seized on the issue of human rights, in marked contrast to the Peronists, and sought to present himself as a champion of human rights by denouncing the military-union pact *(pacto militar-sindical)* that had been rumored since November.[60] The brilliance of this move was that, whether or not a pact ever existed, such a denunciation picked up what were increasingly perceived as real elements of Peronism and served to define the profile of the soon-to-be two main presidential candidates[61] by casting Luder and the Peronists as representatives of a past that included the outgoing military rulers and Alfonsín and the UCR as representatives of the future and the real opponents of military rule. Alfonsín was ably taking advantage of the lack of concern about the possibility of an authoritarian regression—due to the weakness of the hard-line elements within the military, and the closer relationship of the Peronists to the military rulers, to launch an all-out electoral competition in which the portrayal of the UCR's former partners within the Multipartidaria as defenders of the old order would allow Alfonsín to ride the wave of antimilitary sentiment (Fontana 1987:177–78; Cavarozzi 1992a:227–32).

The divide that Alfonsín introduced persisted in the wake of his denunciation of the military-union pact in April 1983, as for a third and final time the military insisted on closing the door on their record of human rights violations. This time they did not present any type of document to garner the support of society, but resorted to the unilateral sanction of an amnesty law, which was made public on July 26 and eventually sanctioned, as Law No. 22924, the Law of National Pacification, on September 22 (Fontana 1987:182–83; Melo 1989:93).[62] As with the earlier documents, the announcement of the amnesty law triggered much criticism and provoked a debate within society that served to clarify the positions of key actors on the military's record of human rights abuses (Centro de Investigaciones sobre el Estado y la Administración 1984a:285–92; Fontana 1987:183–85). For a third time, the human rights movement, which would settle for nothing less than outright moral and legal condemnation of the military's repressive activities, staged a demonstration that gathered some 40,000 protesters on August 19. Also, as in the context of the "Final Document" earlier in the year, there was a clear differentiation between the two leading presidential candidates. Luder was hedging his bet with two apparently contradictory statements on the proposed amnesty law, saying in effect that "from the juridical point of view, its effects are irreversible." Alfonsín retorted that the proposed amnesty was "not irreversible, because . . . it can be attacked as unconstitutional" (quoted in Fontana 1987:183–84).[63] Even though Luder would eventually reverse his statement, claiming that he would strike down the amnesty law if elected, the dividing line was clear.[64] The Peronists' own acts, which to large segments of the population stood for a past they sought to reject,[65] gave credibility to Alfonsín's denunciation of a military-union pact while bolstering Alfonsín's portrayal of himself as a credible alternative to the military rulers.

This dynamic, in the end, was reflected in the October 30 election, an election that produced a surprising and significant outcome. It was surprising in that the electoral results gave Alfonsín a resounding victory by the margin of 52 to 40 percent of the vote.[66] Indeed, in handing the Peronists their first electoral defeat in a free election for the presidency, Alfonsín had more than doubled the historical vote of the UCR. Alfonsín's victory was also a significant outcome in that it meant that the military's attempt to condition the transition by means of their rapprochement with the Peronists had failed.[67] But if the electoral results that defeated the military's last hope to condition the transition went counter to what was widely expected, it is still important to emphasize that the victory was not merely a result of chance. Alfonsín's victory, and the military's unsuccessful search for assurances concerning their human rights record, can be accounted for in terms of the political dynamics that characterized Argentina's transition.

The failure of the military to condition the transition process was basically the result of the two factors that defined Argentina's mode of transition as a reform through rupture—the primarily confrontationist strategy of societal opposition actors, and the virtual disappearance of an antichange disposition within the governing elites. Because of the primarily confrontationist strategy of societal opposition actors, a factor enabled by the weakness of the outgoing rulers, the agenda of the transition process was basically dictated by the opposition. This resulted in a set of rules that allowed for a truly free and fair electoral contest.[68] The military were simply too weak to gain the guarantees they sought by conditioning the form in which the future government would be constituted, either by reforming the constitution—something the military had not been able to achieve at the peak of their power and that, in the post-Falkland/Malvinas war context, was simply out of the question—or by negotiating a pact with a broad spectrum of opposition forces, something that was unlikely because the military rulers had nothing to offer the opposition as a whole in return for the guarantees they were seeking. There was simply no incentive for the opposition to adopt an accommodationist strategy and compromise with the outgoing rulers.[69] Because of the virtual disappearance of an antichange disposition within the governing elites, moreover, the uncertainty concerning the successful completion of the transition was reduced, and the danger of an electoral strategy that divided former allies in the antiauthoritarian movement was removed.

The problem for the military rulers was that, despite their ability to establish a belated rapprochement with the Peronists, their pact was based on the weakest of foundations. First, the military's attempt to gain assurances in a backdoor manner hinged on a very risky procedure: a free and fair election. Rather than embed their demand for assurance in a constitutional document, which would place their need for guarantees firmly beyond the whims of electoral tides, or in a pact that encompassed all main political forces, which would not be threatened by the electoral success of any single political force, Argentina's military rulers had had to settle for a pact with a single political force, which left everything hinging on the electoral fortunes of a single party in a free election. Second, because the election was to be carried out in a context that was not shaped by the fear of an authoritarian regression, any political force that took an accommodationist stance toward the rulers of the old order would necessarily be handicapped in the electoral contest. Because the uncertainty about the successful completion of the transition was reduced, the danger of an electoral strategy that divided former allies in the antiauthoritarian movement was removed, and an incentive for an electoral strategy that sought to accentuate the polarization of the electorate and that rejected any accommodation with the outgoing rulers was generated. The military's attempt to gain assurances by means of a rapprochement with the Peronists, in sum, not only was premised on the riskiest of procedures, a free and fair election, but actually hinged on the results of an electoral contest in which the preferred electoral strategy ran counter to the accommodationist stance of the Peronists. While the military's ability to condition the transition could not be ruled an impossibility, the systematic forces at work ran counter to the military's hopes.[70]

In this scenario, Alfonsín took advantage of the opportunities that were offered to him. Even though labor was one of the most victimized sectors under military rule, and even though labor's opposition to military rule seemed to put Peronist leaders in an ideal position to capitalize on the wave of antimilitary sentiment, Alfonsín was the leader who best understood the dynamics of the transition and who capitalized on these dynamics by highlighting the manner in which the Peronist leadership appeared to have compromised with the old rulers and by presenting himself as the candidate most able to bring about change, positioning himself in a way that would attract voters that rejected the military. Thus, while Alfonsín's victory was a surprise in that it broke with a pattern of Peronist victories, it was not a fluke. It reflected the importance of an electoral strategy that depended not only on the traditional following of a party, which was all the Peronist leaders appeared to believe was necessary, but also on the appropriateness of an electoral strategy given the political dynamics of the very moment in which the election was held.[71]

The brilliance of Alfonsín's denunciation of the military-union pact was that it served to mark a clear distinction among political parties that had previously formed a unified opposition within the Multipartidaria,[72] and to fully identify Alfonsín with the demand for citizenship that was so widespread in the electorate. This made a crucial difference in the outcome of the election. The Peronists could count on a loyal following, although this secure basis of support had shrunk somewhat as a result of the economic policies of the military rulers. But beyond that loyal following, voters responded to the messages put forth by politicians, and this is where Alfonsín picked up key votes. His message was particularly attractive to the five million new voters under the age of twenty-eight, with whom the Peronists' discourse about the glorious old days of Peronism found little resonance, as well as to women. It is significant that, even though Alfonsín did not have the support of workers qua workers, given the unchanged Peronist dominance of unions,[73] he was able to make significant inroads, winning votes of workers as citizens—that is, those who responded to Alfonsín's discourse on citizenship over the Peronists' appeal to organized interest. Moreover, as the campaign became increasingly shaped by Alfonsín's message concerning the stark choice the electorate faced between a past, represented by the Peronist candidate Luder, and the future, represented by himself, a marked polarization of the electorate benefited Alfonsín as voters that typically voted for left-wing and right-wing candidates shied away from the eleven other candidates, besides Alfonsín and Luder, running in the presidential race.[74] The election results, in short, were less of a reflection of the past shape of the electorate—the electorate on which assumptions of a Peronist victory were based—than of the dynamics of the transition process.

In the end, the last hope for gaining assurances that a future government would not prosecute the military because of their record of human rights violations failed because the pact with the Peronists was swept away by the political dynamics that resulted from the two basic factors that were the truly defining features of the modality of the transition that was initiated with the defeat in the Falkland/Malvinas Islands war. The military had been forced to seek a pact with the Peronists, rather than with a broad array of political forces, because it did have something to offer Miguel—certain favors that would help him establish his dominance with Peronism—but it did not have anything to offer all major political forces. It was evident that, despite some military bluffs, a transition was going to occur. The military's pact with Miguel did not do anything to change this. Just as there was no basis for a quid pro quo between the military and all political forces, there was no reason for the electorate to accept the constraints on the future government, which voting for Luder would mean, when they had other alternatives in an election that was free and fair.

Following the October 30 election, there was little left for the military to do. In their last sign of weakness, the date for Alfonsín to assume power, originally January 30, 1984, was moved forward, to December 10. Then, five days before handing over power, the military junta dissolved itself. Finally, when Alfonsín assumed power on December 10, the relatively brief but extremely painful experience of military rule opened with the coup of 1976 came to a close. Thereafter, a new era in Argentine politics began. Indeed, just as in the case of the 1976 coup, the installation of Alfonsín as president and the reopening of Congress were the launching points of a new attempt at regime founding. Now that the military rulers had abysmally failed to institutionalize a bureaucratic authoritarian form of rule, the central challenge of Argentine politics would center on the prospects of party politicians to consolidate a democratic form of government.

Conclusion

Argentina's transition from bureaucratic authoritarianism during 1982–83 has been the subject of a heated polemic among analysts of transitions, who have sought to explain why the transition was initiated in June 1982. As discussed, military defeat in the Falkland/Malvinas war was an important catalyst in the triggering of the transition. But in some sense the fate of the military rulers was cast as soon as the invasion was launched on April 2. Thus, what was most important about the Falkland/Malvinas war was the very decision to engage in such a risky venture. In this regard, the argument in this chapter is that the elements highlighted by the political-institutional model provide the soundest explanation for the initiation of the transition. To be succinct, Argentina's transition was a result of the formation of a societal actor that sought to displace the military rulers from power and that drove the increasingly weak military rulers to pursue an ever riskier strategy. In the end, as a result of military defeat at the hands of the British, the military rulers were further weakened and, after assessing the risks of continued involvement in the management of the state, changed their orientation, abandoning their commitment to military rule and accepting the opposition's basic demand to start a transition.

The process of transition itself, a second fundamental question in the study of transitions, was shaped by two key factors. First, because the outgoing rulers had been so weakened as a result of their performance in government, the transition was characterized by the opposition's openly confrontational strategy toward the outgoing rulers. The agenda of the transition process was basically dictated by the opposition. Second, the change in orientation by the military rulers, who joined the societal opposition in accepting the need for a transition, and the resulting virtual disappearance of an antichange disposition within the governing elites, meant that the transition would be sought both by the outgoing military rulers and by societal actors. Argentina's mode of transition, therefore, could be characterized as a reform through rupture. Although the military were able to engineer a rapprochement with the Peronists, that did not alter the process of transition. Because the military were so weak, there was no reason for societal forces to seek such an accommodation with the outgoing rulers. The strategy of accommodation never became a dominant strategy, and the forces that made concessions to the outgoing military rulers were punished in the general election. These concessions were widely perceived as unnecessary, due to the lack of a credible threat of an authoritarian regression, and a population seeking to break with the stranglehold of military rule punished the accommodationist forces and undermined the conditions for the military-union pact. Argentina's transition ended as it began, with the military lacking any real ability to control events and secure the guarantees they sought.

Part V
Conclusion

Chapter 7

The Argentine Case in Comparative-Historical Perspective

This book has provided an in-depth analysis of Argentina's experience with bureaucratic authoritarianism during 1976–83, identifying the key phases into which the entire episode of bureaucratic authoritarianism can be divided, and explaining the political dynamics in each phase. In doing this, a key goal has been to weave the explanatory factors highlighted by the political-institutional model with the challenges that are peculiar to bureaucratic authoritarianism as a form of rule. Having completed that task, this chapter seeks to go beyond a focus on Argentina during the 1976–83 period to consider the comparative implications of the argument developed on the basis of the Argentine case and to put Argentina's experience with bureaucratic authoritarianism in historical perspective.

To elaborate a comparative perspective, the chapter begins with a summary of the arguments about the Argentine case developed in Chapters 3 through 6 and a discussion of two other cases of bureaucratic authoritarianism: Chile (1973–90) and Brazil (1964–85). In a second section, this book's arguments about the political dynamics of bureaucratic authoritarianism are restated in light of the comparative perspectives offered by the cases of Chile and Brazil. In a third section, bureaucratic authoritarianism as a form of rule is placed in historical perspective. While the military rulers' failure to reach their goals is emphasized, special consideration is given to the impact of bureaucratic authoritarian rule after the experience with bureaucratic authoritarianism per se came to an end. To illustrate the significance of the legacies of bureaucratic authoritarianism for the democracies that emerged from the transitions from bureaucratic authoritarianism, the impact of Argentina's episode with bureaucratic authoritarianism on the country's subsequent political developments is discussed. Finally, returning to the point of departure of this book, the fruitfulness and applicability of regime analysis as a research program is briefly addressed.

Bureaucratic Authoritarianism in Comparative Perspective

The Argentine Case Summarized

Bureaucratic authoritarian rule began in Argentina with the March 1976 coup. Faced with what was perceived as a grave threat, as Chapter 3 shows, the military rulers moved immediately and with great determination against actors who could offer resistance. Because the military perceived the degree of opposition offered by the displaced forces to be potentially quite strong, they initially responded with a large dose of repression. But quite rapidly, as the guerrillas were roundly defeated and the threat they posed receded at the end of 1976, and as labor began to be viewed less as a threat and more as potentially malleable, a new strategy vis-à-vis society began to emerge. The military rulers initiated an opening to society, albeit one that was quite restricted and carried out at the same time that repression continued to be used, particularly against leftist elements. The clear intent was to gain support for the new political order the military sought to introduce.

This new strategy had serious consequences for the political dynamics of Argentina's experience with bureaucratic authoritarianism. While it was advanced by the sectors of the military that acknowledged what was referred to in Chapter 2 as the problem of representation—the need to acknowledge a legitimate political role for excluded societal actors if the military is to successfully lay the basis of a new political order—it was also opposed by other important sectors of the military. Thus, as Chapter 4 shows, the military split between a hardline sector that saw no role for compromise with societal forces, and a soft-line sector that sought to foster "responsible" allies within the labor arena—allies that could, at an appropriate time, become participants in the military's project and broaden the support for the military. As a result, the military rulers were unable to shape the new institutions that would serve as the basis for a new political order, and thus tackle the challenge of constitutional definition, in a concerted and determined manner.

The lack of cohesion within Argentina's military rulers, due to their particular response to the problem of representation, was only compounded by the interim institutional arrangement adopted by the military upon assuming power. The interim institutional arrangement adopted in 1976, as discussed in Chapter 3, had two key aspects that were particularly negative from the perspective of the military's cohesion. Because it included a declaration of a temporary "state of exception," whereby the commander-in-chief of the army would serve temporarily both as a member of the junta and as president of the country, it introduced a point of contention that would be the focus of a series of heated negotiations within the armed forces. Moreover, because the interim institutional arrangement envisioned the full-scale "colonization" of the state apparatus, whereby the three branches of the military participated directly in the management of the state, an incentive for each service to focus on its own particular interests was provided. Rather than ensuring the unified backing of all services for the government's policies, this arrangement resulted in the feudalization of the state, which generated a tendency for factious power-struggles rather than unified action.

As a result of their inability to act as a cohesive body, the capacity of Argentina's military rulers to respond resolutely to the political challenge raised by the task of constitutional definition—that is, the need to define an institutional framework that embodied their vision of a new political order—was severely hindered. The military's response to the challenge of constitutional definition, as Chapter 4 shows, was both a hesitant and ultimately partial one, because the military had not been able to agree on an institutional model that could be supported by all branches of the military. As the "Political Foundation of the Armed Forces for the Process of National Reorganization" showed, the divisions within the military could even prevent a precise definition of a set of institutional rules. Where the military did succeed in laying out a clear legal framework, as with the Law of Professional Associations, other problems were apparent. In this case, the fact that the new labor code would severely hamper the power of the very labor leaders that certain sectors of the military had courted as potential allies raised doubts about just how committed the military as a whole would be to the institutionalization of the proposed model of industrial relations. If the sanctioning of these two foundational documents in late 1979 was sufficient to bring an end to the debate on the matter of constitutional definition, and thus bring the phase of origin to a close, the very institutional framework that was proposed was a clear sign of military weakness that prevented the military from moving into the next phase with any sustained momentum.

The problems that Argentina's military rulers faced as they sought to tackle the challenge of institutionalization at the heart of the phase of evolution were thus in part prefigured by their response to the challenge of constitutional definition. The attempt to institutionalize their project was hampered because the institutional arrangement proposed by the military rulers was rejected, as a matter of principle, by some key societal actors that were gradually being reconstituted and strengthened. That is, the very institutional arrangement envisioned by the military's two foundational documents, which proposed a restricted democracy and a new model of industrial relations that eliminated politics from the labor arena while reducing the political power of the Peronist-dominated unions, was not accepted by societal actors, who rejected them as illegitimate and responded by opposing them in a principled fashion. That rejection was significant in that the actors who refused to accept the proposed constitutional order were central enough to the functioning of society to be relevant to the institutionalization of bureaucratic authoritarianism and strong enough to disrupt and block the process of institutionalization.

But, as argued in Chapter 5, the problem facing the military rulers went beyond the legitimacy or lack of legitimacy of the institutional arrangement they proposed. The military rulers continued to be divided over just how to deal with society, injecting this intramilitary struggle into the issue of presidential succession during much of 1980, and as a result of this ongoing lack of cohesiveness they lacked the resolve and determination to implement the project they had made public in late 1979. The possibility of founding a legal order that had the solid backing of the military rulers, even if societal actors saw it as illegitimate, was thus squandered. Politics was patterned by the institutionally unmediated interaction between rulers and ruled in which even the collaborationist labor leaders grouped in the CNT, who had been courted by the soft-liner elements within the military, failed to fully accept the legality of the new labor code and sought instead to play on the divisions within the military to circumvent and eventually subvert the aims of the new legal framework.

In short, continuing the trend set during the phase of origin, the military rulers were undecided about an appropriate response to the problem of representation, oscillating between the options of recognizing key actors such as trade unions and political parties, and then, fearing the activation of opposition such a policy seemed to foster, ignoring or even repressing these societal actors. As a consequence, the military rulers wound up with the worst of both worlds. Divisions over how to respond to societal groups prevented the military from backing a legal framework with any convincing degree of resolve, and the military's disunity provided an opportunity for opposition forces to reorganize. To be sure, the military rulers were clearly the dominant actor, continuing to exercise control over the government and to rule through the institutional arrangement they had agreed to in 1976 as an interim solution. But if the military was clearly still in control, as a result of their failures vis-à-vis the challenge of institutionalization, the military rulers' had not been able to consolidate their power by founding a new political order or political regime, generating instead what could be characterized as a tenuous authoritarian "political situation."[1]

The political dynamic that took shape during the phase of evolution was particularly dangerous from the perspective of the rulers, for it allowed for the gradual reorganization of opposition forces in society—or what has been called the "resurrection of civil society"—which, in turn, further accentuated the divisions within the military rulers. The destabilizing nature of this dynamic rapidly took its toll on the military rulers, as evidenced in late 1981 by the palace coup that sought to bring about a "return to the sources"—that is, to the kind of policies the military had advanced upon taking power in 1976. The problem was that while the hard-line elements within the military rulers were seeking to curtail the growth of a principled opposition, by breaking with the military's own institutional arrangement for management of the state, their response actually plunged the country into a political crisis. The issue facing Argentina was increasingly less about the military's ability to consolidate their power and more about their capacity to prevent a transition from occurring.

The roots of Argentina's transition can be found in the political crisis that developed throughout 1981. There can be no doubt that military defeat in the Falkland/Malvinas war was an important catalyst in the triggering of the transition in June 1982. But, as argued in Chapter 6, it is crucial to understand the political dynamics behind Argentina's decision to invade the Falkland/Malvinas Islands, given that this decision in effect sealed the fate of the military rulers. From this perspective, the transition was a result of the formation and gradual strengthening of a societal actor that sought to unseat the military rulers and that drove the increasingly weak military rulers to pursue an ever riskier strategy that exposed them to ever greater loses of power. This was, in essence, the political dynamics behind the decision to invade the Falkland/Malvinas Islands. In the end, as a result of military defeat at the hands of the British, the military rulers were further weakened, and when they assessed the risks of continued involvement in the management of the state, they changed their orientation, abandoning their commitment to military rule and accepting the opposition's basic demand to start a transition. The initiation of the transition was in effect the final consequence of the conflicting imperative to which the military rulers were subjected to as a result of the problem of representation. That imperative led them to acknowledge the need to open channels for representation of excluded forces, in order to provide the basis for a new political order but also to resist any such opening, because of its negative impact on the cohesiveness of the military rulers and the opportunities such openings provide opposition groups in society.

Once the transition had begun, the process of transition itself was shaped by the two factors that define the mode of transition: the joint acceptance on the part of the societal opposition and the outgoing military rulers that a transition was desirable, and the dominance of an openly confrontational strategy toward the outgoing rulers, a strategy made possible by the relative weakness of the antichange sectors within the military. Indeed, these two factors, which defined Argentina's transition as a clear case of "reform through rupture," would shape a particularly precipitous transition. Thus, the agenda of the transition process was basically dictated by the opposition and, as the key legal documents that regulated the transition show, the military were quite unable to control the process of transition and ensure the emergence of political forces favorable to the military. Even when elements within the Peronist Party sought to make certain gains by adopting an accommodationist strategy toward the outgoing military rulers, the very logic of the transition doomed such a strategy and undermined the conditions for a military-union pact. Essentially, the electorate perceived such concessions to the outgoing military rulers as unnecessary and punished the accommodationist forces in the general election of October 1983. The end of the transition, which occurred when the military transferred power to Raúl Alfonsín, the candidate of the UCR, in December 1983, thus brought about a clean break with military rule.

Comparative Perspective I: Chile Under General Pinochet

If the Argentine case bears out the argument that bureaucratic authoritarian rulers face a peculiar challenge that prevents these military rulers from founding a stable political order, and that the political dynamics of bureaucratic authoritarianism as a form of rule can be accounted for in terms of the general factors highlighted by the political-institutional model presented in Chapter 1, a comparison of Argentina's experience with bureaucratic authoritarianism with the comparable experiences of Chile and Brazil allows us to consider the generalizability of these arguments (see Figure 7.1).[2]

Chile's experience with bureaucratic authoritarianism began with the September 1973 military coup that displaced the democratically elected government of President Salvador Allende. If, as in Argentina, the military that staged the coup were responding to what they saw as a grave threat, associated in this case with the Marxist agenda of Allende and the Popular Unity (Unidad Popular), the coalition of leftist political parties that backed Allende, in the Chilean case the threat was actually greater and the perceived malleability of the actors the military were reacting against was lower than in the case of Argentina.[3] This was significant, in that the greater degree of opposition to the new governing elite offered by the displaced forces had important consequences for the way in which Chile's military rulers dealt with the problem of representation and for the ability of Chile's rulers to remain a cohesion actor. The most basic consequence was that while, as in Argentina, Chile's military rulers launched an all-out campaign of terror in the initial period after they assumed power, unlike what happened in Argentina, they did not see the possibility of gaining the support of excluded sectors through the type of dialogue Argentina's rulers initiated quite soon after taking power. As a result, Chile's military rulers continued to rely on repression for a longer time and benefited from the kind of internal consensus and cohesion that their Argentine counterparts had also generated around purely reactive objectives for a more prolonged period of time.[4]

If the blunt refusal to deal with the problem of representation allowed Chile's rulers to remain cohesive and avoid the early splits that weakened Argentina's rulers, their sense of cohesion was also aided by the type of interim institutional arrangement they had adopted in the wake of the 1973 coup.[5] In this case, power was initially located in a four-man military junta organized on the basis of the equality of power of the army, navy, air force, and national police (the Carabineros). Partly on the consideration of age, the junta named General Augusto Pinochet, commander-in-chief of the army, to the office of president, which was conceived as a rotating position. But Pinochet rapidly began to centralize power in his hands.[6] In June 1974, the Statute of the Military Junta firmly placed executive power in Pinochet's hands, in effect doing away with the notions of a rotating presidency and a relative parity among the three major services. Adding to this power, as a

	ARGENTINA	CHILE	BRAZIL
PHASE OF ORIGIN			
The Seizure of Power	1976-77	1973-80	1964-68
The Challenge of Constitutional Definition	1977-79	1977-80	1967-69
Degree of opposition by the displaced forces	Medium	High	Low
Interim institutional arrangement	Factional rule	Personalized rule	Collective rule
Degree of cohesion of the new governing elites	Low	Very high	Moderately high
Outcome	Partial and hesitant response: Vague institutional framework	Resolute response: Rigid institutional framework	Resolute response: Flexible institutional framework
PHASE OF EVOLUTION			
The Challenge of Institutionalization	1980-82	1981-88	1970-82
Degree of cohesion of the governing elites	Low	High	Medium
Institutional arrangement	Vague institutional arrangement	Rigid institutional arrangement	Flexible institutional arrangement
Orientation and strength of societal actors	Principled opposition by relevant actors	Principled opposition by relevant actors	Principled opposition by relevant actors
Outcome	Authoritarian tenuous political situation	Authoritarian political situation	Authoritarian political situation
PHASE OF TRANSITION			
The Challenge of Removing the Old Governing Elites	1982-83	1988-90	1982-85
Orientation (vis-à-vis the institutional arrangement) and strength of the old governing elites and societal actors: Identity of the agent of change	Rejection of old order by contending societal actors and weak governing elites: Change from within and outside the governing elites	Rejection of old order by contending societal actors: Change from outside the governing elites	Rejection of old order by contending societal actors and strong governing elites: Change from within and outside the governing elites
Relative power of the antichange sectors within the governing elites vis-à-vis the agent of change: Strategy of the agent of change	Weak: Strategy of confrontation	Very strong: Strategy of accommodation	Moderately strong: Strategy of accommodation
Outcome	Reform through rupture	Reform from below	Reform through transaction

Figure 7.1. Bureaucratic Authoritarianism in Argentina, Chile, and Brazil

result of the creation of the intelligence agency DINA (Dirección de Inteligencia Nacional), also in June 1974, Pinochet gained control over all security functions, which he used not only against opponents in society, but also to control potential rivals. Pinochet was thus able to transform the military institution into the "obedient and nondeliberative instrument of the policies" that he favored, and to personalize power in such a way that politicization of the military that had weakened the hold on power by Argentina's rulers was avoided.[7]

These significant differences between Chile and Argentina had a clear impact on the ability of Chile's rulers to respond to the challenge at the heart of the phase of origin: the challenge of constitutional definition. In contrast to the hesitant and partial response mustered by Argentina's divided rulers, the military rulers in Chile were able to resolutely advance a forward-looking agenda, or foundational project, embodied in the 1979 labor code and a new constitution approved in a plebiscite in 1980.[8] Unlike in Argentina, both those documents contained a precise definition of a set of institutional rules that were, moreover, backed by a cohesive governing elite. There could be no doubt that these documents provided a legal basis for the new order the military sought to introduce, as Chile's military rulers entered the phase of evolution and tackled the challenge of institutionalization with significant momentum.

But these documents also opened up new issues that had dangerous implications from the perspective of the future stability of military rule, because the response to the challenge of constitutional definition entailed an acknowledgment on the part of the military rulers of the problem of representation.[9] If Chile's military rulers had until then dealt with the excluded sectors through repression, and even though they continued using repression, if more selectively, after 1980, the two foundational documents did provide for the first time certain spaces that would serve as sites for the reconstitution of actors that did not perceive the new order as legitimate.[10] In the case of the labor code, which aimed at decentralizing and weakening the power of trade unions, the impact was quite immediate, as this new if restricted legal space provided an opportunity for rank-and-file workers to participate in union affairs and reactivate union life. While channeling workers' activities, the new labor code also unwittingly provided an arena for the opponents to military rule.[11]

The impact of the new constitution was slow in coming, for it ratified, at least in the short term, "the freezing of political exclusion" (Garretón 1986b:173). The very institutional order that this constitution enshrined, however, contained elements that worked against the long-term stability of the new order. For example, while the new constitution secured Pinochet's position, extending his presidential term until 1989 and allowing him to continue enjoying dictatorial powers in a way that definitively placed him above the military junta and the military institution (Arriagada 1988:46–48, 111–12),[12] by personalizing power to such an extent it introduced the issue of presidential succession as the weak link in the new institutional order and gave opponents to military rule an easy target and a rallying point around which they could cement the much needed unity of opposition forces (Garretón 1986b:173, 176–77; 1987: chaps. 3, 4).[13] Moreover, even as the new constitution did advance "a personalized conception of political power," it also put limits on the arbitrary power of the government and revived the old idea of a constitutional army (Arriagada 1988:136, 115; Valenzuela 1995:22), and it provided an important opening for opposition forces to affect future developments. In particular, the armed forces became committed to supporting a legal structure and a specific timetable, which included a plebiscite to be held in 1988 to ratify or reject Pinochet in the role of president.[14] If, from the perspective of those who sought a return to democracy, the prospects in 1980 were grim—given that Pinochet had already been able to prevail in two plebiscites[15] and that a new victory in 1988 would ratify Pinochet as president until 1997—by seeking to justify Pinochet's permanence in power the new constitution had actually introduced certain limits on the governing elites, and certain rigidities that provided some crucial strategic possibilities to opposition forces.

Thus, Chile's military rulers responded to the challenge of constitutional definition very differently from their Argentine counterparts. In effect, they initially ignored the problem of representation, but then provided a response to the challenge of constitutional definition, as a cohesive force and in a unilateral fashion, that shaped a precise legal framework with a measured but significant acknowledgment of the problem of representation. Chile's governing elites had avoided the problems that resulted from the early, even premature, overture to society carried out by Argentina's rulers: the generation of schisms within the military that thwarted, in turn, the definition of and subsequent commitment to a legal order. Because the perceived lack of malleability of societal actors ruled out such direct and early contact between governing elites and excluded sectors, Chile's rulers avoided such entanglements and presented society with a set of institutional rules as a fait accompli, delivered from high and without consultation,[16] which Pinochet's opponents could take or leave but, unlike the

Argentine case, were expected to receive the full backing of a cohesive military actor.

This more successful response to the challenge of constitutional definition prefigured a more successful phase of evolution for Chile's military rulers. Beginning in 1981, Chile would avoid the problems that plagued Argentina's rulers from the very outset of the phase of evolution. However, because Chile's new order was far from being legitimate in the eyes of key actors in society, and because this illegitimacy raised questions about the long-term survival of the new institutional framework, Chile lacked a defining feature of a political regime, a more consolidated or legitimate form of rule, and is best characterized, as it moved into the post-1980 period, as a relatively stable authoritarian political situation (Valenzuela and Valenzuela 1986b:5, 9–10).

The problem was that, despite their successes and comparatively more secure position vis-à-vis society in contrast to their Argentine counterparts, Chile's military rulers had endangered their hold on power by the very constitutional proposals that sought to consolidate their power. Inasmuch as the new institutional framework constituted an acknowledgment of the problem of representation, it unwittingly provided the means for a disloyal opposition, which sought to bring military rule to an end, to advance its agenda. The new legal order was still perceived as illegitimate and did nothing to instill pragmatic orientations conducive to institutionalization. If not generating support within society, the new institutions did, however, provide opportunities that societal actors could and would use to oppose Pinochet. This did not mean that Chile's military rulers would be threatened from within or that they were vulnerable to confrontationist demands from the outside, as Argentina's rulers were. Indeed, Pinochet's opponents made a mistake in pushing the demand that Pinochet step down during the cycle of protests in the 1983–86 period (Garretón 1987:106–7, 88, 131, 135). Unlike in Argentina, the military had not only set down clear rules concerning the management of the state and abided by them, but they had also defined and supported a legal framework for interaction between state and society. In the face of pressure for change, then, the military rulers remained cohesive and stood by their preestablished legal framework, refusing to allow the course of events to be dictated by the unmediated interaction between state and society. In other words, only inasmuch as the opposition acknowledged that it was possible to make a distinction between the legitimacy and the legality of the order the military rulers had created and unified behind an accommodationist strategy that sought change by operating through the very institutional framework the military had created, would they become a force that was strong enough to effectively contend for power.[17] In short, while Chile's military rulers appeared to have a firm grip on power, the response to the problem of representation embodied in their foundational documents made them vulnerable to an accommodationist opposition movement operating within the very rules of the game. As powerful as Pinochet appeared, time was on the side of the opposition.

Chile's transition was indeed brought about through legal channels, specifically the constitutionally mandated plebiscite of October 1988. What was crucial in initiating the transition was that, in the wake of the failure of the cycle of protest in the mid-1980s, Pinochet's opponents adopted a strategy of accommodation that led them to desist in their efforts to circumvent the 1980 constitution and to center their efforts on contesting the 1988 plebiscite. If this meant waiting, at least they would meet Pinochet on grounds where they stood a chance of victory, for the opposition's strategy helped them overcome previous divisions and unite the actions of a broad and erstwhile divided set of political parties and groups that, despite their heterogeneous composition and political views, rejected the exclusionary nature of military rule.[18] This more unified and thus stronger force would then be able to take advantage of the rigid institutional framework that had been created as a result of the personalistic nature of power in Chile.

Because Pinochet had worked hard to commit the military as an institution to the institutional framework envisioned by the 1980 constitution, as a way to consolidate his personal hold on power, now the military institution's acceptance of these institutional rules limited the potential use of arbitrary power on Pinochet's part. Thus, once the plebiscite was finally held, public uncertainty concerning the government's willingness to accept defeat was quickly put to rest when Air Force General Fernando Matthei went to the Palacio de la Moneda, the Government House, to force Pinochet to admit the opposition's victory.[19] At this point, the military backed the legal force of the 1980 constitution and proved unwilling to annul a vote on what was seen as Pinochet's personal gamble. In sum, advantage of the rigidities of the system Pinochet had constructed, the opposition had been able to prevail and to trigger the initiation of a transition as a result of their victory in the 1988 plebiscite.

The process of transition advanced much as it had begun, with the impetus for change coming from outside the governing elite—that is, from groups that had been excluded under the authoritarian system—very much in the face of resistance by the top military leader, General

Pinochet (Valenzuela 1992:75, 77; Garretón 1995a:254). Another key characteristic of the transition was that even though the old rulers were defeated, inasmuch as they were unable to avert a transition they remained a powerful force, exerting a great degree of control over the transition and forcing the opposition to advance its agenda through a purely accommodationist strategy (Agüero 1995a:64–67; McGuire 1995:192–95). Chile's mode of transition, thus, is an example of a "reform from below," and, as is characteristic of this mode of transition, the transition proceeded through legal channels. This ensured a smooth process of change, whereby Patricio Aylwin, presidential candidate of the opposition Concertation of Parties for Democracy (Concertación de Partidos para la Democracia), took over power in March 1990 after prevailing in a general election in December 1989 (Angell and Pollack 1990). It also guaranteed, in what is one of the most characteristic features of this mode of transition, that no abrupt break with the past would occur, as had been the case with Argentina's transition. Rather, the very manner in which Chile's transition took place allowed the outgoing rulers to put in place some important safeguards that would in essence project their power into a post-transitional period.[20]

Comparative Perspective II: The Brazil of the Generals

Brazil's experience with bureaucratic authoritarianism, which began with the April 1964 coup, was quite unique in that it was the first case of bureaucratic authoritarianism, and the case that provided a reference point for subsequent cases. Indeed, in part because Brazil did not have a model to follow, but rather partly stumbled across and partly created this model, it diverged markedly from the experiences of both Argentina and Chile. Most notable is that Brazil's military rulers initially envisioned their role as a provisional and merely corrective one, and it was not until late 1968 that the Brazilian military abandoned a time frame for the return to democracy and began to act, as is typical in bureaucratic authoritarianism, as though they had goals but not deadlines (Cardoso 1993:216–18, 220). While the unique and circuitous path Brazil's military rulers followed raises complex issues of interpretation, making it a more difficult case to analyze than either Argentina or Chile, Brazil's episode of bureaucratic authoritarianism still makes sense in terms of the argument advanced in this book. Much of the peculiarity of Brazilian military rule is linked to the considerably lower level of threat faced by the military rulers when they staged the 1964 coup, compared with the threat their counterparts in Argentina, and even more so in Chile, faced.[21]

Brazil's military rulers faced a relatively low degree of opposition from the displaced forces, and, as in other cases, that is important because it affected the timing of the response to the problem of representation. Unlike in Chile and Argentina, where the military seized power as a cohesive hard-line actor that was quite unconcerned, at least in the short run, with the role of societal actors in the institutional order they would put in place, Brazil's military rulers were torn by a conflicting set of goals as soon as they came to power. On the one hand, the military rulers moved against elements of the old system they had just replaced immediately after the coup. Thus, the military carried out "Operation Cleanup," arresting thousands of potentially "subversive" elements from parties on the left, labor organizers, and peasant league organizers. Furthermore, hundreds were tortured, more than four hundred Brazilians saw their political rights suspended and/or their electoral mandate revoked, and hundreds of union leaders were removed from their posts.[22] On the other hand, the military were divided about how far they needed to go to right the wrongs that had provoked them to stage their coup. In particular, despite pressures from hard-line sectors within the military, President General Humberto Castello Branco and his supporters believed that the problems Brazil faced could be fixed by using the power they had granted to the executive through the military's Institutional Act No. 1 for a short period of time (Alves 1985:31–34). They saw no need to ban political parties or even cancel elections, and Congress, rather than being closed, was retained as an institution that would give legitimacy to the military rulers, to the point that Congress itself was granted a role in ratifying the choice of president. Even a return to democracy was envisioned by the very timetable the military adopted.

In short, facing what was perceived to be a relatively low degree of opposition and a set of actors believed to be quite malleable, the new military government was dominated, despite countervailing pressures, by the soft-line sector around Castello Branco and functioned according to an interim institutional arrangement that put power firmly in the hands of the military-dominated executive while not banning, but rather severely restricting, the functioning of Congress, the parties, and elections. The mission of the military rulers was conceived as a corrective intervention that did not even require a full closing-down of the old system.

The predicament that such an early acknowledgment of the problem of representation generated for the military rulers rapidly became evident. Despite the support the military received from the Democratic National Union (União Democrática Nacional [UDN]), a conservative party, and the favorable mood among the population at the time of the coup, the military were unable to exercise full control over the Congress, to guarantee victory even in elections that restricted the rights of opposition leaders, and to contain the reorganization of, and opposition actions by, the student movement, the labor movement, and even guerrilla forces.[23] Predictably, these developments accentuated the divisions within the military, weakening the hand of the military softliners and setting the stage for a steady advance by the hard-line sectors that rejected any timetable for a return to democracy and argued for a more thoroughgoing change than had been envisioned until then. As a result, the government's agenda was increasingly shaped by this hard-line sector.

Landmarks in the advance of the hard-liners included the Institutional Acts No. 2 and No. 3, which were sanctioned in reaction to opposition victories in the October 1965 gubernatorial elections and which abolished existing parties, laid down the rules for new parties to be formed, and made all future elections of president, governor, and state capital mayors indirect elections. Next came a new constitution, which was approved in 1967 and essentially synthesized the previous three Institutional Acts, and a new Institutional Act, No. 5, proclaimed in reaction to the resurgence of societal protest and a noncompliant Congress in late 1968. This new act gave great powers to the executive branch and was particularly significant in that it introduced changes that meant that "for the first time since the coup of 1964, there was no date scheduled for a return to the rule of law" (Skidmore 1988:84; Rouquié 1987a:283–84, 278).[24] Finally, toward the end of 1969, a National Security Law was enacted, the new constitution was revised to further expand the extraordinary powers of the executive, and General Emílio Garrastazú Médici, a hard-liner, was elected as president.[25] By late 1969, the displacement of the soft-liners by the hard-liners was complete and with this newly gained sense of cohesion the Brazilian military put in place a new legal framework that was a clear manifestation of their foundational pretenses.

If the circuitous but ultimately effective response Brazil's military rulers gave to the challenge of constitutional definition makes for a complex interpretation of the phase of origin, the same goes for an analysis of the subsequent phase of evolution. Despite certain problems, Brazil's legal framework worked fairly well for the military rulers. Having sought to avoid the emergence of a caudillo—or, in other words, the personalistic form of rule that characterized Chile,

Brazil's rulers were forced to repeatedly confront the issue of presidential succession, an issue that tended to generate serious divisions within and among the services.[26] Brazil's rulers did not benefit from the institutional arrangement that gave their Chilean counterparts a great sense of cohesion and that helped to stabilize their hold on power, at least in the short run. But, avoiding the problems that beset Argentina's military rulers, once a president was selected and took office the government could act cohesively because the "armed forces, as mandated by the Brazilian Constitution, were . . . subject to the president's authority" (Arriagada 1988:129; Agüero 1995a:129).

The other peculiarity of the institutional framework the Brazilian military set in place, a result of the relatively low degree of opposition they faced, was the direct acknowledgment by the military rulers of the problem of representation. In responding to the challenge of constitutional definition, the military rulers believed there was more to gain, in terms of legitimacy, than would be lost by providing legal spaces to opposition groups (Cardoso 1993:220). Thus, the military allowed Congress to remain in existence, along with elections and a two-party system. Most significant is that the Congress played a role in the context of presidential successions, constituting the most important block of votes in the Electoral College that essentially ratified the military's choice for the presidency, as well as in the approval of legislation. But the opportunities provided for the opposition forces were still minimal. Elections were biased against the opposition, who were handicapped by the loss of political rights of some of their main leaders, the censorship of the media, the use of repression, the careful manipulation of electoral laws, and the use of patronage and clientelistic networks. The powers of Congress relative to the powers of the military-dominated executive, moreover, were seriously diluted as a result of the government's institutional framework. And even if Congress sought to exercise their restricted powers, the military could cancel electoral mandates or, going even further, simply close down Congress, as it did between December 1968 and October 1969 and again in April 1977.

Compared with both Chile and Argentina, therefore, the political dynamics of bureaucratic authoritarianism in Brazil was fairly distinct. More so than in both these other cases, the military rulers had acknowledged the problem of representation, but they had done so, as in Chile, from a position of strength that had allowed them to craft a set of institutional rules that would channel opposition activities. It is thus important to point out that the options Brazil's rulers allowed society were qualitatively different from those provided by Argentina's rulers, in that these options, unlike in Argentina, were clearly circumscribed within legal spaces. This was extremely significant in that it did not allow the opposition to weaken the military rulers' hold on power, as they did in Argentina, by playing on the divisions that developed within Brazil's military, particularly in the context of presidential successions.[27] As in Chile, then, Brazil's military rulers installed what could be accurately characterized as a stable authoritarian political situation.[28]

Nonetheless, there were some differences between Brazil and Chile. Unlike in Chile, Brazil's military rulers had avoided the personalization of power. As a result, Brazil had to confront the presidential succession issue, with its tendency to generate division within the military, on a more regular basis—a potential disadvantage. But the avoidance of the personalization of power also gave Brazil's military rulers certain advantages that their counterparts in Chile did not have. Specifically, it allowed Brazil's rulers to avoid the rigid timetable that Chile had adopted, in large part as a consequence of Pinochet's drive to consolidate power, and that subsequently gave Pinochet little room to maneuver in the face of an advancing opposition. Brazil's rulers could afford to not precommit themselves to managing the succession issue in a particular way to the same extent, and thus allowed themselves room to respond to any unforeseen development with greater flexibility by changing the rules affecting the succession issue as they saw fit (Huneeus 1986:165–80).

From the perspective of the Brazilian opposition, the lack of legitimacy of such an exclusionary system was as evident as the ability of the military rulers to create and enforce the rules this system was based on (Cardoso 1993:177–80, 160–63). Just as in Chile in the mid-1980s, moreover, Brazil's antiloyal opposition was divided as to what strategy to pursue with regard to the legal structure the governing elites had erected, and this division weakened the opposition.[29] The fortunes of opposition forces would only begin to change in 1974, when the emergence of serious splits within the military institution led to a policy of liberalization by the military as government. As the military rulers became more and more embroiled in the task of repression, the security forces had become increasingly powerful and autonomous, routinely ignoring the chain of command and flouting the military hierarchy. To avoid the growing power of the security forces within the military as an institution, recently selected President General Ernesto Geisel initiated a policy of liberalization, in early 1974, as a way for the military hierarchy to begin reasserting its control.[30]

What ensued was a complicated and cyclical process whereby concessions the military soft-liners made to society led to the gradual strengthening of and political advance by opposition forces, which were followed in turn by reactions by hard-line forces. The first such cycle was marked by the holding of the 1974 election under much freer conditions than in the past, by a surprising opposition victory in those elections, and by a reaction from hard-line elements that led to the Falcão Law in 1976 and the April Package in 1977. The first put limits on party use of radio and television, while the latter sought to forestall the opposition's advance in Congress by changing the electoral laws, by increasing representation from the rural areas, generally controlled by the pro-military party, and by making one-third of the Senate seats indirectly rather than directly elected positions. Similarly, to deny the opposition access to governorships, elections for governorships were to be indirect rather than direct.

A new cycle began with the Reform Package, which restored the right of habeas corpus, eliminated some of the extraordinary powers previously granted the executive branch, and formally abolished Institutional Act No. 5, in mid-1978,[31] and with the granting of a partial political amnesty and restoration of political rights to political leaders in 1979. The soft-liners simultaneously sought to stall the opposition's advance by dividing the opposition, and to that end passed the Party Reform Bill of 1979 and another new electoral reform in late 1981. These efforts at electoral engineering, however, did little to assuage the hard-liners who feared the results of the next important election in 1982 and set off a series of bombs in public places in 1980 and early 1981 in an attempt to derail the process of liberalization before it got out of hand. But this time the soft-liners did not backtrack and allowed the November 1982 election to proceed as planned.[32]

The 1982 election represented a crucial opportunity for the opponents of military rule, given that for the first time state governorships would be directly elected and that the results of the election would determine the makeup of the Electoral College that would pick the next president. This election came to represent a watershed in the development of military rule. Overcoming in large part the efforts of the military to split and hence weaken the opposition, the opposition gained a big victory, winning ten of twenty-two governorships, including the powerful states of São Paulo, Rio de Janeiro, and Minas Gerais, and also gaining a majority of seats in the House of Representatives for the first time. The promilitary party, however, still had a majority in the presidential Electoral College,[33] and therefore the military rulers appeared to have retained control over the weakest point in the institutional system they had set up: the mechanism of presidential succession. But it became clear over time that the 1982 election had actually inaugurated a new political dynamic that finally opened Brazil's transition from bureaucratic authoritarianism.³⁴

The significance of the 1982 election was that it had introduced uncertainty concerning the ability and willingness of the military to dominate the process whereby military presidents had been nominated since the beginning of military rule in 1964. Compared with 1974, the opposition had been considerably strengthened by the resurgence of the labor movement in the late 1970s, by the growing linkages between the opposition Party of the Brazilian Democratic Movement (Partido do Movimento Democrático Brasileiro [PMDB]) and a broad variety of grassroots opposition networks, and finally by the defection of erstwhile elite supporters of the military.³⁵ The opposition, in addition, was pursuing an accommodationist strategy that led them to contest power within the legal constraints the military had devised, attempting, as the Chilean opposition would do, to beat the military rulers at their own game.

Such developments affected the military's own view of the situation. The greater strength of the opposition confronted the military rulers with the choice of either adopting the increasingly repressive measures that would be needed to halt the liberalization process or allowing the process of liberalization to become what the opposition wanted all along, a real process of democratization. This was a tough choice. Nonetheless, because the opposition's moderate strategy made them quite acceptable in the eyes of governing elites, increasingly the benefits of a transition seemed to outweigh the costs of continuing in power, and the rulers chose not to oppose democratization (Stepan 1988:60–67).³⁶ The advance of the opposition, moreover, had an impact on the choices made by the party leaders who supported the military rulers. Specifically, the traditional elites who had supported the military rulers began to reassess, in a very opportunistic manner, the costs and benefits of supporting a set of military rulers whose time appeared to be running out.³⁷ As a result of this changing situation, in sum, the military ceased to find the idea of an opposition president unacceptable, and significant numbers of politicians that had been erstwhile supporters of the military defected to the opposition.

These developments finally came to a head when the Electoral College met to decide who would be the next president in early 1985 and when the opposition candidate, Tancredo Neves, received an overwhelming majority of the votes—a result that the military respected.³⁸ Brazil's democratic opposition had finally succeeded in displacing the military from power, as a result of the push for change that came from societal actors but that was eventually accepted by the military rulers (Valenzuela 1992:75, 77). Another key characteristic of the transition was that the outgoing military rulers retained a considerable degree of power to control the transition process, forcing the opposition, as in Chile, to adopt an accommodationist stance and play by the rules the military set down (Agüero 1995a:64–67; McGuire 1995:192–95). Brazil's mode of transition was thus a "reform through transaction."

The Political Dynamics of Bureaucratic Authoritarianism

The summary of the arguments about the Argentine case, along with the discussion of the cases of Chile and Brazil presented above, provides hints of a comparative analysis of bureaucratic authoritarianism. But it stops short of explicitly drawing out the implications that flow from a comparison of the experience with bureaucratic authoritarianism in these three countries. In this section, therefore, we take on the task of restating this book's arguments about the political dynamics of bureaucratic authoritarianism in light of the comparative perspectives offered by the cases of Chile and Brazil.

A central argument that emerges from this comparative analysis is that all cases of bureaucratic authoritarianism are plagued by the problem of representation—the inability of the military rulers to provide a suitable mechanism for interest intermediation for key societal actors. This is a problem in that military rulers seeking to consolidate their power are unable to generate mass support for the political order they seek to institutionalize. Rather than generating a loyal opposition—that is, a system supporting opposition—their project gives rise to an opposition that espouses a disloyal orientation. The problem of representation thus prevents military rulers from turning bureaucratic authoritarianism into a political regime—in other words, from establishing a firmly institutionalized form of government—and forces these military rulers to realistically aspire, at best, to set up a "political situation." This problem is at the root of the processes that eventually bring bureaucratic authoritarianism to an end.

If the problem of representation is an inescapable challenge that haunts all bureaucratic authoritarian rulers, as the cases of Argentina, Chile, and Brazil show, the manner in which military rulers confront this challenge varies quite considerably from case to case. The different responses have significant consequences for the entire life cycle of bureaucratic authoritarianism, determining to a large extent such crucial issues as the extent of repression, the ability of the military rulers to shape a new legal framework, the durability of military rule, and the form in which transitions from military rule eventually occur. A comparative analysis of the political dynamics of bureaucratic authoritarianism must therefore both acknowledge and explain the variable manner in which the common challenge presented by the problem of representation is managed and the variable consequences of different responses. This is a complicated task, but it can be accomplished by bringing the political-institutional model presented in Chapter 1 to bear on the study of bureaucratic authoritarianism.

The Phase of Origin: The Challenge of Constitutional Definition

Starting with the phase of origin, the phase that centers around the challenge of constitutional definition whereby the new governing elite defines a new set of institutions,[39] the first variable that has been used to account for the variable response to the common challenge presented by the problem of representation is the degree of opposition by the displaced forces to the new governing elite during the initial phase of military rule. The impact of this factor, which has been discussed in the literature in different terms—such as the level of threat that precedes the coups leading to bureaucratic authoritarianism, or the degree of malleability that the military rulers perceived in their potential interlocutors in the excluded sectors—is fairly complex. Indeed, as the comparative analysis shows, it affects the capacity of the military rulers to respond to the challenge of constitutional definition both in a direct manner, by shaping the magnitude of the challenge the military rulers face, and in an indirect manner, by affecting a second key explanatory variable: the degree of cohesion of the new governing elite—the military rulers.

The direct and indirect effects of the degree of opposition by the displaced forces operated in the cases of Argentina, Chile, and Brazil in the following manner. In Chile, the military rulers faced the strongest opposition upon taking power. The impact that opposition had was to prod the military rulers to repress the opposition and provide them with no openings whatsoever. By indirectly cementing the cohesiveness of the rulers, the opposition was not able to hamper the military's ability to rule during the initial phase of military rule and move toward a resolution of the challenge of constitutional definition. In Brazil, the military rulers faced a relatively weak opposition. In contrast to Chile, then, the immediate consequence of this factor was that the military was relatively mild in its treatment of the opposition and very divided at the outset. These divisions, in turn, provided the opportunity for opposition forces, weak as they were, to express their dissent in a way that further exacerbated tensions within the military. But the weakness of the opposition was still such that it did little to constrain the military rulers' margin of maneuverability. Brazil's governing elites were therefore able to react in the face of the opposition's actions and change course by displacing soft-liners within the government and establishing cohesion around the hard-liners' agenda.[40]

The situation in Argentina was somewhere in between that of Chile and Brazil, with the military rulers facing an opposition that was considerably stronger than in Brazil but not as strong as in Chile. As a consequence of this medium level of opposition, ironically, Argentina's governing elites did not benefit either from the solid cohesion that characterized Chile's rulers or from the margin of maneuverability that Brazil's rulers enjoyed during the phase of origin. Instead, while Argentina's rulers were initially extremely repressive and cohesive, after the threat represented by the guerrilla movement was rapidly eliminated, there was a sector within the military that moved fairly rapidly to establish contacts with groups that had been excluded from the political arena. As in Brazil, then, internal divisiveness became a problem for Argentina's governing elites during the phase of origin. But unlike in Brazil, the severe splits within the military became harder and harder to solve, given that the strengthening opposition forces could only be brought under control by an increasingly dramatic and costly response by the hard-liners. As a result, Argentina's military rulers began to lose their sense of cohesion early and were unable to resolve their differences as they moved to respond to the challenge of constitutional definition.

Therefore, while military cohesiveness was a function of opposition strength, increasing as the strength of the opposition the military faced increased, the strength of the opposition also had a more complicated or dialectical effect on the ability of the military rulers to remain a cohesive force, affecting the ability of the military to respond to a changing situation and their margin of maneuverability. Overall, military rulers faced most problems when they were confronted with a medium degree of opposition, since that degree of opposition did not solidify military cohesiveness in the way a high degree of opposition did, while simultaneously not reducing the risks associated with a lack of cohesiveness and allowing for mid-course corrections aimed at reestablishing military unity, in the way a low degree of opposition did.[41]

If the degree of opposition strength is a key factor in explaining the military's ability to tackle the challenge of constitutional definition, interacting as it does with another explanatory factor—the governing elites' cohesiveness—it was also affected by a third crucial factor stressed by the political-institutional model: the interim institutional arrangement that the governing elites design as a way to manage governmental affairs until a more permanent arrangement is devised.[42] This factor, as the degree of opposition strength, interacts in a complex manner with, and has an impact on, the cohesiveness of the military rulers. However, because institutional variations are not easily turned into variables and because it is possible that different institutional configurations can be equally conducive to the same end, such as the maintenance of governing elite cohesion, it is extremely difficult to make any easy generalizations concerning the impact of the interim institutional arrangement.

The analysis of the cases of Argentina, Chile, and Brazil does provide, nonetheless, some suggestive conclusions. In Chile, the military's interim institutional arrangement, an arrangement that gradually gave greater powers to a single leader but that connected the military as an institution to the government, delivered the support of the military as an institution to the government without politicizing it. In Brazil, the attempt to avoid the personalization of power meant that the divisive issue of presidential succession had to be confronted quite regularly. To this feature must be added the peculiar feature of a restricted congressional arena and elections, a feature that also gave rise to splits within the military. Indeed, Brazil's interim institutional arrangement was not as conducive as Chile's setup to a cohesive military actor. Nonetheless, two key features that set Brazil apart from Argentina in this regard did ensure the Brazilian military's ability to rule as a relatively cohesive actor. First of all, while splits did emerge over the presidential succession issue, once a president was selected and took office, the military did abide by the considerable power the constitution legally bestowed on the president. Second, because the military were in agreement that if political forces were to have any role in government it would be through the restricted legal spaces they had sanctioned, these divisions did not even become public and could not be exacerbated by civilians who threw their weight behind this or that military faction. Thus, if lacking the positive effect on the governing elites' cohesion of the Chilean arrangement, Brazil's institutional setup did help to secure a relatively cohesive actor.

Finally, in Argentina, as in Brazil, the military had a strong desire to avoid the personalization of power. The solution adopted by Argentina's military leaders, however, was different from the one chosen by their Brazilian counterparts. Indeed, rather than strengthen the presidency, the opposite was done—power was placed firmly in the hands of the military junta, especially after 1978. To further involve the military as an institution in the affairs of government, moreover, the institutional arrangement provided for the full-scale "colonization" of the state apparatus by the military. As a result, a full overlap between military as institution and military as government was ensured, but at the cost of politicizing the military as institution and directly transferring intramilitary disputes into the heart of the government. The military's institutional arrangement, in short, had negative implications from the perspective of the governing elites' cohesiveness. The preeminent role of the military junta in Argentina, as opposed to the enhanced institutional role of the presidency in both Brazil and Chile, played a part in undermining the cohesiveness of the governing elite (Agüero 1995a:129).

The impact of these three explanatory variables can be seen in the way they jointly affected the ability of the military rulers in Argentina, Brazil, and Chile to confront the challenge of constitutional definition, a key step in their attempt to consolidate their newly gained hold on power. Indeed, if all cases of bureaucratic authoritarianism faced at some point in time what we have called the problem of representation, the combination of these three interacting factors—the degree of opposition offered by the displaced forces, the interim institutional arrangement the governing elites designed upon taking power, and the degree of cohesion of the governing elite—helps to account for the significant variations in terms of when this problem was addressed and how this problem affected the manner in which military rulers responded, with varying degrees of success, to the challenge of constitutional definition.

In Chile, due to the opposition's strength, the problem of representation was essentially ignored during most of the phase of origin, in such a way that the potentially destabilizing implications of providing an opening to excluded actors was fully avoided. The cohesiveness that the military rulers generated as a result of the high degree of opposition they faced was reinforced by their interim institutional arrangement. Thus, Chile's rulers moved with great resolve to confront the challenge of constitutional definition, creating an impressive legal framework that constituted the first sign of acknowledgment of the problem of representation and that was to serve as the basis for the new political order they sought to introduce.

In Brazil, the weakness of the opposition led to a prompt acknowledgment of the problem of representation and, as would be expected, the opening provided was used by opposition forces in a way that destabilized the military rulers. However, both the weakness of these opposition forces, which provided the military rulers with a large margin of maneuverability, and the institutional arrangement, which served as a counterbalance to the divisions generated by the low degree of opposition the military faced, did allow the military rulers, as in Chile, to respond in an effective if more circuitous manner to the challenge of constitutional definition. If there were significant differences in terms of the nature of the legal framework that was set in place, differences that were to have an impact on subsequent developments (as discussed below), the military rulers had been able to reestablish themselves as a sufficiently cohesive force to provide a concerted response to the challenge of constitutional definition.

In Argentina, finally, the medium degree of opposition accounts for a distinct response to the problem of representation. While the military initially ignored the problem of representation, as in Chile, they soon began to acknowledge the need to provide a role for the until then excluded sectors. As in Brazil, this response generated important splits within the military. Unlike in Brazil, however, not only did the relatively stronger opposition restrict the governing elites' margin of maneuverability, but the interim institutional arrangement reinforced rather than counterbalanced the divisiveness that originated in the military's response to a moderately strong but not acutely threatening opposition. As a result, in contrast to both Chile and Brazil, Argentina's military rulers were only partially successful at meeting the challenge of constitutional definition. Their vision of a new order was not clearly embedded in a legal framework that would serve as the basis for future interactions among political forces.

The Phase of Evolution: The Challenge of Institutionalization

Although significant in itself, these variable responses to the challenge of constitutional definition were also significant in that to a large extent they prefigured the degree of success that the governing elites would have as they moved on to address the challenge of institutionalization—that is, the transformation of newly created institutional rules into rules that are accepted and routinely used by all major political forces. Indeed, the military rulers' ability to design a legal framework as well as the institutional rules themselves prefigured, in broad terms, the likelihood that the military would succeed in consolidating their hold on power by institutionalizing the new rules of the game and, further down the line, even the mode whereby a transition from military rule was most likely.

But just as a state-centered view, focusing on the governing elites and the institutional arrangements they craft, does not fully explain the political dynamics of the phase of origin, so must the evolution of bureaucratic authoritarianism be understood in terms of the role of societal forces and of the complex dialectic between state and societal actors, or rulers and ruled, and in terms of the interaction between these actors and the institutional rules the military have set in place. In other words, because the issue of acceptance of the new rules by all key political forces comes to the fore once the challenge of constitutional definition has been addressed, the problem of representation achieves even greater importance than during the previous phase, and the potential role of opposition forces becomes even more directly significant for the evolution of military rule. For rather than being a factor that is important primarily in that it affects how the military rulers go about their business, the role of the opposition now directly affects whether the new institutional rules actually become institutionalized—that is, whether they become the basis for a new political order. Thus, as suggested by the political-institutional model, in addition to considering the degree of cohesion of the governing elites and the impact of the proposed institutional arrangement, in analyzing the evolution of bureaucratic authoritarianism it is necessary to also consider the process of actor formation within society and, more specifically, the orientation and strength of societal actors.[43]

The cases of Argentina, Chile, and Brazil bear out the importance of these explanatory factors. In Chile, the evolution of military rule was shaped, on the one hand, by the military rulers, who remained unified and supportive of the institutional framework they had devised. On the other hand, an increasingly important role was also played by societal forces that rejected this institutional framework and constituted themselves as an antiloyal opposition. To be sure, in the early 1980s this antiloyal opposition was quite weak. But at the same time, the very presence of such an opposition was sufficient for the military rulers themselves to acknowledge, even as they went about proposing a new political order, that there was a basic contradiction at the very heart of the system they had designed. In other words, even at the peak of their power the military rulers could not aspire to instituting an authoritarian political regime, which by definition precludes the ex-

The Argentine Case in Comparative-Historical Perspective 191

istence of any major actor that expresses a principled opposition to the rules of the game, and succeeded only in instituting an authoritarian political situation.

Moreover, time was on the side of the opposition, and even though the military rulers remained unified and in support of the 1980 constitution, it was state-society relations that increasingly shaped Chile's political dynamics. Crucial in this regard was the gradually strengthening of the disloyal opposition during the mid-1980s, and the abandonment, in the wake of the failure of the 1983–86 cycle of protest, of a confrontationist strategy that was ineffective inasmuch as it sought to bring about change outside the legal framework that the cohesive military rulers continued to support. The adoption of an accommodationist strategy by Pinochet's opponents was significant because it both strengthened the opposition, by helping them act in a more unified manner, and allowed them to exploit the only real opportunities at hand—those provided them by the same legal rules the military rulers had designed. While Chile's military rulers were firmly determined to uphold the institutional order they had crafted in 1980, that was not sufficient to ensure that they would continue in power, for their response to the challenge of constitutional definition had entailed an acknowledgment of the problem of representation and had therefore granted opportunities to the opposition that worked against the long-term stability of the new order. In the end, it was the opposition's effective use of these spaces that triggered a transition, undermining the military rulers' hold on power by using the very rules they had designed against them.

In Brazil, the evolution of military rule displayed some important parallels, along with some significant differences, with regard to the Chilean case. Initially, Brazil's military rulers remained unified in support of the legal framework they had laid out, while societal forces rejected the legitimacy of the new order and constituted themselves as an antiloyal opposition. As in Chile, then, the military had succeeded in setting up an authoritarian political situation. The evolution of military rule in Brazil, however, was more complicated than in Chile, and over time some differences between Brazil's and Chile's paths emerged. First of all, Brazil's rulers did not remain as cohesive as their Chilean counterparts, and in 1974 an important schism emerged within the military institution. This development had many implications for the opposition, but it did not, as in the Argentine case, open the way for an interaction between state and society outside of circumscribed legal spaces. Rather, Brazil's rulers were able to deal with this new challenge by changing, rather than doing away with, the legal framework that regulated the interaction between governing elites and opposition forces, essentially beginning a process of liberalization that entailed important concessions to society but that allowed them, nonetheless, to respond flexibly to the all-important issue of presidential succession.

What ensued, then, was a protracted process marked by concessions to and advances by the opposition, and military backtracking. From the perspective of the opposition, the impact of liberalization was dramatic. Before 1974, the opposition had been divided, as some elements argued for a strategy seeking to undermine the military rulers by playing by the military's rules, while others sought to bring change from the outside. But now, as the payoff of an accommodationist strategy was difficult to dispute, the opposition united behind a strategy that allowed them to take full advantage of the legal opportunities the military rulers had provided. Having unified the opposition, this strategic choice also strengthened the opposition and thus enabled them to make important political gains that further strengthened them. As in Chile, therefore, the options of the opposition were framed by the governing elites' acknowledgment of the problem of representation, which provided the opportunities for an accommodationist opposition actor to grow in strength and gradually undermine the military's hold on power from within.

But Brazil's military rulers were not precommitted to the sort of rigid timetable that had been adopted in Chile, in large part because of the role of Pinochet, and that prevented Chile's rulers from responding in a flexible manner when the opposition appeared to have the ability to challenge the military's control over the issue of presidential succession. Rather, because of the nonpersonalistic nature of the institutional framework Brazil's military rulers had earlier adopted, they were better able than their Chilean counterparts to react strategically and to introduce frequent changes in laws as a way to stall the opposition's advance and delay the triggering of a transition. In short, while being less successful at remaining a cohesive actor, and despite facing an opposition that confronted them with a similar strategy, Brazil's military rulers were actually more successful than their Chilean counterparts at prolonging the phase of evolution.[44]

These differences between Chile and Brazil aside, the political dynamics in Argentina stood in clear contrast to the pattern set by these other two cases. Argentina's military rulers faced the worst possible manifestation of the problem of representation. They had split over how to deal with the opposition early on, and because of this had not been able to design and support a clear institutional framework. As a result, the disloyal opposition had no incentive even to channel their action within a set of rules. What ensued was an unmediated relationship between the governing elites and the opposition, which, as the opposition grew in strength, further accentuated divisions within the military and in effect pushed them first to break the rules they had agreed to use to manage the affairs of the government, and then to engage in risky endeavors that strengthened the hand of the opposition to the point that the military rulers were virtually forced to call for a transition. What chances the military rulers did have to moderate the actions of the opposition forces, during 1981, hinged on their acceptance of the opposition's call for a transition. And when such an option was turned down by the military, the opposition acted in an increasingly unified manner behind a confrontationist strategy that sought to undermine the military rulers from the outside. Thus, not only were Argentina's governing elites less successful than their counterparts in setting up even an authoritarian political situation, by institutionalizing a legal though not legitimate framework for political interaction; having failed in this regard, they would also be less able to hold on to power for any considerable period of time.

The Phase of Transition: The Challenge of Removing the Old Governing Elites from Power

Just as the dynamics of bureaucratic authoritarianism during the phase of evolution can in part be found in the response provided to the challenge of constitutional definition, so too is an explanation of why and how transitions from bureaucratic authoritarianism occur shaped to a certain extent by the successes and failures the military rulers can claim in confronting the challenge of institutionalization. In other words, the causes of transitions, seen as processes that hinge on the success of emerging elites in removing the old governing elites from power and establishing themselves as the new power holders, need to be sought in the workings and contradictions of the old regime and in the processes of actor formation occurring under the old regime.[45] While these factors can represent fairly long-term developments, however, transitions can also be affected by short-term shifts, such as sudden changes in the orientation of the governing elites in response to a rapidly fluctuating situation, or changes in strategies of actors oriented toward change. The political-institutional model, thus, seeks to weave together these long-term and short-term developments by drawing attention to the orientation and strength of the old governing elites and societal actors, factors that shape who the potential source of change is likely to be, and to the relative power of the antichange sectors within the governing elites vis-à-vis the agent or agents of change, a related factor that determines the strategies used in transitions.

The cases of Argentina, Chile, and Brazil bear out the importance of these explanatory factors. In Chile, societal forces, constituted as an antiloyal opposition from early on, gradually gained strength and finally became a dominant actor when, in early 1987, they adopted an accommodationist strategy that was appropriate to the circumstances they faced—that is, a relatively successful governing elite that had managed to create a legal framework and that remained very much a cohesive force. The transition was triggered by the actions of this opposition force contesting power and prevailing against the military rulers within the very legal framework these rulers had designed, and specifically by winning the 1988 plebiscite, despite the continued resistance to change at the top level of government. As a transition spearheaded by forces outside the governing elites using an accommodationist strategy, Chile's mode of transition was a "reform from below."

In Brazil, the process leading to a transition was more complex than in Chile. As in Chile, societal forces were constituted as a disloyal opposition from early on, and also as in Chile, opposition forces gained in strength when they unified behind an accommodationist strategy, which was similarly appropriate in light of the legal framework the military rulers had managed to erect. The payoff for the opposition was slower in coming in Brazil than in Chile, however, because the institutional rules that Brazil's rulers had adopted allowed them to react with great flexibility to the growing opposition by changing the very rules of the game, overseeing in effect a protracted process of liberalization that successfully preempted a transition for a long time. Unlike what happened in Chile, moreover, the transition began only when Brazil's military rulers eventually chose not to oppose democratization in the wake of the 1982 election—a step that finally allowed the opposition to impose their candidate for the presidency, the linchpin of the military-dominated legal framework. If similar to Chile in that the transition resulted from the push for change by a societal actor using an accommodationist strategy, thus, Brazil's mode of transition was slightly different, as a result of the orientation of the outgoing rulers, who were not opposed to democratization, and is best characterized as a "transition through transaction."

In Argentina, societal forces were constituted from an early date as an antiloyal opposition, as in Brazil and Chile. Unlike in those two cases, however, because the military rulers were unsuccessful at setting up and maintaining a legal framework, the opposition had no incentive to work within the system. So the driving force behind the transition was an opposition that adopted a confrontationist strategy that was the appropriate strategy in light of the military's weaknesses. In this process, the military rulers increasingly became a reactive force. The strengthening of the opposition accentuated divisions among the military rulers and in a real sense pushed them to launch a risky invasion. In the end, defeat at war triggered a transition in 1982, as the military rulers rapidly shifted their orientation and began to support the idea of a transition. Because the transition continued to be dominated by the opposition's confrontationist strategy, even as the societal opposition and the outgoing governing elites backed the idea of a transition, Argentina's mode of transition is properly characterized as a "reform through rupture."[46]

In sum, in all cases of bureaucratic authoritarianism a driving force behind the transitions was societal forces that had constituted themselves as an antiloyal opposition, as an opposition actor oriented toward a change *of* the military-led system rather than seeking changes *within* the contours of this system. This similarity notwithstanding, opposition forces were effective inasmuch as they adopted different strategies or means to their common goal of bringing an end to military rule, strategies that emphasized accommodation where the military rulers had succeeded in installing a legal framework, and confrontation where they had failed to do so. While the selection of an appropriate strategy may appear as a fairly straightforward matter when viewed with hindsight, it presented a particularly acute dilemma for opposition forces in cases where the military rulers succeeded in installing a legal framework. Indeed, in those cases the fine line between using the legal opportunities permitted by the military while simultaneously seeking to deny the legitimacy of the military's legal framework generated many debates and divisions within opposition movements. Once the appropriate strategy was adopted, such a decision about strategy was doubly significant, helping to unify and thereby strengthen the opposition, while also allowing the opposition to exploit every opportunity provided by the military rulers. In a very real sense, it was only through these strategic choices that the contradictions of bureaucratic authoritarianism were brought to the surface.

Yet the military rulers also affected the transitions in a number of ways. First, they had a direct impact on transitions in cases where the military rulers changed their orientation and decided to support, or at least not to oppose, a transition. In addition, through their ability or lack thereof to set up and maintain a legal framework, and through the very content of that legal framework, they indirectly conditioned the strategic choices of their societal opponents and thus the very modality of a transition, as well as the timing of the initiation of the transition. The analysis of transitions from bureaucratic authoritarianism, thus, highlights the importance of societal actors but also of incumbent elites and the institutions they support.

Bureaucratic Authoritarianism in Historical Perspective

The successful transition from bureaucratic authoritarianism brings to an end the study of the political dynamics of bureaucratic authoritarianism and opens new questions concerning the political dynamics of the democratic systems that emerged through these transitions. The analysis of these democracies, just as the analysis of bureaucratic authoritarianism, must be based on a study of the features that are proper to this form of government, a task that goes well beyond the scope of this chapter. The study of bureaucratic authoritarianism is nonetheless pertinent for the analysis of these democracies, because the legacies of bureaucratic authoritarian rule were among the factors that affected these democracies, despite the clear failures of military rulers to shape a new political order. Therefore, without seeking to offer a full analysis of postbureaucratic authoritarianism democracies, this section points to some links between bureaucratic authoritarian and democratic regimes by considering bureaucratic authoritarianism in historical perspective. This is done by assessing the failures of governments, and also the legacies these regimes generate, and by discussing the legacies of bureaucratic authoritarianism in the case this book has focused on: Argentina. The complex question of how to conceptualize these legacies is also given consideration.

Failures and Legacies

The first and probably most important point to make in carrying out a general evaluation of the various episodes of bureaucratic authoritarianism that have been discussed in this chapter is that they were actually failures when viewed from a historical perspective: they failed in their attempt to install a new and authoritarian order and were displaced as a result of the gathering strength of democratic movements. In other words, while bureaucratic authoritarianism originated as a right-wing reaction to the tensions of the politics of industrialization and to the perceived deficiencies of democracy, it did not offer a workable political formula and did not become a viable alternative for late modernizers in the twentieth century.[47] The sense in which bureaucratic authoritarianism was a failure as an authoritarian capitalist response to the challenges of modernization, however, deserves some elaboration, because the fact that not all cases of bureaucratic authoritarianism were failures in the same way or to the same extent could conceal this basic commonality.

The root cause of this failure is, as argued in this book, the inability of bureaucratic authoritarian rulers to get around the problem of representation—that is, the need to acknowledge a legitimate political role for excluded societal actors within the new political order. This problem manifested itself in different ways across cases, and these differences had important implications. In this sense it is valid to argue that Chile's military rulers were relatively more successful than their Brazilian counterparts, and that the military rulers in both these cases were much more successful than Argentina's rulers. This does not mean, as some authors have implied, however, that in a case like Chile the military rulers were successful in reaching their goals and that they simply retired from power once their mission was completed (Touraine 1989:408; Loveman 1991:35–74). Such an assessment hinges on a post hoc revision of the military's goals that obscures the fact that the military's failure in their project "to re-create the relations between the state and society . . . does not mean [that such a project] was not [their] basic goal" (Garretón 1992:16).

From a historical perspective, bureaucratic authoritarianism was a right-wing attempt to remedy what was seen as a crisis of democracy, rooted in the growing power of labor and left political movements, by installing what was usually labeled a "restricted democracy" or an "authoritarian democracy." And in this regard, bureaucratic authoritarian rulers uniformly failed, because these rulers were never able to reconcile the conflicting imperatives that the problem of representation gave rise to and to lay the foundation for a new political order. As argued above, the response to these conflicting imperatives varied from case to case, with greater or lesser negative consequences for the military rulers. But in all cases these conflicting imperatives worked themselves out, inexorably leading to a transition from bureaucratic authoritarianism that represented a defeat of the project spearheaded by the military rulers by societal opposition forces.[48]

If bureaucratic authoritarianism represents, from a historical perspective, a failed attempt to respond to the political challenges of regime founding, it is crucial nonetheless to stress that bureaucratic authoritarianism was installed by military rulers with foundational pretenses and thus represented much more than a transitional form of government. The basic shortcoming of these military rulers—their failure to lay the basis of a new political order—should therefore not detract attention from the momentous experience of bureaucratic authoritarianism and the sweeping changes that, as the direct and indirect result of this experience, made bureaucratic authoritarianism a significant twentieth-century political phenomenon. In other words, it is crucial to stress the impact that bureaucratic authoritarianism had on countries like Argentina, Chile, and Brazil by acknowledging that there are important legacies of bureaucratic authoritarianism that affect the democracies that emerged from the transitions from bureaucratic authoritarianism (Hagopian 1993).

Analyzing the legacies of bureaucratic authoritarianism is hardly a simply task. For example, while most analysts would agree that the experience of bureaucratic authoritarianism is likely to shape the initial conditions faced by postbureaucratic authoritarian democratic governments, there is some debate about how lasting these legacies will be.[49] Even more complicated is the issue of just how to conceptualize the linkage between the predemocratic period and the democratic period itself. Because diverse authors have stressed such a broad range of possible linkages, it is difficult to provide a coherent sense in which the legacies of bureaucratic authoritarianism affect postbureaucratic authoritarian democracies.

The list of legacies that are explored in the literature on bureaucratic authoritarianism, as well as the broader literature on democratization, is impressive. Stressing the institutional nature of the old regime, some authors have argued that the type of old regime from which democracy emerges helps to determine who the key actors in a post-transitional setting might be and what resources they might enjoy.[50] The role of the old regime in the economy is also seen to have an impact, in more structural terms, on the basic profile and strength of key actors, such as business and labor. Others, meanwhile, have sought to draw attention to less structural and direct ways in which the old regime generates legacies, arguing, for example, that the ability of the old governing elites to manage the economy, as well as such factors as the level of repressiveness of the old regime, affect the learning process of key actors and have the potential to reshape the orientation of such key actors as business elites and labor and left leaders toward authoritarianism and democracy.[51]

The debate about the legacies has also focused much attention on the potential impact of the mode of transition from authoritarian rule. In some cases, these arguments have combined elements of the old regime and the mode of transition—as in the argument that the level of repression under the old regime, as well as the degree of success the military rulers had in consolidating their power and in controlling the process of transition, partially shape the pattern and problems of civil-military relations under democracy.[52] Focusing solely on the mode of transition, others have stressed the manner in which different modes of transition affect both the democratic institutional rules within which actors interact and the pattern of the interaction among actors.[53]

This is not the place to show how a diverse set of arguments about the linkages between features of the old regime and the mode whereby a transition from authoritarianism takes place can be brought together to provide a coherent or integrated sense in which the legacies of bureaucratic authoritarianism affect postbureaucratic authoritarian democracies. However, it is important to stress two points that should guide the study of the legacies of bureaucratic authoritarianism. Most fundamental is that it is necessary to avoid a common tendency in the literature to equate legacies solely with constraining conditions that postbureaucratic authoritarian governments inherit as a result of the policies of the outgoing military rulers, and to conceive of legacies instead in a broader sense as both positive or negative, constraining or enabling, and even as intended or unintended consequences of military rule. In addition, for the sake of providing some order to such a discussion, it is useful to distinguish, very broadly, between short-term and long-term consequences of bureaucratic authoritarianism. These two guiding ideas, indeed, are sufficient to demonstrate the varied and significant legacies of bureaucratic authoritarianism, as an analysis of the Argentine case clearly shows.

The Argentine Case

The importance of stressing the legacies of bureaucratic authoritarianism is nowhere clearer than in the Argentine case. When viewed from a historical perspective, the failure of its military rulers was evident. Not only had the military rulers failed to install a new political order, but they had failed to such an extent that the Peronists, whom the military had blamed for many of the country's problems and whom they had displaced from power through the 1976 coup, remained one of the country's main political forces by the time military rule came to an end. Even more humiliating, the military rulers were forced to turn, during their last days, to Peronist leaders in an effort to seek guarantees that the new civilian government would not seek to prosecute them for human rights violations. As the military retreated to the barracks, such continuities with the prebureaucratic authoritarian period were a sign of the generic limits of bureaucratic authoritarianism as a transformative force.[54] But even in this case, where the failure of bureaucratic authoritarianism was so easy to grasp, significant legacies testified to the momentous nature of bureaucratic authoritarianism.

Probably the most distinctive legacy of the Argentina's experience with bureaucratic authoritarianism during the 1976–83 period was the short-term impact that resulted from the combination of an old regime that was extremely repressive but not able to control the transition process. As a result of the transition, then, there emerged a civilian government that was able to take important steps to punish the former military rulers for human rights violations but that at the same time triggered a number of rebellions by disgruntled middle-ranking officers within the army.[55]

As a result of the relatively unconstraining mode of transition, Argentina also began its post-transitional phase with few undemocratic features, either in terms of military prerogatives or in terms of a restrictive constitutional structure and electoral law. By virtue of the same characteristics that allowed Argentina to make a fairly clean break with authoritarian rule, however, Argentina's post-transitional politics were quite confrontational. Indeed, because of the particular mode of transition, the main political parties lacked any incentive to moderate their claims, which would be necessary to ensure the success of the transition in the context of other modes of transition, and the first democratic administration was marked by the attempt of Alfonsín to transform his victorious Radical Civic Union into a hegemonic party, a move that pushed the Peronist party into a position of uncompromising opposition (Cavarozzi and Grossi 1992).[56] Much of the immediate post-transitional dynamic was, in short, to a large extent shaped by features of the old regime and mode of transition.

As significant as these legacies were, certain long-term consequences of bureaucratic authoritarianism would prove to be even more critical to Argentina's politics. Most important in this regard was the impact that the military rulers had on the economic system. The military rulers had come to power intending to bring about a change in the old import-substituting industrialization (ISI) model of development, through the neoliberal policies pursued by Minister of Economy Martínez de Hoz. This reorientation of economic policies did not last long, for in the wake of a financial crisis, which in turn triggered a wave of capital flight, in early 1980, the military abandoned and reversed Martínez de Hoz's economic program. Thereafter, the attempt to return to the type of policies pursued by Martínez de Hoz under General Leopoldo Galtieri was stalled by the Falkland/Malvinas conflict and totally discarded in the context of the transition (Smith 1989:231–49; Damill and Frenkel 1992:5–24). This failure to restructure the economy notwithstanding, the very attempt to bring change did have its effect. If nothing else, the military had succeeded in undermining the conditions that had allowed for the reproduction of the ISI model (Kosacoff 1993:21–23; Cavarozzi 1995:16–18). In effect, while the military rulers had not shaped the future, they had at least ensured that there would be no return to the past.

Going beyond this systemic dimension, the military's policies also brought about changes at the level of key actors of the economic system, such as business and labor. Those changes were significant in that they indirectly prepared the way for the radical economic changes that would be introduced, starting in 1989, under Peronist President Carlos Menem. Business was affected in a number of ways by the experience of bureaucratic authoritarianism. First of all, there was a process of concentration and centralization of capital, whereby the prime beneficiaries and supporters of the original ISI policies—capitalists with a small number of firms that lacked any significant degree of vertical and horizontal integration—lost out, while a small number of national conglomerates *(grupos económicos)* that owned a diversified set of firms and that had access to the financial markets and external credit grew in strength.[57] Along with the rise and consolidation of these *grupos económicos,* the experience with bureaucratic authoritarianism also had an effect on the very orientation of business groups toward military rule. Despite certain benefits that were clearly derived from military rule, business elites were troubled by the military's poor economic performance—and, even more important, by their exclusion from decision-making and by the government's propensity for making erratic decisions, as with the invasion of the Falkland/Malvinas Islands. As a result of the entire experience of military rule, "the armed forces became a risky actor . . . in the eyes of capitalists," leading business sectors to reassess the costs and benefits of authoritarianism and democracy and to abandon their traditional proauthoritarian orientation (Acuña 1993:59; 1995).

Conclusion

The changes affecting labor and its allies were also sweeping and profound. As a result of the military's economic policies, industrial employment fell dramatically in areas where labor had traditionally been strong, such as Greater Buenos Aires, Córdoba, and Santa Fe. Even though this decline in industrial employment was compensated for by new jobs opening up in areas of the interior of the country, a result of the military's regional industrial promotion program, this process of regional deindustrialization and industrial relocation signified a blow to labor, because the geographical dispersion of the new industries along with the lack of a tradition of unionization in these areas of the interior made it difficult to unionize the new labor force.[58] Other consequences of the government's economic policies, such as the shift of industrial employment from large to smaller firms, increasing dispersion of wages, and the growing heterogeneity of the popular sector, worked in the same direction—in effect reducing the unionized labor force.[59]

To these factors one must add the consequences of the repressive policy of the military rulers. Repression had a number of effects. The most direct was that, by eliminating the guerrilla movement as well as activists close to the rank and file of the labor movement, it destroyed the force behind the radicalization of labor in the 1960s and 1970s. In addition to ensuring that labor would be deradicalized, military repression had an indirect effect in that it provided the context for a reevaluation of political democracy both within leftist political parties and among labor's main political allies, the Peronists. The result of this learning process was that Peronist politicians began to push for a growing differentiation between the Peronist party—which had always been a somewhat amorphous entity and had been in a state of flux since the death of Juan Perón in 1974—and Peronist trade unions.[60] In sum, reinforcing the structural weakness imposed by the military's economic policies, labor emerged from military rule as an actor bereft of its radical tendencies, which gradually ceased to be the backbone *(columna vertebral)* of Peronism and lost the central influence it had had in politics in the mid-1970s (Palomino 1995:213–18).

Jointly, then, these long-term changes had a tremendous impact on Argentine politics.[61] In negative terms, by weakening organized labor and those sectors of domestic capital that had been at the core of the old ISI system, and by altering the orientation of key actors toward authoritarianism and democracy, a key legacy of bureaucratic authoritarianism was that the basic political forces behind Argentina's "impossible game," a game whereby key actors were driven by a calculus that constantly pushed them to undermine democracy, were almost totally done away with.⁶² In positive terms, moreover, the legacies of bureaucratic authoritarianism had also prepared the way for the radical free-market economic reforms that would later be carried out by Carlos Menem, after taking power in 1989. Indeed, by weakening of labor and strengthening the new *grupos económicos,* the military rulers had in some way made these reforms possible.⁶³

In sum, while Argentina's military rulers had clearly demonstrated the limits of bureaucratic authoritarianism as a transformative force and failed to shape a new political order, they did leave multiple legacies that affected how others—the very politicians that had managed to defeat the project spearheaded by the military—would go about defining a postbureaucratic authoritarian political order. This is probably the most critical factor that, despite the failure of bureaucratic authoritarianism to offer a viable formula for political stability for late modernizers in the twentieth century, gives contemporary historical significance to bureaucratic authoritarianism as an authoritarian capitalist response to the challenges of modernization, over and above other less ambitious forms of authoritarianism.

Conclusion: Regime Analysis and the Political-Institutional Model

This chapter has gone beyond the analysis of Argentina's experience with bureaucratic authoritarianism during 1976–83, first by considering this book's arguments about the political dynamics of bureaucratic authoritarianism on the basis of the comparative perspectives offered by the cases of Chile and Brazil. Then, it went beyond this book's substantive focus by placing bureaucratic authoritarianism as a form of rule in historical perspective, emphasizing in particular the legacies of bureaucratic authoritarianism in post-1983 Argentina. By way of conclusion, this attempt to put the study of bureaucratic authoritarianism in Argentina in a broader perspective is taken one step further by briefly restating the link between the study of bureaucratic authoritarianism and the overall agenda of regime analysis.

As stated at the outset, the task this book set out to tackle was a double one: first, to develop a general conceptual framework—the political-institutional model—on the basis of a synthesis of a broad range of literature generated by students of political regimes and regime change; and second, to combine this general framework with an understanding of the specific characteristics of one particular attempt at regime founding: bureaucratic authoritarianism. This book has sought to combine, then, the general and the specific, the abstract and the concrete, and in doing so shed light on the substantive issue of bureaucratic authoritarianism as a political phenomenon while also making the study of bureaucratic authoritarianism part of the broader agenda of regime analysis through the explicit use of a general framework for the analysis.

The implications of such an analytical strategy are very significant. Such a strategy allows the analyst to acknowledge and address the specifics of different instances of the same problem, such as transitions from authoritarianism and transitions from democracy, and it facilitates comparisons between different phenomena by providing the general framework within which such comparisons could be carried out. In other words, this strategy provides a foundation for the broader agenda of regime analysis by enabling analysts to address the specifics of the problems they may be interested in while providing a way to compare findings that emerge from such studies with findings that emerge from studies other political regimes.

This book has sought to show the value of such a strategy to the study of bureaucratic authoritarianism by shedding light on the peculiar problems faced by military rulers when they tackled the generic challenge all regime founders confront. But the implications of such a strategy for the study of democratization, a topic currently of great concern to regime analysts, are not difficult to spell out. One of the great challenges faced in the study of democratization is the need to broaden the empirical scope of theorizing—which was originally based on the study of Latin American and Southern European cases—to encompass comparable cases from Eastern Europe and the former Soviet Union. Such an ambitious comparative enterprise offers regime analysts the opportunity to develop and test a range of new ideas that could add to the already substantial body of knowledge that regime analysts have accumulated over the past two and a half decades. However, some specialists in Communist and post-Communist politics have resisted engaging in such theorizing, in part for fear that the peculiarities of these societies would be lost from sight under the umbrella of the broad comparisons some regime analysts have proposed. As the analytical strategy employed in this book suggests, however, regime analysts are not forced to choose between what is general and what is specific. Rather, the strength of this analytical strategy is its ability both to capture what is specific and to provide the conceptual language within which these specific aspects can be compared against each other. In other words, the analytical strategy employed in this book for the study of bureaucratic authoritarianism has important implications beyond bureaucratic authoritarianism, providing in particular some suggestions that can help regime analysts as they tackle the daunting analytical challenges raised by the study of democratization.

Appendix A

Summary Chronology of Events

1976

March 24 — A military coup is staged and a new government is constituted, headed by a military junta formed by the three commanders-in-chief of the armed forces: Army General Jorge Rafael Videla, Navy Admiral Eduardo Emilio Massera, and Air Force Brigadier General Orlando Ramón Agosti. Videla is also President.

1977

March — The Group of 25 or Commission of 25 (Grupo de los 25 or Comisión de los 25) is formed.

April–June 1977 — President Videla states the need for a political proposal.

1978

April — The Labor Action Commission (Comisión de Gestión y Trabajo [CGyT]) is formed.

June — The Peronist Syndical Movement (Movimiento Sindical Peronista [MSP]) is constituted.

August 1 — Videla is redesignated President, now as a retired officer; Division General Roberto Eduardo Viola becomes Commander-in-Chief of the Army and assumes Videla's position on the military junta.

August — The National Labor Commission (Comisión Nacional de Trabajo [CNT]), which incorporates the CGyT, is formed.

September 15 — Admiral Armando Lambruschini becomes Commander-in-Chief of the Navy, replacing Massera in the military junta.

1979

January 24 — Brigadier Omar Graffigna becomes the Commander-in-

	Chief of the Air Force, replacing Agosti in the military junta and completing the full replacement of the first junta.
April 27	A general strike, organized by the Group of 25, is staged.
August–September	The Commission of 20 (Comisión de los 20), also called the Group of 20 (Grupo de los 20), is constituted.
September 10	The United Leadership of Argentine Workers (Conducción Unica de Trabajadores Argentinos [CUTA]) is formed.
November 16	Law No. 22105, the Law of Professional Associations (Ley de Asociaciones Gremiales de Trabajadores), is sanctioned.
December 19	"The Political Foundation of the Armed Forces for the Process of National Reorganization" (Bases Políticas de las Fuerzas Armadas para el Proceso de Reorganización Nacional) is publicized.
December 28	General Leopoldo Galtieri replaces Viola as Commander-in-Chief of the Army and assumes the army's seat in the military junta.

1980

March 27	An official "political dialogue" between government officials and select "personalities" of society begins.
April	A financial crisis erupts.
April	The United Leadership of Argentine Workers (CUTA) ceases to exist.
April 17	Lorenzo Miguel, former head of the metal workers' union (UOM) and the 62 Organizations (62 Organizaciones), regains his freedom.
October 2	Viola is nominated to succeed Videla as President.
November 24	The General Labor Confederation (Confederación General del Trabajo [CGT]) is reconstituted around the unions gathered in the Group of 25.

1981

March 29	Retired General Roberto Viola assumes the presidency in replacement of Videla.

April	The Intersectorial CNT-20 (Intersectorial CNT-20), combining unions from the CNT and the Commission of 20, is formed.
July 14	The Multipartidaria, a front made up of the country's five main political parties, is constituted.
July 22	A second general strike is called, by the CGT. Most parties support the general strike.
September 9	Ricardo Balbín, the top leader of the Radical Civic Union (Unión Cívica Radical [UCR]), dies.
September 11	Admiral Jorge Isaac Anaya takes over as Commander-in-Chief of the Navy, thus replacing Lambruschini in the military junta.
October 13	Lorenzo Miguel revives the 62 Organizations.
November 7	The CGT organizes the "March of Work," a demonstration backed by political parties.
December 11	President Viola is displaced through a palace coup.
December 16	The Multipartidaria releases a comprehensive critique of military rule entitled "Before It Is Too Late."
December 22	General Leopoldo Galtieri assumes the presidency, retaining his post in the military junta.
December	Brigadier Basilio Lami Dozo takes over as Commander-in-Chief of the Air Force, replacing Graffigna in the junta.

1982

March 30	A massive demonstration, initiated by the CGT with full backing of the Multipartidaria, is held in the Plaza de Mayo.
April 2	Argentina invades the Falkland/Malvinas Islands.
May 20	The Intersectorial CNT-20 becomes the General Confederation of Labor-Azopardo (Confederación General del Trabajo-Azopardo [CGT-Azopardo]).
May	The CGT is renamed as the General Confederation of Labor-Brasil (Confederación General del Trabajo-Brasil [CGT-Brasil]).
June 14	Argentina surrenders to Britain, thus ending the Falkland/Malvinas Islands war.

June 18	Galtieri resigns his post as Commander-in-Chief of the Army and is replaced by General Cristino Nicolaides, who thereby joins the military junta.
June 22	Retired General Reynaldo Bignone is designated President, to assume the office on July 1, while the navy and the air force withdraw from the military junta.
July	The President signs law No. 22617, which relegalizes political activities.
August 17	Lami Dozo is replaced as Commander-in-Chief of the Air Force by Brigadier Augusto J. Hughes.
August 26	The Statute of Political Parties, providing the basis for the relegalization of party activities, is approved.
September	Vice-Admiral Rubén Franco is nominated to replace Admiral Anaya as Commander-in-Chief of the Navy, beginning on October 1.
September 21	The military junta is reconstituted.
September 22	The "Bread, Peace, and Work" march, leading to a mass concentration of workers in the Plaza de Mayo, is organized by the CGT-Brasil.
October 3	The "March for Life," organized by eight human rights organizations, is staged.
November 11	The military junta publicizes a fifteen-point document to guide the transition.
November	Press reports on a "military-union pact" begin to circulate.
December 6	A third general strike, called by the CGT-Azopardo and supported by the CGT-Brasil, is staged.
December 10	The "March of Resistance," a twenty-four-hour demonstration, is organized by human rights groups.
December 16	The Multipartidaria organizes the "March of the People for Democracy and National Reconstruction." While the CGT-Brasil joins the march, the CGT-Azopardo supports it but does not attend in an organized manner.

1983

January 13	The CGT-Azopardo announces the formation of its own 62 Organizations (62 Organizaciones Azopardistas). The organization is not formally constituted until March 19.

Appendix A: Summary Chronology of Events 211

February 12	The CGT-Brasil is renamed as the CGT of the Argentine Republic (CGT de la República Argentina [CGT-RA]).
February 28	The definitive timetable for national elections is announced.
March 28	A fourth general strike is called by the CGT-Azopardo and is supported by the CGT-RA.
April 28	The military junta announces its "Final Document of the Military Junta on the War Against Subversion and Terrorism."
May 20	A march in repudiation of the "Final Document" is organized by human rights organizations.
May	The National Movement of Union Renovation (Movimiento Nacional de Renovación Sindical [MNRS]) is formed to support Alfonsín's candidacy.
June 3	The right to strike is legalized by Law No. 22825.
June 23	An electoral law, No. 22838, is approved.
June 24	Law No. 22839, reestablishing the legal status the CGT and other third-level workers' organizations, is approved.
June	A law to enable the devolution of the CGT to workers is approved.
July 19	Valentín Erudinio Suárez is appointed as "normalizing delegate" of the CGT.
July 28	Raúl Alfonsín is proclaimed as the presidential candidate of the UCR.
August 9	Lorenzo Miguel regains control of the metal workers' union (UOM).
August 19	Human rights organizations organize a march to repudiate a proposed amnesty law.
August 22	Italo Luder is proclaimed as the presidential candidate of the Peronist party.
September 21	The "March of Resistance" is organized by the Mothers of the Plaza de Mayo. The CGT-RA adheres to the march.
September 22	A self-amnesty law, No. 22924, the Law of National Pacification, is sanctioned.
October 4	A fifth general strike is simultaneously though still unilaterally called for by the CGT-RA and the CGT-Azopardo.

October 14	The "unity of the Argentine labor movement" is proclaimed by both the CGT-RA and by the CGT-Azopardo.
October 30	National elections are held.
December 10	Alfonsín is inaugurated as President, and military rule comes to an end.

Appendix B

Number of Affiliates of Major Labor Unions, Argentina, 1979 and 1982/83

	No. of Affiliates
Confederación General de Empleados del Comercio de la República Argentina (CGEC)	408,000*
Unión Obrera Metalúrgica de la República Argentina (UOM)	287,587
Unión Obrera de la Construcción de la República Argentina (UOCRA)	186,614
Federación de Asociaciones de Trabajadores de la Sanidad Argentina	170,900
Unión Ferroviaria	170,647
Federación Trabajadores de Industrias de la Alimentación	148,783*
Unión del Personal Civil de la Nación	133,188*
Asociación Obrera Textil de la República Argentina (AOT)	127,928
Asociación Bancaria	125,000
Asociación Trabajadores del Estado (ATE)	110,000
Sindicato de Mecánicos y Afines del Transporte Automotor (SMATA)	72,403
Federación Argentina de Trabajadores de Luz y Fuerza (FATLyF)	69,952*
Federación de Sindicatos de Trabajadores Municipales de la Provincia de Buenos Aires	66,000*
Unión de Obreros y Empleados Municipales	65,866
Unión de Trabajadores Gastronómicos de la República Argentina	65,000
Federación Obrera de la Industria del Vestido y Afines (FONIVA)	45,318*
Federación de Obreros y Empleados Telefónicos de la República Argentina	39,888*
Federación Unica de Viajantes de la Argentina (FUVA)	38,261*
Unión Tranviarios Automotor	37,784
Federación Gremial del Personal de la Industria de la Carne y sus Derivados	37,667*
Unión Trabajadores de Entidades Deportivas y Civiles	30,712
Federación de Obreros y Empleados de Correos y Telecomunicaciones (FOECYT)	28,370*
Federación de Sindicatos Unidos Petroleros del Estado	26,568*
Federación Argentina de Trabajadores de Aguas Gaseosas y Afines	23,000*
Sindicato Gráfico Argentino	22,500

Federación de Obreros y Empleados de la Industria del Papel, Carton, Químicos y Afines	22,000*
Asociación Obrera Minera Argentina	20,000
Unión Obreros y Empleados Plásticos	18,993
Federación Nacional de Trabajadores de Obras Sanitarias	18,930*
Unión Trabajadores de la Industria del Calzado de la República Argentina	18,000
Unión Docentes Argentinos	17,640*
Asociación Argentina de Telegrafistas, Radiotelegrafistas y Afines	14,200
La Fraternidad	13,403
Federación Argentina de Trabajadores de Industrias Químicas Petroquímicas	12,881*

SOURCE: Data reported by the unions to the ministry of labor, as recorded in Ministerio de Trabajo y Seguridad Social, Dirección Nacional de Recursos Humanos y Empleo, *Estructura Sindical en la Argentina* (Buenos Aires: Ministerio de Trabajo y Seguridad Social, 1987), 91–199.

NOTE: Figures followed by an asterisk (*) indicate data are for 1982–83.

Appendix C

Basic Economic Indicators, Argentina, 1976–83

	1976	1977	1978	1979	1980	1981	1982	1983
GDP Growth	−0.5	6.3	−3.3	6.5	1.0	−7.0	−5.8	2.6
Inflation	349.0	160.0	169.0	140.1	87.5	131.2	209.7	433.6
Fiscal Deficit/GDP	−7.1	−2.8	−3.2	−2.6	−3.5	−9.1	−7.5	−12.7
Current Account/GDP	1.2	2.2	2.8	−0.5	−3.1	−3.8	−4.1	−3.8
Foreign Debt	8,279	9,678	12,496	19,034	27,162	35,671	43,634	45,069
Public Sector Foreign Debt as Percentage of Total	62.7	62.5	66.8	52.3	53.2	56.1	65.5	70.4
Investment/GDP	27.1	27.2	23.9	22.6	22.7	18.3	16.9	17.3
Unemployment	4.4	2.7	2.3	2.4	2.5	5.3	4.6	3.9
Real Wage	−32.7	−1.5	−1.8	14.9	11.8	−10.6	−10.6	25.5

SOURCES: Banco Central de la República Argentina (BCRA), Instituto Nacional de Estadística y Censos (INDEC), Economic Commission for Latin America (ECLA), the World Bank, and International Monetary Fund (IMF), as reproduced in Roberto Frenkel et al., *Argentina: Evolución Macroeconómica, financiación externa y cambio político* (Madrid: Fundación CEDEAL, 1992), 63, 65; World Bank, *Argentina: Economic Memorandum*, vol. 2: *Statistical Appendix* (Washington, D.C.: World Bank, 1985), 285; Stephen Haggard and Robert Kaufman, *The Political Economy of Democratic Transitions* (Princeton: Princeton University Press, 1995), 47.

NOTE: Foreign debt figures are in millions of dollars; real wage figures are for manufacturing wages.

Notes

Chapter 1: The Political-Institutional Model

1. A short list of works on regime analysis would include the following. On the breakdown of democracies and the nature of authoritarian regimes, see O'Donnell (1973), Collier (1979a), Collier and Collier (1991), Perlmutter (1981), Linz (1975), and Linz and Stepan (1978). On transitions from authoritarian rule, see O'Donnell, Schmitter, and Whitehead (1986), and Higley and Gunther (1992). On democratic consolidation, see Mainwaring, O'Donnell, and Valenzuela (1992a), Gunther, Diamandouros, and Puhle (1995), and Przeworski (1995). Important works covering more than one of these major issues include Moore (1966), Dahl (1971, 1973, 1989), Mouzelis (1986), Przeworski (1991), Huntington (1991), Luebbert (1991), Rueschemeyer, Stephens and Stephens (1992), and Linz and Stepan (1996). Some of the most useful broad conceptual discussions of the issues raised by regime analysis include Garretón (1987:23–58), Morlino (1990, 1995a), and Schmitter (1995b). A parallel and supplementary body of literature is that on social revolutions. See, among others, Skocpol (1979, 1994: chap. 11) and Wickham-Crowley (1992). The supplementary nature of the literature on revolutions and transitions is pointed out by Skocpol (1994:334–35).

2. Such an effort is fairly daunting, given the sheer number of contributions and the breadth of concerns they address. Necessarily, then, such an effort emphasizes what are considered to be the most fundamental elements in a broad-ranging literature, leaving out and many times not even acknowledging and addressing other elements. No doubt different authors would go about this task differently, but such is the nature of syntheses.

3. For an attempt to analyze the central concepts in regime analysis that complements the current one, see Munck (1996).

4. Schmitter with Karl (1994:173–77), Schmitter (1995a:12–13), O'Donnell and Schmitter (1986:3–5).

5. This distinction between two different types of political processes—the fluid politics of transitional moments, and the structured politics of more "normal" moments—is recognized by other authors, who provide insights that are useful in formulating a regime analysis agenda. The distinction is the key insight behind the critical juncture model of Collier and Collier (1991) and is at the heart of the work by Unger (1987a) on cycles and formative contexts as well as of Giddens's (1984) structuration theory. Zolberg (1972:205–6) highlights this distinction in arguing that "moments of madness" or "moments of political enthusiasm" are always followed by "the restoration of boredom."

6. Similarly, in his discussion of authoritarian regimes, Linz (1964:324) refers to the "emergence, evolution and breakdown" of regimes. A similar breakdown of phases is developed by Morlino (1990:99–107, 1995b:573–74). See also Garretón (1984).

7. Although regime analysts have not always begun their analysis by considering the phase of origin, that is the logical starting point in a comprehensive framework for the study of regimes. By adopting the proposed distinction between three phases, and by beginning our analysis with a consideration of the phase of origin, we are better able to draw connections that the literature has tended to overlook between the different phases in the overall life of a regime.

8. If the manner in which power is seized can help to explain the shape and prospects of any new regime, a full explanation of why power is seized as it is belongs to

an analysis of the phase of transition and can be legitimately taken as a given in theorizing about the phase of origin. Thus, for example, while studies of new democracies may consider the impact of the manner in which the transition from authoritarianism affects a country's democratic institutions and prospects, an explanation of the manner in which the transition from authoritarianism occurs is something that needs to be addressed within a theory of the breakdown of authoritarianism.

9. Certain aspects of the process by which new elites seek to shape a new regime, such as the choice of institutions, can be carried out before the transition from the old regime is completed. This is the case, for example, in democratic transitions, in which such basic institutions as electoral laws must be defined before a full transfer of power can take place. But even in those cases, only after power has changed hands can such institutional choices cease to be mere promises by authoritarian rulers and be seen as potential bases for a new political order.

An important point implicit in this discussion of the seizure of power is that the unit of governance, which regime analysts have always taken to be the modern state or the nation-state, is already predefined. That is, talk about the seizure of power assumes that different elites share a common definition of the state. As various analysts have recently recognized (Linz and Stepan 1996: chap. 2; Przeworski 1995: chap. 1), conflicts over the definition of the state can affect the process of regime transition and should thus be considered as a potential causal factor within regime analysis. But, it is important to stress, while the processes that regime analysts try to explain may be affected by the processes that define where power is to be located, these are two distinct processes with very different political stakes. Regime analysis has a legitimately defined object of study.

10. Although for clarity I reserve the term "transition" to indicate transitions from old regimes rather than transitions to new regimes, this conceptualization is quite similar to O'Donnell's (1992:18) distinction, which was developed in the context of democratic transitions, between two transitions: a transition from authoritarian rule leading to the installation of a democratic government, and a transition from this newly installed democratic government to a consolidated democratic regime. Przeworski's (1991:67) distinction between "extrication" from the old regime and "constitution" of a new regime corresponds closely to O'Donnell distinction between two transitions, even though the moment of "constitution" refers only to the design of new institutions and not to their consolidation. Garretón (1986a:98–99, 107) develops a similar distinction, in the context of his discussion of bureaucratic authoritarianism, between "reactive" and "transformative" or "foundational" dimensions. That distinction, however, is conceived in broader and less institutional terms than either O'Donnell and Przeworski do.

11. A key reason for separating these two phases is to allow for a clearer consideration of the independent effect of the institutions themselves on the challenge of institutionalization.

12. As Sartori (1994:202, 198) puts it, "Constitutions are 'forms' that structure and discipline the state's decision-making processes . . . [or] instruments of government which limit, restrain and allow for the control of the exercise of power." In a parallel formulation, Riggs (1990:212) refers to the creation of a "constitutive system." Unger (1987a:6–7, 33–34, 58–61, 68–69) elaborates a more expansive notion of "formative context," which refers to "the basic institutional arrangements and imaginative preconceptions that circumscribe . . . routine practical or discursive activities and conflicts and that resist their destabilizing effect." A political order also entails an informal aspect, which Unger calls the imaginative counterparts to institutional rules within a formative context, or what Foley (1989) calls the gaps and abeyances in constitutions. As Foley argues, there are important ways in which constitutions do not shape policy-making, but as Unger (1987a:103, 58–61, 100–115, chap. 3) argues, while there is "no one-to-one re-

lation between the institutional and imaginative aspects of a formative context," there remains a very definite connection between institutional and imaginative elements that shape the large-scale options of social life.

13. In his 1973 study of authoritarianism, Linz (1973b:234) argues for the need to study the all-important and understudied "process by which rulers proceed to consolidate power, once they have gained it." This assessment of the literature is probably still correct today, if less so, for much work is being done on institutional choices in new democracies (Przeworski 1991:79–88; Lijphart 1992; Sisk 1995: chap. 1; Geddes 1996). But, as Mainwaring (1991:43) indicates in his discussion of electoral laws, "most analysts have focused on the political consequences" of institutional rules, while "the issue of [the] political origins [of these institutions] has received less attention." This is certainly the case with Lijphart's (1984:220–21) classic *Democracies*, where the problem of the origin of institutions is discussed only in the last two pages of the book. It remains the case in Lijphart's (1994: chap. 7) most recent book, where only the last chapter deals with the problem of the origins of electoral laws. And the same point applies to Sartori's (1994) recent book, which despite its title only addresses the issue of "engineering" in the last chapter, reserving the rest of the book for a discussion of the consequences of constitutional structures. In sum, while not every question in the agenda of regime analysis needs to be addressed within a particular work, it is problematic that the problem of institutional design should be so understudied.

14. This factor has been stressed by O'Donnell (1973:99–106) and Collier (1979b:29).

15. If there is a limiting case that invalidates the impact of sequential effects, it would be a transition through revolution. But even in such cases, where there appears to be little overlap between the process by which the old governing elites are displaced and the process whereby the new governing elites set out to consolidate power and construct a new order, it would be a mistake to talk about the construction of the new order, as McFaul (1993:13–14) does in the case of postcommunist Russia, starting "from a clean slate [or] tabula rasa." While a transition necessarily implies a break or lack of continuity, a move in a new direction, where a country is coming from has an impact on where it may go through the sequential effects the past generates. As Unger (1987a:313) points out, "The sequential influence never determines particular outcomes . . . [but] it makes certain lines of transformation more likely than others." In the case of Russia after 1991, this would mean acknowledging the way in which the construction of a new order is shaped by the fact that it is a postcommunist order. The notion of "sequential effects" is developed by Unger (1987a:312–19), while a similar notion of "confining conditions" is elaborated by Kirchheimer (1969).

16. Various versions of this thesis concerning the relative degree of power of the outgoing and incoming power holders are found in Rokkan (1970:157), Lijphart (1992), and Przeworski (1991:81–88). This thesis figures prominently, in a slightly different context, in the work of Moore (1966) and Collier and Collier (1991), both of whom stress the relative degree of power different classes have in transitional processes. It has also been the key notion behind the distinction among "modes of transition" and the related issue of "birth marks" and "enclaves" stressed by Karl (1990), Garretón (1989a:51–63), and Valenzuela (1992:64–66), as well in Skocpol's (1979:172) argument concerning how "the specific way in which each old regime broke down politically had important consequences . . . [in that it] shaped and limited the efforts and achievements of the statebuilding revolutionary leadership." Of course, the classical reference to the legacies of transitional processes is due to Tocqueville (1945:28), who wrote: "[All nations] bear some marks of their origin. The circumstances that accompanied their birth and contributed to their development affected the whole term of their being."

17. The linkage between the two tasks in the phase of origin—the seizure of power,

and the challenge of constitutional definition—can be complex, because of the variable ways in which the old and the new come together and, specifically, the variable timing when the challenge of constitutional definition is addressed. The challenge of constitutional definition may be settled before, and as a condition of, the seizure of power by a new elite. In that case, the seizure of power is the first test of the new constitutional structure. However, this situation, characterized by a perfect overlap in time between the destruction of the old and the construction of the new, is unlikely to be all that common. In most cases, indeed, the situation is likely to be less tidy. There is likely to be an interim period in which the old has been set to rest but the challenge of constitutional definition that is to lay the ground for the new has not been completed.

18. In discussing Russia around 1992, Schmitter (1993:31) makes the point that the form in which power was seized affected the manner in which the challenge of constitutional definition was addressed. Linz has also recently stressed the importance of interim arrangements in the process of democratization (Shain and Linz 1995; Linz 1990: 149–50; Linz and Stepan 1992).

19. If success and failure are thus but the two opposite poles on the continuum of possible outcomes of an elite's attempt to tackle the challenge of constitutional definition, it is important to recognize the difficulty of determining just what constitutes a sufficiently successful response to the challenge of constitutional definition. The key point, nonetheless, as Schmitter (1973:219) argues, is that "no political system can persist without some minimal constitutionalization of its decision-making procedures."

20. To give an example that crops up in the literature on democratic consolidation, democracy can be considered a consolidated regime at the point in time when such key actors as the military and business elites cease envisioning military coups as a course of action (O'Donnell 1992:18–24, 48–49).

21. As Mainwaring (1992:305, 304–8) puts it, "The way conflicts within the ruling bloc emerge and are handled ultimately cannot be divorced from the question of legitimacy." Lamounier (1989:53, 75) makes the same point in criticizing Skocpol. See also Portes and Kincaid (1985:72), Bobbio (1989:69–88), and Linz and Stepan (1996:48–49, 51).

22. This is a central implication of Lijphart's classic work on consociational democracy, where he argues that issues of institutional design can have a great effect, making the difference between a workable democracy and an ungovernable polity (Lijphart 1977, 1984; see also Horowitz 1991).

23. The point that control is not only or primarily a matter of repression, but rather a function of both coercion and legitimacy, has been expressed in a variety of ways. But it essentially comes back to the argument that "no amount of violence . . . can abolish the consensual minimum required by every system of rule" (Unger 1987b:85). The coercion and legitimacy dualism is a central theme of Gramsci's work, as well as Giddens's (1987:11) notion of the "dialectic of control."

24. The need to look beyond the governing elites when considering problems of regime formation is something regime analysts have recently become more emphatic about. Indeed, while regime analysts have generally been in agreement over the basic idea that for institutionalization to occur, the proposed institutional rules must be understood and accepted by actors that pattern their behavior according to these rules (Mainwaring 1992:296), there has been a shift concerning the fundamental issue of which actors must accept the proposed institutional rules for there to be institutionalization. Not long ago, narrow definitions stressing the importance of the governing elites were common. An example of this is apparent in the definition of regime offered in 1986 by O'Donnell and Schmitter (1986:73, emphasis added), where they state that a regime "necessarily involves institutionalization, i.e., to be relevant the patterns defining a given regime must

be habitually known, practiced, and accepted, *at least* by those which these same patterns define as *participants* in the process." But, as O'Donnell and Schmitter themselves indicate through their subsequent definitions of regime, this understanding of the actors deemed to be relevant to the process of institutionalization need not be so restrictive. In an 1991 article, Schmitter states that institutionalization is accomplished when the patterns that constitute a regime are "habitually known, practiced, and accepted by *most, if not all, actors*" (Schmitter and Karl 1991:76, emphasis added). Similarly, in a 1992 publication, O'Donnell (1992:48–49, emphasis added) stresses that the consolidation of democracy hinges upon the requirement that "*social and political actors who control significant power resources* . . . habitually subject their interrelations to the institutions specific to political democracy." The basic idea behind these redefinitions, then, is that the institutional rules of the game must be accepted and practiced not only by the governing elites but also by "the major actors in the political system" (Mainwaring 1992: 296; see also Przeworski 1991:x, 26, 39–39).

25. Two aspects of this argument deserve clarification. First, the implicit assumption behind this conceptualization is that because conflict is a constant in all societies, what matters from the perspective of the process of institutionalization is not whether there is or is not opposition, but rather what type of opposition governing elites face. Second is the more complex issue concerning the special problems associated with the use of institutions as a factor in an argument about their institutionalization. The issue is that this type of argument runs the danger of falling prey to the problem of endogeneity, whereby the consequence of a certain process is confused with its cause (King, Keohane, and Verba 1994:107–8, 185–95). This is a real danger, but it is still possible to legitimately argue that an institutional arrangement itself affects the likelihood of its institutionalization via the *pull effect* of institutions on actors. Indeed, soft functional arguments, such as the one presented here, avoid the problem of endogeneity by spelling out the causal mechanism—the type of orientation that different institutional arrangements generate in actors on the basis of the ability of institutions to manage the conflicts that emerge within a society—whereby the functionalist force produces an outcome (Unger 1987a:280, 294–300, 332–37). There still is a problem in that this causal mechanism entails a prospective argument, whereby the orientation of actors hinges on these actors' knowing what the effects of different institutional designs are even before such institutions have been used. There are many skeptics, such as Elster (1988:308), who emphasize the "massive difficulty of predicting the consequences of major institutional changes." But, as Sartori (1994:201) argues by way of a rebuttal of Elster's views, there are many examples of "a predicted effect that was predictable *ex ante*, that was, we know *ex post*, well predicted."

26. An elaborate attempt to distinguish among the types of opposition is carried out by Linz (1973a, 1978), but his distinctions are regime specific. He distinguishes between "loyal" or "constitutional" and "disloyal" opposition in the context of democracy, and between "semi-," "pseudo-," "alegal," and "illegal" oppositions in the context of authoritarianism. Although these distinctive terms are quite useful when studying particular regime types, it is imperative for the purpose of a general model to use terms, such as principled and pragmatic oppositions, that get at the concept that underlies these more specific terms.

27. Spelling out the point made by Skocpol in the quotation discussed above, Przeworski (1986:54, 50–53, 1991:5) underlines the importance of "organized" as opposed to "diffuse" opposition, stating that "what is threatening to authoritarian regimes is not the breakdown of legitimacy but the organization of counterhegemony." This formulation is useful in that it serves as a corrective to studies of political culture that focus on

attitudes on an individual level but say nothing about how these attitudes inform the behavior of actors constituted as such. But while Przeworski uses this argument to reject the usefulness of the concept of legitimacy for regime analysis, it is important to notice that the perceived legitimacy, or lack thereof, of a regime plays a role in the very ability of groups to organize and become effective forces of opposition, which is Przeworski's concern (Tarrow 1994: chap. 7). It is therefore not necessary to reject the notion of legitimacy in order to draw attention to the variable strength of opposition actors.

28. This argument raises an important methodological issue. While most analysts would agree that the distinction between principled and pragmatic opposition orientations can be determined through careful analysis, there are bound to be disputes that would severely weaken the analytical usefulness of this argument, concerning how to assess the strength of societal opposition actors and how to determine how strong an actor must be to be relevant from the perspective of the process of institutionalization.

My solution is to follow an objective criterion for identifying relevant actors, viewing actors as relevant inasmuch as they express a main cleavage in a society. It is important to stress that such a criterion does not say anything about specific actors, given that the actors will vary, according to the type of cleavage and the associated issues these actors express. For example, as Lipset and Rokkan (1967) argue, European political development can be understood in terms of four cleavages—the center-periphery, state-church, land-industry, and owner-worker cleavages—that generated actors with different types of conflicting interests. For the purpose of a general framework for regime analysis, however, the specifics are not central. While the nature of the conflict may vary, and the stakes of the dispute may be different, the key issue is that cleavages serve to generate the central political struggles. Thus, while the particular nature of the conflict and the actors involved should certainly be developed in a substantive theory of a particular regime type, for the purpose of a general theory it is crucial to see how the generic issues raised by opposition actors affect regime dynamics.

29. The stable persistence of a regime does not mean the absence of change, but rather incremental or evolutionary change. As Whitehead (1994:327) states, "A regime can be said to persist, or to reproduce itself, so long as the inevitable changes in institutions and rules that occur over time come about incrementally, without changing the basic principles of the system."

30. As Linz (1978:86, chap. 5; 1990:147–48) argues, deinstitutionalization could be followed in turn by reequilibration. See also O'Donnell and Schmitter (1986:23–24).

31. While the task of reproducing consolidated institutions does not proceed automatically and continues to depend on the choice of actors to use them, the risks are lower. For one, what is at stake is only the continuation of a pattern of behavior, something that is made easier by sunk costs, habit, and so on. Moreover, what adjustments do have to be made to adapt to a changing environment are aided, institutionally, by the built-in legitimate role allowed to opposition forces.

32. What is peculiar about a "political situation" is that the governing elites have not lost control over the direction of government, as is the case in a political crisis, but also have not consolidated their power through an institutionalized order, as in the case of a political regime. If there is not a single mechanism whereby actors gain access to government and exercise governmental power, as in a regime, there is nonetheless one procedure regulating the exercise of political power that is clearly dominant, over and above the procedures advanced by other actors. Thus, in a "political situation" it is not the authoritarian or democratic character of the government that is in doubt. Rather, it is the acceptance of the proposed institutional rules by all relevant actors that is at issue.

Scholars have characterized the middle ground between successful regime formation and outright political crisis in other ways. To acknowledge the lack of institutionalization of various attempts at regime foundation in Latin America, Chalmers (1977:37) suggests talking about "experiments" in democracy and authoritarianism. Lamounier (1989:54, emphasis added) also stresses the need "to capture the *experimental* and incremental aspect" of the processes of institutionalization in such cases as Brazil in the 1970s. Finally, Mainwaring, O'Donnell, and Valenzuela (1992b:3, 11) refer to the difference between "transitional" and "consolidated" democracies, and also to "stunted" regimes. As Collier and Levitsky (1997) show, students of democratization have come up with a large number of terms to acknowledge the possibility of a less than fully institutionalized politics.

33. The labels of "stable persistence," "unstable persistence," and "crisis" are from Morlino (1990:101), who presents an analysis similar to the one offered here.

34. A political crisis can give way either to a new attempt on the part of the same governing elites to complete the unfinished process of regime formation, or to the deepening of a crisis that makes displacement of this elite—that is, a transition—increasingly likely.

35. For analytical reasons, the use of the term "transition" is limited to the process whereby the established governing elites lose power and a new set of elites seize power, instead of encompassing both this process and the process by which the new elites define an institutional order, as is common in the recent literature on democratization. Of course, the process whereby an emerging elite displaced the established elites can chronologically coincide or overlap with the process whereby this emerging elite confronts the challenge of constitutional definition. Indeed, it is rare that these two processes would not intermingle. Yet, in order to be able to acknowledge the distinctiveness of these processes, as well as to study the potential interaction between the two processes, it is useful to use the narrower and clearer definition of transition proposed here. This is not a new observation. For example, Linz (1990:144) makes this point clearly in the context of democratic transitions, when he states: "It is essential to emphasize that the crisis and breakdown of nondemocratic regimes is a process that should be kept analytically separate from that of transitions to political democracy." See also O'Donnell and Schmitter (1986:65).

36. Although in many ways O'Donnell and Schmitter's book marks the beginning of the "transitions literature," many of the arguments they develop are prefigured in the works of Rustow (1970) and Linz (1978).

37. While these two approaches have sometimes been called the "elitist" and "social movement" approaches to transitions (Tilly 1993/94:2; Whitehead 1992:154; Foweraker 1994:218; Mainwaring 1992:302–4; Tarrow 1995a:204–9), it is necessary to clarify that what is at issue is whether change originates within the governing elites or whether it is promoted by a counter-elite constituted in society. Although those who criticize the elitist perspective seek to stress the role of mobilized masses, it is only inasmuch as the masses are constituted as an actor, which means that they are led by a counter-elite, that they play a role in transitions. It is probably more accurate, thus, to contrast "statist" and "societal" approaches to transitions rather than "elitist" and "social movement" approaches. On the role of leaders in social movements, see Garretón (1989b:261, 262, 275), Munck (1990a, 1995:675–81), Alberoni (1991:283–91), Offe (1991:883), Foweraker (1993, 1994), and Tarrow (1995a, 1995b).

38. One position may be more accurate than the other in terms of assessing the source of change in a specific transition, but the positions represent only partial positions within a general theory of transitions. Various authors have warned about the dangers of a sterile counterposition of "top down" versus "bottom up" approaches. See Przeworski

(1991:56–57), Mainwaring (1992:298–302), Cardoso (1984:51), and Whitehead (1994: 333–34). For attempts to combine these approaches, see Collier and Collier (1991: chap. 5) and Karl (1990).

39. The descriptive status of the transitions literature in this regard is well illustrated by the oft-repeated argument that splits within the governing elites are a factor in accounting for the initiation of transitions (O'Donnell and Schmitter 1986:19; Skocpol 1979:49, chap. 2; Mann 1993:168, 220, 222; Mainwaring 1992:299; Haggard and Kaufman 1995:12, 37). This may be true, but this literature has still done little to advance an understanding of the process whereby governing elites lose cohesion, as recognized even by some of the same authors that stress the importance of this factor (Skocpol 1994:311; Haggard and Kaufman 1995:5–7, 365–66, 12).

40. While much recent literature pays scant attention to the dynamics of the old regime, some notable exceptions include Linz, Stepan, and Gunther (1995), Linz and Stepan (1996: chap. 4), Whitehead (1994), and Middlebrook (1995).

41. Part of the problem with this argument has to do with the difficulty in assessing *ex ante* how strong an actor must be to become what I label a "dominant" actor. If the predictive power of this argument is thus seriously impaired, that is probably due more to the very contingent nature of the process under consideration than to a defect inherent in this line of thinking.

42. Let me offer a word of clarification about this notion of governing elite cohesion and splits. In discussing the phases of origin and evolution, a key assumption about the governing elites has been that when the governing elites come to power they are a relatively cohesive force. Assuming cohesion of the governing elites, therefore, as a default position, the analysis hinged on any deviation from that position, seeing lack of cohesion as a factor that weakened the degree of elite *support* for the creation and institutionalization of a new political order. In thinking about the role of governing elites in the context of transitions, however, the key consideration is whether a split within the governing elites leads some sectors of the governing elites to actually *oppose* the institutional framework of government. To avoid confusing these two quite different forms of the problem of governing elite cohesion, the discussion of governing elites in the context of transitions refers not to elite cohesion but to the orientation of the governing elites and, specifically, whether a sector of the governing elites adopts an orientation of principled opposition.

43. While the literature on modes of transition has generally conceptualized this dimension in terms of the degree of control that outgoing rulers exert over the process of transition, the current formulation frames the issue from the perspective of the contending elites, as does Karl (1990:8–9). The terms "confrontation" and "accommodation" come from Collier and Collier (1991:748). For a more detailed discussion about modes of transition and a justification for this conceptualization of modes of transition, see Munck and Leff (1997).

44. For example, despite being accused of advancing a voluntaristic notion of choice, O'Donnell and Schmitter (1986) state clearly that while some options, such as confrontation, have been available to opposition actors in other times and contexts, in the context of the cases they are studying the decisions of democratic opposition forces are structured by consideration of the actions of the military and the bourgeoisie in such a way that compromise is the only strategic option. Yet, as they acknowledge at the outset, these structural factors remain in the background of their analysis (O'Donnell and Schmitter 1986:4–5).

45. This argument represents an adaptation of Moore's (1966) argument about the variable coalitional opportunities that the power of landlords made available to an

emerging bourgeoisie, and of Collier and Collier's (1991) argument that the power of the oligarchy shaped the strategies that the middle-class reformers could pursue vis-à-vis labor. In both cases, it is the power of the old governing elites that shapes the strategic options confronted by emerging elites. On the manner in which the old regime delimits the strategic options of challenging elites, see also Goodwin and Skocpol (1989:500–501).

Chapter 2: The Political Dynamics of Bureaucratic Authoritarianism

1. The same could be said about the short-lived democracies in interwar Europe, as well as of the experience with democracy in several Latin American countries during the 1945–70s period. The advantage of focusing on cases of authoritarianism is that regime analysis really began with the study of the breakdown of these democracies.

2. Linz's effort to define the attributes of authoritarianism in the context of a broader attempt to distinguish among nondemocratic regimes in the twentieth century is developed in various articles (Linz 1964, 1975). The connection between O'Donnell's conceptualization of bureaucratic authoritarianism and Linz's work on authoritarianism is stressed by O'Donnell (1973:94–95). For a more skeptical view of the connection between bureaucratic authoritarianism and Linz's notion of authoritarianism, see Angell (1984:121–25).

3. O'Donnell (1973:53–55, 92–95, 1988:31–33), Collier (1979a:399; 1979b:24).

4. On the use of the concept of bureaucratic authoritarianism within the South American context, see O'Donnell (1978a, 1981), Collier (1979a), Garretón (1979, 1983), Remmer and Merkx (1982), Valenzuela and Valenzuela (1986b:3–7), Fontana (1987: 7–22), Melo (1989:10–15, 18), and Cardoso (1993: chap. 9). On the use of the concept outside the South American region, O'Donnell (1973:92–93; 1978a:28–31) suggested that the concept of bureaucratic authoritarianism can be applied to Mexico as well as to Spain, Turkey, and Greece. Greece during the period of military rule (1967–74) is discussed as a case of bureaucratic authoritarianism by Mouzelis (1986:177–81). The notion of bureaucratic authoritarianism has been used in the context of South Korea during the period 1961–87 by Im (1987:231–57) and Cumings (1989), and of East Asia more broadly by Woo-Cumings (1994). The Philippines under Marcos has been characterized as a case of bureaucratic authoritarianism by Hawes (1987:45). China under Deng Xiaoping is referred to as a case of bureaucratic authoritarianism by Joseph (1993:132) and Hamrin and Zhao (1995:xxv–xxvi). Both China and the Soviet Union after Stalin's death in 1953 are labeled as cases of bureaucratic authoritarianism by Andrain (1994: chap. 8).

5. If the problem of conceptual stretching was avoided in most studies that used the concept of bureaucratic authoritarianism through such a reconceptualization, even this broad contrast between a modern and bureaucratized, as opposed to traditional, form of authoritarianism is not made by all authors. Andrain (1994:24), for example, blatantly disregards even this most abstract meaning of the concept of bureaucratic authoritarianism and not only includes Confucian China as a case of bureaucratic authoritarianism but asserts that "the bureaucratic-authoritarian regime has been the dominant [type of political system] during the last three thousand years" of Chinese history. This is clearly a case of conceptual stretching, where the defining attributes of the original conceptualization, such as the importance of industrial class conflict and the exclusion of labor, have been abandoned or transformed in a way that bears no resemblance to the phenomenon originally discussed. On conceptual stretching, see Sartori (1970).

6. As Sartori (1984:34–35) points out, a conceptual analysis involves establishing the component element or attributes of a concept and the cases that are referents of a concept or, stated in other words, the intension and extension, respectively, of a concept.

7. Linz stresses a third factor—the distinction between ideologies and mentalities—but drops it from his typology of authoritarian regimes because, he states, the difficulty of studying mentalities makes this dimension "turn out in practice to be less helpful" than the dimensions of limited pluralism and limited mobilization. A fourth factor that Linz invokes in his definition of authoritarianism, the extent to which leaders exercise power in a predictable manner, is never systematically addressed in his writings. Linz (1975:277, 179–80, 191–96, 264–66, 269–74, 277–81, 1964:297–301, 304–11).

8. For the purpose of empirical analysis, the focus is on the defining or necessary attributes as opposed to the central or contingent ones. See Sartori (1984:32–35, 54–57, 1993:14–15).

9. This way of generating subtypes of authoritarianism differs in part from the way suggested by Collier. As Collier argues, while all subtypes are "derivative" concepts that are formed with reference to, and as a modification of, some other concept, the generation of subtypes has generally proceeded in two ways. On the one hand, "classical" subtypes are generated by a process of "addition," which increases the information already conveyed by the root concept, while, on the other hand, "radial" subtypes are generated by a process of "subtraction"—through the weakening or elimination of some of the attributes of the core or original concept. In this book, however, following the procedure used by Linz in his efforts at building a typology of political regimes, the concept of bureaucratic authoritarianism is derived from that of authoritarianism through a process of "specification"—that is, by specifying the "particular" forms through which a "general" defining attribute manifests itself. Collier and Levitsky (1997), Collier and Mahon (1993), Linz (1975:179–80, 265, 269, 277–81). For an extended discussion of the procedures for generating subtypes, see Munck (1996).

10. This definition, it should be pointed out, constitutes little more than a briefer version of the original definition proposed in O'Donnell (1973:31–33).

11. This feature was highlighted by O'Donnell (1973:95, 111–14), Stepan (1971), and others (Cardoso 1979:35; Fontana 1987:7–9), who saw bureaucratic authoritarianism as a new form of authoritarianism in South America, compared with more traditional forms of military rule in which a military officer, often retired, controlled the executive while the military as an institution was not involved in government and restricted its actions to backing the executive. It is important to acknowledge, as will be discussed in Chapter 7, that the extent to which the military as institution and the military as government overlapped varied considerably between one case of bureaucratic authoritarianism and another. This feature, nonetheless, does serve to distinguish what is a defining feature of bureaucratic authoritarianism as opposed to other forms of military rule or authoritarianism. See also the distinction between regimes in which the governing military elite is hierarchical or nonhierarchical in Linz, Stepan, and Gunther (1995:85–86, 116) and the confirming analysis of Agüero (1995a:55–58).

12. The coup coalition that helps to inaugurate bureaucratic authoritarianism has generally been seen to include the military, big domestic capital and their international partners, and certain segments of the middle class. Collier, for example, refers to the "alliance of military, technocrats, and transnational capital" as an attribute of bureaucratic-authoritarianism (Collier and Mahon 1993:850; Collier 1979b:24). Bresser Pereira (1993:70, 1981) refers to a "political coalition . . . based on a fundamental agreement between the bureaucrats, particularly the military, and capitalists." See also Kaufman (1986:89). The term "bureaucratic rings" was coined by Cardoso (1993:171–74).

13. This characteristic is stressed by O'Donnell (1973:53, 92–94, 1978a:13–14) and Collier (1979b:19–25). See also Collier and Collier (1991: chap. 7). The same characteristic is highlighted by Linz (1975:289–90) in his discussion of "bureaucratic-military authoritarian regimes" and by Huntington (1968:219–37) in his discussion of "veto" coups. Stressing this reactionary thrust, Touraine (1989:373–75) goes as far as to propose the label of "anti-popular dictatorships" for the regime types being discussed here.

14. Various labels, such as "traditional," "personalistic," "sultanistic," and "neopatrimonialism," have been elaborated to describe these cases. The problem with drawing a neat boundary between the concept of authoritarianism and these traditional-personalistic forms of rule, however, is exemplified by Linz's discussion of sultanism. Thus, while he consistently stresses that sultanism is "in some respects [a] more modern form of personal rulership," he first argues that "the roots and function of [sultanistic] regimes are radically different" from democracy, authoritarianism, or totalitarianism—the three main types of modern political systems (Linz 1975:253, 252–64)—but subsequently appears to conceptualize sultanistic rule as a subtype of authoritarianism (Linz 1993:62). More recently, however, Linz appears to again conceive of sultanism as a regime type in itself and not as a subtype of authoritarianism (Linz, Stepan, and Gunther 1995:81–83). The distinction between bureaucratic authoritarianism and previous forms of military rule in Latin America is discussed by O'Donnell (1973:95, 111–14) and Collier (1979a). The distinction between bureaucratic authoritarianism and Central American sultanism is discussed by Skocpol (1994:268–75). See also Maira (1986:14–23).

15. On the extension of the concept of bureaucratic authoritarianism to these cases, see Collier (1979c:395–97, 1993:97). The Peruvian 1968–80 case has been conceptualized as a case of organic statism by Stepan (1978). On the distinctiveness of Mexican authoritarianism vis-à-vis bureaucratic authoritarianism, see Kaufman (1977) and Whitehead (1994:327–34). O'Donnell has sometimes included Mexico as a case of bureaucratic authoritarianism, while at other times he has not. Where he does include Mexico as a case of bureaucratic authoritarianism, he does so by distinguishing between types of state and types of regime, and by reformulating the concept of bureaucratic authoritarianism so that it would be rooted in the overarching concept of type of state. On the changing usage of the concept of bureaucratic authoritarianism in O'Donnell's writings, see O'Donnell (1973:95–97, 1978a28–31, 1988:6). This reformulation of the concept of bureaucratic authoritarianism by O'Donnell was brought to my attention by David Collier in a personal communication, June 1, 1993. On reconceptualization efforts that entail a shift in the overarching concept, see Collier and Levitsky (1997:445–48). For an argument concerning the usefulness of retaining the link between the notion of bureaucratic authoritarianism and the concept of political regime, see Fontana (1987: 14–22).

16. China under Deng Xiaoping is better conceived as an example of a post-totalitarian subtype of authoritarianism. On this subtype, see Linz (1975:336–50) and Linz, Stepan, and Gunther (1995:82–83).

17. As Linz (1975:265) and Collier (1979a:402–3) argue, it is important to define regimes in procedural and political terms that are independent of the policies pursued by particular rulers. On the need to dissociate economic policies from the definition of bureaucratic authoritarianism, see also Touraine (1989:369–75).

18. While I use the label "bureaucratic authoritarianism," other efforts to conceptualize the same South American cases have used other terms. For the sake of avoiding the communication problems generated by the proliferation of terms with the same meaning, as well as to acknowledge the pioneering effort by O'Donnell to conceptualize the peculiarities of this political phenomenon, I adopt the better known term "bureaucratic au-

thoritarianism." Some of the other terms used to refer to the same phenomenon include "military-technocratic-bureaucratic authoritarian" regime (Linz 1975:293), "techno-bureaucratic-capitalist authoritarian" regime (Bresser Pereira 1993:70, 1981), "military authoritarianism" (Angell 1984), "modern military authoritarian regime" (Munck 1984: 287–95), "anti-popular dictatorships" (Touraine 1989:369–78), and the "Southern Cone Model" (Whitehead 1985). On the problem of language usage in the social sciences, see Sartori (1984:35–40).

19. This is the manner in which Linz characterizes the subtype of authoritarianism that he labels "bureaucratic-military authoritarian regimes" and that is based on a coalition dominated by army officers and bureaucrats, lacking a commitment to a specific ideology and both forgoing and prohibiting the creation of a mass single party. Linz's definition does not overlap directly with the definition of bureaucratic authoritarianism I have provided and encompasses a broader set of cases than the concept of bureaucratic authoritarianism. Indeed, Linz sees bureaucratic-military authoritarian regimes as occurring more frequently than any of the other subtypes of authoritarianism that he identifies with the labels "organic statist," "post-democratic and post-colonial mobilizational," "personal," and "post-totalitarian." But as Linz's discussion of bureaucratic authoritarianism within the context of his elaborations on bureaucratic-military authoritarian regimes shows, Linz certainly considers cases of bureaucratic authoritarianism as encompassed by the concept of bureaucratic-military authoritarian regimes. His comment concerning the paradigmatic status of bureaucratic-military authoritarian regimes therefore also applies to bureaucratic authoritarianism (Linz 1975: 281, 277–350; 1993).

20. This fact probably accounts in part for the significance of the debate on bureaucratic authoritarianism within comparative politics as a whole, and regime analysis in particular, and for what would otherwise clearly be the unjustifiable influence on our thinking of a small set of cases. On the distinction between members that are more-or-less central to a concept, and on typical examples, see Lakoff (1987: chap. 2, 86–87, 267, 288–89).

21. By advancing our understanding of the challenge associated with the problems authoritarian rulers face after taking power, this study seeks to fill a relative gap in the study of authoritarianism. As Linz stated back in 1975—and little has changed in this regard—"the analysis of many authoritarian regimes has been limited by the perspective introduced by a one-sided emphasis on the origins of such regimes as cases of military intervention in politics without further analysis of their functioning after having been established by a coup" (Linz 1975:284). Studies of transitions from authoritarian rule have thus been quite weak when it comes to spelling out the link between the previous regime type and the transitional process. A notable exception is Linz and Stepan (1996: chap. 4).

22. The distinctiveness of bureaucratic authoritarianism, and authoritarianism more generally, is stressed by O'Donnell (1973:94) and Linz (1964:293–95, 1975:178–79).

23. A similar argument is advanced by O'Donnell (1979), Schmitter (1973:231–32), Stepan (1978:296–97, 301–16), Unger (1990:94–109), and Drake (1996:44–52). See also Linz (1973a:202–5), Barrera and Valenzuela (1986:230–31), Smith (1989:160), and Hagopian (1994:38–39, 45–46).

24. On the notion of conflicting imperatives, see Gould (1994).

25. The solitude of bureaucratic authoritarian rulers is aptly described by O'Donnell (1979:311) as "that of a state that, from the apex of its institutions, loudly proclaims the importance of the tasks it is performing and announces a future of greatness, and yet does not receive in return even the echo of its voice. This discourse is lost in the silence

of the excluded and coerced sectors. . . . That such a discourse is merely a monologue suggests to the rulers the depth of the mystery regarding what is in fact occurring behind the silence of civil society." See also Oszlak (1987:35, 38).

26. In the context of bureaucratic authoritarianism, splits within the governing elite can assume a number of forms. As Stepan (1971:253–66, 1988:30–44) has proposed, it is possible to distinguish between three basic aspects of the military as an actor in these military-based authoritarian regimes: the military as government, the security community, and the military as institution. Although most analyses of bureaucratic authoritarianism stress the split between the military as institution and the military as government, divisions can also emerge both within the military as institution and within the military as government, as well as across any of these three different aspects.

27. Besides Imperial Germany, Linz (1973a:204) refers to the negative integration performed by the social democratic opposition parties in the nineteenth century and by the Communist parties in the 1970s. For his part, Morlino (1995b) sees the role of the Communist trade unions in Italy during the 1950s as a clear example of negative integration.

28. In other words, rather than use these channels to represent interests, and given the option to express their attitude toward the military's project, workers will use their voice to change the entire system. Drawing on Hirschman's (1970, 1992:89–94) concepts of exit, voice, and loyalty somewhat loosely, given that he links the exit option to the market realm and not to the political realm, workers are never given any reason to be loyal under bureaucratic authoritarianism and, given the option of exercising their voice, they use it not to introduce changes *within* the system but to advance a change *of* the system. In this case, therefore, the option of voice and exit are mutually reinforcing rather than mutually exclusive, as Hirschman seems to imply. For applications of these concepts to authoritarian regimes, see Misztal (1993). On the impossibility of negative integration in the context of authoritarianism, see Linz (1973a:204, 1975:294).

29. Giddens (1987:250–51) develops this argument in a different manner. He argues that the endurance of forms of rule like bureaucratic authoritarianism depends on the government's gaining "a considerable measure of popular legitimacy. . . . The more it achieves such legitimacy, the more it becomes enmeshed in an administrative order distinct from the military sphere through which governmental control was obtained."

30. Rouquié (1986:111) stresses that "the 'doctrine of national security' which in one form or another is shared by these military governments, provides a discourse or language that serves temporarily to disguise their illegitimacy, but it is incapable of generating a new and permanent source of legitimacy. . . . Briefly, the theory of national security cannot substitute for a legitimating ideology." Nonetheless, it does perform "the internal function of forging and mobilizing a consensus within the military institution." See also Linz (1973b:235, 240), Stepan (1971:172–87), O'Donnell (1976:207–13, 222–23), and Touraine (1989:370–71). Much has been written on the Doctrine of National Security. Some important sources are Arriagada and Garretón (1978), Comblin (1980), Arriagada (1981), Varas and Agüero (1984), Alves (1985: part 1), and Pion-Berlin (1989: chap. 5).

31. On the problem of legitimizing formulas in the context of authoritarianism and on the military's attempt to justify their break of the constitutional order through the promise of democracy in the future, see Linz (1964:322, 1973a:186–87, 1973b:239), Rouquié (1986:110–11, 1987a:345–50), and O'Donnell (1979:289–90).

32. Others have argued, in a complementary formulation, that this unresolved "legitimacy problem" constitutes "the Achilles' heel of these types of regime" (O'Donnell and Schmitter 1986:15). The dovetailing of the analysis of the dynamics of bureaucratic au-

thoritarianism and its demise is not coincidental. As Cardoso (1986:151) correctly points out, "the transition from an authoritarian regime . . . tells us something about the dynamics of authoritarian regimes."

33. The response to the problem of representation shapes—to use a notion developed in social movement theory—the political opportunity structure of labor.

34. While the illegitimacy of bureaucratic authoritarianism does not directly lead to its downfall, as Przeworski (1991:54–55) argues, the continued illegitimacy of the project of negative integration can be seen to have an impact on the formation of labor as a political actor and on the role of labor as an opposition force under bureaucratic authoritarianism. Thus, the illegitimacy of bureaucratic authoritarianism has an impact on the political dynamics of this form of government, not through the link of public opinion as measured at the individual level, an approach that would be consonant with the political culture literature of the 1960s, but rather through the process of actor formation and the constitution of a counterhegemonic force (Tarrow 1994:120–22, 1992:181–86). The process by which labor is reconstituted as a political actor, indeed, is part of what Garretón (1989b:273) refers to as the "invisible transition to democracy."

35. See also Linz (1975:266, 1964:300), Cardoso (1979:43–44), and Perlmutter (1981:169).

36. This argument represents an adaptation of Sabel's (1981) model of internal union politics to an authoritarian context. See also Barrera and Valenzuela (1986:231, 236–40).

37. If the rulers sought to gain legitimacy by reaching out to society in an attempt to reincorporate the excluded sectors, even if in a managed manner, they would have to allow societal organizations certain freedoms, especially so that their leadership could be renewed or confirmed as representative. For without the support of forces that could be deemed representative, the rulers would remain just as isolated as they were at the beginning. Once representative forces do emerge, however, they are difficult to manage—that is, they are likely to turn into an antisystem opposition force. This argument is hardly novel. Indeed, a key finding in the study of labor politics has been that labor tends to adopt more "radical"—antisystem—postures when confronted by authoritarian and arbitrary forms of rule. On the thesis that labor becomes more radical in the face of intransigent rulers, see Lipset (1983), Collier and Collier (1991), Mann (1993:28–29, 510–12, 680–82, 724–29, chaps. 17 and 18), and Hall (1994:42–47).

38. Stated in terms of the distinction introduced by Mann (1986a:113, 1993:59–61), the problem that bureaucratic authoritarian rulers face is that while they are able to advance their goals on the basis of the state's despotic power, they are unable to develop the state's infrastructural power. On the importance of considering the connection between both types of power, see Hall (1994:xi–xii).

39. Kaufman (1986:89–100) argues that the withdrawal of support by economic elites is a key factor explaining the demise of bureaucratic authoritarianism, while Linz (1975:290) also stresses the central importance of the governing elite's allies to the stability of such forms of government. See also O'Donnell (1978a), Faucher (1981:18–34), and Martins (1986).

40. In Chile, the persistently high level of fear among the economic elites accounted for their continued support of the Pinochet-led government, but a transition from bureaucratic authoritarianism occurred nonetheless. On the Chilean case, see Silva (1992/93).

41. Various authors have pointed out that one of the things the civilian technocrats offered the military was an ideology in the form of an economic discourse that would disguise their own lack of an ideology that could legitimate their rule. For example, Pion-Berlin, writing on the Argentine case, argues that "the junta was in missionary search

for an economic formula that would not only lead to recovery but that would automatically induce support for the Proceso, sparing it the burden of political discourse and practice" (Pion-Berlin 1989:118; see also O'Donnell 1981:207–10). As O'Donnell (1988: 191–95) writes, however, the economic discourse never displaces the military's supremacy in policy, for the armed forces always retained, via the coup they engineered, the "right of access to the institutional apex of the state."

42. Some authors see the withdrawal of business support for bureaucratic authoritarianism as indicating a split within bureaucratic authoritarianism, but it is important to avoid the potential confusion associated with such usage. In this book, the common thesis concerning splits "within the regime" is taken to refer to a split within the governing elites and not within the broader coalition that supports the governing elites.

43. Mann (1986b:521) makes the same point in stating: "Autonomous 'despotic' powers exercised by a centralized political elite . . . are precarious and temporary."

Chapter 3: The Installation of Military Rulers, and the Assault on Labor in Argentina, 1976

1. There was a first meeting of the coup-plotters on July 1, 1974, the very day Perón died, and contacts between the military and the civilians that would eventually prepare the way for the March 1976 coup started in August 1975, when Martínez de Hoz began to propose his economic program to high military officers. In early October 1975, Dr. Ricardo Yofre, who would become President Videla's general subsecretary, approached General Suárez Mason with a political plan for a future military government. Subsequently, a team with two representatives from each of the three branches of the armed forces was formed to harmonize the divergent proposals concerning the nature of the military's intervention in government. These discussions led to the elaboration of a document entitled "Basis for the Intervention of the Armed Forces" ("Bases para la Intervención de las Fuerzas Armadas"). On the July 1974 meeting, see Canitrot (1983:20). On Videla's Christmas speech, see Kandel and Monteverde (1976:150–52, 209–10). On the contacts between the military and civilians and the intramilitary discussions, see Epstein (1987:89), Fraga (1988:246–47, 258–62), Vázquez (1985:19–28), and Jordán (1993: 37–38). The "Basis for the Intervention of the Armed Forces" document is reproduced in Junta Militar (1980:13–24).

2. Much has been made of O'Donnell's (1973) supposedly deterministic structural explanation of the origins of bureaucratic authoritarianism, an explanation that is usually counterposed to Linz's (1978) more probabilistic theory of the breakdown of democracy. But as O'Donnell's (1973:147–48) game theoretic analysis of Argentina's 1966 coup shows, what O'Donnell emphasizes are the structural and macro factors that constrain the behavior of political actors and lead a certain set of actors, as rational actors pursuing their interests, to support a coup. What is missing in O'Donnell's theory of the origins of bureaucratic authoritarianism is an explicit consideration of the variable ability of different political systems to manage the tensions associated with the capital-labor cleavage, a matter fully addressed in the magisterial work by Collier and Collier (1991).

3. "Incorporation," as Collier and Collier (1991:3) define it, refers to "the legalization and institutionalization of a labor movement sanctioned and regulated by the state."

4. O'Donnell (1973: chaps. 3 and 4, 1978b), Waisman (1987), Collier and Collier (1991:484–97, 721–42).

5. The coup against Perón in 1955 opened a complex picture. Now that Peronism had lost control of the state, unions developed in a more autonomous manner, but they were

still firmly Peronist unions. This means that because of the electoral proscription of the Peronist party, the 62 Organizations, formed in 1957, acted as a political actor substituting for the Peronist party. If recovering some aspects as a social actor, the union movement became the organizational core of a political movement (Abós 1983).

6. In the wake of the Cordobazo, which triggered the replacement of General Onganía and raised the spectrum of much broader and radical change, Perón eventually prevailed. He had made himself indispensable—only he could hold together the centrifugal forces that the military were unable to contain. Thus, President Lanusse held talks with Perón, and the talks soon led to the lifting of the political ban that had prohibited Peronists from running for the presidency since 1955, and to the end of Perón's eighteen-year exile in late 1972. On the transition from military rule, see O'Donnell (1988: chaps. 8 and 10).

7. Because of an exclusionary clause in the electoral law that framed the transition in 1972–73, Perón himself was not allowed to run for office. He thus decided to stay in Spain during late 1972 and early 1973, while national elections, held in March 1973, led to a Peronist government headed by Héctor Cámpora. Perón then returned to the country on a permanent basis on June 20, 1973. New elections were quickly held in September 1973, and, having won 62 percent of the votes, Perón assumed the presidency in October 1973. On the 1973–76 period, see De Riz (1981), Torre (1983a), Munck with Falcón and Gallitelli (1987: chap. 14), and Jordán (1993: chap. 1).

8. While in exile, Perón had encouraged the formation of leftist unions and a guerrilla organization as a way to prevent the consolidation of power by those sectors of Peronism that might seek to pursue the option of promoting a "Peronism without Perón," as some prominent union leaders, such as Augusto Vandor, sought to pursue. On changes within Peronism during 1955–73, see O'Donnell (1988:230–35), Collier and Collier (1991:493–97, 723–27, 731, 737–39), James (1988), and McGuire (1997: chaps. 4 and 5). On the Peronist left, see James (1976), Gillespie (1982), and Moyano (1995).

9. The new Law of Professional Associations, approved in November 1973, granted important powers to the central bodies located in Buenos Aires to remove leaders of union locals or regional branches. On the move against Tosco, see Roldán (1978) and Brennan (1994).

10. These decrees are reproduced and discussed in Deheza (1981:100–103).

11. According to O'Donnell (1988:24–28, 142, 302–5, 1981:202), who distinguishes between five levels of crises, the crisis preceding Argentina's 1976 coup corresponded to a "crisis of social domination," the highest level of crisis he distinguishes. See also Munck (1989:68). For an assessment that sees a lower degree of threat, see Drake (1988: 375–76).

12. An insider's account is that of Minister of Defense Deheza (1981). Negotiations between the military and various party leaders are chronicled, from the perspective of the army, by Fraga (1988: chap. 5).

13. I use the phrase "war against subversion" in the place of the Spanish phrase "lucha contra la subversión." In doing so, I do not intend to subscribe to the same diagnostic and policy prescription underlying Argentina's "dirty war." Rather, I seek to retain the sense of a phrase that the military used to define a "problem area."

14. The reconstruction of these events is based on accounts in newspaper reports, as well as on accounts provided by journalists (Kandel and Monteverde 1976; Vázquez 1985); by the minister of defense at the time of the coup, who provides an account of the two meetings he held with the three commanders-in-chief during the course of March 23 (Deheza 1981:236–44); by the minister of labor, Miguel Unamuno (1982); and by the general secretary of the CGT at the time of the coup, Casildo Herreras (1985, 1987).

15. Although an explanation of the peculiar interim institutional arrangement set up by the Argentine military goes beyond the aim of this book, it is worth pointing out that the arrangement entailed a fairly complex set of rules that had been discussed and decided on in the period leading up to the coup and that made sense in terms of the previous experiences in government of the military as well as the military's perception of the nature of the problems against which they were reacting.

16. Rouquié (1982b:15, 19, 1987:294–96) still places the 1966–73 military period in the same category as the 1976–83 one. Both are named as "constituent dictatorships" *(dictaduras constituyentes)*, in contrast to the "provisional" or "caretaker" military experience between 1955–58 and the experience with military rule under a civilian guise in 1962. On the military's corporate pact, see Fontana (1987:40–41).

17. The most important documents are the "Proclamation of the Process of National Reorganization" (March 24, 1976), the "Act for the Process of National Reorganization" (March 29, 1976), the "Purpose and Basic Objectives of the Process of National Reorganization" (March 24, 1976), the "Statute for the Process of National Reorganization" (March 24, 1976), and Law No. 21256 (March 24, 1976). The first four of these documents are reproduced in Troncoso (1984:107–11) and Junta Militar (1980:7–12, 25–28). Law No. 21256 is reproduced in Vázquez (1985:218–22).

18. It should be kept in mind that the phrase "commander-in-chief" of each branch of the armed forces refers to a translation of *comandante en jefe*, a position in the direct line of command.

19. In contrast to the fate that befell Congress, the Supreme Court was not abolished. The independence of the Supreme Court was severely limited, because in accepting the constitutive powers of the junta the court rendered itself incapable of interpreting the constitution independently, engaging perforce in juridical debates within a reality where the law had little relevance. While seeking to maintain the fiction of an independent judiciary, the government clearly conceived of its political power as being "without juridical nor factual limits" and always acted as if it were invested with attributes and powers of an implicit and generic nature, not limited by the law. Groisman (1987a:63, 67). Not only had the military rulers asserted—in one of their basic legal documents, the "Statute for the Process of National Reorganization"—that their actions were based on a constituent power *(poder constituyente)* that placed the "Statute" as well as the "Purpose and Basic Objectives of the Process of National Reorganization" over the constitution itself. Beyond this, in the day-to-day practice, the military used unrestricted discretion at every step—and that was most evident in their holding of citizens in detention, at the disposition of the Executive Power, without ever going through ordinary procedures of accusation, presentation of evidence, and sentencing. In these cases of arrests, the discretionary power of the Executive was invoked, in effect saying that this power was not subject to rules, not juridically controllable, and finally, not requiring any foundation or basis whatsoever. It is not surprising that the extreme cases of arbitrariness were found in the interaction between urban guerrillas and the armed forces. On these grounds, a legalistic discourse rapidly and easily turned into a discourse of summary justice. Thus, underlying the uncertain legal status of many activities carried out by the military was the existence of a power that did not recognize limits. In certain instances, the military did not even go along with its own norms. Indeed, as Linz (1975:287) argues, in the case of "bureaucratic-military authoritarian regimes" there is a "distortion or perversion of legality."

From the point of view of a government that only partially recognized limits of a legal nature and that was accustomed to acting on the basis of "reasons of state" with great discretion, the Supreme Court did not represent a threat. In cynical fashion, the role of this court was seen as granting a modicum of legitimacy to the military rulers, which its abolition would have erased. The cost of leaving the Supreme Court in operation was seen as fairly insignificant. Nonetheless, to avoid the possibility of unfavorable rulings upon taking power, the military rulers removed from the Supreme Court and high tribunals judges deemed to be suspicious. On the justice system, see Groisman (1987b:14, 6), Inter-American Commission on Human Rights of the Organization of American States (1980:22–34), Comisión Nacional sobre la Desaparición de Personas (1985: chap. 3), Foro de Estudios Sobre la Administracion de Justicia (1985), Guest (1990:25–27), Jordán (1993:46, 49), and Ietswaart (1980).

20. For a further discussion of the powers of the junta, see Vanossi (1976:45).

21. Because the faculties of the CAL were reduced to advice, lacking any political power, its importance derived from its function as a representative of military opinion. The participation of the three branches was ensured by the regulatory norms that made the presidency of the body rotate each year, called for the formation of subcommittees, demanded the presence of all three branches for the body to meet, and required that decisions be approved by an absolute majority. The impact of the CAL was given or circumscribed by the classification of a proposed law or bill as of "transcendental significance" or not. Although bills could be submitted by either the Executive Power or the junta, the power to decide what classification was given resided ultimately in the junta. Bills deemed not to be of "transcendental significance" could be ratified and promulgated immediately—that is, signed into law by the Executive Power. Those of "transcendental significance" went to the CAL and needed the "provisional opinion" of the corresponding subcommittee and the "definitive opinion" of the plenary session of the CAL. Thereafter, in cases where the Executive Power shared the view approved by the CAL, the bill was signed into law. When there was a discrepancy in views, it was the criterion of the junta that ultimately prevailed. On the CAL, see Castiglione (1992:35–37).

22. There was a slight variation in cases where military issues were to be considered. In those cases, the Joint Chief of Staff took the place of the secretaries general.

23. The matter would not be resolved until August 1978, at which time the presidency began to be occupied by a retired officer.

24. Subsequently, in October 1976, a ninth ministry was created. This ministry, the ministry of planning, was occupied by General Ramón Genaro Díaz Bessone. García Delgado and Stiletano (1988:71–73), Buchanan (1987:352–53), Jordán (1993:51–55).

25. Memories of the previous experience with bureaucratic authoritarianism, which had been seriously undermined by the Corbobazo uprising and widespread labor militancy, were still close to the surface.

26. On the selection process whereby the commanders of the armed forces selected Martínez de Hoz as minister of economy from among various candidates between the end of 1975 and beginning of 1976, see Fontana (1985:100) and Epstein (1987:89).

27. In the case of the governorships, the army received 50 percent of the governorships, with the other half being evenly split between the navy and the air force. These positions were occupied by retired officers, with the exception of the province of Tucumán and the national territory of Tierra del Fuego, Antarctica, and the Islands of the South Atlantic. A detailed and complete breakdown of the distribution of secretaryships, governorships, and other important public posts is in García Delgado and Stiletano (1988:74–77, 79–87). For further details on military and civilian participation in the government, see Carta Política (1976a), Buchanan (1987:351–53), Ricci and Fitch (1990), and Castiglione (1992: chap. 3). The lack of civilian participation is noted in Jordán (1993:38–39, 50–51).

28. As some military officers later admitted, this attempt to share power equally

among the three services can account for many of the flaws of Argentina's experience with military rule. See Bignone (1992:60), Fitch (1988:A32–A33), and Oszlak (1987:39).

29. On the importance of the previous level of threat, see O'Donnell (1988:142, 24–31, 138–44, 1978a:7–9), who argues: "The crisis that preceded the June 1966 coup was much less severe than the one that preceded the coup of March 1976." The greater degree of internal cohesion displayed by the military in 1976, in contrast to 1966, is stressed by Deheza (1981:186–210) and by Fraga (1988:253, 261).

30. The lack of coordination at the top was dramatized most patently in the desperate and frustrated search for information by relatives of the *"desaparecidos"* (disappeared).

31. Compared with the other branches of the military, the army had a greater degree of participation and responsibility in the "war against subversion." The task was carried out along the lines of four military zones, each headed by a corps commander or division general. Each zone consisted of some five provinces, and within these zones all military personnel, including police forces, responded directly to the corps commander. Even the provincial governors had to respond to army division generals. On the logistics of the military's terror machine, see Inter-American Commission on Human Rights of the Organization of American States (1980), Comisión Nacional sobre la Desaparición de Personas (1985), Guest (1990:36–48), Fernández (1983), Mittelbach (1986), Moyano (1991: 56–64), Pion-Berlin (1989:102-4), Brysk (1994:36–40), and Verbitsky (1996). For the intellectual background for such actions, see Hodges (1991: chaps. 5–7) and the writings of the minister of planning following the 1976 coup, General Díaz Bessone (1986).

32. On March 24, 1976, the activities of all political parties were suspended and many organizations, as well as a number of political parties—such as the Revolutionary Communist Party (Partido Comunista Revolucionario), the Socialist Workers Party (Partido Socialista de los Trabajadores), the Trotskyist Worker Party (Partido Obrero Trotskista), and the Marxist-Leninist Communist Party (Partido Comunista Marxista-Leninista)—were simply dissolved. Finally, a long list of people lost their political and union rights when the military junta passed an Act of Institutional Responsibility (Acta de Responsabilidad Institucional) on June 23, 1976. That act was subsequently regulated by Law No. 21650 on October 19, 1977. Inter-American Commission on Human Rights of the Organization of American States (1980:16–20, 245–47), Jordán (1993:46).

33. D'Abate (1980), Decker (1983:94–100), Fernández (1985:60–68), Gallitelli and Thompson (1982:146–49), Kogan, Bialakowsky, and Micieli (1986:360–61).

34. The military overseers or trustees *(interventores)*, who were named by the labor minister, were vested with all the legal and statutory attributions of the union's executive and deliberative bodies. Military "intervention" of a union usually consisted of one military overseer and four or five military advisers. On April 23, 1976, resolution No. 106 of the labor ministry set the powers of the military overseers. These included both deliberative and executive powers. On December 3, 1976, Decree No. 898 provided for even broader powers.

One of the main reasons given for the removal of labor leaders was that they were unrepresentative, as could be substantiated by the evidence of corruption in managing of union funds. This accusation was not new in Argentine union politics and was later to be launched against the military overseers themselves—for example, in the case of the auto workers' union (SMATA). For the case of SMATA under military control, see Rodríguez (1983). More frequently than not, the military would announce that it was conducting some investigation into the corrupt management of unions, only to never present any conclusive evidence later on. For an example of a typical accusation made by the military, see the report of the military overseer of the bank workers' union (Asociación Bancaria), reproduced in *Informes Laborales* (Documentación e Información Laboral-DIL), no. o. 196/7 (June–July 1976): 1/722–1/723. This report was made public in July 1976 by the labor ministry as proof of the "irregularities" in the management of union affairs. Similar accusations were made by the military overseers of the metal workers' union, the port workers' union, the meat workers' federation (Federación Gremial de la Industria de la Carne), and others.

35. In May 1976, furthermore, two laws dissolved other politically oriented labor groups: the Movement for Labor Unity and Coordination (Movimiento de Unidad y Coordinación Sindical), the Base Union Movement (Movimiento Sindical de Base), the Union Bloc of Authentic Peronism (Bloque Sindical del Peronismo Auténtico), and the Peronist Working Youth (Juventud Trabajadora Peronista).

36. Among the five initially affected were the electrical workers' union, the Union of Public Employees of the Province of Córdoba (Sindicato de Empleados Públicos de la Provincia de Córdoba), and the state workers' union (ATE).

37. The most important unions put under government control on March 31 included the telephone workers (FOETRA), the metal workers (UOM), the construction workers (UOCRA), the journalists union (FATPREN), the state oil workers (Federación de Sindicatos Unidos Petroleros del Estado), the textile workers (AOT), the auto workers, the meat workers (Federación Gremial del Personal de la Industria de la Carne y sus Derivados), and the longshoremen (Federación de Estibadores Portuarios Argentinos). Some of the more important new organizations put under trusteeship in April were those belonging to teachers (Unión Docentes Argentinos), maritime workers (Sindicato Argentino de Obreros Navales), state gas workers (Federación Argentina del Personal de Gas del Estado and Sindicato de Trabajadores de Gas del Estado-Capital Federal), light and power workers (FATLyF and the Sindicato Luz y Fuerza-Capital Federal), printing workers (Sindicato Gráfico Argentino), railroad workers (Unión Ferroviaria), bank workers (Asociación Bancaria), and municipal workers (Unión de Obreros y Empleados Municipales-Capital Federal). By the end of 1976 the number of "intervened" unions had risen to fifty-seven. *Informes Laborales* (DIL), no. 195 (May 1976): 1/709–1/710; *Informes Laborales* (DIL), no. 196/7 (June–July 1976): 1/713–1/714; Trabajadores y Sindicalistas Argentinos en el Exilio (1979:54–55).

38. The only large union not affected was the confederation of commerce workers (Confederación General de Empleados del Comercio de la República Argentina [CGEC]).

39. As a central element of the labor ministry's carrot-and-stick policy, Law No. 21356, sanctioned on July 22, 1976, empowered the labor ministry both to extend the mandate of elected union leaders at the head of their organizations and to remove the leaders of said organizations. The extension of the mandate of elected union leaders was part of the government's arsenal of options to selectively reward compliant union leaders.

40. The number and names of detained union leaders remained unknown for a long time, even though the government promised to release this information. By the end of May 1976 there was still no official count. *Informes Laborales* (DIL), no. 195 (May 1976): 1/704. Based on data provided by Fernández (1985:113–34), the number of union leaders arrested declined from 268 in 1976, to 69 in 1977, to 7 in 1978, to 10 in 1979, and to 9 thereafter. See also Epstein (1989:180).

41. The union's social service network, funded through the government-mandated employer withholding of a percentage of workers' wages and salaries, constituted an invaluable source for workers to access health care. In fact, it was in many cases the key reason for a worker to join a union and pay dues. It was also one source of the unions' economic power, and the corruption of union leaders. The social service network was one of the few aspects of union life that continued to function after the 1976 coup, even

though changes were introduced in the management of the Obras Sociales. With the "intervention" of unions, their corresponding Obras Sociales were also taken over by the military overseers, although some unions still under labor control likewise lost control over their Obras Sociales. All in all, 90 percent of all Obras Sociales ceased to be directly controlled by unions, their administration depending on the National Institute of Obras Sociales (Instituto Nacional de Obras Sociales [INOS]), which was in turn put under military control. The motivation for this policy was the military's perception that control over the vast financial resources represented by the Obras Sociales gave labor leaders too much power and leverage. Along a somewhat different line, the military also saw the issue of the Obras Sociales as a useful battle horse. Pointing to the corrupt management of these funds by some union leaders, a blanket criticism of corruption was made, with the purpose of undermining the prestige and credibility of all labor leaders in the eyes of union members. Cortés (1985), Neri (1982:131–39).

42. Because the activities concerned with the internal administration of unions and their Obras Sociales were legally allowed, the labor ministry could authorize the holding of assemblies and congresses for these purposes.

43. Collective bargaining, regulated by the Law of Collective Bargaining (Ley de Convenios Colectivos de Trabajo), was prohibited under Decree No. 9/76, which canceled collective bargaining schemes for an indefinite time. With this prohibition, labor unions lost one of their main raison d'être. Yet the loss of this mechanism does not reveal the whole picture. The military came up with a complex and changing scheme for setting wages. Although the government set general wage levels—primarily through a "wage sheet" (planilla) method that used the format of pre-1976 collective bargaining agreements as a guideline to establish base wages industry by industry—starting in March 1977 a feature known as the "flexibility margin," which allowed employers to increase wages by a certain percentage above the wage-sheet maximums, was introduced. Such flexibility margins were increased from 10 percent to 75 percent by August 1978, before being freed in September 1979. The significance of this wage-setting scheme is that the negotiations that previously took place on an industry-wide basis *(por rama)*, between the unions or federations and business chambers, now occurred within each particular firm, where shop stewards engaged in deliberations with management over wages. (Law No. 21356 granted shop stewards a restricted right to engage in this type of bargaining.) The task of collective bargaining was effectively decentralized, and the centralized power of unions and federations was weakened. For a detailed discussion of the complex and ever-changing wage policy pursued by the military rulers, see Munck (1990b: 445–50), Decker (1983:59–66), and Slodky (1987).

44. On the previous legal framework of industrial relations, see Munck (1990b: 84–93).

45. The report of the Comisión Nacional sobre la Desaparición de Personas (1985:296) states that 30 percent of the disappeared were workers, while another 18 percent were employees.

46. Short of using state terror, the military could control worker representatives through legal means. The labor ministry's discretionary power, indeed, reached beyond unions into the workplace, where it could replace shop-stewards *(delegados)* and members of the factory *(comisiones internas)*.

47. Blacklisting of employees was practiced in several firms, but the record of business varied greatly. Some employers would paternalistically warn certain workers that they "had better leave"—that is, resign from their employment for their own good. This behavior could be cynically seen as in the interest of business, as just another way of rationalizing production during a downturn in the business cycle. But at the time, firings

could be practiced with little or no pretext, and in the case of marked workers many times the only other option was an exit of a more permanent nature. In other cases, employers participated willingly in the repression. The variation had much to do with the size of the firm and the nationality of the ownership, with the worst horror stories coming out of transnational corporations, such as Ford. Personal conversation with Héctor Palomino, Buenos Aires, 1987, Pion-Berlin (1989:111–12), Pozzi (1988a:145–48), Fernández (1985:56), Abós (1984:12–13), Agrupación Clasista 1o. de Mayo (1986:18).

48. The number of employees in the national administration, having increased from 583,000 in 1970 to 732,000 in 1975, fell to 666,000 by 1980. Similarly, the number of employees in state enterprises and public banks, which increased from 370,000 in 1970 to 444,000 in 1975, fell to 315,000 by 1980. The job decline in the state enterprises was higher than the overall level of 16 percent, being in the order of 30 percent for the period between 1975–80. (The figures correspond to the end of the year.) Fundación de Investigaciones Económicas Latinoamericanas (1987:102). For data on individual state enterprises, see Dimase (1981).

49. Canitrot (1980, 1981, 1983), Smith (1989: chap. 9), Schvarzer (1987a), Foxley (1983).

50. Various economists agree that the monetarist approach to the balance of payments, starting in December 1978, both dealt the death blow to a model of economic accumulation that had been supported by the Peronist coalition and at the same time led to the growth of that coalition. Kosacoff (1993:21–23), Damill and Frenkel (1992:5–19).

Chapter 4: The Military's Project and the Reconstitution of Labor in Argentina, 1976–1979

1. For official statements that confirm such a perception, see Fontana (1987:63, 105–6). Notwithstanding this shared sense that the threat had been contained, as figures that estimate the number of casualties of state terror show, high levels of repression continued until at least late in 1977. Thus, using data of the National Commission on Disappeared People (CONADEP), Moyano (1991:53) estimates that, while 3,485 people were kidnapped and presumed killed in 1976, the figure was 2,544 in 1977, down to 830 in 1978, and at 148 in 1979. See also Fernández Meijide (1988:26–32).

2. This public statement was made in June 1977. Earlier, on April 4, 1977, President Videla had issued a statement in which he argued that his government had completed "the fundamental stage of basic ordering" (quoted in Troncoso 1985:13–14). (These quotations from Spanish sources, as well as all subsequent ones, have been translated by the author.)

3. It is important to stress that the decisions regarding the fundamental course of the Proceso were always left to the military rulers themselves. There was certainly a functional convergence between the technocrats that made up the economic team around Martínez de Hoz and the military, based on the complementarity between the goals of Martínez de Hoz's economic program and the military's general goals. But such a functional convergence did not prevent basic disagreement between the military and the economic team from emerging. What is crucial, therefore, is that the resolutions of these disputed areas were given according to the internal power struggles within the military itself. That is, Martínez de Hoz's power hinged on the support he could gain within the military, rather than on any independent source of power. I therefore agree with Fontana (1985:96–98, 1987:52–59, 59–60), who places political power squarely in the hands of the military corporation, a point he underlines by arguing that the civilian

proposals of a political economic plan were subordinated to the dictates of the National Security Doctrine.

4. In April 1977, President Videla had explicitly referred to the kind of interlocutors the government had in mind for any future dialogue: "We believe today, now that we have passed the fundamental stage of basic ordering, that it is possible and necessary to open a dialogue that only excludes the corrupt, the economic delinquent or the subversive delinquent" (quoted in Troncoso 1985:13–14). In August 1977, moreover, President Videla gave some indication of the purpose of such a dialogue: "The Armed Forces consider that to start a new instance in the history of the country it is necessary to conceive a political project which, drawing on previous experiences, would be capable of structuring a convergence between civilians and soldiers behind a common project. . . . The concretization of the proposal will also imply the gradual participation of civilians in the 'Process of National Reorganization'; only the subversives and the corrupt will be excluded, and participation will be on an individual basis and not through groups" (quoted in Troncoso 1985:50–51).

5. President Videla did refer again to the political proposal and the role of a dialogue within it in March 1978, but there was little overt reference to such a proposal until early 1979.

6. The study of state-labor relations actually provides a more suitable way of addressing the problems associated with the military's search for responsible allies than the study of the formation of a much rumored official party—the Movement of National Opinion (MON)—to embody the civilian-military convergence that Videla referred to on several occasions and that was envisioned as the vehicle through which the military would create a permanent political legacy. The problem with focusing on the MON is that the formation of such an official party was never seriously addressed, so there was nothing comparable to the rich record of state-labor relations during this period. For this reason, I address the challenge the military confronted in seeking allies, by focusing on the military's attempt to fashion a labor actor that would support its project.

7. A dialogue between officers of the armed forces and the unionists was not an unusual occurrence in Argentine labor history. It had been a central characteristic of the union movement ever since its initial contacts with Perón in 1943, and it was never interrupted, even during periods of repressive military rule. The familiar Spanish phrase "jugar la interna militar" captures the importance of the military's internal politics within union strategizing, which makes sense in terms of "el sueño del coronel propio" (the dream of one's own colonel) which, Rouquié (1982c:68, 1982b:28) argues, afflicts all sectors of society. Delich (1982a:145–46, 1982b:110).

8. On April 1, 1976, a meeting initiated by unionist Otto Calace took place, with more than fifty unionists and the military overseers *(interventores)* of the (CGT) participating. The following day there was another meeting, smaller in size, of the same unionists, who decided to petition to have an interview with the CGT's military overseers, the labor minister, and the president. A six-member commission (Comisión de 6) was formed, led by Calace, Rivas, Pérez, Raviti, Maldonado, and Blanco. On April 7, in another meeting, the formation of a liaison commission (Comisión de Enlace) to establish contacts with military authorities was announced. There had been a debate between two options. One option was to form an Advisory Committee (Comisión Asesora) to the CGT's military overseers, which by entering into dialogue with the authorities hoped to affect their actions. The second option, which gained majority support, was to form a liaison commission made up of twelve members, which would interact with the military overseers of the CGT while maintaining greater independence and distance from the government. The Group of 8 (Grupo de los 8), which also maintained early contacts with mili-

tary officers, remained at the margin of these developments. Two weeks later, they would unsuccessfully attempt to hold a plenary meeting of labor organizations as a step preceding official contacts with the government. *Informes Laborales* (DIL), no. 194 (April 1976): 1/686–87; Fernández (1985:73).

9. These offices were largely preserves of the army. During the entire Proceso the labor ministers were General Liendo (March 1976–February 1979), General Llamil Reston (February 1979–March 1981), Brigadier Julio César Porcile (March 1981–July 1982), and Héctor Villaveirán (July 1982–October 1983). The military overseers of the CGT were Colonel D. Emilio Alfredo Fabbrizzi (March 24, 1976–April 28, 1976), Colonel Juan Alberto Pita (April 28, 1976–May 30, 1976), Commodore Julio César Porcile (June 15, 1976–January 30, 1978), Colonel José Hipólito Nuñez (January 30, 1978–January 17, 1979), and Colonel Rolando Valentín Rojas (January 17, 1979–November 29, 1979). After the new Law of Professional Associations was sanctioned, Colonel Rolando Rojas acted as administrator of the former CGT and later was designated the CGT's "liquidator" *(liquidador)*. Finally, on July 20, 1983, Valentín Suárez was named "normalizing delegate" *(delegado normalizador)* in charge of normalization of the CGT.

10. There were also mini-dialogues within individual unions, between military overseers and unionists acting in their capacity as advisers.

11. There is some question about whether the military made up for this lack of a discourse for society by adopting an economic discourse. Fontana (1985:96–98) argues that a prime factor accounting for the alliance between the armed forces and the technocrats was that the armed forces simply lacked a political discourse for civil society. O'Donnell (1981:207–10, 224–26), likewise, argues that the civilian liberal economists offered the governing military, under the guise of a political-economic program, nothing else than a political ideology. But the technocratic economic program, as the National Security Doctrine, was also apolitical, in the sense that it did not address the military's need to fashion an answer to the problem of representation, which was an essentially political problem.

12. The importance of considering the distinct tasks around which military cohesion must be built is a point made by O'Donnell (1976:204) in the context of his analysis of the Argentine experience with bureaucratic authoritarianism in the wake of the 1966 coup. In a distinction similar to the one made in this book, he refers to a "consensus of termination" that is "strictly limited to the replacement of the existing regime," as distinct from the question of "the new rules to be introduced."

13. The link between the intramilitary and state-society dimensions was clearly demonstrated when, in mid-July 1977—the same time President Videla was referring to a dialogue, Interior Minister General Albano Eduardo Harguindeguy clearly dissented from Videla with respect to the opening of political activities and adopted a hard-line position, stating: "The country will have to forget about political parties for a long time, and I want to make clear that no member of the Armed Forces talked about an opening of a dialogue with political parties. There has not existed, nor does, nor will be, any dialogue with political parties for a long time" (quoted in Troncoso 1985:45). See also Fontana (1987:76–79).

The timing of the military's decision to debate a political proposal and to seek allies in society also coincided. As indicated, military contacts with labor started before the first public announcements by Videla concerning the need for a political proposal and a dialogue with civilians. But if the Argentine military went public with the issue of a political proposal in the second quarter of 1977, the military had actually been debating a political project drafted by General Ramón Genaro Díaz Bessone's since October 1976. Eventually, this proposal failed to gain full backing among the military, and that failure was confirmed by the resignation of Díaz Bessone as minister of planning in December 1977 and by his retirement soon after. The debate on the "political proposal" that was eventually made public in December 1979 thus began within the military junta and the high commands in December 1977, although it took a back seat to other issues the military were confronting until early 1979. Díaz Bessone's proposal is partially reproduced as "Proyecto nacional" (Documento de trabajo) in Vázquez (1985:299–327). See also Fontana (1987:60–63, 110) and Jordán (1993:53–55).

14. The retreat of union leaders was well symbolized by Casildo Herreras, secretary general of the CGT at the time of the coup, when he supposedly uttered to a journalist in Uruguay the famous phrase, "No sé nada; estoy desconectado de todo, me borré . . . " (I do not know anything; I'm out of touch with all of it, I'm out of here . . .). On the few instances of resistance, see Pozzi (1988a:70–71).

15. As if to lay any possible doubts to rest, when several militants acted against the new restrictive legislation, the first sentences, of three to ten years in prison, were handed down by the War Council at the end of April 1976. *Informes Laborales* (DIL), no. 194 (April 1976): 1/683, 1/688.

16. Even though the process whereby relevant actors are constituted is critically important for understanding the process of regime formation and regime change, it is rarely addressed in the literature. Most analyses simply take this process as a given and focus on the interaction among preconstituted actors.

17. In the following paragraphs I draw on unpublished material by Fraga (1980).

18. In terms of political "sectors," the removal of labor leaders from large unions meant that the "verticalist" *(verticalista)* sector—those that had supported Isabel Perón—lost out to the leaders of small unions that favored political sectors that had been relatively uninfluential during 1973–76: the Group of 8 or "anti-verticalists" (Grupo de los 8 or *antiverticalistas)*, led by Donaires and Racchini; the "participationists" or "New Current of Opinion" *(participacionistas* or Nueva Corriente de Opinión), led by Mico and Barrionuevo; and the "independents" *(independientes)*, led by Baldassini, Echezar, and Horvath.

A few words on the genealogy of these different sectors are necessary to put this information in context. The "verticalists" traced their origins to the 62 Organizations, which was formed in 1957 and became the labor branch of the Peronist Party, serving as a political coordinator of Peronist-controlled unions. Led by Lorenzo Miguel in 1975, the 62 Organizations was one of Isabel Perón's main supporters. The "orthodox" sector *(ortodoxos)*, which shall be referred to later, had supported Raimundo Ongaro against Augusto Vandor in 1968 but had moved closer to the "verticalists" after Vandor's death and Perón's reelection in 1973. The "participationists" originated in 1967 during the military government led by Onganía, with which it shared a common vision of the proper role of labor. The Group of 8 was created in 1969, when they were expelled from the 62 Organizations and were close to the "participationists." During the government of Isabel Perón, they were led by Victorio Calabró and known as the "antiverticalists" *(antiverticalistas)*. Finally, the "independents" *(independientes)* were created in 1958 as a mostly non-Peronist labor sector. Abós (1984:34–35), Fernández (1985:77–82, 138), Pozzi (1988b: 137–38).

Paying attention to the various political sectors within Argentine labor is important because—although Argentine labor has been unified under a single peak organization, the CGT, since 1930—after Perón's fall in 1955, union politics, muffled in part during 1946–55 by Perón's presence and his authoritarian hand in dealing with dissenters, was channeled through union or labor groupings *(nucleamientos sindicales* or *agrupamientos político sindicales)*. Indeed, since 1955, labor groupings had a more independent life than the CGT, which had been in the process of being "normalized" more than it had been actually functioning. Labor groupings consist of union leaders that come together, as representatives of union members, to express certain political positions or tendencies. The study of labor groupings is therefore indispensable for understanding how labor is constituted as an actor, and labor politics more generally. Dimase (1964, 1972), Fernández (1988), Miedzir, Peixoto, Fernández, and Lucita (1988), and Balvé (n.d.).

19. The distinction between first- and second-line unionists corresponds to the distinction in the Argentine union structure between second-level entities, which encompass unions with a national scope and federations, and first-level entities, which encompass leaders of union locals, leaders of unions belonging to federations, and union leaders from the provinces in the interior of the country. Third-level entities correspond to confederations, such as the CGT. On the trade union structure, see Abós (1985) and Ministerio de Trabajo y Seguridad Social (1987).

20. However, different military overseers had quite different styles of management, and the role of unionists as collaborators with the military overseers was an uneven phenomenon across unions.

21. The displacement of the old leadership within the "intervened" unions created a significant vacuum, because in many cases the top leadership had not changed hands since the late 1950s. There had been little turnover and few new faces since the generation of the Revolución Libertadora (1955–58).

22. A characteristic of this group of leaders, which followed from their retention of their legal posts, was that, having something to lose, they were susceptible to the carrot-and-stick game played by the labor ministry. On the one hand, there was the ever-present threat of "intervention," which eventually befell many unions. On the other hand, there was the promise of extending the mandate of union leaders as long as elections were not held. This mechanism allowed many union leaders to remain at the head of their organizations for some ten years without ever having to contest an election. It also gave certain unionists a considerable advantage when the time came to reopen the electoral process as part of the normalization of union life. The "Group of 8" and the "participationists" saw the advantages of this scenario early. Fraga (1980:47).

23. The unions that adhered to the CGT had been divided into six groups of approximately twenty unions apiece. In late 1976, a seventh group was formed as a group for unions that had not belonged to the CGT previously.

24. On these numerous commissions, see Munck (1990b:194–209).

25. Even though Labor Minister Liendo began a dialogue with labor leaders some six months after taking office, with the clear goal of derailing or neutralizing the attempts by union leaders to call a clandestine plenary meeting, the government's insistence on the ban on union activities did not create any significant problem for the government at this time. The push for a plenary meeting was favored, in particular, by unionists who had been displaced as leaders of their unions and who were trying to retain their status as spokespersons for their unions. But the unionists who remained as leaders of their unions, who numerically outdid the more established and politically oriented union leaders who had been removed from their posts at the head of unions, were well aware of the government's power to appoint overseers in their unions and were unwilling to jeopardize their tenuous position.

26. The most general and shared condition was the drastic wage drop, brought about within the framework of Martínez de Hoz's program, of 30 to 40 percent in the March–September 1976 period. The single best source on labor conflicts throughout the Proceso, although covering only the Videla period, is Falcón (1982); also useful is Pozzi (1998a: chap. 3). On the wage drop, see Beccaría and Orsatti (1985:20).

27. Pozzi (1988a:78–83) does point to semiclandestine forms of solidarity in the form of *coordinadoras*.

28. On the basis of the few cases in which this law, approved on September 8, 1976, was actually implemented, it appears that it was primarily used to dissuade and pressure workers and their leaders in order to avoid strikes or other forceful measures before they occurred.

29. Among those fired were eight members of the leadership board of the Federal Capital local of the light and power workers' federation. The union leadership had already been displaced at the federation level.

30. On the SEGBA strike, see Pion-Berlin (1989:114–16), Pozzi (1988a:71–81), Baizán and Mercado (1987), Dimase (1981:33–61), and Verbitsky (1985b:69–72).

31. The special regimes, which regulated the activities of state workers as part of collective bargaining agreements, were attacked by the military as undue privileges. They were done away with through both general and piecemeal legislation. Most important, in mid-December 1976 the Executive Power passed Law No. 21476, which introduced substantial changes in the norms set out in the collective bargaining agreements, as they affected state enterprises and the public sector. By means of other piecemeal legislation, all forms of worker participation in the running of state enterprises, such as *co- and auto-gestion*, were eliminated.

32. The stakes in these conflicts were high, because little could be expected in terms of containing labor militancy within the private sector—where an important sector of business came to disagree with Martínez de Hoz's economic program owing to the negative consequences it had for their firms—if the military rulers themselves could not control the enterprises they were running. It could be argued, nonetheless, that the "special" treatment that workers in the state sector received, because the goal of restructuring the state was central to the rulers' general aims, increased the level of the problems the government had to face. Not only were state workers targeted by the Law of Redundancy, and Law No. 21476, which modified the regulations affecting the activities of state workers, but wages in the state sector also suffered a decline even greater than that affecting workers as a whole. Even though a Technical Advisory Commission on Wage Policy for the Public Sector was formed in early July 1976, state workers were singled out in Martínez de Hoz's antistatist philosophy. For example, on November 10, 1976, when Martínez de Hoz announced that wage increases were soon going to be granted for certain sectors that had been falling behind relative to other sectors, he explicitly said: "The public sector is not included; at least it is not included in our proposal. . . . It has to wait for better times." "Inminente decisión sobre salarios," *La Nación*, November 18, 1976, 4. It is not surprising that state workers were prone to conflicts, particularly in the initial stages of military rule, which included strikes by electrical power, telephone, and railroad workers.

33. It is difficult to read too much into the Smith case, because apparently his disappearance was partly linked to a dispute over jurisdiction among different branches of the armed forces. Baizán and Mercado (1987), Abós (1984:22–28), Senén González (1984:65–73).

34. The importance of labor peace reflected the problems that had undermined the military's previous experience in government and led to a series of measures, such as the expulsion of foreign workers from Bolivia and Chile. In this way, the military sought to prevent unemployment from becoming a source of labor unrest. On unemployment levels, see Appendix C and Pozzi (1988a:50–62).

35. It is unclear whether the majority decided to go ahead and publish the document, or whether it was leaked to the press as it was being discussed, presenting a sector of

unionists with a fait accompli. Parcero (1987:185), for example, talks about a leak to the press; Senén González (1984:69) puts the emphasis on a majority decision.

36. The first and temporary name of the Group of 25, which initially gathered twenty unions, was the Commission of 20 (Comisión de los 20). The constituent unions were those organizing soda water workers (Federación Argentina de Trabajadores de Aguas Gaseosas y Afines), railroad workers (Unión Ferroviaria), food workers (Federación Trabajadores de Industrias de la Alimentación), food service workers (Unión de Trabajadores Gastronómicos de la República Argentina), state workers (ATE), light and power workers (FATLyF), telegraph workers (Asociación Argentina de Telegrafistas, Radiotelegrafistas y Afines), mining workers (Asociación Obrera Minera Argentina), naval conductors (Sindicato de Conductores Navales de la República Argentina), auto workers (SMATA), truck drivers (Federación Nacional de Trabajadores Camioneros y Obreros del Transporte Automotor de Cargas), telephone workers (FOETRA), commerce workers (CGEC), traveling salesmen (Federación Unica de Viajantes de la Argentina), postal workers (Federación de Obreros y Empleados de Correos y Telecomunicaciones [FOECYT]), tire workers (Sindicato Unico de Trabajadores del Neumático Argentino), paper workers (Federación de Obreros y Empleados de la Industria del Papel, Carton, Químicos y Afines), health workers (Federación Nacional de Trabajadores de Obras Sanitarias), locomotive engineers and firemen (La Fraternidad), and state oil workers (Federación de Sindicatos Unidos Petroleros del Estado). All in all, there were five unions currently under government control and fifteen unions led by trade unionists.

There continued to be a great degree of overlap between the Group of 25 and the previous commissions, such as the Group of 8, the Commission of 21, and the Commission of 7, which arose from the CGT's seven groups. Also, the formation of the Group of 25 in no way superseded the CGT, which continued to function.

37. After the January document, the government reacted with considerable displeasure, condemning the document and cutting off the dialogue it had maintained with these union leaders. But, clearly heartened by the conciliatory view of the government's actions expressed by some of the key leaders of the Group of 25, the government moved toward resumption of the dialogue as preparations for the July ILO conference began. The government needed to put together a delegation that, as had always been the case, included worker representatives. Given their concern with the government's international image, and specifically a possible condemnation of their labor policy within the ILO forum, government authorities negotiated with representatives of the Group of 25, which had gained international recognition as the "provisional leadership" of the Argentine labor movement in the face of the government's control of the CGT, even though the Group of 25 was not legally recognized by the military government.

38. Three commissions were established to deal with three major areas of concern: the revisions of the Law of Professional Associations, the revisions of the law regulating the union-run social service network (Obras Sociales), and union housing plans.

39. As is discussed below in more detail, although the Group of 25 comprised primarily unions still under labor control, some of its leaders were first-line unionists who belonged to unions that had been "intervened." The government's attempt to bring second-line labor leaders into more prominent positions was obviously also threatening to the top leaders who had been displaced from their posts and who felt that such a move would give greater permanence to their displacement.

40. Abós (1984:35–36), Fernández (1985:91), Pozzi (1988a:84–86), Verbitsky (1985b: 94–96).

41. As before the coup, top labor leaders presented themselves as "bulwarks against Marxist penetration in the unions." *Review of the River Plate,* September 30, October 21,

October 29, November 18, 1977; Pozzi (1988a:85–86, 118, 120–21, 153–55); García (1980:58–59); Falcón (1982:126–30).

42. The process of reaffiliation, in response to the government's Decree No. 385/77 of March 1977, was carried out toward the end of 1977.

43. The Group of 25, which by this time far exceeded the original twenty-five unions, was divided into five smaller subgroups or sectors that traced their origins to a not very distant past and that had distinct political profiles. The "verticalist" sector included twenty unions; the "orthodox" ten and the "independent" and "participationist" sectors jointly added twenty-two unions; and the Group of 8 added ten. (On the background of these sectors, see note 18.) In addition to these sixty-two unions, a series of dissident unionists, congregated in "groups" *(agrupaciones)* and belonging to unions under military control, participated in the activities and debates of the Group of 25. Abós (1984:37).

44. While most of the big unions that had been more prominent during 1973–76 had been "intervened," and had in many cases been handicapped by the imprisonment of their leadership, the bulk of the unionists comprising the Group of 25 came from small unions still under the control of labor leaders. This factor is crucial in explaining why they, and not other unions, were at the forefront of unionism's regrouping and reorganization following the coup. Precisely because they were small and their leaders had been of lesser political stature during the 1973–76 period, they were least affected by the measures that were introduced immediately after the coup. This element of continuity within a sea of change allowed them to rapidly regain a certain degree of initiative.

45. When the formal announcement of the formation of the new labor grouping was made on April 7, the initial list of members had been expanded to include unions representing railroad workers (Unión Ferroviaria), auto workers (SMATA), meat workers (Federación Gremial del personal de la Industria de la Carne y sus Derivados), telephone workers (FOETRA), traveling salesmen (Federación Unica de Viajantes de la Argentina), health workers (Federación de Asociaciones de Trabajadores de la Sanidad Argentina), port workers (Sindicato Unido Portuarios Argentinos), grain loaders (Unión Recibidores de Granos y Anexos de la República Argentina), municipal workers (Union Obreros y Empleados Municipales-Capital Federal), chemical workers (Federación Argentina de Trabajadores de Industrias Químicas y Petroquímicas), and workers in sports and civic entities (Unión Trabajadores de Entidades Deportivas y Civiles). Soon thereafter five new unions were added: the oil workers' union (Sindicatos Unidos Petroleros del Estado-Capital Federal), the food service workers' union (Unión de Trabajadores Gastronómicos de la República Argentina), the bank workers' union (Asociación Bancaria), leather workers (Sindicato de Obreros Curtidores), and the auto club workers' union (Sindicato Unico de Trabajadores del Automóvil Club Argentino). Polosecki (1978); Abós (1984:37–38); Senén Gonzalez (1984:85). On the size of these unions, see Appendix B.

46. Of the unions that spearheaded the formation of the CGyT, the metal workers, textile workers, construction workers, and light and power workers had been put under military control; the commerce workers and the plastics workers were still led by unionists.

47. Initially, the fact that the CGyT was made up of many unions under government trusteeship and that many of the CGyT leaders were not legally at the head of their unions made relations with government, in the form of an open dialogue, more difficult than in the case of the Group of 25. Even though the CGyT jockeyed for position to gain access to government authorities, in the short run the Group of 25 still had an important advantage in that most of its leadership was legally recognized as union leaders. Thus, the creation of the CGyT did not bring to an end the dialogue between the government and the Group of 25. Partly because of the heterogeneity of this grouping and the pres-

ence of moderates in its leadership, the Group of 25 maintained a fairly fluid dialogue with the government, although with certain interruptions, during 1978. It is significant that the legal standing of Group of 25's leaders, as well as the fact that they never lost their international reputation as the representatives of the Argentine labor movement, allowed the Group of 25 to imposed its list of candidates as workers' representatives in the official delegation to the 1978 ILO conference. But labor minister Liendo also met, in that context, with some leaders of the CGyT in what were their first public negotiations with the government. Abós (1984:38); Senén Gonzalez (1984:87). Beyond the implications that the rise of leaders who had been displaced from their post had for government-labor relations, as the discussion below will spell out, the emergence of the extremely polemic issue of leadership legality would constitute an increasingly contested issue in the dispute among labor leaders.

48. While the Group of 25 had contacts mainly with the nationalist sectors within the army and the navy, Triaca, of the plastics workers' union, and Cavalieri, of the commerce workers' union, had particularly fluid relations with more powerful leaders. In fact, Triaca and Cavalieri had frequent and secret meetings with Generals Videla and Viola. "Panorama Laboral," various issues, 1978–79; Fraga (1980:80); and Bignone (1992:74).

49. From the beginning, dissension with the Group of 25 led to the emergence of two positions. One position, held by unionists who were less compromised with defined political views, and more open to changes in the leadership of the workers' movement, maintained that it was tactically convenient to restrict activities to union matters while formulating an autocritique of the actions of unions before March 1976. The other position was held by unionists who believed that both union and broader political issues were interrelated and must be considered jointly. In terms of the sectors within the Group of 25, the Group of 8 and the "participationists," as well as the "independents," held a narrower view of the proper role of unionism, as opposed to the overtly political stance of the "verticalist" and the "orthodox" sectors. As Fernández (1985:73) points out, this division can be seen emerging already in April 1976, over the merits of a liaison commission (Comisión de Enlace) versus an advisory committee (Comisión Asesora).

50. The formation of the MSP in June 1978 clearly upset the government authorities, because within the MSP were such leaders as Miguel Gazzera, Roberto Digón, and Carlos Cabrera, who in 1968–69 had belonged to the CGT of the Argentines (CGT de los Argentinos), a combative labor grouping that had militantly opposed Argentina's previous military rulers. Using as a pretext an unauthorized plenary meeting held by the MSP, the government reacted by banning the MSP's activities in September 1978. As Dr. Daireaux (1980:11), the national director of labor relations within the ministry of labor in 1979, wrote, "In contrast to the Group of 25 and the CNT [a labor grouping the CGyT would shape], the MSP never was accepted, either formally or informally, as a representative labor grouping by the government."

51. A group of "verticalists," upset over the formation of the MSP, coalesced into a new sector called the "dissident verticalists" *(verticalistas disidentes)* and broke with the Group of 25 in August 1978. Later, in October, the "independents" also broke with the Group of 25. Defections were also carried out on an individual basis, such as that of Hugo Barrionuevo, who belonged to the "participationist" sector.

52. Besides the CGyT, represented by fourteen mostly large unions under government control, the remainder of the unions in the new labor grouping belonged to the "independent" sector, which was made up of twenty-nine unions; the "dissident verticalists," which included twenty-six unions; and a few odd unionists representing the "participationist" sector. Abós (1984:39–40), Senén Gonzalez (1984:91), Fernández (1985:138).

53. The impetus for these meetings came from various sectors, particularly at the in-

termediate levels of the union structure. In late 1978, various expressions of pressure on the national labor leaders to unite came from the rank and file and from intermediate levels of union organizations. This prompted the CNT to send a note to the Group of 25 calling for unity between the two groupings. During the first two weeks of March 1979, unionists from the provinces of Mendoza, San Juan, and San Luis traveled to Buenos Aires with the intention of bringing the two wings into which the union movement had divided closer together. Thereafter, the unionists from the interior acted as go-betweens for the CNT and the Group of 25. Additional pressure was put on the national leadership level by a couple of joint declarations by regional labor leaders. The public calls for unity by leaders of individual government-controlled unions that competed with each other and that had thrown their support behind the rival labor groupings, as was the case of the metal workers' union and the textile workers' union, was also important. The combined impact of all these moves cleared the way for talks between the two groupings. But after repeated contacts and meetings, and in the face of warnings by government authorities about the legal restrictions on union activity, the positions of the two groupings were not any closer. Even though the "independents," the "participationists," and the Group of 8 within the Group of 25 were in favor of immediate union with the CNT, the "verticalist" and "orthodox" sectors—that is, the MSP—maintained that it was necessary to take a principled position, even at the cost of foregoing what they called a "unity without substance" *(unidad sin contenido)*.

54. There were many rumors that certain sectors within the military had given union leaders a "green light"—that is, expressed their support for the general strike. Specifically, a group of nationalist colonels and Retired Admiral Emilio Massera are mentioned. Nonetheless, the decision to arrest the strike organizers, which was adopted by the labor minister in consultation with the president and the interior minister, showed the negative reaction within the key sectors of the military. "Panorama Laboral," April 16, 1979, and April 23, 1979.

55. On the preparations for the 1979 general strike, see the interviews with Pérez (1984) and Albanese (1984). On the general strike itself, see Abós (1984:49–55) and Senén Gonzalez (1984:116–17).

56. See the CNT's "Reflexiones para una Propuesta Económica" (Reflections for an Economic Proposal), a document released by the CNT in November 1978 and reproduced in Abós (1984:126–31). A move toward a more critical stance was evident in 1979, and in the speech delivered by the leader of the workers' delegation and key CNT leader, Jorge Triaca, to the 1979 ILO conference in Geneva. This speech, which was openly critical of the military's economic policies, caused uneasiness within government circles. Senén Gonzalez (1984:119–21), Abós (1984:56–59).

57. For the demands of the Group of 25, see "Análysis de Coyuntura de Salarios" (Conjunctural Analysis of the Wage Situation), a document released in December 1978 and reproduced in Senén Gonzalez (1984:107–9). A critical message read by Saúl Ubaldini at a dinner attended by some 300 Peronist leaders at the end of 1978 is also indicative of the demands of this labor grouping (Grupo de los 25 1978). See also Senén Gonzalez (1984:107–12) and Carazo and Audi (1984:78–83).

58. The meager union activity that was carried out at the firm level, particularly as a result of deliberations between shop stewards and management over wages, only reinforced the lack of connection between workers within firms and national union leaders.

59. Plant-level activism was crucial to the 1969–74 period, and while the left was weeded out at this level during the 1974–76 period, unions still maintained a strong presence within the workplace, as, for example, the role given to factory committees within the 1974–75 collective bargaining agreements attested. Abós (1983:85–86, 99, 106–9, 136–37, 173–74), Gilly (1978), Fernández (1982).

60. In some of the larger unions, such as the metal workers (UOM), textile workers, auto workers, and construction workers (UOCRA), the reduction in the number of shop stewards reached 60 to 70 percent. Daireaux (1980:6–7). The reduction in sheer numbers of members of factory committees and shop stewards is illustrated by a report by the general secretaries of UOM locals in the Greater Buenos Aires area. They report that in late 1979, after three and a half years of military rule, there was a 50 percent reduction in shop stewards and no new incorporation of workers to union activity (cited in Fraga 1980:54). A starker but nonrepresentative figure is that reported in 1978 for the Ford plant in Córdoba, where the number of shop stewards had dropped from 300 to 6. Boggs and McLellan (1978:16); see also Munck with Falcón and Gallitelli (1987:211).

61. Although the Montoneros organized the CGT in the Resistance (CGT en la Resistencia) in August 1976, that body did not have a major presence in the following two years. Subsequently, in 1979, the Montoneros' Special Agitational Troops (Tropas Especiales de Agitación [TEA]) were set up to take their actions into the labor field in the context of a military offensive. However, the death of Armando Croatto, one of the leaders of the CGT in the Resistance, in September 1979, signified the effective end of the TEAs. Gillespie (1982:237–38, 262–65), Fraga (1980:35–37).

62. Even in democratic contexts, representative leaders maintain some autonomy from those they represent. Indeed, leaders are not representative only inasmuch as they simply reflect certain predetermined and fixed interests. Representative leadership is best conceived as entailing a dialogue between leaders and followers, in which leaders listen and teach and can help change the mind of those they represent about what is in their best interest. Because the exercise of leadership entails the use of autonomous power, questions about the legitimacy of a leader's decisions are always likely to be part of a leader-follower relationship. What is essential to representative leadership, and what distinguishes a situation where we can talk about the autonomy of leaders as opposed to the hyperautonomy of leaders, is the capacity that the rank and file retain to sanction their leaders. This capacity was precisely what was lacking in the authoritarian context of Argentina, and it is what gave rise to a hyperautonomous leadership.

63. As pointed out in Chapter 3, the labor ministry had the power both to displace leaders from their union posts and to extend the legal mandate of elected union leaders at the head of their organizations.

64. Early on, the unresolvable issue of leader representativity was not that much of a problem. In the beginning, the leaders of the Group of 25 essentially claimed that, as elected heads of the unions they represented, they could speak for labor with more authority than those second-line leaders organized within the ambit of the government-controlled CGT. With the rise of the CGyT, and its successor CNT, however, the issue became more complex. Now leaders of unions formally controlled by military overseers began to participate actively in the politics of labor groups. And increasingly, the problem associated with leaders who did not retain a legal mandate as union heads was not restricted to the CGyT and then the CNT. The conflicting claims on the part of leaders who saw themselves as leaders of this or that union multiplied for a number of reasons.

First, the passage of time weakened whatever legitimacy labor leaders could claim solely on the grounds that the military allowed them to legally retain their positions without facing election. Second, some leaders of big unions under government control moved into the Group of 25, in some cases after being released from prison. Third, over time more unions, including the original unions of the Group of 25, were militarily "intervened." If fifty-seven unions had been put under military control by the end of 1976, by 1979 this number had risen to 223 out of a total 1,293 labor organizations that had legal recognition or "legal personality" *(personería gremial)*. Fraga (1980:4). Eventually, this problem reached the point where the competing leadership would align themselves in different labor groupings. Thus, a number of unions, including those representing metal workers, state workers (ATE), construction workers (UOCRA), textile workers, light and power workers, auto workers, food service workers (Unión de Trabajadores Gastronómicos de la República Argentina), state oil workers (Federación de Sindicatos Unidos Petroleros del Estado), and railroad workers, were simultaneously aligned in the two main competing labor groupings.

This confusing scenario did not prevent the two main groupings from making claims regarding their relative strength. Thus, while the Group of 25 could count on some sixty-two unions, the CNT claimed the support of seventy-one unions and, given its support among large unions, could boast a far superior number of affiliates. In a context in which union actions were curtailed, however, such comparisons were somewhat meaningless. Abós (1984:40), Fernández (1985:138), Carta Política (1979:5), Pozzi (1988b:134).

65. In the late 1960s, radicalized workers found a coherent proposal in the revolutionary populism of the CGT of the Argentines (CGT de los Argentinos), which helped structure the conflict between an entrenched bureaucratic leadership and their antibureaucratic opponents. In the late 1970s, both labor groupings were made up of leaders who belonged to a leadership level that was disconnected from rank-and-file workers.

66. On the culture of fear in Argentina, see O'Donnell (1983) and Corradi (1987). On the significance of protests as a manner of breaking with state imposed fear, see Martínez (1992).

67. Those who supported Martínez de Hoz included President Videla and General Albano E. Harguindeguy. An early but typical statement by Videla came immediately after Martínez de Hoz made a public announcement, in September 1976, stating the reasons he was against granting wage increases. Videla said simply: "The economic program is that of the national government and has the support, backing and understanding of the Armed Forces" (quoted in Troncoso 1984:70). Opposition to Martínez de Hoz came from Generals Roberto Eduardo Viola and Liendo, who managed the link between the military and labor and who repeatedly clashed with Martínez de Hoz. In general, while Martínez de Hoz would have been happy to see trade unions disappear, for all practical purposes, the army representatives in the labor ministry, by contrast, helped to preserve the union structure, if only by "freezing" all activities. Their target was not unions per se, but a certain kind of unionism. Thus, their approach is better seen as selective, while that of the ministry of economy was destructive, entailing an all-out offensive against unions. For an early statement on the main positions, see Carta Política (1976b). For later discussions, see Cermesoni (1978a, 1978b), Mora y Araujo (1979, 1980), and Velazquez (1979a).

Also opposed to Martínez de Hoz, but for different reasons, were Generals Luciano Benjamín Menéndez and Carlos Guillermo Suárez Mason, who were nonetheless opposed to any dialogue with labor. The most extreme opposition, however, came from the navy, where Admiral Massera was obstinately opposed to President Videla and attacked Martínez de Hoz as a way of expressing his opposition to Videla. For the importance of these divisions, see Fontana (1987:52–59, 104) and Jordán (1993:40–41, 43, 128). For Menéndez's views, see Menéndez (1981:32–51). On the tensions between Videla and Massera, and the latter's political aspirations, which led him to have close contacts with Montonero leaders, see Uriarte (1992:103–7, 119–20, 123–32, 141–77, 189–92, 195–200, 229–52), Bignone (1992:60, 62–63, 78), and Guest (1990:23–25, 70–75). For Massera's critique of Martínez de Hoz's economic program, see Massera (1979, 1980).

68. The main proponent of a dialogue was General Viola, while those opposed included primarily General Albano E. Harguindeguy, and, during 1979, the commander-

in-chief of the navy, Admiral Lambruschini and the commander-in-chief of the air force, Brigadier Graffigna. Not only opposed to a political opening, but also arguing for an extension of the use of repression, were Generals Menéndez and Suárez Mason. Meanwhile, President Videla maintained a position in between these two groups, clearly seeking to broaden the military's basis of support, but, as his support of Martínez de Hoz indicated, not with the same determination as General Viola. Fontana (1987:71, 76–77, 82–83, 85–87, 137–39).

69. The announcement that Videla had been redesignated President came in May 1978. In July, Division General Roberto Eduardo Viola was appointed commander-in-chief of the army and the next representative of the army in the junta as of Videla's retirement date, July 31. Subsequently, the navy and air force representatives were also replaced. In September, Admiral Armando Lambruschini became commander-in-chief of the navy, thus replacing Admiral Massera in the junta. In January 1979, Brigadier Domingo Graffigna took over as commander-in-chief of the air force, replacing Agosti in the junta. Thus, the "state of exception" came to an end in August 1978, and by January 1979 a fully new junta presided over the Proceso. Subsequently there was also a restructuring of the cabinet, as well as new designations. The army retained the ministries of the interior, still headed by General Harguindeguy, and labor, where General Llamil Reston replaced General Liendo in January 1979. The air force received the ministry of foreign relations; while the navy received the ministry of defense and social welfare. Martínez De Hoz continued as minister of economy, and a civilian was appointed minister of justice. Jordán (1993:129–34), García Delgado and Stiletano (1988).

70. Many examples of the contradictory policies that emanated from the government as a result of the splits among its members were provided by the government's labor policy. Indeed, the clashes between important sectors of the military, which put emphasis on security concerns as a result of the experience of the Cordobazo in 1969, and the economic team, which was seen by these sectors within the military as quite dogmatic, were repeated. An early clash between the labor minister and the economy minister occurred during April 1976 over Law No. 20744, the Labor Contract Law (Ley de Contrato de Trabajo), which set out the contractual relations between employers and employees. While Martínez de Hoz wanted to simply do away with the entire law, the labor minister argued that the legal vacuum created by this drastic approach would only exacerbate social discontent and strengthen leftist influence among workers. In this case, a compromise solution was reached whereby the old law was not repealed but only modified by Law No. 21297, sanctioned on April 23, 1976, which eliminated twenty-five articles, including those dealing with the right to strike and to engage in other forms of direct action, and modified ninety-eight articles of the old law. But the conflicts continued. Thus, while the military sought to avoid excessive unrest by securing low rates of unemployment, much of the thrust of Martínez de Hoz's economic program made it more difficult for the military to cultivate support or even exercise control in the labor arena. Similar differences of opinion led to numerous confrontations over wage levels between Martínez de Hoz and the labor ministry.

71. A series of incidents rocked the government in the months just before to the military's final response to the challenge of constitutional definition. These incidents revealed the deep split within the military with regard to the option of a political opening. First, in the context of a September 1979 visit by the Inter-American Commission on Human Rights of the Organization of American States (ICHR-OAS) to study the human rights situation in the country, there was a crisis within the military over the advisability of releasing journalist Jacobo Timerman from prison. After a decision was made to expel Timerman from the country, General Luciano Benjamín Menéndez, commander of

the Third Army corps in Córdoba, staged a rebellion. This rebellion was put down and General Menéndez, who not only opposed the release of Timerman but also opposed any political opening and called for an extension of the use of repression, would soon pass into retirement and thereafter lose influence within the government. Fontana (1987:85–88), Jordán (1993:167–69), Simpson and Bennett (1985:245–67). For the critical report of the ICHR-OAS, see Inter-American Commission on Human Rights of the Organization of American States (1980). For Timerman's own indictments of the military's use of state terror, see Timerman (1981).

72. This document is reproduced in Junta Militar (1980:43–63). On the foundational pretense of the "Political Foundation of the Armed Forces," see Jordán (1993:171–72), González Bombal (1991:12–14, 130–31). For a definition of the military's project, see de Ipola and de Riz (1982:86–89).

73. Justification for the usurpation of power had been spelled out both in terms of the autocratic creation of norms during the situation of constitutional crisis that led up to the coup and the power of the military institution within such a context, and in terms of the transitory character the military assigned to their task. Thus, in the "Statute," the military junta invoked a constituent power *(poder constituyente)* that placed the "Statute," as well as the "Purpose and Basic Objectives," over the constitution itself. But because the junta did not want to break totally with traditional liberal forms of legitimation, it introduced the notion of transitoriness. Given that the military government had come to be through a unilateral and nonconsensual act, it could not claim to be based on a form of popular sovereignty brought about through representative mechanisms such as a Constituent Assembly. So it justified its rule, over and above the constitution, on the grounds that the exercise of power was only a temporary aberration called forth by the situation of emergency or crisis. The source of legitimacy of their constituent power resided, in other words, in the temporary character of its exercise, given that the principle of democratic legitimacy was not explicitly rejected, but seen as the end point of the regime. Indeed, the "Purposes of the Process of National Reorganization" stated explicitly that the military's goal was to carry out a number of fundamental changes "so as to assure the later installation of a republican, representative and federal democracy." "Acta para el Proceso de Reorganización Nacional," reproduced in Troncoso (1984: 110–11). Unwilling to reject the notion of "the people" *(el pueblo)* as a source of legitimacy in a permanent manner, the military offered a complex and ultimately contradictory formulation of the bases of state power. Vanossi (1976:43), O'Donnell (1979).

74. What can be reconstructed from various sources is that there were four main competing projects. Differences in substantive content aside, and ultimately more important, these projects were conceived with the goal of finding support from certain actors within civil society. Thus, various officers and groups of officers pushed their particular visions and engaged in private contacts with individual labor leaders, party leaders, and prominent members of society, in order to build support for their views. This process necessarily brought out, more markedly than before, differences within the military and the government. This statement is supported by the entire personal archive of Rosendo Fraga, adviser to Labor Minister General Liendo during 1976–78, chief of advisers to Interior Minister Liendo in 1981, and adviser to President Bignone in 1983. Some of the debate concerning the competing projects filtered out from government circles and made its way into discussions on the course and future of the Proceso, published in articles of magazines close to the government. See, for example, a series of key articles in *Carta Política* (1977a, 1977b, 1977c, 1978a, 1978b). See also the writings of the director of *Carta Política*, Mariano Grondona (1983), and the analysis of this monthly magazine by de Ipola and de Riz (1982). For a characterization of the decision-making process behind

the "Political Foundation of the Armed Forces," and the various alternative political projects considered by the military, see Vázquez (1985:66–105), Fontana (1987:79–90), Pion-Berlin (1989:118), González Bombal 1991:7–8), and Bignone (1992:84–87).

75. The enabling legislation for the new labor law (*decreto reglamentario* no. 640/80) was not sanctioned until March 1980. The text of Law No. 22105, along with the enabling legislation, is reproduced in D'Abate (1980:85–117). For a view that sees the Law of Professional Associations as a confident move by a government reaching a phase of institutionalization, inserting its social plan into its larger economic plan, see Pion-Berlin (1989:116–18).

76. The sole detention of a labor leader, an all too common occurrence in the life of those involved in union matters, was enough to disqualify someone.

77. The project to change the legislation on Obras Sociales was to be announced simultaneously with the new Law of Professional Associations but was delayed until August 1980.

78. D'Abate (1980), Portantiero (1980), Abós (1984:63–68), Fernández (1985:63–65), Delich (1982a:142–45, 1982b:108–10), Gallitelli and Thompson (1982:157–62), Pozzi (1988a:143–52, 157–59).

79. The elaboration of Law No. 22105 spanned more than three and a half years. The steps that its elaboration went through are the following. Between April and November 1976, the labor ministry did a study on the convenience of drawing up a new law. As part of this process, starting in August 1976, the ministry of labor organized a series of consultation meetings with former labor ministers: Alfredo Allende, labor minister under Frondizi; Horacio Aguirre Legarreta, labor minister under Aramburu; Bernardo Bas, labor minister under Guido; and Rubens San Sebastián, labor minister under Onganía and Lanusse. The first guidelines of the future law were unveiled in November 1976.

Between November 1976 and April 1977, the military junta started consideration of the project, discussing the main outlines of the law, and in April 1977 the military junta outlined the remaining steps the bill would have to follow until it was sanctioned into law. In August 1977, after a full year of consideration, the labor ministry gave the military junta the definitive draft of the bill.

Thereafter, a team of interservice compatibilization (Equipos de Compatibilización Interfuerzas) analyzed the project between September and December 1977, and by January 1978 the secretaries general of the three branches had finished the job of harmonizing various proposals. In February, the military junta resolved that the promulgation of the Law of Professional Associations would follow the same steps other bills went through, and in March the military junta resolved that the Law of Professional Associations be made compatible with the law on Obras Sociales.

In May 1978, the team of interservice compatibilization considered the status of second-level organizations, and between May and June the secretaries general of the three branches approved the final guidelines on second-level organizations and some other corrections to the bill. After a lengthy halt in the debate about this bill, the secretaries general of the three branches analyzed suggestions elaborated by the team of interservice compatibilization during January and February 1979, and in March the junta gave its stamp of approval to the bill. In April, Labor Minister General Reston handed the bill to President Videla.

Following a new postponement in the debate in May 1979, debate started up again in July, with the reception of the definitive bill by the Legislative Advisory Commission (CAL). Finally, during July, the military officers of the CAL interviewed various labor leaders, and Labor Minister Reston met in August with the delegation of workers that went that year to the ILO conference in Geneva, to discuss the position of the unionists with respect to the future law.

Chapter 5: The Dynamics of a Political Situation in Argentina, 1980–1982

1. Even though the military junta began to address the issue officially only at the beginning of September 1980, presidential succession actually became a matter of internal debate within the military as early as April 1980.

2. It is significant that the announcement came on December 4, 1979, only two weeks before the public release of the "Political Foundation of the Armed Forces." Galtieri succeeded Viola as commander-in-chief on December 28.

3. Viola was known as a man open to dialogue with broad sectors of society, and had earned himself a reputation as a "populist" who was "overly friendly with the unions." The belief that Viola was unlikely to continue the economic program of Martínez de Hoz was rooted in firm knowledge about Viola's preferences. General Viola was known to have links with Lorenzo Sigaut, an economist who favored a more inward-oriented economic model, as well as with generals like Horacio Tomás Liendo, who were fairly well disposed toward negotiations with labor.

4. Fontana (1987:121, 123–24) appears to contradict himself when he first argues that intramilitary opposition to Viola "reflects a factious dispute rather than politico-ideological cleavages," but then immediately goes on to argue that Viola and Galtieri "represent divergent political orientations." There were certainly factors that came into play that cannot be reduced to a division between soft-liners and hard-liners. Indeed, Videla's support of Viola's nomination, certainly an important factor, is better explained by the fact that Viola followed Videla in seniority and had shared primary responsibility with Videla for the planning of the coup, and that he had always supported Videla in his positions as commander-in-chief of the army and as president, despite their differing views on Martínez de Hoz's economic program and the need for a political opening. But, as Fontana (1987:70–71, 124) himself discusses, Viola also had support among the young generals of the Class of '76, who provided a crucial counterweight to the army "high command"—the division generals in the army, who had assumed a hard-line orientation opposed to Viola. See also Fraga (1988:229), Bignone (1992:79–81), and Jordán (1993: 263–64).

5. In April 1980 two private banks, Promosur and the Banco de Intercambio Regional (BIR), went bankrupt. Thereafter, between April 1980 and March 1981, the government either took control of or liquidated some sixty-two financial institutions, which jointly controlled 20 percent of deposits.

6. Fontana (1987:125, 151), Peralta-Ramos (1987:55–57), Portantiero (1987:266–67), Acuña (1995:241–43), Frieden (1991:214–15, 225). Since 1978, the military had increasingly lost support among its original social base, to the point that it was increasingly isolated from society. In a landmark development, the government-imposed overseer of the Argentina Industrial Union (UIA), Eduardo V. Oxenford, publicly criticized the economic policies of Martínez de Hoz in September 1980. Throughout 1980, in short, economic interests pressured the military on the issue of whether the government that would assume power in 1981 should continue Martínez de Hoz's program.

7. The initial reason for the high number of labor conflicts was the "flexibilization" in wage-setting mechanisms allowed in September 1979. This meant that workers were given some discretion to exceed wage guidelines set by the government. A rationale for striking existed, given that now something could be won.

8. Various sources provide an estimate of the magnitude of this wave of conflicts. The only source that considers trends since 1976 puts the number of strikes at 188 for 1979 and at 261 for 1980, compared with an annual average of 76 strikes for the three-year

1976–78 period. Based on data from *Vencer*, no. 8 (May–June 1981): 6–7, reproduced in Munck with Falcón and Gallitelli (1987:229). According to another source, the number of labor-related conflicts reported to the labor ministry increased by 80 percent from 1978 to 1980. At any rate, the strike wave beginning in October 1979 represented a new peak of labor militancy since the wave of conflicts in November–December 1977. For an overview of labor conflicts during this entire phase, see Munck with Falcón and Gallitelli (1987:216–19) and Pozzi (1988a:87–95, 156).

9. There were still more political sources of conflict, as in late 1976 and early 1977, such as the introduction of changes in the special regimes affecting particular groups of workers. The number of workers affected in 1980 were considerable, as changes in legislation covered state workers, rural workers, insurance and banking workers, port workers, bakery workers, and journalists. Finally, the move to privatize state enterprises within the framework of Law No. 2177, sanctioned on March 5, 1980, led to a series of protest actions by maritime workers starting at the end of March. But in a clear sign that the government itself attributed economic and not political reasons to the strike wave, beginning in October 1979 and for the first time since the 1976 coup the government published official data on labor conflicts. The reason for making these data available, according to sources within the labor ministry and Interior Minister Harguindeguy, was that official recognition of the number of labor conflicts would help to avoid a distortion of the number and nature of conflicts. On the cause of strikes, see Vencer, no. 8 (May–June 1981): 6–7, in Munck with Falcón and Gallitelli (1987:229) and Pozzi (1988a:42–45). The "anxiety-provoking" effect of the strikes is discussed in Pion-Berlin (1989:122, 127) and Falcón (1982).

10. *Review of the River Plate*, June 11, 1980, 835; Munck with Falcón and Gallitelli (1987:219). The risks of labor conflicts in the absence of established leaders with which to negotiate was also perceived within the government, as is clear from a paper written by Daireaux (1980:12), the national director of labor relations within the ministry of labor in 1979.

11. In addition, Viola's selection did not solve the problems the military were facing in maintaining support from the original coup coalition. While Viola's selection was well received by national industrialists, the more internationally oriented sectors of business that sought a continuation of the economic policies of Martínez de Hoz reacted negatively. Viola's likely access to the presidency had introduced uncertainty among this sector of supporters of the military even before the October announcement of Viola, and this uncertainty became even more pronounced in the months between Viola's selection and his assumption of the presidency. In effect, the abandonment of the policies begun by Martínez de Hoz in December 1978 occurred even before Viola assumed power, when the peso (the national currency) was devalued on February 2, 1981. On the increasing uncertainty surrounding the issue of presidential succession, see Carta Política (1980), Massera (1979, 1980), and Schvarzer (1987a:102–9).

12. Acuña (1980), Jordán (1993:228–30), González Bombal (1991:25–31), McGuire (1995:184).

13. On August 27, Harguindeguy met for some six hours with labor leaders Juan Racchini, Ramón Valle, Mario Cala Gómez, and Luis Etchezar. At this meeting, Valle, leader of the insurance union (Sindicato de Seguro de la República Argentina), gave Interior Minister Harguindeguy a document expressing the views of one labor sector on the "Political Bases" document released by the government in December 1979. Valle (1980). A new round of talks with labor leaders two months later included Jorge Triaca, Rubén Marcos, Enrique Venturini, and Ramón Baldassini. Senén González (1984:138–40), Pozzi (1988b:132–33).

14. As Jordán (1993:230) concludes, Harguindeguy, the interior minister who served as the government's point man in this "political dialogue," "would end his term [on March 1981] without being able to show one single government order that was the result of the conversations" he conducted.

15. Important signs of liberalization included the relaxation of press censorship and the release of political prisoners. Concerning press censorship, the appearance of magazines and books, and published interviews with prominent politicians, provided some indication of the changing times (López Saavedra 1983, 1984; Moncalvillo 1983; Avellaneda 1989; Graham-Youll 1979). Concerning political prisoners, even though Isabel Perón was not released until July 1981, the release of former Undersecretary of Foreign Relations Jorge Vázquez and of the former governor of the province of La Rioja, Carlos Saúl Menem, in January 1980, as well as of two important labor leaders, Lorenzo Miguel, former head of the metal workers' union and the 62 Organizations, and Diego Ibañez, former head of the state oil workers' union (Federación de Sindicatos Petroleros Unidos del Estado), in April 1980, was significant.

16. Only a few days after the initiation of the "political dialogue," Interior Minister Harguindeguy repeated the commonly used phrase "The Process of National Reorganization does not have deadlines" *(el Proceso no tiene plazos)*, stressing that "only when the sought objectives have been attained will a solution which will give continuity to these goals be instrumented" (quoted in Redacción 1980:64). Again, as if to dampen any expectations among opponents to the government that the political dialogue would lead to elections in the short term, the very next day after the beginning of the talks, Army Commander-in-Chief Leopoldo Galtieri announced: "The ballot boxes are well stored and will remain well stored" (quoted in Redacción 1980:65). The military seemed clear about what they did not want, but the military's difficulties in controlling the agenda were also becoming clear. Thus, for example, an important and rising leader of the UCR, Raúl Alfonsín, responded to Galtieri's comments by demanding "the immediate convocation to elections," arguing with bravado that "if general Galtieri, commander-in-chief of the Army and member of the junta, has said that the ballot boxes are well stored and will remain that way for a good time, we respond to him that they should start dusting them because we will fill them with votes" (quoted in Redacción 1980:65).

These exchanges allowed various party leaders to clarify their positions and thereby give new life to dormant party organizations. Thus, while Balbín, head of the UCR, had met with the interior minister in early May 1980, Alfonsín's less conciliatory position was an important trigger for the reactivation of debate within the party. In the case of the Peronist party, while some minor figures had accepted the government's invitation to participate in the "political dialogue," Deolindo Bittel, first vice-president of the Peronist party and first in line after imprisoned Party President Isabel Perón, rejected the government's overtures, stating that certain conditions would have to be met before a dialogue with government authorities would be considered. As we shall see below, by forcing politicians to take positions with regard to an official "political dialogue," the military had provided the context for reactivating the traditional links between the Peronist party and trade unions. On the response of political parties to the "political dialogue," see González Bombal (1991:36–82).

17. In the course of the negotiations that would unify Argentina's labor leaders, the dissident bloc of the Group of 25—the unions that were not a part of the Peronist Syndical Movement (MSP)—split and formed its own group: the Commission of 20 or Group of 20 (Comisión de los 20 or Grupo de los 20). The Commission of 20 was also opposed to the new labor law. Polosecki (1979). For its part, the National Inter-union Movement (Movimiento Nacional Intersindical), which gathered a number of unionists linked to

the traditional left, announced its "total support" for the CUTA's plan to oppose the labor code. Velázquez (1979b). One of the few voices favorable to the new labor code was that of the 32 Democratic Unions (32 Gremios Democráticos), a traditionally anti-Peronist labor grouping formed in 1957 in opposition to the Peronist 62 Organizations. On the formation and subsequent activities of the CUTA, see Munck (1990b:239–45, 274–84), Abós (1984:60), and Senén González (1984:122).

18. Ironically, the virtual breakup of this body became public knowledge on April 1, a week after the government announced the enabling legislation of the Law of Professional Associations, which had provided the raison d'être for the unification of the labor leadership in the CUTA. The enabling legislation for the Law of Professional Associations (*decreto reglamentario* no. 640/80) was sanctioned on March 23, 1980.

19. Only a few labor leaders were consulted in the preparation of the Law of Professional Associations, and even this meager participation did not make any difference. This consultation took place in the latter phase of the discussion about the law and had no impact on its final form. Thus, even the CNT leadership felt excluded.

20. The perceived intransigence of the military's labor code was reconfirmed when the government approved Law No. 22269 of Obras Sociales, which abolished the old Law No. 18610 favored by unionists and drastically reduced the economic power of trade unions. The new law, approved on August 15, 1980, did not alter in any major way the functioning of the system of Obras Sociales, but it did introduce changes in the status of the property encompassed by the Obras Sociales as well as their juridical personality *(personería gremia)*. The resources of the system and the patrimony of the Obras Sociales were to be considered of a public nature, thus becoming delinked from the unions. Furthermore, the Obras Sociales were not to be administered by unions any more; rather, they were to be managed exclusively by state entities, coordinated by the National Institute of Obras Sociales (Instituto Nacional de Obras Sociales [INOS]). The net effect was to withdraw a crucial source of economic power from unions. On the debate over the new laws of Obras Sociales, see Mera (1978, 1979), Pascual (1980), and Pozzi (1988a:159–60).

21. The link between the issue of presidential succession and the process of union normalization was stated explicitly, in a July 1980 paper, by Daireaux (1980:14), the national director of labor relations within the ministry of labor in 1979.

22. The original February 29, 1980, deadline for presenting the petitions for new jurisdictions, as mandated by the Law of Professional Associations, was met by only one-third of the unions. Thus, it was only after this deadline was extended by a month that most unions presented their petitions to the labor ministry. Fraga (1980:4).

23. Once petitions for new jurisdictions were submitted to the labor ministry, the timetable imposed by the new law included the following other steps: (1) A ninety-day lapse for the readjustment of the zones of jurisdiction and the union statutes, (2) an estimated four to five months for the granting of new "legal personalities" (personería gremial), and (3) an estimated ninety-day period for holding union elections.

24. In a paper presented to an ILO conference, Mantilla (1980:37–38) writes that by the end of 1980 some 2,300 requests had been presented to the labor ministry but that new jurisdictions had been approved for only 505 unions. Of 2,943,722 union affiliates, only 912,520 were covered by the decisions—that is, decisions affecting the vast majority of affiliates, the more than two million workers belonging to the major unions, remained pending.

25. The same trend was evident with regard to another key piece of labor legislation, that affecting the Obras Sociales. As with the Law of Professional Associations, after the law was sanctioned a period of expectation began regarding the regulation of the law and, finally, its implementation. As it turns out, the military never provided the en-

abling legislation that was necessary, and thus the state never took over the Obras Sociales belonging to the unions, except in those cases where unions were run by government-appointed trustees.

26. Despite the general opposition within labor to the new labor law, the expectation that its implementation would not affect all unions equally was divisive and accounts for the continued rivalry between two main union groupings and the eventual breakup of the CUTA in April 1980.

27. Both the Peronist party and the UCR publicized separate documents criticizing the new labor law. Support for the unionists' position also came from elements within the church. The church's view was made public in two documents released in August and December 1979: the Equipo Episcopal de Pastoral Social's "Comunicado sobre Agremiación" and the Comisión Permanente de la Conferencia Episcopal Argentina's "Declaración sobre la Ley 22,105," both of which are reproduced in Abós (1984:132–35). The Centro de Investigación y Acción Social (CIAS) sponsored a debate on the church's position with respect to the new law and published critical articles on it in a special issue of their journal (Centro de Investigación y Acción Social 1980).

28. The call for an all-encompassing meeting did not receive unanimous backing. Although the church backed the call, among the political parties the UCR, the MID, and the Federal Party (Partido Federal), rejected the initiative. Furthermore, not all business sectors gave their support.

29. The inclusion of labor in the "political dialogue" was made official through an announcement of the labor minister on March 19, 1980.

30. Immediately after Deolindo Bittel, head of the Peronist party, rejected the government's invitation to dialogue, the MSP resolved in a plenary meeting of 110 representatives of 60 organizations to support the position expressed by Bittel. On the Peronist party position on the "political dialogue," see Bittel (1983:35–49). The position of the MSP on the "political dialogue" can be found in Movimiento Sindical Peronista (1980).

31. The CGT was formed by elements of the Group of 25, the "dissident verticalists"—a sector that two years earlier had left the Group of 25 to join the CNT and that had recently defected from the CNT—and by a sector from the Commission of 20, the labor grouping formed as a spin-off from the Group of 25 in August 1979. The forces behind the formation of the CGT also included a single leader, Lorenzo Miguel. As head of the powerful metal workers' union and the 62 Organizations, Miguel had been the single most important labor leader in Argentina at the time of the 1976 coup. Following the coup, he had been imprisoned, and since September 1978 he had been under house arrest. But with his release in April 1980, Miguel would reemerge as a preeminent figure whose role in labor politics and within the Peronist party during the years 1980–83 cannot be overestimated. All sectors of labor immediately had to take into account what Miguel thought about this or that matter. But it was the Group of 25 that always responded faithfully to his wishes; conversely, the CNT and its major figures—Triaca, Cavalieri, and especially Miguel's UOM rival, Rubén Marcos—saw Miguel as a competitor. Indeed, Miguel was closer to the Group of 25 because his rival within the UOM was affiliated with the CNT. His chances of regaining control over the UOM therefore depended on winning enough support among general secretaries of UOM locals to force a realignment of the UOM from the CNT to the Group of 25.

32. Immediately after its formation in late November, the CGT released its first public message, and at the end of December the newly selected board of directors *(consejo directivo)* crafted a new and critical document (the messages are reproduced in Senén Gonzalez 1984:145–47). These actions helped give a political orientation to the conflicts that had erupted at the rank-and-file level. Under conditions that severely restricted the

margins of action of unionists, however, the links between the rank and file and leadership could not be rapidly reconstituted. This factor remained the most severe handicap faced by labor as an opposition force.

Nonetheless, as the CGT drew attention to itself, the government's displeasure at this new development was obvious. The government response included the temporary jailing of some CGT leaders from the interior, warnings against the holding of public activities, and some isolated cases of union "interventions." Furthermore, some meetings of the CGT were prohibited by order of the ministry of the interior, which reminded unionists that the CGT, as a third-level organization, was forbidden by the new Law of Professional Associations.

33. This process of reactivation was given an unequivocal political bent through two meetings of the top leaders of Argentina's two main political parties—Ricardo Balbín of the UCR and Deolindo Bittel of the Peronist party—in late November 1980 and late April 1981. Earlier, in March 1980, the Peronists had sought to form a multiparty alliance and took an important step in this direction by signing a declaration that was strongly critical of the military government with a loose gathering of leaders from political parties that had been excluded from the "political dialogue." The signatories consisted of Deolindo Bittel, for the Peronist Party; Alende, for the Intransigent Party (Partido Intransigente); Solano Lima, for the Popular Conservative Party (Partido Conservador Popular); Simón Lázara, for the Unified Socialist Party (Partido Socialista Unificado); Enrique de Vedia, for the De Vedia and Auyero line of the Popular Christian Party (Partido Popular Cristiano); and Víctor García Costa, for the Popular Socialist Party (Partido Socialista Popular). It is significant that the UCR's reluctance to join forces with the Peronists prevented the formation of a unified party front at that point in time. But developments in late 1980 and early 1981 would bring the Peronists and the UCR closer together, and that would eventually lead to the formation of the Multipartidaria, which met formally for the first time in July 1981. González Bombal (1991: 44–48, 58, 90–95).

Going beyond these political parties, the process of recovery for society included the constitution and activities of human rights organizations, some of which had led the earliest demonstrations in opposition to the military government and now received international recognition through the award of the 1980 Nobel Peace Prize to human rights activist Adolfo Pérez Esquivel. The human rights movement had made its first appearance on April 30, 1977, when a group of women with white handkerchiefs on their heads marched around the Pyramid of the Plaza de Mayo, in front of the Casa Rosada, demanding to see their "disappeared" sons and daughters. Thus began a ritual march every Thursday and what later became known as the Mothers of the Plaza de Mayo (Madres de la Plaza de Mayo) a human rights organization that stood alone in challenging the military government at this early phase. While the Mothers of the Plaza de Mayo came to symbolize Argentina's human rights movement, there were at least nine other organizations that formed part of this movement (Brysk 1994: chap. 3; Guest 1990: chap. 4, 208–15, 298–302, chap. 26; Veiga 1985). Nonetheless, one distinctive characteristic of Argentina's human rights movement, in contrast to that of Brazil and Chile, is that it had few links with the Catholic church, given the latter's close links with the military rulers (Mignone 1988).

34. If the Group of 25 sought to subvert the military's new labor code from the outside, the CNT's strategy was to subvert the new labor code from within.

35. Although there had been discussions in mid-1979 about the possibility of cutting short Videla's terms, this option did not transpire. Fontana (1987:149).

36. On the Viola presidency, see Fontana (1987:125–36), Pion-Berlin (1985:64–68), and Baloyra (1987:119–24).

37. The ministry of economy was reorganized into five different ministries: economy and finance, agriculture and livestock, commerce and maritime interests, industry and mining, and public works and services. Most indicative of Viola's economic orientation was the appointment of Lorenzo Sigaut as minister of economy and finance. But the close ties that were developed between the other ministries and different sector of the business class were as significant. Fontana (1987:242–43), Jordán (1993:269–71, 273), and Acuña (1995:244). Meanwhile, the labor ministry passed from the army to the hands of the air force in the person of former CGT overseer Brigadier Julio César Porcile, while the ministry of the interior remained under control of the army with the appointment of former Labor Minister General Horacio Tomás Liendo, a close friend of Viola. In the makeup of the cabinet, there was a trend toward a demilitarization of the cabinet, with seven of the thirteen ministries going to civilians, compared with two out of eight in Videla's first cabinet. In one of his last decisions as president, on March 28, Videla had signed a new Law of Ministries, which expanded their number from eight to thirteen. García Delgado and Stiletano (1988:73), Jordán (1993:271–76).

38. The term "liberalization" is used here consistent with O'Donnell and Schmitter's (1986:7–11) use—that is, as referring to "the process of making effective certain rights that protect both individuals and social groups from arbitrary or illegal acts committed by the state or third parties." It is crucial, then, to distinguish liberalization from democratization, for if liberalization is initiated as a way to strengthen the hold on power by the governing elites, democratization entails the process whereby the old rulers are replaced by a new set of rulers.

39. Fontana (1987:127), González Bombal (1991:69–30, 83–85, 87), McGuire (1995: 186).

40. For a partial version of the text of the secret "Guidelines" issued by the military junta, entitled "Pautas de la Junta Militar al Poder Ejecutivo (para el ejercicio de la acción de gobierno 1981/84)," see Junta Militar (1985).

41. During this period, political parties released a series of documents critical of military rule. The most important documents are reprinted in Multipartidaria (1982). Documents issued by the Peronist party are collected in Bittel (1983). Other important opposition statements are those of Alende, Vicente, Storani, and Rosa (1981). The Peronist debate about their role in the Multipartidaria is the focus of two interviews published in *Línea* (1981a, 1981b). The Communist Party's position on the Multipartidaria is discussed in two articles in Comentarios (1981a, 1981b) and Kohen (1981).

42. With the formation of the Intersectorial, the realignment of unions that had begun with the breakup of the CUTA in April 1980 and led to the formation of the CGT in November 1980 was completed. The resulting lineup of unions by sector is presented in Senén González (1984:145).

43. Most parties, with the exception of the UCR, supported the CGT's call to strike. For the CGT's call to a general strike, see Confederación General del Trabajo (1984a). On the strike itself, see Abós (1984:78–81) and Senén González (1984:155).

44. On one front, the continued advancement of the government's project to take over the Obras Sociales prompted a critical communiqué from the Intersectorial. With regard to the issue of wages, after a series of meetings between government authorities and the Intersectorial, the government announced a wage increase in late September. But the very next day, the Intersectorial publicly rejected the offer as insufficient. All the Intersectorial had received from the government were vague promises that the process of returning the unions to the workers would be carried out by the Viola administration. The hardening of the Intersectorial's position in light of the repeated failure of their overtures toward the government led to the reinitiation of contacts with the CGT, with the aim of cementing labor's unity. Nothing came from this initiative, however, because as

soon as Lorenzo Miguel moved to consolidate his position within the union movement by reconstituting the 62 Organizations in mid-October, all talks were broken off. The problem was that the resuscitated labor branch of the Peronist movement, banned immediately after the 1976 coup, was made up solely of CGT members, and that the Intersectorial would have a difficult time entering any negotiations on an equal footing. The failure of these intralabor negotiations aside, the Intersectorial's very willingness to consider entering into such talks was a sign of its frustrations with the government.

45. If Viola's labor allies felt increasingly alienated from the government, key business supporters, who had supported him as an alternative to the continuation of Martínez de Hoz's economic plan, started to waver. It is significant that, in late August, a key representative of big national industry known for his criticisms of the Martínez de Hoz program, Eduardo Oxenford, resigned from the post of minister of industry and mining.

46. On September 15, Retired General Harguindeguy, now in the role of adviser to President Viola, announced: "There [will] be no presidential elections in 1984; the president will be designated by the junta and the current power scheme will be maintained" (quoted in González Bombal 1991:100). A similar statement was made by General Galtieri in October. Fontana (1987:130).

47. Balbín died in September. On Balbín's moderating influence and the importance of his death to the prospects of agreements between the military rulers and political parties, see González Bombal (1991:36–44, 99–100) and McGuire (1995:187).

48. Viola was forced to resign under the pretext of an illness, for which he was confined on November 9. After a brief presidential interregnum of the minister of the interior, General Liendo, between November 20 and December 11, Viola was forced to resign. There followed another brief interim period, which ended with General Galtieri's nomination by the junta as president and his assumption of the office on December 22. Galtieri retained his positions as commander-in-chief of the army and a member of the military junta, but two new officers shared power alongside General Galtieri in the junta. Admiral Jorge Isaac Anaya had replaced Admiral Lambruschini as commander-in-chief of the navy in September 1981. Then, Brigadier Basilio Lami Dozo assumed the position held until then by Brigadier Omar D. Graffigna in December 1981.

49. Institutionally, as Fontana (1987:121, 132, 137–39) argues, this split between soft-liners and hard-liners can be conceptualized in terms of a schism between the military as an institution and the military as government, where the latter is conceived as centered on the president and his cabinet. However, given that the basis of military opposition to President Viola was within the very military junta, which according to the institutional rules set down in 1976 had extensive powers of government, it is appropriate also to see the splits between soft-liners and hard-liners as being institutionally manifested in a split *within* the military as government. On the impact of these divisions on the power of the state, see Stepan (1985:329).

50. As the literature on transitions shows, while all attempts at liberalization, such as the one attempted by Viola, fail, there is more than one way for the tensions to which it gives rise to be "resolved." If in Argentina, liberalization led to a coup by the hard-liners, there is another way in which the split between soft-liners and hard-liners in the context of liberalization could be resolved. That would entail the conversion of liberalizers into reformers, which in essence accept the demand for democratization by societal actors and align with democratizers in society against the hard-liners. Such an alliance appeared to be viable in Argentina during 1981, especially given the initial moderation and willingness to reach an accommodation with Viola on the part of political parties. But Viola never "took the plunge" and remained a liberalizer set on recomposing the

basis of support for military rule. As his power weakened, the backlash by the hard-liners led to an authoritarian regression. On the dynamics of liberalization and the option of an authoritarian regression, as opposed to the option whereby liberalizers become reformers and liberalization flows into democratization, see O'Donnell and Schmitter (1986:23–24) and Przeworski (1991: chap. 2).

51. Cavarozzi (1982:14–15), Damill and Frenkel (1992:19), Garretón (1992:16, 20–21).

Chapter 6: Reform Through Rupture and Democratization in Argentina, 1982–1983

1. The return to neoconservative economics was carried out by Minister of Economy Roberto Alemann. Within Galtieri's new cabinet, set up according to the changes in the Law of Ministries approved on December 15, there were also a few signs of continuity. Viola's labor minister, for example, was reconfirmed in his post. García Delgado and Stiletano (1988:74), Jordán (1993:308–14).

2. The continuity in the CGT's strategy across the Viola and Galtieri presidencies is highlighted in the comments of CGT leader Saúl Ubaldini: "The labor sector is unconcerned about the current institutional situation. . . . It demands the return of the state of law. . . . The access of Galtieri to the presidency does not create any expectations among workers" (quoted in Senén González 1984:159).

3. The consensus is particularly strong with regard to emphasizing state- or ruler-centered factors as opposed to societal factors. Cavarozzi (1986:168), for example, writes: "Neither the UCR nor the Peronist movement . . . had any significant impact on the political processes leading to the collapse of the military regime, nor for that matter did other opposition forces." Virtually identical quotes can be found in the work of many other analysts. Thus, de Riz (1982:1218) writes: "The transition appears not as a consequence of a process gestated in civil society and in its political organizations, but as a decision of the military." Similarly, Gómez and Viola (1984:31) argue: "The collapse of the military-authoritarian regime was not provoked by a significant mobilization of civil society . . . but due to an accelerated process of implosion." For G. Di Tella (1984:105, 107), the transition in Argentina "is not the consequence of the actions of the opposition to the government but is due, rather, to the crisis within the alliance of government. . . . This democratic opening is a totally autonomous decision, in which the opposition is still a passive spectator of what is happening." For Landi (1988:61), "the collapse of the military government installed in 1976 was the product of its own failure to perform than of great opposition mobilizations." Finally, for Smith (1989:265), it was "primarily the military's own political incompetence and internal contradictions that finally brought the regime to its knees, not irresistible pressure from an aroused citizenry." See also Rouquié (1987b:270). The importance of external factors is stressed by Cheresky (1985: 22) and Melo (1989:25–26).

4. It is worth noting that many of the same observers that stress state- or ruler-centered factors in their explanation of Argentina's transition at the same time mix into their account of the transition references to activities in society. Thus, while Fontana (1987:160, 1984:123–24) states that the transition was "not so much a result of the interaction between the political actors of civil society and the politico-military power, but rather a consequence of the regime's internal dynamics," he also argues that following that massive demonstration of opposition to the government in late 1981 and March 1982, "the rapid erosion process undergone by the government in the terrain of its relation with the society created the danger of a greater fragmentation inside the military

corporation." This is a far cry from statements about the transition being explained in intramilitary terms that avoid reference to the activities of actors within society, and comes very close to the view presented in this book. The basic point is that while the internal politics of the military rulers was a primary determinant of the transition, intramilitary issues cannot be understood in isolation from the dialectics of state-society relations.

5. Cardoso, Kirschbaum, and van der Kooy (1992:21–22), Guest (1990:2, 337), Fontana (1987:123).

6. The topic of the Falkland/Malvinas Islands became a priority for the military junta as soon as Viola was removed from power in late 1981. First, the navy began to resurrect its old plans sometime between December 15 and 23. Then, a decision to invade was made by the military junta during the first two weeks of January 1982. But the actual date of the invasion was only decided on March 26, when the situation in the South Georgia Islands, apparently triggered by the navy in a manner that was autonomous from the junta, forced the immediate decision to invade the Falkland/Malvinas Islands, in advance of the projected date for the invasion, so as not to lose the surprise factor. On the decision-making process, see Cardoso, Kirschbaum, and van der Kooy (1992:19–97), Comisión Rattenbach (1988), Freedman and Gamba-Stonehouse (1991:39–70, 104–9), Piñeiro (1992:15–23), Burns (1987: chap. 4), and Norden (1996: 69–71). For a discussion of the developments leading up to the April 2 invasion, from the perspective of a key participant, Argentina's foreign minister, see Costa Mendez (1993: 75–186).

7. Fontana (1987:123, 140–41), Cardoso, Kirschbaum, and van der Kooy (1992:34–40), Guest (1990:338), Burns (1987:30)

8. The one constant was the military's reliance on small conservative political parties from the provinces. Makin (1985:163–64), McGuire (1995:187, 184), Fontana (1987: 141–44).

9. Fontana (1987:142), McGuire (1995:187), Cardoso, Kirschbaum, and van der Kooy (1992:39, 43–44, 93, 108, 337), Rock (1985:374–75), Guest (1990:338), Moneta (1984: 126–27), de Camargo and Vasquez Ocampo (1988:309–12), Portantiero (1987:272–73). In an interview with an anonymous protagonist of the war, presumably General Galtieri, the interviewee refers to the expectations of political gain that a victory in the Falkland/Malvinas Islands would bring (Montenegro and Aliverti 1982:23).

10. While explaining why the decision to invade was not made before, as a result of the army's failure to back the navy's desires, the urgency of responding to the growing opposition, something quite evident in late 1981, also explains why the decision was not postponed. If a prudent strategy, in line with Argentine interests, would have been to wait for the results of the U.N.-sponsored negotiations concerning the issue of sovereignty over the Falkland/Malvinas Islands, the timing of the military's decision appeared more influenced by their pressing need to respond to their growing problems vis-à-vis society. One of the best historical overviews of the legal disputes over the Falkland/Malvinas Islands is Beck (1988).

11. Stressing that "the contradictions and internal dynamics of authoritarian states are, in themselves, principal determinants of international violence," Borón (1988:135, 140) argues not only that the impetus for the invasion was the military's need "to repair the critical internal front," but also that the strategic errors made by the military were rooted in the very political dynamics of military rule.

12. The expectations concerning the United States were based on what President Galtieri saw as the understanding that had developed between him and Ronald Reagan, after the latter had become president of the United States in January 1981. The basis

for this relationship was rooted in the way Galtieri assisted the Reagan administration in its anticommunism crusade in Central America. The Argentine military contributed trainers for the Contras fighting the Sandinistas in Nicaragua and sent advisers to El Salvador to help the Salvadorean military fight the FMLN guerrillas, allowing Reagan to get around congressional limits on U.S. advisers in the region. Reagan's election had undoubtedly led to a dramatic shift in U.S. policy toward Latin America and Argentina, away from the condemnation of human rights abuses committed by military governments to their support as anticommunist allies. Rapidly, such sanctions as the ban on the sale of arms to Argentina, in effect since 1977, were lifted by the U.S. Senate, and the pressure that President Jimmy Carter had put on the military became a thing of the past. But, as even the most casual of observers of political trends could tell, during the early 1980s Reagan had no more "special relationship" than that with his conservative soul-mate Margaret Thatcher. On the Argentine military rulers' expectations and misperceptions, Cardoso, Kirschbaum, and van der Kooy (1992), Burns (1987:32–36), Verbitsky (1984:80–109), Dabat and Lorenzano (1984:80–81, 93), Feldman (1985), Borón (1988:141–43), Guest (1990: chap. 25), McGuire (1995:188), and Norden (1996:71–75). On Thatcher's role in the Falkland/Malvinas Islands war, see Barnett (1982).

13. On the Argentine military campaign on the Falkland/Malvinas Islands themselves and the blunders in fighting, see Freedman and Gamba-Stonehouse (1991: chaps. 16–23), Kon (1982), and the governmental investigation into the conduct of the war by the Comisión Rattenbach (1988). While much was made in Argentina of the U.S. decision to support Britain in military terms, the U.S. contribution was quite minimal and did little to alter the military equation. Dabat and Lorenzano (1984:116–17).

14. To start off, on April 6, labor leaders from both the Intersectorial and the CGT, as well as leaders from the major political parties, were flown to the Falkland/Malvinas Islands to witness the installation of General Benjamín Menéndez as governor. Among those who participated in the ceremony were Former President Videla; party leaders including Deolindo Bittel, head of the Peronist party, A. Robledo, F. Cerro, and Carlos Contín, head of the UCR; and unionists including Jorge Triaca, Ramón Baldassini, Rodolfo Soberano, and Luis Etchezar, of the Intersectorial, and Saúl Ubaldini and Fernando Donaires, of the CGT. After this ceremony, both wings of labor sent their leaders on a series of trips abroad to Europe and the United States, where they voiced their support for "Argentina's actions." On the actions of Argentine parties and unions on behalf of the war effort, see Cardoso, Kirschbaum, and van der Kooy (1992:152–53, 161–62, 164) and Verbitsky (1985c:164–67). The positions assumed by diverse organizations on the Falkland/Malvinas conflict are discussed in Dabat and Lorenzano (1984:104–9), Fernández (1982:41–57), and Gilly (1984). These two last essays are reprinted in Plá (1984).

15. Cardoso, Kirschbaum, and van der Kooy (1992:153, 165, 323), Aznárez and Calistro (1993:112–17).

16. The CGT criticized the government through two communiqués publicized on April 8. In them, they asked for an end to layoffs and suspensions, reactivation of the productive apparatus, and improvement in wages, emphasizing that support for the Falkland/Malvinas effort in no way lessened the urgency of providing an adequate response to the socioeconomic problems affecting workers. Within the labor camp, the usual differentiation of positions was evident. Thus, while the CGT and the 62 Organizations stated their reservations toward the government in no uncertain terms, the Intersectorial embraced this newest cause of the military rulers. The government's bias toward the Intersectorial resulted in the formation of a delegation for the upcoming ILO conference that excluded the CGT leaders. The CGT responded to its marginalization by declaring itself in a "virtual state of mobilization" to resist the permanence of the military govern-

ment. Abós (1984:87–88), Senén González (1984:164–67). For the CGT's documents, see Confederación General del Trabajo (1984b, 1984c).

17. Fontana (1987:164–65), Cardoso, Kirschbaum, and van der Kooy (1992:152, 192, 217, 336).

18. Mann (1987:350–52) stresses the import of war in determining the durability of different forms of rule and considers the unsettling proposition that fascism might have endured to the present had it not been for the contingent result of World War II. In the Argentine case, one could argue that the result was not all that contingent. "What if" types of questions are indeed less legitimate, because the Falkland/Malvinas invasion was not really a gamble that could have gone either way.

19. Another counterfactual situation that helps in assessing the impact of war is a case in which war was not even fought and in which the Argentine rulers would thus not have to deal with the effects of military defeat. Although it is likely that such an outcome would have probably increased the durability of military rule, while also ensuring that a future transition would not be carried out by an extremely debilitated military, it is unlikely that the basic dynamics behind the decision to launch the Falkland/Malvinas invasion would not have led to a transition under fairly similar conditions.

20. Such an interpretation is echoed by Pion-Berlin (1985:56), who states that "while the Malvinas War hastened the military's downfall, it was not . . . the cause," and by Borón (1988:144–45), who argues: "The disintegration of the military regime, which had begun *before* the Malvinas War, acquired an accelerated rhythm and irreversible character after the defeat at the hands of the British forces."

21. As O'Donnell and Schmitter (1986:23–25) argue, all processes of transition entail a crucial element of uncertainty because of the reversibility of the process. But, as Przeworski (1991:67) points out, where the hard-line elements collapse, the problem of an authoritarian regression almost disappears.

22. For the makeup of Bignone's cabinet, see Reinaldo García (1985:176–77). For the testimony on this period by the president himself, see Bignone (1992:125–86).

23. On the various interim arrangements that have been adopted in the recent democratization experiences, see Shain and Linz (1995:1–123). McGuire (1995:192–202) provides a detailed analysis of the factors affecting the type of interim government that oversaw Argentina's transition. Although he emphasizes the not inconsiderable power of the military rulers, he also stresses the extent to which party leaders did not want to get involved in any interim arrangement, for fear of being tarnished by association with the military rulers, and the extent to which they could still dominate the agenda without actually being in government. On the relatively low degree of control over the transition process exercised by the Argentine military, in contrast to their Brazilian and Chilean counterparts, see Fontana (1987: chap. 4), Varas (1988: chap. 4), Agüero (1995b:146–47), and McGuire (1995:193, 208–10).

24. President Bignone made this promise to lift the ban on political activities in a meeting with representatives of the main political parties on June 25, 1982, a few days before he took office. At the same meeting, he told party leaders that his administration would follow an economic program similar to the one outlined by the Multipartidaria. An abbreviated transcript of this meeting is reproduced in Bignone (1992:241–50). The Multipartidaria's program, issued on June 23, 1982, is reproduced in Multipartidaria (1982b).

25. Although President Bignone had announced that elections would be held during the last trimester of 1983 on December 1, 1982, the precise date of the election was only made public on February 28, 1983. One other sign of the military's ability to delay the pace of events was their refusal to lift the state of siege that had been originally decreed

on November 6, 1974, by President Isabel Perón and that had been prolonged indefinitely, on October 1, 1975, by Provisional President Italo Luder. The state of siege was not lifted until October 29, 1983, the day before the election.

26. The Statute of Political Parties required parties to reregister their members, while stipulating that parties had to have a minimum membership in order to be on the ballot and that they could not seek the overthrow of the democratic system. The new electoral law proposed a proportional representation system, according to the D'Hont method. The president would be elected in a single round by an electoral college. Parties had to gain at least 3 percent of the vote within a particular province to win a seat in the Chamber of Deputies. Unlike the electoral law used in the 1972–73 transition, no overt restrictions, such as the one that did not permit Juan Perón to run, were included in the 1983 law. On the reforms to the electoral law introduced by Decree-Law No. 22847 and 22838, see Botana and Mustapic (1991:58–59), McGuire (1995:190, 199), and Melo (1989:43–44).

27. As O'Donnell and Schmitter (1986:28–36) correctly stress, in the context of transitions from authoritarianism the problem of the military's human rights record is many times a critical issue in the transition. On the impact of the relative extent of human rights violations on the transition process, see the interesting discussion of the Greek and Argentine cases in Huntington (1991:211–31) and McGuire (1995:196).

28. The military junta was reconstituted after the members of the junta that had launched the Falkland/Malvinas had been replaced. Immediately thereafter, the junta emitted a declaration justifying the role of the armed forces in the "dirty war." Then, on October 20, President Bignone announced "five points" on which "agreements" with society could be reached. These five points covered the "war against subversion," the Falkland/Malvinas Islands war, the border issue with Chile, the economic crisis, and the electoral law. Finally, on November 12, the junta presented its "fifteen topics for concertation," which included the prior five points and a heterogeneous group of ten more issues. On the reconstitution of the junta, see Melo (1989:33–35) and Fontana (1987:172). For the text of the junta's declaration justifying the armed forces' role in the "dirty war," issued on August 25, 1982, see Junta Militar (1982a). The fifteen-point document, issued on November 11, 1982, is reproduced in Junta Militar (1982b).

29. These demonstrations were part of a broader wave of protests the military rulers faced toward the end of 1982, which culminated in what has been referred to as "hot December" (Gilly 1983; Dabat and Lorenzano 1984:152–53). The other protest measures included a general strike on December 6 and a neighborhood-based form of protest between October and December 1982 called the Vecinazos (González Bombal 1988). It is important to stress that, while these protests were related in that they all contributed to a growing sense of weakness on the part of the government, there were not only scarce links between the Vecinazos and the labor movement (García Delgado and Silva 1985:72–73, 78; González Bombal 1985:105), but also little connection between the December general strike and the efforts to repudiate the military's attempt to condition a post-transition government. It is noteworthy, nonetheless, that the CGT fully supported the Multipartidaria's "March of the People," and that even though the Intersectorial, now renamed as the CGT-Azopardo, did not bring out its supporters in an organized manner, it was persuaded to adhere to the measure. The church was alone in publicly calling for "national reconciliation" (Conferencia Episcopal Argentina 1982).

30. As Fontana (1987:174) writes, in the wake of the events of December 1982, it was clear that "the government [had] little to offer its civilian counterparts. . . . From that point on the soldiers [knew] that they [could not] count on a joint commitment by political and union leaders in order to guarantee the future situation of the Armed Forces and

the judicial immunity for their members." See also Portantiero (1987:273–74) and Melo (1989:89–93).

31. The military rulers also considered the possibility of a new coup d'état or a prolonged postponement of the electoral process, but, as Fontana (1987:175–76, 180–83) argues, "the deep internal crisis [excluded] such possibilities." However, this did not preclude attempts to resurrect the notion of a new subversive threat, which led to various kidnappings and killings after July 1982. The most publicized of these actions was the assassination of two political militants, Oscar Cambiasso and E. Pereyra Rossi. Dabat and Lorenzano (1984:149–50, 194), Melo (1989:36).

32. At the time, the Peronist party was less a political organization dominated by a real political class than an association that gathered diverse political sectors connected with various labor groupings. The dominance of labor was based on the traditional role of labor as the backbone (*columna vertebral*) of Peronism, and the fact that Perón, wanting to use the party as a vehicle for his own goals, had always avoided institutionalizing Peronism as a party. The death of Perón had not changed this, in that the crisis that ensued was rapidly followed by the military coup of 1976. As had been the case during previous episodes of military rule, and despite the drastic weakening of labor in the wake of the 1976 coup, labor retained a level of organizational strength that Peronist politicians lacked. Unionists therefore occupied a privileged position as party leaders or as a basis of support for competing leaders. Indeed, during the transition from authoritarian rule, union politics and Peronist party politics overlapped to a large extent, as labor politics shifted toward the interior of the Peronist party, and the party became another arena in which the contest between labor groupings was carried out.

33. The name CGT-Azopardo was selected as a clear demonstration that the members of the Intersectorial were claiming to be the "historical" representatives of the Argentine labor movement. To distinguish themselves from the other CGT, they tagged on the name of the street where they were headquartered. The CGT-Azopardo was constituted during the course of the Falkland/Malvinas war, on May 20, 1982.

34. In May 1982, in order to more clearly differentiate itself from the newly formed CGT-Azopardo, the CGT renamed itself, on the basis of the name of the street where it was headquartered, as the CGT-Brasil.

35. The internal sectors within Peronism and their origins are discussed in Corbière (1981), Dabat and Lorenzano (1984:156–58), and Jordán (1993:399–400).

36. On March 6, 1976, the Congress of the Peronist party had selected a National Council that included Isabel Perón as president, Deolindo Bittel as first vice-president, and Lázaro Roca as general secretary. With the banning of party authorities following the coup, no changes occurred in this lineup of party authorities. Moreover, because Isabel Perón was imprisoned following the coup until July 1981, and had moved to Spain upon her release, Bittel in effect held the top leadership post, a position that was ratified by the National Justicialist Congress on March 5, 1983.

37. As discussed in Chapter 5, the leadership of the Peronist party and this wing of labor began working together in 1980 in the context of their opposition to the government-initiated "political dialogue." Once Miguel resuscitated the 62 Organizations, in mid-October 1981, the 62 Organizations and the CGT-Brasil worked closely together. Immediately following the Falkland/Malvinas defeat, on June 17, 1982, the CGT-Brasil and the 62 Organizations of Miguel called on the Peronist party to put itself at the head of the wave of popular protest. The basis for understandings between the CGT-Brasil and Miguel's 62 Organizations, on one side, and the Peronist party, on the other, were further reaffirmed in the next days as both party leaders and unionists called for immediate elections. This separate but coincident announcement led the Peronist party to

state that as long as the split between the two wings of the labor movement endured, it would support the CGT-Brasil, and Miguel's 62 Organizations, as the political expression of the Peronist workers' movement.

38. Some three months earlier, when their demands for wage improvements were not being readily met, the CGT-Azopardo had called for a general strike. Given that the CGT-Brasil had called for a demonstration as part of their "struggle plan" *(plan de lucha)* there was, moreover, an attempt to coordinate the two protest measures. But a government concession, in the form of a wage increase and the promise of rapid union normalization, made the CGT-Azopardo back down. The CGT-Brasil, for its part, went ahead with its planned action and staged a march leading to a mass concentration of workers in the historic Plaza de Mayo under the motto "Bread, Peace, and Work" *(Pan, Paz, y Trabajo)* on September 22. Throughout November, the CGT-Azopardo again continued to seek some form of accommodation with the government in exchange for greater control over the normalization process. To this end, they met with the minister of economy and his advisory team on a number of occasions. But after a period of waiting, as it became clear that the government was not forthcoming with a positive response to their wage demands, and as the CGT-Brasil moved ahead with their plan of mobilization, holding their first public act in the interior of the country on November 21, the CGT-Azopardo finally decided to call the general strike.

39. There was confusion regarding the Multipartidaria's support for the measure, because after the secretaryship of the Multipartidaria had stated its support for the general strike, the UCR's president, Contín, denied such support. Abós (1984:91–92).

40. After the general strike, the CGT-Azopardo continued to pressure the government, revealing their adoption of a two-pronged strategy. They continued to meet with government authorities, and most frequently with the labor minister, while still raising the threat of a new general strike. The payoff came in late December, when the government decreed a wage increase, after a meeting between the CGT-Azopardo and the minister of economy. Even though the CGT-Brasil deemed it an insufficient measure, the CGT-Azopardo accepted the offer as a sign of goodwill.

41. By this point in time, the CGT-Brasil had changed its name, once again, and was now know as the CGT of the Argentine Republic (CGT de la República Argentina [CGT-RA]).

42. On Miguel's role during the entire period of military rule, see Aznárez and Calistro (1993:95–174) and Carpena and Jacquelin (1994:15–50, 189–200, 215–25).

43. Before the meeting, called by the "hard-liners" and held on October 19 at the stadium of the Atlanta football club with some 30,000 Peronists present, Miguel referred to sectors that attempted to draw a line between the people and the armed forces, implicitly accusing supporters of Saadi's Intransigence and Mobilization sector. Rejecting this not-too-subtle conciliatory overture to the military by Miguel, parts of the crowd responding to Saadi's sector booed and hissed when Miguel spoke. The tensions continued after the act, as Miguel and Saadi traded accusations, with Miguel rejecting *"montonerismo,"* a reference to those who supported the Peronist Montonero guerrilla group and those who criticized the military, while Saadi accused Miguel by name of being an accomplice of the military. That was not the first time Miguel had voiced such views. Shortly after regaining his freedom in 1980, Miguel had warned against the dangers of "subversion" on occasion of a ceremony in honor of Vandor. Aznárez and Calistro (1993: 100, 123–27).

44. However, it is important to recall that the CGT-Brasil was not a monolithic organization and that the Miguelistas, represented by the unions supporting Miguel, coexisted alongside the more confrontational Group of 25.

45. On September 29, 1982, Miguel got himself ratified as general secretary of the 62 Organizations, in the first legal meeting of the group since its dissolution in 1976. A total of 117 union organizations participated in the meeting. Miguel's 62 Organizations was made up solely of CGT members.

46. After the end of the Falkland/Malvinas war, the UOM entered a period of debate and heightened divisiveness. The UOM, led by Marcos and Guerrero, voted to remain within the CGT-Azopardo. Efforts at reunification of the UOM floundered toward the end of June, as Marcos and Guerrero remained in the CGT-Azopardo, while thirty-seven locals gathered in the Agrupación "Augusto Vandor" voted to form a competing leadership to be headed by Miguel. The Marcos/Guerrero sector recognized the split but claimed to have a majority of support.

47. Besides Nicolaides and Miguel, other rumored signatories of the pact were Generals Jorge Suárez Nelson and Juan Carlos Trimarco and unionists Diego Ibañez, Herminio Iglesias, Diego Ibañez, and Rogelio Papagno. On the military-union pact, see Cordeu, Mercado, and Sosa (1985:76–78), McGuire (1995:189), Dabat and Lorenzano (1984:157), Aznárez and Calistro (1993:126, 130–31), and Carpena and Jacquelin (1994: 215–25).

48. From the beginning of the transition, the Bignone government had searched for goodwill among labor leaders in order to ensure an orderly transition. It had also appointed Héctor Villaveirán, a person known to have close contacts with labor leaders and who was well respected by them, as labor minister. To gain labor support, the government took some important steps. It legalized the right to strike through Law No. 22825, in early June 1983; it recognized the legal existence of the CGT through Law No. 22839 later that same month; and it took a concrete step to return the CGT to workers' hands by appointing Valentín Suárez as "normalizing delegate" of the CGT on July 19.

From the unionists' perspective, however, the union normalization process was a top priority, and progress to this end was extremely slow. Military control of certain unions did come to an end, but the selected unions tended to be small and generally from the interior of the country. Indeed, with regard to the state of the union normalization process, the pattern of delay that had characterized the process since it started in early 1980 continued. Even though in mid-May 1983 Labor Minister Villaveirán asserted that trade unions would be in the hands of unionists before the national elections of October 30, and sought to accelerate the normalization process, full normalization of the union structure would not take place until the majority of unions held elections after the military relinquished power. Thus, in October 1984, when the process of union elections began under the new democratic government, 355 of 1,172 labor unions registered with the ministry of labor had been normalized under the military's legislation, 612 had retained the leadership they had had at the time of the 1976 coup, 111 were under the control of "transitory commissions" *(comisiones transitorias)* appointed during the last months of military rule, and 94 were run by "normalizing delegates." Gaudio and Domeniconi (1985).

If the union normalization process was a slow one, the trend with regard to what little was done was still clear. Initially, the military displayed favoritism toward the CGT-Azopardo, in particular by allowing them to gain greater influence within the "transitory commissions" that were set up to oversee the electoral process. Particularly after they lifted a planned September 22 general strike, the CGT-Azopardo seemed to be gaining ground. But toward the end of 1982, a change in government policy took shape, and by May 1983 the roles were reversed and the CGT-Azopardo was protesting the lack of fairness in the process of normalization. Melo (1989:38–39), Munck with Falcón and Gallitelli (1987:222), Cordeu, Mercado, and Sosa (1985:75–76).

49. This organization, known as the "62 Organizaciones Azopardistas," was announced on January 13, 1983, but not formally constituted until March 19.

50. While Cafiero and the Group of 25's political arm, MUSO, expressed their backing of Miguel's 62 Organizations, the reincorporation into the CGT-Brasil of a series of unions representing the "non-aligned" *(no-alineados)* and "independent" *(independientes)* sectors that had moved toward the CGT-Azopardo during the Falkland/Malvinas war produced discomfort among Group of 25 leaders. Specifically, they objected to the loss of the combative image that had characterized the CGT-Brasil. Aznárez and Calistro (1993:127–28).

51. Along with Miguel, the political rights of twenty-three other persons were restored on April 14, 1983.

52. As was traditional within the Peronist party, the selection of the Peronist presidential candidate responded to a veiled procedure. Primary elections—which were marked from the very beginning by a clear predominance of the "hard-liners" associated with Miguel and the CGT-RA over the "moderates" of Robledo, who was explicitly supported by Matera and the 62 Organizations formed by the CGT-Azopardo—did help to narrow down the field. By late June, then, Luder and Cafiero, who was backed by the MUSO, emerged from the pack as the most likely candidates. If by late July Luder had moved into the lead, there ensued almost a whole month of internal debates, which delayed the launching of the Peronist candidates. The whole process, after relying on a mixture of negotiations and the gauging of public support, culminated in a party convention dominated by a dozen or so party leaders and union bosses. Here Miguel's support for Luder over Cafiero was crucial to the definition of the Luder-Bittel formula on August 22. The formula was formally announced on September 5, and new party leaders were chosen at the same time. Good accounts of the candidate selection process can be found in Cordeu, Mercado, and Sosa (1985) and Cavarozzi (1986:156–58). See also Palermo (1986).

53. On the Peronist's campaign, see Cordeu, Mercado, and Sosa (1985).

54. This declaration of unity was clearly made for public consumption, for there was no new unified leadership. The two wings of the union movement disputed whether such a joint leadership should be unipersonal, as the CGT-RA insisted, or collegial, as the CGT-Azopardo wanted, and the disagreement impeded even the easier task of forming a commission to take over the CGT. The unity of the labor movement would have to wait until the end of 1984, while the CGT was not returned to union hands until June 1985 and finally reconstituted through a normalizing Congress *(Congreso normalizador)* held in November 1986. Senén González (1984:195).

55. Cordeu, Mercado, and Sosa (1985:96), Centro de Investigaciones sobre el Estado y la Administración (1984a:393–94), Landi (1988:59).

56. Unlike the fifteen-point declaration issued in November 1982, this document was less ambitious, focusing solely on the issue of human rights violations. On the document and societal reactions to it, see Centro de Investigaciones sobre el Estado y la Administración (1984a:151–63), Fontana (1987:175–80, 188–89), and McGuire (1995:188–89).

57. In this march as well as in later ones, a novel element of Argentine political culture, related to the forms of these mass demonstrations, became apparent. For one, street mobilizations stopped being a monopoly of the Peronists, as both supporters of human rights organizations and supporters of the UCR took to the streets in large numbers. Also, and closely linked to the first point, there was a change in the public spaces chosen for mass demonstrations. Thus, demonstrations were held not only at the classic Plaza de Mayo, traditionally linked to a Peronist movement that could practically claim it as its birthplace. Now, other meeting places such as the Congress, the Obelisk of the

Plaza de la República, and the Tribunales and the Cabildo, were selected. The obvious symbolic significance of the choice of new sites lay in their association with the representative, popular, and legal aspects of government, rather than with the executive branch. Romero (1985:262–66).

58. Given that the Multipartidaria was created with the purpose of denying the military the option of negotiating separately with one or another party, the rapprochement between the Peronists and the military in late 1982 was a first clear step that undermined the Multipartidaria. But starting in March 1983, as party leaders began focusing on how to win the upcoming elections, and as any uncertainty that it was going to be held could be laid to rest, the role of the Multipartidaria predictably decreased even further in importance. A party arena initially defined by the Multipartidaria, in which all major parties were clustered, gave way to a scenario centered around the two main and well-differentiated parties. Thus, one of the last significant acts of the Multipartidaria was publication of a document critical of military rule in early February (Multipartidaria 1984; Fontana 1987:175–76). Thereafter, until the day before the October 30 elections, when the members of the Multipartidaria signed a Democratic Charter (Carta Democrática) that reaffirmed their defense of a democratic form of government, the political dynamics of the transition was given more by interparty competition than by the logic of a broad party front (Melo 1989:88, 50–51).

59. Luder was caught in the awkward position of having been provisional president in 1974, when certain key decrees allowing for the expansion of military powers so that they could better fight the guerrillas were signed. Moreover, while human rights organizations had sought support from the two main union groupings for their May 20 protest march, no labor contingency made an appearance.

60. The denunciation was made on April 25, just before the government's document was publicized but at a time when its content was known and its release was imminent. On the issue of the existence of such a pact, the historical record remains unclear. However, as Landi (1988:46, 69–72, 113–15) argues, even though it is unlikely that a formal pact as such ever existed, that did not really matter, for the debate that this alleged pact triggered had the most important political consequences. Arfuch (1987) and Melo (1989:48–49). For the text of Alfonsín's denunciation of the pact, see Alfonsín (1984). On the reactions to Alfonsín's denunciation, see Aznárez and Calistro (1993:133–38) and Carpena and Jacquelin (1994:215–25). The context of the pact is discussed by P. Sánchez (1983), J. Sánchez (1983:10–11), and Torre (1983b). The perspective of various unionists can be found in Taccone (1982) and Claves (1984:17–18).

61. Because open political activity was suspended during military rule, and because, as with the Peronists, the UCR had lost their main leader when Balbín died in September 1981, the UCR also faced a leadership struggle. Nonetheless, the impact of the loss of Balbín on the UCR was different, in that the UCR was a more institutionalized party. The key contestants were Alfonsín, representing the Movement of Renovation and Change (Movimiento de Renovación y Cambio) sector, and Fernando de la Rúa, representing the National Line (Línea Nacional). By mid-June, the candidacy of Alfonsín was for all practical purposes ensured, and on July 28 the Alfonsín-Víctor Martínez formula was proclaimed. As discussed above, the Peronists presidential candidates were not defined until August 22. On Alfonsín's rise, see Acuña (1984:213–30).

62. This law gave amnesty to those engaged in the "war against subversion," for actions committed during the period from May 25, 1973, to June 17, 1982, "no matter what the nature of these actions may have been." In a sign of the military's increased lack of control over the transition process, this third attempt at securing guarantees was not only not associated with an effort to pursue what seemed like a futile endeavor—to gain

the support of society. In addition, this attempt gave rise to considerable internal disagreement among the three branches of the armed forces.

63. Both comments were made in early August. This illuminating exchange continued in mid-August, with Alfonsín stating that if he were elected president he would annul the amnesty law, but that different levels of responsibility should be distinguished. Alfonsín's "theory of levels," which would eventually figure prominently in his approach to the human rights policy of his administration, is discussed by Verbitsky (1987:43–66, 384–91).

64. Given that even the military-appointed judges declared the law unconstitutional, Luder's belated reconsideration lacked much credibility.

65. Besides the Peronists' equivocations concerning the military's attempt to put the human rights record beyond the reach of future governments, a couple of incidents reinforced this image of the Peronists. One incident was a fistfight in which the leadership of the CGT-RA attacked the Mothers of the Plaza de Mayo in early September, a disgraceful event that was only partly righted when Ubaldini and Bonafini, the heads of the CGT-RA and the Mothers of the Plaza de Mayo, respectively, publicly embraced during a demonstration organized by the Mothers with the CGT-RA's support on September 21. Another episode, which gained more exposure, was the burning of a burial box with the UCR acronym on it by Herminio Iglesias, the Peronist gubernatorial candidate in Buenos Aires, at the Peronists' campaign closing rally. This event, shown on national television, appeared to symbolize the Peronists' inclination toward violence and intolerance. By this point, the fact that the Peronist party had been the only political force that had publicly denounced the military's violation of human rights to the visiting delegation of the Inter-American Commission on Human Rights of the Organization of American States in September 1979 had faded from memory. Melo (1989:50), González Bombal (1991:54, 60–62), Aznárez and Calistro (1993:150–52, 164–65). On the links between human rights organizations and labor groups, see Veiga (1985:36, 41, 46, 84, 98) and Dabat and Lorenzano (1984:157).

66. Besides winning the presidency, the UCR won an absolute majority in the Chamber of Deputies, gaining 130 of a total of 254 seats while the Peronists won 110. The Peronists did win a majority in the Senate, with 24 seats to the UCR's 16 seats of a total of 46, and also won a majority of the provincial governorships.

67. As a sign of what was to come, in one of the first measures following the transfer of power, the military's self-amnesty law, Law No. 22924, the Law of National Pacification, was annulled. Melo (1989:93).

68. All the military had achieved by way of improving their fortunes was a slight bias toward the small provincial parties that had supported the military by lowering the minimum threshold for gaining representation. This raised a faint possibility that these parties may hold key votes in the presidential Electoral College, but such a possibility never materialized. McGuire (1995:190).

69. Unlike the controlled transitions of Brazil and Chile, the Argentine transition was characterized by a weakened military that had little to offer societal actors willing to engage in a dialogue with them. The basic condition for a pacted transition to democracy—that is, that the outgoing military rulers should have something the civilians wanted—was truly lacking in the case of Argentina (Fontana 1987:174). That the military wanted to retreat to the barracks was evident to everyone. There was therefore no reason for a body like the Multipartidaria to accept any conditions to gain access to the government when such a prize could be achieved at no such cost. Of course, individual parties could still find it to their advantage to bargain with the government behind the back of the Multipartidaria, as apparently was the case with the Peronists. And this would have an

impact on the transition. But no pact with all major political actors was in the making. The argument in this chapter is thus based on the understanding that pacts must be comprehensive—involve all actors that could realistically have an impact on the policy issues the pact covers—and that pacts must entail a quid pro quo—that is, that all signatories must gain something and have something to offer.

70. In interpreting Argentina's transition, McGuire (1995:181–82, 189–90, 193) emphasizes the contingent nature of the Peronist's electoral defeat and states: "Had the Peronists won the elections, Argentina's transition would have been interpreted as a carefully staged, incumbent-controlled one on the Brazilian, Chilean, or Spanish model." Without denying the unpredictable role of chance, this book's argument stresses, in contrast, the extent to which the very dynamics of the transition—which was shaped by the two factors that define its modality—undermined the viability of the military-Peronist pact. The possibility of a pacted transition was open during the Viola period. But once the backlash by hard-liner elements within the military closed the option of transition based on the conversion of liberalizers into reformers and an accommodation between these reformers with the opposition forces in society, the preconditions for a pacted transition vanished. González Bombal (1991:117, 132–33).

71. As various authors have argued, while Argentine politics had previously centered around the antinomies of the people versus oligarchs, or liberation versus dependency, Alfonsín clearly perceived the operative cleavage as between authoritarianism and democracy and cast himself in the role of defender of democracy. The Peronists, meanwhile, continued to stress the social conquests made by Perón in the 1940s, without really acknowledging the extent to which the populations were not responding to such appeals. Cavarozzi (1983, 1986:169–70), Portantiero (1987:275–76), Verbitsky (1985c: 43–50).

72. Actually, the Peronists had taken the first step that began to undermine the Multipartidaria by entering into a dialogue with the military rulers, because the Multipartidaria was created with the purpose of denying the military the option of negotiating separately with one or another party. In this sense, that error on the part of the Peronists created the opportunity for Alfonsín to associate the Peronists with the old order.

73. As before 1976, unions remained solidly Peronist-dominated. The one exception was a small group of unionists that formed the National Movement of Union Renovation (Movimiento Nacional de Renovación Sindical [MNRS]) to support Alfonsín's candidacy in May 1983. Redacción (1983a).

74. Alfonsín and Luder won 92 percent of the total vote. A list of all the party candidates in the presidential race is reproduced in Redacción (1983b). On the electoral strategy of minor parties, see Dabat and Lorenzano (1984:156–63) and Jordán (1993:401–2, 404–7). For an analysis of the election results, see T. Di Tella (1984), Catterberg (1985), Maronese, de Nazar, and Waisman (1985), Canton (1986), Jorrat (1986), Delich (1986: 149–56), Mora y Araujo (1986), and Rock and E. Avellano (1986).

Chapter 7: The Argentine Case in Comparative-Historical Perspective

1. On distinctions between a political regime and a political situation, see Chapter 1.

2. For the purposes of this comparison, the link between the military rulers and the broader category of excluded sectors is considered, instead of focusing primarily on the relationship between the military rulers and labor. For a comparative analysis that

specifically stresses the role of labor under bureaucratic authoritarianism, see Drake (1996). The role of labor in transitional processes is discussed in Valenzuela (1989) and in Collier and Mahoney (1997). The role of labor in the democratization of a distinct type of regime, postrevolutionary authoritarianism, is discussed in Middlebrook (1995: chap. 8).

3. The degree of opposition to the new governing elites offered by the displaced forces, the variable highlighted in the political-institutional model, has been discussed in the literature in various terms, such as the level of threat that precedes the coups leading to bureaucratic authoritarianism, and the degree of malleability the military rulers perceived in their potential interlocutors in the excluded social forces. Ranking cases according to the degree of threat or malleability provides us with a way to assess the relative degree of opposition to the new governing elites in the cases under consideration. In this regard, O'Donnell distinguishes primarily between the relatively low degree of threat that characterized the cases of Brazil in 1964 and Argentina in 1966, and the relatively high degree of threat that characterized the cases of Chile in 1973, Uruguay in 1973, and Argentina in 1976. Moving beyond this broad contrast between the experiences with bureaucratic authoritarianism that originated in the 1960s, as opposed to those that emerged in the 1970s, other authors distinguish among cases that had coups in the 1970s, stressing the greater threat associated with the Chilean case as compared with both the Argentine and the Uruguayan cases. While such an assessment diverges slightly from O'Donnell's that the challenge to the dominant classes was "no less intense" in Argentina in the 1970s and Uruguay compared with Chile, it does draw on the distinction O'Donnell made between a threat provoked by armed organizations that challenged the state's coercive supremacy, as in Argentina and Uruguay, and a threat in which leftist political parties in control of the executive branch of government sought a fundamental change in the social order, as in Chile. It is also worth stressing that the actor seeking change in Chile was more rooted in society and broadly based, and hence less malleable from the perspective of the military rulers, than the actors seeking change in Argentina and Uruguay. O'Donnell (1988:24–31, 142; 1982:42–43), Collier (1979c:389–90), Remmer and Merkx (1982:10–14), Stepan (1985:320, 325, 339–40), Drake (1988:370–76; 1996: chap. 2), Falabella (1989:59–61), Remmer (1989:26–31, 116–17), Frieden (1991:88–89, 103, 135, 143–45, 150, 175–76, 178–79, 206–11, 228), Hagopian (1994:48–49), Valenzuela (1995:24).

4. Garretón (1984:13) sees Chile's rulers as pursuing a repressive or "reactive" approach during 1973–1976/77, stressing "foundational" goals during the subsequent 1976/77–1980/81 period. Others argue that even though there are signs of change starting in 1978, the reactive phase actually continued until 1980 (Brunner, Barrios, and Catalán 1989: chap. 2). Drake (1988:376–84; 1996:76–90, 117–80) documents the backlash against labor and its allies in the Chilean case, comparing the measures adopted in Chile with those employed both in Argentina and in Brazil. See also Barrera and Valenzuela (1986:235–36). Estimates of the number and type of people affected by the repression in Brazil, Argentina, and Chile are presented in King (1989) and Kaufman (1995).

5. For an attempt to compare the institutional setup of military rule across cases of bureaucratic authoritarianism, see Huneeus and Olave (1987), Rouquié (1987a: chaps. 8, 9), Arriagada (1988: chaps. 10, 11), Remmer (1989:34–42, 178–82), Valenzuela (1995: 22–23), Ricci and Fitch (1990:66–67), Agüero (1995a:56–57, 129), and Haggard and Kaufman (1995:37–43, 78–80). For a comparison of the organization of repression and the role of security forces in Chile, Argentina, and Brazil, see Fagen (1992) and Stepan (1988:23–25).

6. Having been named commander-in-chief of the army by President Allende only

nineteen days before the 1973 coup, and having joined the conspiracy against Allende at the last moment, Pinochet was, first of all, in a weak position with respect to his own branch of the military, the army. A Decree Law passed by the junta on September 21, 1973, however, gave Pinochet, as commander-in-chief of the army, the exclusive power over promotions and retirements within the army for a period of one year. With his newly gained power, Pinochet moved to displace officers who could challenge him, and to promote those whom he considered loyal. Valenzuela (1995:32–33).

7. Pinochet's genius was to draw on the military institution's traditional of professionalism and to manipulate it in order to distance the military from political power. In effect, Pinochet separated the roles of the military as government and the military as institution, in a way that avoided the military's politicization, which so weakened the military regime in neighboring Argentina. Key policy decisions were made by Pinochet and his staff, ministers, and advisers, while the military junta participated in policy-making only occasionally. Moreover, the power of the military corporation as a whole was effectively denied by Pinochet's rapid use of his authority to make all cabinet appointments, and through his veto power over junta actions, as a result of his participation in the junta and the requirement for unanimous agreement. The armed services and the Council of Generals, in turn, were explicitly excluded from the decision-making process. Appointment of officers to government positions was therefore conditional on their taking a leave of absence from their military duties. The military as an institution was more clearly a basis of support for the government, rather than the administrator of the state. At the same time, a potentially destabilizing split between these two roles was contained due to the effective bridging of the roles of the military as government and the military as institution in Pinochet's person, as head of both the government and the military institution. Arriagada (1988: chaps. 1, 2, and 10–14, 111), Valenzuela (1995:22–50), Remmer (1989:38–39, 121–45), Huneeus (1986:150–56), Varas (1987:186–87).

8. The need to advance a foundational project was first proclaimed in the so-called Speech of Chacarillas of July 9, 1977. The labor plan of June 1979 was the first of an ambitious plan baptized as "the seven modernizations," launched toward the end of 1978 and 1979. On the overall plan, see Tironi (1990:136–38, 149–51). On the labor plan, see Barrera and Valenzuela (1986:248–58). On the Speech of Chacarillas and the elaboration of the new constitution, see Valenzuela (1995:50–54), Arriagada (1988:33–34, 43), Garretón (1986b:160–63), and Varas (1987:75–80).

9. As in the other cases of bureaucratic authoritarianism, the conflicting imperative created by the problem of representation was evident in Pinochet's argument, presented in the Speech of Chacarillas, "for both the institutionalization of the military regime and the promise of a long-run return to democracy." This tension was embedded in the very goal of the 1980 constitution, the foundation of a "protected and authoritarian democracy" (Garretón 1986b:159, 161).

10. Garretón (1986b:164) makes this point nicely when he states that the Labor Plan and other key government measures "signify not only the 'consolidation' of the historical program of the regime . . . but also the site of new social contradictions and conflicts and, therefore, of new forms of social movement." On the formation and strengthening of the opposition, see the chapters by Valenzuela and Valenzuela, Barrera and Valenzuela, and Smith in Valenzuela and Valenzuela (1986a); the chapters by Maria Valenzuela, Angell, and Garretón in Drake and Jaksic (1995); Campero and Cortázar (1988); Schneider (1995); and Oxhorn (1995).

11. The Labor Plan severely restricted the right to strike, made union membership completely voluntary, allowed collective bargaining only on the part of plant-level unions, and restricted the types of issues that unions could address. On the effect of

the new labor legislation, see Barrera and Valenzuela (1986:259–60) and Barrera, Henríquez, and Selamé (1985).

12. As a result of the personalization of power in Chile, how to categorize Chile under Pinochet is in dispute. For example, McGuire (1995:194) suggests classifying Chile as a "personal" type of regime, and Remmer (1989:38, 144, 178–79) refers to Chile as a case of "sultanist form of military rule," "neopatrimonial rule," and "personal dictatorship." Meanwhile, Huntington (1991:111–13) also characterizes Chile as a "personal dictatorship," although he acknowledges that it shared many features of the cases he labels "military regimes." Without denying the peculiarity of Chile's institutional setup, I here follow Valenzuela's (1995:22–23) argument that "the preeminence of Pinochet as ruler did not mean that the Chilean regime was a personalistic dictatorship" and that the "armed forces in Chile constituted the fundamental pillar of the regime," a feature of bureaucratic authoritarianism. Thus, Chile under Pinochet is distinguished from "sultanistic" or "neopatrimonial" regimes, terms that, as Linz (1990:145–46) argues, generally refer to forms of "personal rule with loyalty to the ruler" in which "the ruler exercises power without restraint . . . unencumbered by rules." On the form of government of Chile under Pinochet, see also Valenzuela and Valenzuela (1986b:3–7) and Agüero (1995a:57).

13. The very illegitimacy of the 1980 plebiscite, which Pinochet claimed to have won with 67 percent of the votes, indirectly aided the process of unity of opposition among Christian Democrats and Socialists. Thereafter, the very focused goal of getting rid of Pinochet played an important role in the unification of a previously divided opposition and the formation of a coalition that, most important, brought together Christian Democrats and one wing of the Socialists.

14. The 1980 constitution did not mention Pinochet by name. Rather, in 1988 a single presidential candidate to serve eight years was to be selected by the commanders-in-chief of the armed forces and ratified through a plebiscite. However, it was almost a foregone conclusion that Pinochet would be the candidate.

15. In addition to the 1980 plebiscite on the new constitution, the government had also claimed the support of 75 percent of the voters in a plebiscite held in 1978 to reassert Pinochet's position in light of international criticisms of human rights abuses.

16. Initially, the military rulers entered into a dialogue with nonleftist labor leaders of what came to be known as the Group of 10, but this dialogue "did not, however, remain cordial for very long." Nothing similar to the extensive contacts between top military leaders and labor leaders that characterized state-labor relations in Argentina occurred in Chile (Barrera and Valenzuela 1986:231, 236–48).

17. For a more expanded discussion of these points, see Munck (1992). On the interplay between legality and legitimacy in democratic transitions, see Shain and Linz (1995:14–21) and Rupnik (1995:64–66).

18. Given that the right-wing parties had supported the 1973 coup and Pinochet throughout, the main opposition political parties were those to the left and center of the political spectrum. This encompassed a broad number of organizations representing quite distinct interests. In particular, a strong tension had divided the left-wing parties that had made up Allende's Popular Unity coalition and the centrist Christian Democrats (Partido Demócrata Cristiano [PDC]), which had been seriously compromised in the demise of Allende's government and the democratic system. Over time, the PDC and the Socialist party (Nuñez faction), united in their opposition to Pinochet, had mended fences. But the Chilean opposition had remained divided during the 1983–86 protest cycle. Specifically, the various moderate groupings, such as the Democratic Alliance and the National Accord, had always excluded the elements of the left that continued to sup-

port an insurrectionary strategy. This last obstacle was resolved, however, when the opposition decided to accept the legality of the 1980 constitution. On the one hand, the framing of the choice entailed by the 1988 plebiscite, which amounted to a referendum on Pinochet, was the impetus for a set of sixteen moderate but still disparate political parties and groups to come together in February 1988 as the Concertation of Parties for the No (Concertación de Partidos por el No), a broad front of opposition to Pinochet's attempt to ratify his position as president for another eight years. But going beyond these groups, the decision to contest the 1988 plebiscite provided the basis for an even broader unity of action that included the more radical opposition groups. Indeed, even the still illegal Communist Party, which was excluded from the Concertation of Parties for the No, issued a declaration calling on its supporters to join forces with this opposition front.

19. The results gave Pinochet 43 percent of the vote, with 54.7 percent going to the opposition. On the plebiscite, see Drake and Valenzuela (1989).

20. Specifically, the democratic opposition had to accept such overtly undemocratic features as Pinochet's right to remain as army commander-in-chief for eight years more, and thereafter as Senator for life, the presence of nine appointed senators, a National Security Council with strong powers and military representation, and a packed supreme court, as well an electoral law that was drawn up by the military to favor right-wing parties and that almost ensured that the constitution could not be amended against the will of the forces that had supported Pinochet's regime. As a result of a bargain between the opposition and the democratic right that until then had supported Pinochet, some changes were introduced in the 1980 constitution after the 1988 plebiscite. These constitutional amendments, approved in a July 1989 plebiscite, made the mechanisms for revising the constitution more flexible, reduced the mandate of the first president to four years, diminished the importance of the designated senators, changed the composition and powers of the National Security Council so that the tutelary role of the military was diminished but not excluded, and eliminated the proscription against the Communist Party. If some of the more conditioning aspects of the 1980 constitution were thereby softened, a series of new preemptive and confining measures was taken by the Pinochet government in the year following the 1988 plebiscite, including laws affecting the Central Bank, elections, and television, as well as appointments within, and the budget of, the armed forces. Valenzuela (1992:62–67).

Because of the significant authoritarian legacies that Pinochet was able to impose on the civilian rulers who took power in 1990, there is some disagreement about the precise timing of the end of Chile's transition. Thus, some authors argue that in 1990 Chile's transition is best characterized as being "incomplete" (Garretón 1995a:28, 32–38, 111–12, 253–54; Linz, Stepan, and Gunther 1995:78–79, 116). But the difference in interpretations of when Chile's transition ends is attributable more to authors' different definitions of what constitutes a transition than on disagreement about the basic facts of Chile's political history. Specifically, the divergent views on this matter hinge on the emphasis put on the rise to power of a new actor, or on the definition of the set of institutional rules that shape the contours of the regime and that are not intended merely as a transitory arrangement. In line with the conceptual framework in this book, 1990 is seen as the end of the transition because at that point power shifted from military to civilian hands.

21. Skidmore (1973:4), Linz (1973b:238), Mainwaring (1988:96, 1995:363). See also the sources cited in note 3.

22. Skidmore (1988:24–27, 34), Alves (1985:34–48, 51–53), Mericle (1977).

23. Alves (1985:60–61, 81–95), Skidmore (1988:42–43, 47, 49–51, 73–81).

24. This feature was to distinguish bureaucratic authoritarianism from previous

forms of military intervention in South America, which were conceived of only as temporary interruptions of normal politics. The phrase that captured the refusal of the military to accept a time frame for their actions was the statement commonly used by the military rulers themselves to the effect that they had "goals but not deadlines." Valenzuela and Valenzuela (1986c:185), Valenzuela (1995:51, 59), Arriagada (1988:43).

25. Alves (1985:62–66, 70–75, 77–79, 95–100, 105–6, 117–19), Skidmore (1988:46–49, 56–57, 81–84, 93–101, 107).

26. The military's High Command selected the presidents, but the procedure was not clearly established. Skidmore (1988:63–64, 97–99, 109, 150), Alves (1985:105–6), Arriagada (1988:105).

27. As Skidmore (1988:64, 108–9) points out, these divisions did not become public and could not be exacerbated by civilians who threw their weight behind this or that military faction.

28. Linz (1973b:235), Lamounier (1989), Skidmore (1988:150, 156–59).

29. In the case of Brazil, the division was between those that worked within the system, trying to advance their cause by working with and voting for the opposition party, the Brazilian Democratic Movement (Movimento Democrático Brasileiro [MDB]), and those that sought to oppose the government from the outside, questioning the validity of using the limited legal opportunities the rulers had provided. Skidmore (1988:114–16).

30. Stepan (1988: chaps. 2, 3), Skidmore (1988:117–35, 160–71), Alves (1985:119–32).

31. Although this reform abolished Institutional Act No. 5, a series of emergency powers did much to reestablish many of the arbitrary powers the Act had established. Lamounier (1989:71).

32. Alves (1985: chaps. 7, 8, Conclusion), Skidmore (1988:171–78, 188–92, 197–203, 217–22, 227–30, 233–36).

33. The constitution of the Electoral College, just as the electoral and party laws, had changed over time. The Electoral College that would select the next president in 1985 had 680 members that included all senators and federal deputies and 132 state deputies (six representatives appointed by each of the twenty-two state legislatures). The promilitary party had secured a clear majority—359 votes, to the 321 votes of the combined opposition.

34. There is confusion in the literature about when Brazil's transition began. Most analyses pinpoint 1974 as the beginning of regime change in Brazil, but 1982 is probably more accurate. Before 1982, Brazil had undergone a process of liberalization—that is, a process aimed at broadening the social base of the authoritarian system. But, as Przeworski (1991:54–66) argues, "liberalization does not always lead to transition." It is therefore crucial to clearly distinguish between a process of liberalization, which does not change the fundamentals of an authoritarian system, and one of democratization, which does entail a transition from authoritarian rule. The importance of not confusing the policies initiated in 1974 with a transition to democracy is stressed by Alves (1985:119, 167–68, 171, 259) and Cardoso (1993:226). On the nondemocratic aims of Brazil's liberalizers and on the significance of the 1982 election, see Stepan (1988:36–37, 62–64), Martins (1986:88–91), and Lamounier (1989:71–72).

35. On the formation and strengthening of the opposition, see Alves (1985:174–210; 1992), Stepan (1985:332–38), Cardoso (1986), and the chapters by Della Cava, Mainwaring, Alvarez, and Keck in Stepan (1989).

36. The costs of remaining in power had become quite evident the last time the military rulers had to confront the presidential succession issue, in 1977–78. In that instance, there was a struggle between hard-liners and soft-liners that ended with President Geisel not following the process for selection of presidents. He simply imposed

General João Figueiredo as the official nominee, without conferring with the High Command. Stepan (1988:43), Alves (1985:170–71).

37. As Hagopian (1992:247–61) argues, the 1982 election had an important impact on the traditional elites that had supported the military, because by their defeats they lost control over political patronage and were therefore willing to use their power in Congress and the presidential Electoral College as a bargaining tool for recapturing the positions they lost in 1982.

38. In the case of Brazil, as with Chile, there is some dispute over when the transition actually ended. While 1985 brought an end to military rule, it is also accurate to point out that it was only as a result of elections for a Constituent Assembly in 1986, the approval of a new constitution in 1988, and finally the first direct election for president in November 1989 and the assumption of power by Collor de Mello in March 1990, that a new set of institutional rules had been put in place. Again, the different interpretations hinge on the analysts' desire to stress actors or institutional rules in the definition of a transition, and again, in line with the conceptual framework in this book, the emphasis here is on the point at which power shifted from military to civilian hands, which leads to 1985 as a cutoff date. On the difficulty of defining an end to Brazil's transition, see Shain and Linz (1995:9, 83, 84–86).

39. As argued in Chapter 3, while the challenge of constitutional definition is the first issue to address in any study of an attempt to set up a bureaucratic authoritarian regime, such a task presupposes, first, a clear seizure of power—that is, installing in power a new set of governing elites and completing the transition from the previous form of rule. A full explanation of the seizure of power, however, belongs to a theory of the breakdown of democracy rather than to a theory of the origin and evolution of, and transition from, bureaucratic authoritarianism.

40. The attempt by military rulers to return to a closed political context after a political opening has been made is an extremely difficult task. The attempt to "return to the sources" is much more difficult than the original installation of the military, because the original sense of purpose is hard to regain and because a policy of liberalization enables the "resurrection of civil society" that is usually more united in confronting the military than at the time of the coup. Indeed, the problems with such mid-course corrections are clearly illustrated by the attempts by General Leopoldo Galtieri in Argentina to reverse the policies initiated by General Roberto Viola. In the case of Brazil, however, such a problem was avoided in large part because of the weakness of the forces that organized in opposition to the military even when the government's agenda was fairly liberal, as was the case during the 1964–67 period. On attempts at closing liberalization episodes, see O'Donnell and Schmitter (1986:48–56).

41. This argument draws on and is broadly consonant with O'Donnell's (1973:99–103; 1978a:7–9) argument concerning the link between the degree of threat and class polarization immediately preceding the bureaucratic authoritarian coups and the cohesiveness of the military rulers. For a critique of this view, however, see Remmer and Merkx (1982).

42. As Remmer (1989:25–35, 43) and others (Philip 1985:38–42, 49, 54–57; Fontana 1987:10–13) argue, in a study of the political dynamics of bureaucratic authoritarianism, it is important not to focus solely on the impact of societal forces on the military rulers and to explicitly consider the institutional dimensions of government. If cohesion is a characteristic pertaining to the military, and thus an intramilitary matter, it is important nonetheless not to abandon a focus on societal forces and seek to explain the military's cohesiveness solely in intramilitary terms (Rouquié 1987a:10–12; Valenzuela 1995:24). A key point of the political-institutional model this book elaborates, thus, is the

need to acknowledge the impact of both state- and society-centered issues and to study their mutual interaction.

43. One of the few authors to draw attention to this process, which has been ignored all too often in the study of bureaucratic authoritarianism, is Garretón, who refers to the recomposition of civil society as an "invisible transition to democracy." The key point of such a notion is that social actors emerge and develop according to their own rhythms and within a distinct social realm. It is crucial to stress, nonetheless, the significant role played by political-strategic issues, and that mobilizing the masses themselves is not enough to undermine military rulers. As Garretón (1989b:273, 261, 262, 275; 1987: 40–50) states, "the political significance of the mobilizations depends on the effect they have on the state. . . . Social mobilizations do not in themselves bring about transitions from authoritarian rule to democratic rule. They can play a critical role in such a transition, but they are not the source of change. . . . Political direction and coordination are also essential." The importance of political-strategic issues for social movements is also stressed in Munck (1995:675–81).

44. A word on Remmer's (1989:34–43) attempt to correlate the diverse institutional arrangements adopted by military rulers and the durability of military rule is in order here. As in the present analysis, Remmer argues that military rule lasted longer in Brazil than in Chile. But she finds that when one considers a broader number of cases, the type of institutional arrangement adopted in Brazil is less durable than the type adopted in Chile. There are, however, a number of differences with regard to how I have proceeded in this book and how Remmer tests her argument. Remmer tests her argument by comparing cases that fit the broad category of military rule, instead of by comparing the impact of diverse institutional arrangements on cases that can be classified as examples of bureaucratic authoritarianism. In addition to this problem of classification, there is the problem of measurement. Remmer argues that military rule lasted twenty-one years in Brazil (1964–85) and sixteen years in Chile (1973–89), using the date when the military rulers handed power over to civilians rather than dating the end of bureaucratic authoritarianism when the transition phase begins. A final point that deserves to be raised is that it is important to avoid an excessively statist view that sees the durability of bureaucratic authoritarianism solely in terms of institutional arrangements. Although these factors are important, as this book's analysis seeks to show, it is important to address the impact of societal forces on the dynamics and durability of bureaucratic authoritarianism. Because Remmer objects to analyses of bureaucratic authoritarianism in terms of such factors as the level of class polarization, and seeks to account for the dynamics of bureaucratic authoritarianism in terms of state institutions, however, such societal factors do not figure prominently in her attempt to explain the durability of bureaucratic authoritarianism.

45. Because most theories of transition do not offer an analysis of these issues, their arguments are more descriptive than explanatory. An important example is the role of divisions among soft-liners and hard-liners that plays such an important part in recent thinking about transitions. In most cases, these divisions are simply taken as givens, while little is done to explain why such key actors emerge in the first place. See, for example, O'Donnell and Schmitter (1986:19–21). Przeworski (1991:56–57) does point us in the right direction when he argues that the source of these divisions is rooted in the relationship between state and society—which is another way of referring to the political dynamics of the old regime. However, little to address such a key issue in a more systematic and thorough manner has been offered. Thus, the attention this book pays to the political dynamics of the old regime and the processes of actor formation addresses a gap in the recent literature.

46. While Argentina's transition can be appropriately categorized—along with the case of Greece (1967–74) for example—as a transition initiated as a result of military defeat by a foreign power, it is important both not to overdo the causal impact of external factors and not to overlook the manner in which the impact of external factors always works its way through domestic factors. First of all, short of military defeat leading to foreign occupation, as was the case with Germany and Japan following World War II, external factors do not have to lead to regime change, as the case of Iraq following the Gulf War shows. But even then, the deeper roots of regime change lie in the political dynamic that leads these countries to adopt an aggressive foreign policy. Thus, while acknowledging a variety of foreign influences on transitions, as analyzed by a growing body of literature, the view advanced in this book coincides with O'Donnell and Schmitter's (1986:18) emphasis on domestic factors and the political dynamic within a country. See also Huntington (1991:112). On the importance of international factors in transitions, see Whitehead (1986, 1996a, 1996b), Stepan (1986), and Schmitter (1996). On the linkage between international and domestic factors, see also Munck and Kumar (1995).

47. The military's failure to carry their project through to completion is stressed by Garretón (1995a:184–85), Borón (1988:134), and Hagopian (1993:467–68, 1994:37–39, 50). On the difficulties of institutionalizing bureaucratic authoritarianism in the age of mass politics, see Mouzelis (1986:179–83) and Diamandorous (1986:145–55). On other right-wing forms of government during the twentieth century, see Hobsbawm (1996: chap. 4).

48. It is important to note that even if the military's goals are defined in negative terms—that is, in terms of their attempt to "eliminate politics, [and] not to found a new political order," as Rouquié (1987a:269) suggests—it remains the case that such an apolitical ideal is a form of political order and, moreover, that the very resurgence of politics and the eventual transitions represented a defeat of such a goal.

49. The debate over the durability and hence the importance of legacies has hinged primarily on the impact of the variable modes of transition. The alternative positions in this debate are well summarized in Przeworksi's (1991:51, 98; 1995:48–49) statements to the effect that a transition's "final destination depends on the path" but that a transition's legacies "can be gradually wiped away."

50. Linz, Stepan, and Gunther (1995), Linz and Stepan (1996), Huntington (1991: 120). While Przeworski's (1991:95–99) critique of the attempts to link the old regime and the problems and prospects of democracy may be proper in many cases, this does not appear to be the case when such linkages are based on the kind of refined typology developed by such scholars as Juan Linz.

51. On the assessment of costs and benefits of authoritarianism and democracy made by business elite as well as by the broader population, see O'Donnell (1992:31–37). In addition to the importance of economic performance, Payne and Bartell (1995:268–71) stress how business elites assess the old regime in terms of the extent to which it allowed business elites to influence policy-making and adhered to free-market tenets. On the process of learning more broadly, see Bermeo (1992).

52. Huntington (1991:211–31), Pion-Berlin (1994), Norden (1996: chap. 8), Agüero (1995a: chap. 9).

53. Karl (1990), Schmitter and Karl (1992), Lijphart (1992), Munck (1994a:364–65), Haggard and Kaufman (1995: chap. 4), Munck and Leff (1997).

54. Even in Chile—the most successful case of bureaucratic authoritarianism—the continuities between the pre-1973 and the post-1990 are quite remarkable (Scully and Valenzuela 1993; Valenzuela 1994:110–15). In Brazil, as Hagopian (1994:37–40, 50–53; 1992:250) shows, the poor showing of the promilitary political party in the 1974 election

led the military to revive clientelism and resurrect the traditional political elites, so that when the military relinquished control over the executive in 1985 it was evident that "the bureaucratic authoritarian regime did not ultimately revamp the way politics was practiced in Brazil."

55. Norden (1996: chaps. 4, 5, 6), Osiel (1986), Pion-Berlin (1991), Acuña and Smulovitz (1995). In other cases of bureaucratic authoritarianism, even where the old regime had been very repressive, as in Chile, the more controlled mode of transition allowed the military to retain prerogatives that essentially put a review of their record of human rights off limits. Thus, while Linz, Stepan, and Gunther (1995:85–86) are correct in arguing that in cases where the old regime was led by a hierarchical, as opposed to nonhierarchical, military elite, the problem of civil-military relations is likely to be a particularly ominous one, it is necessary to stress that the military are not always able to retain prerogatives and establish reserve domains that run counter to the subordination of the military to popularly elected authorities, as Linz, Stepan, and Gunther imply. The impact of the nature of the old regime on postbureaucratic authoritarian politics is mediated, rather, by the mode of transition. Thus, while in cases of controlled transitions the problem of civil-military relations is rooted in the attempt of a fairly unified military institution to retain undemocratic powers at the expense of the civilian authorities, in the case of uncontrolled transitions, military insubordination to civilian rule was rooted instead in military factionalism and challenges to a military hierarchy that cooperated with the civilian government. On the link between the mode of transition and military prerogatives under postbureaucratic authoritarian democracies, see Stepan (1988: chaps. 6, 7) and Haggard and Kaufman (1995:109–18). On postbureaucratic authoritarian civil-military relations, see Pion-Berlin (1992, 1994), Zaverucha (1993), Hunter (1994), Agüero (1995a), and Acuña and Smulovitz (1996).

56. For a discussion and comparison of the short-term impact of the mode of transition in Argentina, Chile, and Brazil, see Cavarozzi (1992a), Munck (1994b), McGuire (1995:202–10), and Munck and Leff (1997).

57. Azpiazu, Basualdo, and Khavisse (1986), Basualdo (1987), Schvarzer (1983), Nun (1987a), Smith (1989:249–55).

58. While it is clear that the country's industrial profile changed dramatically during the 1976–83 period, whether there was an overall process of deindustrialization is under dispute. Thus, while much data show Argentine industry as a percentage of total GDP declining from around 29 percent in 1974 to 22 percent in 1981 and only partially regaining lost ground, going back up to 24.5 percent, by 1983, data from the 1985 economic census show an increase in the order of 3.8 percent in the number of industrial workers over the 1973–84 period, as well as a slight increase in total industrial output over the same period. What accounts for this apparent discrepancy is the simple fact that the process of deindustrialization was a relative one—that is, relative to the previous rates of growth of industry and of the growth rates in the other areas of the economy.

If it is more accurate, then, to talk of a process of "relative deindustrialization," these aggregate figures still hide a real process of regional deindustrialization. For if total figures remained more-or-less constant, the military's economic policies did have a devastating impact on industry in the traditional strongholds of industry (Greater Buenos Aires, Córdoba, and Santa Fe). These losses were made up only by the growth of new industry in areas of the interior of the country, a result of the military's program of regional promotion of industry. What took place, in sum, was a process of "relative deindustrialization" conjoined with a process of regional deindustrialization, and spatial reconfiguration and dispersal.

The figures indicating a process of deindustrialization come from Smith (1989:253) and Nun (1987a:100). For the 1985 economic census and discussions of the new data, see Instituto Nacional de Estadísticas y Censos (1989:15). On the process of relative deindustrialization and the military's regional industrial promotion program, see Gatto, Gutman, and Yoguel (1987), and Schvarzer (1987b).

59. For a general overview of these trends, see Munck (1982) and Villarreal (1987). Shifts in occupational structure are covered in Palomino (1987). On the trend toward geographical dispersion, see Nun (1987a:106–9) and Quintar (1989). On the overall reduction of firm size, see Nun (1987a:108), Gatto, Gutman, and Yoguel (1987: table 13), and Instituto Nacional de Estadísticas y Censos (1989:13). On wage dispertion, see Beccaría and Orsatti (1985:23–28) and Villarreal (1987:80–81). On heterogenization, see José Nun (1987b:125–32). On unionization levels, see Abós (1985:67–78).

60. On the Peronist renewal movement, see De Ipola (1987) and McGuire (1997: chap. 17). On the learning process on the left, see Hodges (1993).

61. As with the short-term legacies of bureaucratic authoritarianism, the long-term legacies are likely to vary across cases. On the impact of bureaucratic authoritarianism on the old import-substituting industrialization model of development, see Garretón (1995a:22, 47–49, 182–85) and Touraine (1989:375, 377–78, 407–8). On changes at the level of key actors in the economic system in Chile, see Eugenio Tironi (1990: chap. 5), Scully (1992:186–202), Munck (1994c:195–202), and Garretón (1995a:201–9); in Brazil, see Bruneau and Faucher (1981) and Reis and O'Donnell (1988). On the impact of bureaucratic authoritarianism on the orientation of business toward authoritarianism and democracy in Chile, see Silva (1992/93); in Brazil, see Payne (1994). On the economic performance of military rulers in Argentina, Chile, and Brazil, see Hartlyn and Morley (1986) and Remmer (1989:197–200). On the learning process on the left in Chile, see Faúndez (1988), Walker (1990), and Garretón (1995b:214–32); in Brazil, see Weffort (1989); more broadly, see Cavarozzi (1992b).

62. This became clear when Argentina's new democracy faced its first crisis, the Holy Week military uprising in 1987. Not only did all political parties sign a democracy pact that condemned the incident and defended the country's democracy, but the main business organizations also opposed the military uprisings and supported democracy. Cavarozzi and Grossi (1992:184–85), Acuña (1995:269). On the "impossible game," see O'Donnell (1973: chap. 4, 1978).

63. Although the first democratic president, Alfonsín, had a chance to carry out structural reforms, that did not happen, because the diagnosis of the crisis facing Argentina was distorted, and because of other more structural impediments. It would therefore be up to Menem, a Peronist president, to introduce a new economic model. On the distorted diagnosis of the crisis under Alfonsín, see Canitrot (1993:81), Damill and Frenkel (1992: 26–28), and Cavarozzi (1995:25–28). On the more structural impediments, see Munck (1994d). On the reforms introduced by Menem, see Acuña (1993) and Palermo and Novaro (1996).

References

This listing of references is arranged in three sections: Newspapers; Periodicals; and Books, Articles, Manuscripts, and Unpublished Documents.

Newspapers

Clarín. 1976–83.
La Nación. 1976–83.
La Opinión. 1976–83.
La Prensa. 1976–83.
All the above sources were published in Buenos Aires.

Periodicals

El Bimestre Político y Económico. 1982–83.
Búsqueda de un País Moderno. April 1981 (vol. 1, no. 1)–August 1983 (vol. 3, no. 22).
Cabildo. 2nd epoch, August 1976 (vol. 1, no. 1)–December 1983 (vol. 8, no. 71).
Carta Política. May 1976 (no. 31)–May 1980 (no. 77).
CIAS: Revista del Centro de Investigación y Acción Social. April 1980 (vol. 29, no. 1)–September 1983 (vol. 32, no. 326).
Claves. January 1984 (vol. 1, no. 1)–December 1984/January 1985 (vol. 1, no. 11).
Comentarios. February 1978 (vol. 1, no. 1)–March 1983 (vol. 6, no. 3).
Compañero. December 1982 (vol. 1, no. 1).
Confirmado. May 1978.
Convocatoria: Organo Oficial del Movimiento Sindical. February 1980 (vol. 1, no. 1).
Criterio. 1976–83.
Cuadernos Gremiales: Revista de Capacitación Sindical del Centro de Estudios Laborales. January 1984 (no. 1)–1984 (no. 7).
Informativo CLAT. July 1979 (vol. 4, no. 37)–November 1982 (vol. 7, no. 67); 2nd epoch, April 1984 (no. 1)–November/December 1985 (no. 19).
Informes Laborales (Documentación e Información Laboral). January 1976 (no. 191)–September–October 1976 (no. 199/200).
Línea. July 1980 (vol. 1, no. 2)–November 1983 (vol. 4, no. 49).
Movimiento para la Revolución Nacional y Popular. December 1982 (vol. 1, no. 1)–March 1983 (vol. 1, no. 4).
El Porteño. January 1982 (vol. 1, no. 1)–December 1983 (vol. 2, no. 24).
Redacción. January 1980 (vol. 8, no. 83)–April 1985 (vol. 13, no. 146).
The Review of the River Plate. January 12, 1977–December 30, 1977.

All the above sources were published in Buenos Aires.

Books, Articles, Manuscripts, and Unpublished Documents

Abós, Alvaro
- 1983 *La columna vertebral: Sindicatos y peronismo* (Buenos Aires: Editorial Legasa).
- 1984 *Las organizaciones sindicales y el poder militar, 1976–1983* (Buenos Aires: Centro Editor de América Latina).
- 1985 *Los sindicatos Argentinos: Cuadro de situación, 1984* (Buenos Aires: Centro de Estudios para el Proyecto Nacional).

Acuña, Marcelo Luis
- 1984 *De Frondizi a Alfonsín: La tradición política del radicalismo*, 2 vols. (Buenos Aires: Centro Editor de América Latina).

Acuña, Carlos H.
- 1980 "El 'diálogo' del gobierno," *Revista del Centro de Investigación y Acción Social* (Buenos Aires), 29, no. 295/296 (August–September): 19–53.
- 1993 "Politics and Economics in the Argentina of the Nineties (Or, Why the Future No Longer Is What It Used to Be)," 31–73, in William C. Smith, Carlos H. Acuña, and Eduardo A. Gamarra (eds.), *Democracy, Markets, and Structural Reforms in Latin America: Argentina, Bolivia, Brazil, Chile, and Mexico* (New Brunswick, N.J.: Transaction/ North-South Center).
- 1995 "Intereses empresarios, dictadura y democracia en la Argentina actual (O sobre por qué la burguesía abandona estrategias autoritarias y opta por la estabilidad democrática)," 231–82, in Carlos H. Acuña (ed.), *La nueva matriz política Argentina* (Buenos Aires: Ediciones Nueva Visión).

Acuña, Carlos H., and Catalina Smulovitz
- 1995 "Militares en la transición Argentina: Del gobierno a la subordinación constitucional," 153–202, in Carlos H. Acuña (ed.), *La nueva matriz política Argentina* (Buenos Aires: Ediciones Nueva Visión).
- 1996 "Adjusting the Armed Forces to Democracy: Successes, Failures, and Ambiguities in the Southern Cone," 13–38, in Elizabeth Jelin and Eric Hershberg (eds.), *Constructing Democracy: Human Rights, Citizenship, and Society in Latin America* (Boulder, Colo.: Westview Press).

Agrupación Clasista 1o. de Mayo
- 1986 *La ocupación de Ford: 18 días que conmovieron la Argentina* (Buenos Aires: Ediciones Agrupación Clasista 1o. de Mayo).

Agüero, Felipe
- 1995a *Soldiers, Civilians, and Democracy: Post-Franco Spain in Comparative Perspective* (Baltimore: Johns Hopkins University Press).
- 1995b "Democratic Consolidation and the Military in Southern Europe and South America," 124–65, in Richard Gunther, P. Nikiforos Diamandouros, and Hans-Jürgen Puhle (eds.), *The Politics of Democratic*

Consolidation: Southern Europe in Comparative Perspective (Baltimore: Johns Hopkins University Press).

Albanese, Pascual
1984 "[Interview with Pascual Albanese]," 189–93, in Osvaldo Calello and Daniel Parceco, *De Vandor a Ubaldini*, vol. 2 (Buenos Aires: Centro Editor de América Latina).

Alberoni, Francesco
1991 *Gênese* (Rio de Janeiro: Rocco).

Alende, Oscar, Nestor Vicente, Conrado Storani, and José María Rosa
1981 *El ocaso del "proceso"* (Buenos Aires: El Cid Editor).

Alfonsín, Raúl
1984 "El pacto," 237–38, in Centro de Investigaciones sobre el Estado y la Administración (CISEA), *Argentina 1983* (Buenos Aires: CISEA/Centro Editor de América Latina).

Alves, Maria Helena Moreira
1985 *State and Opposition in Military Brazil* (Austin: University of Texas Press).
1992 "Cultures of Fear, Cultures of Resistance: The New Labor Movement in Brazil," 184–211, in Juan E. Corradi, Patricia Weiss Fagen, and Manuel Antonio Garretón (eds.), *Fear at the Edge: State Terror and Resistance in Latin America* (Berkeley and Los Angeles: University of California Press).

Andersen, Martin Edwin.
1993 *Dossier secreto: Argentina's Desaparecidos and the Myth of the "Dirty War"* (Boulder, Colo.: Westview Press).

Andrain, Charles F.
1994 *Comparative Political Systems: Policy Performance and Social Change* (Armonk, N.Y.: M. E. Sharpe).

Angell, Alan
1984 "The Soldier as Politician: Military Authoritarianism in Latin America," 116–43, in Dennis Kavanagh and Gillian Peele (eds.), *Comparative Government and Politics: Essays in Honour of S. E. Finer* (London: Heinemenn).

Angell, Alan, and Benny Pollack
1990 "The Chilean Elections of 1989 and the Politics of the Transition to Democracy," *Bulletin of Latin American Research* 9, no. 1:1–23.

Arfuch, Leonor
1987 "Dos variantes del juego de la política en el discurso electoral del 1983," 27–52, in Eliseo Verón et al., *El discurso político: Lenguajes y acontecimientos* (Buenos Aires: Hachette).

Arriagada Herrera, Genaro
1981 *El pensamiento político de los militares (Estudios sobre Chile, Argentina, Brasil y Uruguay)* (Santiago, Chile: Centro de Investigaciones Socioeconómicas).
1988 *Pinochet: The Politics of Power* (Boston: Unwin Hyman).

Arriagada H., Genaro, and Manuel A. Garretón
1978 "Doctrina de seguridad nacional y régimen militar," *Estudios Sociales Centroamericanos* (San José, Costa Rica) part 1 in vol. 7, no. 20 (May–August): 129–53; part 2 in vol. 7, no. 21 (September–December): 53–82.

Ash, Timothy Garton
1990 *The Magic Lantern: The Revolution of 1989* (New York: Random House).

Avellaneda, Andrés
1989 "The Process of Censorship and Censorship of the Process," 23–47, in David W. Foster (ed.), *The Redemocratization of Argentine Culture, 1983 and Beyond* (Tempe: Center for Latin American Studies, Arizona State University).

Aznárez, Carlos, and Julio César Calistro
1993 *Lorenzo: El padrino del poder sindical* (Buenos Aires: Tiempo de Ideas).

Azpiazu, Daniel, Eduardo Basualdo, and Miguel Khavisse
1986 *El nuevo poder económico en la Argentina de las años 80* (Buenos Aires: Editorial Legasa).

Baizán, Mario, and Silvia Mercado
1987 *Oscar Smith: El sindicalismo peronista ante sus límites* (Buenos Aires: Puntosur).

Baloyra, Enrique
1987 "Argentina: Transición o disolución," 87–136, in Carlos Huneeus (ed.), *Para vivir la democracia* (Santiago de Chile: Centro de Estudios de la Realidad Contemporánea).

Balvé, Beatriz
n.d. "Los nucleamientos político-ideológicos de la clase obrera: Composición interna y alineamientos sindicales en relación a gobierno y partidos, Argentina, 1955–1974," *Serie Estudios,* no. 51 (Buenos Aires: Cuadernos del CICSO).

Barnett, Anthony
1982 "Iron Britannia," Special Issue of *New Left Review,* no. 134 (July–August).

Barrera, Manuel, Helia Henríquez, and Teresita Selamé
1985 *Sindicatos y estado en el Chile actual* (Santiago: UNRISD-CES).

Barrera, Manuel, and J. Samuel Valenzuela
1986 "The Development of Labor Movement Opposition to the Military Regime," 230–69, in Arturo Valenzuela and Samuel Valenzuela (eds.), *Military Rule in Chile: Dictatorship and Oppositions* (Baltimore: Johns Hopkins University Press).

Basualdo, Eduardo M.
1987 *Deuda externa y poder económico en la Argentina* (Buenos Aires: Editorial Nueva América).

Bartell, Ernest, and Leigh A. Payne (eds.)
1995 *Business and Democracy in Latin America* (Pittsburgh: University of Pittsburgh Press).

Beccaría, Luis A., and Alvaro Orsatti
1985 *La evolución del empleo y los salarios en el corto plazo: El caso Argentino, 1970–1983* (Buenos Aires: CEPAL, Documento de Trabajo no. 14).
Beck, Peter
1988 *The Falklands Islands as an International Problem* (London: Routledge).
Beltrán, Virgilio R.
1987 "Political Transition in Argentina, 1982 to 1985," *Armed Forces and Society* 13, no. 2 (Winter): 215–33.
Bermeo, Nancy
1992 "Democracy and the Lessons of Dictatorship," *Comparative Politics* 24, no. 3 (April): 273–91.
1995 "Classification and Consolidation: Some Lessons from the Greek Dictatorship," *Political Science Quarterly* 110, no. 3 (Fall): 435–52.
Bignone, Reynaldo B. A.
1992 *El último de facto: La liquidación del Proceso, Memoria y testimonio* (Buenos Aires: Planeta).
Bittel, Deolindo F.
1983 *Peronismo y Dictadura* (Buenos Aires: Editora del Movimiento).
Bobbio, Norberto
1989 *Democracy and Dictatorship: The Nature and Limits of State Power* (Minneapolis: University of Minnesota Press).
Boggs, Michael D., and Andrew C. McLellan
1978 "Sindicatos Argentinos," *AFL-CIO Free Trade Union News*, no. 33: 4–5, 16.
Borón, Atilio
1988 "The Malvinas War: Implications for an Authoritarian State," 133–48, in José Silva-Michelena (ed.), *Latin America: Peace, Democratization, and Economic Crisis* (London: Zed Press).
Botana, Natalio, and Ana María Mustapic
1991 "La reforma constitucional frente al régimen político Argentino," 47–87, in Dieter Nohlen and Liliana de Riz (eds.), *Reforma institucional y cambio político* (Buenos Aires: Editorial Legasa/CEDES).
Botana, Natalio R., et al.
1985 *La Argentina electoral* (Buenos Aires: Editorial Sudamericana).
Bousquet, Jean P.
1983 *Locas de la Plaza de Mayo* (Buenos Aires: El Cid Editor).
Brennan, James P.
1994 *The Labor Wars in Córdoba, 1955–1976: Ideology, Work, and Labor Politics in an Argentine Industrial City* (Cambridge, Mass.: Harvard University Press).
Bresser Pereira, Luiz Carlos
1981 *A Sociedade Estatal e a Technoburocracia* (São Paulo: Brasiliense).
1993 "Efficiency and Politics of Economic Reform in Latin America," 15–76, in Luiz Carlos Bresser Pereira, José María Maravall, and

Adam Przeworski, *Economic Reform in New Democracies* (New York: Cambridge University Press).
Bruneau, Thomas C., and Philippe Faucher (eds.)
  1981 *Authoritarian Capitalism: Brazil's Contemporary Economic and Political Development* (Boulder, Colo.: Westview Press).
Brunner, José Joaquín, Alicia Barrios, and Carlos Catalán
  1989 *Chile: Transformaciones culturales y modernidad* (Santiago: FLACSO).
Brysk, Alison
  1994 *The Politics of Human Rights in Argentina* (Stanford, Calif.: Stanford University Press).
Buchanan, Paul G.
  1987 "The Varied Faces of Domination: State Terror, Economic Policy, and Social Rupture During the Argentine 'Proceso,' 1976–81," *American Journal of Political Science* 31, no. 2 (May): 336–81.
Burns, Jimmy
  1987 *The Land That Lost Its Heroes: The Falklands, the Post-War, and Alfonsín* (London: Bloomsbury).
Calello, Osvaldo, and Daniel Parceco
  1984 *De Vandor a Ubaldini,* 2 vols. (Buenos Aires: Centro Editor de América Latina).
Campero, Guillermo, and René Cortázar
  1988 "Actores sociales y la transición a la democracia en Chile," *Colección Estudios CIEPLAN,* no. 25 (December): 115–58.
Camps, Ramón J. A.
  1982 *Caso Timerman: Punto Final* (Buenos Aires: Tribuna Abierta).
Canitrot, Adolfo
  1980 "La disciplina como objetivo de la política economica: Un ensayo sobre el programa económico del gobierno Argentino desde 1976," *Desarrollo Económico* (Buenos Aires), 19, no. 76 (January–March): 453–75.
  1981 "Teoría y práctica del liberalismo: Politica antiinflacionaria y apertura económica en la Argentina, 1976–1981," *Desarrollo Económico* (Buenos Aires), 21, no. 82 (July–September): 131–89.
  1983 "Orden social y monetarismo," *Estudios Cedes* 4, no. 7 (Buenos Aires: CEDES).
  1993 "Crisis and Tranformation of the Argentine State, 1978–1992," 75–102, in William C. Smith, Carlos Acuña, and Eduardo Gamarra (eds.), *Democracy, Markets, and Structural Reforms in Latin America: Argentina, Bolivia, Brazil, Chile, and Mexico* (New Brunswick, N.J.: Transaction).
Canton, Darío
  1986 *El pueblo legislado: Las elecciones de 1983* (Buenos Aires: Centro Editor de América Latina/CICSO).
Carazo, Alfredo, and Rodolfo Audi
  1984 *Siete años de lucha contra la dictadura* (Buenos Aires: Editorial Nuevo Horizonte).

Cardoso, Fernando Henrique
1975 *Autoritarismo e democratização* (Rio de Janeiro: Editora Paz e Terra).
1979 "On the Characterization of Authoritarian Regimes in Latin America," 33–57, in David Collier (ed.), *The New Authoritarianism in Latin America* (Princeton: Princeton University Press).
1984 "A Democracia na América Latina," *Novos Estudos Cebrap* (São Paulo), no. 10 (October): 45–56.
1986 "Entrepreneurs and the Transition Process: The Brazilian Case," 137–53, in Guillermo O'Donnell, Philippe Schmitter, and Laurence Whitehead (eds.), *Transitions from Authoritarian Rule: Comparative Perspectives* (Baltimore: Johns Hopkins University Press).
1993 *A Construção da Democracia: Estudos sobre política* (São Paulo: Editora Siciliano).
Cardoso, Fernando Henrique, and Enzo Faletto
1979 *Dependency and Development in Latin America* (Berkeley and Los Angeles: University of California Press).
Cardoso, Oscar R., and Rodolfo Audi
1982 *Sindicalismo: El poder y la crisis* (Buenos Aires: Editorial Belgrano).
Cardoso, Oscar Raul, Ricardo Kirschbaum, and Eduardo van der Kooy
1992 *Malvinas: La trama secreta* (Buenos Aires: Planeta).
Carpena, Ricardo, and Claudio A. Jacquelin
1994 *El intocable: La historia secreta de Lorenzo Miguel, el último mandamás de la Argentina* (Buenos Aires: Editorial Sudamericana).
Carta Política
1976a "La cúpula cívico-militar," *Carta Política* (Buenos Aires), no. 32 (June): 32–35.
1976b "Sindicatos: Estrategia o submisión," *Carta Política* (Buenos Aires), no. 35 (September): 19–21.
1977a "Vuelve la política," *Carta Política* (Buenos Aires), no. 40 (February): 15–19.
1977b "Hay que llenar el vacío," *Carta Política* (Buenos Aires), no. 41 (March): 23–29.
1977c "¿Qué pasa en la Junta?" *Carta Política* (Buenos Aires), no. 48 (October): 32–40.
1978a "¿Otro o el mismo?" *Carta Política* (Buenos Aires), no. 55 (June): 38–42.
1978b "El plan político: Los puntos sobre las íes," *Carta Política* (Buenos Aires), no. 61 (December): 32–37.
1979 "Un mes repetido," *Carta Política* (Buenos Aires), no. 64 (March): 4–8.
1980 "Más allá de Videla," *Carta Política* (Buenos Aires), no. 76 (April): 30–36.
Castiglione, Marta
1992 *La militarización del Estado en la Argentina, 1976/1981* (Buenos Aires: Centro Editor de América Latina).

Catterberg, Edgardo Raul
   1985 "Las elecciones del 30 de Octubre de 1983: El surgimiento de una nueva convergencia electoral," *Desarrollo Económico* (Buenos Aires), 25, no. 98 (July–December): 259–67.
Cavarozzi, Marcelo
   1982 "Argentina at the Crossroads: Pathways and Obstacles to Democratization in the Present Political Conjuncture," *Working Papers,* no. 115 (Washington, D.C.: Wilson Center).
   1983 *Autoritarismo y democracia, 1955–1983* (Buenos Aires: Centro Editor de América Latina).
   1986 "Peronism and Radicalism: Argentina's Transition in Perspective," 143–74, in Paul Drake and Eduardo Silva (eds.), *Elections and Democratization in Latin America, 1980–1985* (San Diego: CILAS, Center for U.S.-Mexican Studies, IOA).
   1989 "El esquema partidario Argentino: Partidos viejos, sistema débil," 297–334, in Cavarozzi and Manuel Antonio Garretón (eds.), *Muerte y resurección: Los partidos políticos en el autoritarismo y las transiciones en el Cono Sur* (Santiago: FLACSO).
   1992a "Patterns of Elite Negotiation and Confrontation in Argentina and Chile," 208–36, in John Higley and Richard Gunther (eds.), *Elites and Democratic Consolidation in Latin America and Southern Europe* (Cambridge: Cambridge University Press).
   1992b "The Left in Latin America: The Decline of Socialism and the Rise of Political Democracy," 101–27, in Jonathan Hartlyn, Lars Shoultz, and Augusto Varas (eds.), *The United States and Latin America in the 1990s* (Chapel Hill: University of North Carolina Press).
   1995 "Oportunidades perdidas y aprendizajes en curso: La política Argentina," XIX International Congress of the Latin American Studies Association (LASA), Washington, D.C., September 28–30, 1995.
Cavarozzi, Marcelo, and Manuel Antonio Garretón (eds.)
   1989 *Muerte y resurección: Los partidos políticos en el autoritarismo y las transiciones en el Cono Sur* (Santiago: FLACSO).
Cavarozzi, Marcelo, and María Grossi
   1992 "Argentine Parties Under Alfonsín: From Democratic Reinvention to Political Decline and Hyperinflation," 173–202, in Edward Epstein (ed.), *The New Argentine Democracy: The Search for a Successful Formula* (New York: Praeger).
Caviedes, Cesar N.
   1984 *The Southern Cone: Realities of the Authoritarian State* (Totowa, N.J.: Rowman & Allanhead Publishers).
Centro de Investigación y Acción Social (CIAS)
   1980 Special Issue on the Church's Position on the Law of Professional Associations, *Revista del CIAS* (Buenos Aires), 29, no. 291 (April).
Centro de Investigaciones sobre el Estado y la Administración (CISEA)
   1984a *Argentina 1983* (Buenos Aires: CISEA/Centro Editor de América Latina).

1984b "Del colapso militar al triunfo de Alfonsín," *Cuadernos del Bimestre*, no. 3 (Buenos Aires: CISEA).
Cermesoni, Jorge Raúl
1978a "¿Pero hacen falta, en verdad, los sindicatos?" *Carta Política* (Buenos Aires), no. 53 (April): 16–18.
1978b "Frente a una ley de Asociaciones Profesionales," *Carta Política* (Buenos Aires), no. 60 (November): 72–73.
Chehabi, H. E., and Alfred Stepan (eds.)
1995 *Politics, Society, and Democracy: Comparative Studies* (Boulder, Colo.: Westview Press).
Cheresky, Isidoro
1985 "Hacia la Argentina postautoritaria," 21–31, in Isidoro Cheresky and Jacques Chonchol (eds.), *Crisis y transformación de los regímenes autoritarios* (Buenos Aires: Editorial Universitaria de Buenos Aires).
Cheresky, Isidoro, and Jacques Chonchol (eds.)
1985 *Crisis y transformación de los regímenes autoritarios* (Buenos Aires: Editorial Universitaria de Buenos Aires).
Claves
1984 "Hablan los enemigos de la burocracia [Interview of Andrés Framini and Julio Guillán]," *Claves* (Buenos Aires), 1, no. 4 (April): 12–21.
Collier, David (ed.)
1979a *The New Authoritarianism in Latin America* (Princeton: Princeton University Press).
Collier, David
1979b "Overview of the Bureaucratic-Authoritarian Model," 3–32, in David Collier (ed.), *The New Authoritarianism in Latin America* (Princeton: Princeton University Press).
1979c "The Bureaucratic-Authoritarian Model: Synthesis and Priorities for Future Research," 363–97, in David Collier (ed.), *The New Authoritarianism in Latin America* (Princeton: Princeton University Press).
1993 "Bureaucratic Authoritarianism," 96–98, in Joel Krieger (ed.), *The Oxford Companion to the Politics of the World* (New York: Oxford University Press).
Collier, David, and Steven Levitsky
1997 "Democracy With Adjectives: Conceptual Innovation in Comparative Research," *World Politics* 49, no. 3 (April): 430–51.
Collier, David, and James E. Mahon
1993 "Conceptual 'Stretching' Revisited: Alternative Views of Categories in Comparative Analysis," *American Political Science Review* 87, no. 4 (December): 845–55.
Collier, Ruth Berins, and David Collier
1991 *Shaping the Political Arena: Critical Junctures, the Labor Movement, and the Regime Dynamics in Latin America* (Princeton: Princeton University Press).
Collier, Ruth Berins, and James Mahoney
1997 "Adding Collective Actors to Collective Outcomes: Labor and Recent

Democratization in South America and Southern Europe," *Comparative Politics* 29, no. 3 (April): 285–303.
Comblin, Joseph
  1980   *A Ideologia da Segurança Nacional: O Poder Militar na América Latina* (Rio de Janeiro: Editora Civilização Brasileira).
Comentarios
  1981a "La multisectorial y los comunistas," *Comentarios* (Buenos Aires), 4, no. 9 (September): 6–8.
  1981b "Gobierno de transición cívico-militar," *Comentarios* (Buenos Aires), 4, no. 11 (November): 5–7.
Comisión Nacional de Trabajo (CNT)
  1984   "Reflexiones para una Propuesta Económica," 126–31, in Alvaro Abós, *Las organizaciones sindicales y el poder militar, 1976–1983* (Buenos Aires: Centro Editor de América Latina).
Comisión Nacional sobre la Desaparición de Personas (National Commission on Disappeared People [CONADEP])
  1985   *Nunca Más: Informe de la Comisión Nacional sobre la Desaparición de Personas* (Buenos Aires: Editorial Universitaria de Buenos Aires).
  1986   *Nunca Más (Never Again): A Report by Argentina's National Commission on Disappeared People* (London and Boston: Faber & Faber/Index on Censorship).
Comisión Permanente de la Conferencia Episcopal Argentina
  1984   "Declaración sobre la Ley 22,105," 132–35, in Alvaro Abós, *Las organizaciones sindicales y el poder militar, 1976–1983* (Buenos Aires: Centro Editor de América Latina).
Comisión Rattenbach
  1988   *Informe Rattenbach: El drama de malvinas* (Buenos Aires: Ediciones Espartaco).
Conferencia Episcopal Argentina
  1982   "Camino de Reconciliación," *El Bimestre Político y Económico* (Buenos Aires), 1, no. 4 (July–August): 64–67.
Confederación General del Trabajo (General Labor Confederation [CGT])
  1984a "La segunda huelga general," 138–39, in Alvaro Abós, *Las organizaciones sindicales y el poder militar, 1976–1983* (Buenos Aires: Centro Editor de América Latina).
  1984b "El 30 de marzo y las Malvinas," 140–43, in Alvaro Abós, *Las organizaciones sindicales y el poder militar, 1976–1983* (Buenos Aires: Centro Editor de América Latina).
  1984c "CGT: Ante la guerra," 143–45, in Alvaro Abós, *Las organizaciones sindicales y el poder militar, 1976–1983* (Buenos Aires: Centro Editor de América Latina).
Corbière, Emilio J.
  1981   "El peronismo en su hora más difícil," *Búsqueda de un País Moderno* (Buenos Aires), no. 6 (November): 20–29.

Cordeu, Mora, Silvia Mercado, and Nancy Sosa
- 1985 *Peronismo: La mayoría perdida*, 2nd ed. (Buenos Aires: Sudamericana/Planeta).

Corradi, Juan E.
- 1987 "The Culture of Fear in Civil Society," 113–29, in Mónica Peralta-Ramos and Carlos Waisman (eds.), *From Military Rule to Liberal Democracy in Argentina* (Boulder, Colo.: Westview Press).

Corradi, Juan E., Patricia Weiss Fagen, and Manuel Antonio Garretón (eds.
- 1992 *Fear at the Edge: State Terror and Resistance in Latin America* (Berkeley and Los Angeles: University of California Press).

Cortázar, René, Alejandro Foxley, and Víctor E. Tokman
- 1984 *Legados del Monetarismo: Argentina y Chile* (Buenos Aires: Ediciones Solar).

Cortés, Rosalia
- 1985 "La seguridad social en la Argentina: Las obras sociales," *Documentos e Informes de Investigación*, no. 28 (Buenos Aires: FLACSO, September).

Costa Mendez, Nicanor
- 1993 *Malvinas: Esta es la historia* (Buenos Aires: Editorial Sudamericana).

Cumings, Bruce
- 1989 "The Abortive Abertura: South Korea in the Light of Latin American Experiences," *New Left Review*, no. 173 (January–February): 5–32.

Dabat, Alejandro, and Luis Lorenzano
- 1984 *Argentina: The Malvinas and the End of Military Rule* (London: Verso).

D'Abate, Juan Carlos
- 1981 *El antipoder sindical* (Buenos Aires: Editorial IUS Consultores).

Dahl, Robert
- 1971 *Polyarchy* (New Haven: Yale University Press).
- 1989 *Democracy and Its Critics* (New Haven: Yale University Press).

Dahl, Robert (ed.)
- 1973 *Regimes and Oppositions* (New Haven: Yale University Press).

Daireaux, Emilio
- 1980 "El sector laboral," mimeographed, July 18, 1980.
- 1981a "Relaciones del trabajo: Las convenciones colectivas de trabajo y los conflictos laborales," mimeographed, February 19, 1981.
- 1981b "Cursos de acción posibles en materia de actividad sindical," mimeographed, March 3, 1981.

Damill, Mario, and Roberto Frenkel
- 1992 "Malos tiempos: La economía Argentina en la decada de los ochenta," 3–70, in Roberto Frenkel et al., *Argentina: Evolución Macroeconómica, financiación externa y cambio político* (Madrid: Fundación CEDEAL).

de Camargo, Sonia, and José Maria Vasquez Ocampo
  1988 *Autoritarismo e democracia na Argentina e Brasil: Uma decada de política exterior, 1973–1984* (São Paulo: Editora Convívio).
de Ipola, Emilio
  1987 "La difícil apuesta del peronismo democrático," 333–74, in José Nun and Juan Carlos Portantiero (eds.), *Ensayos sobre la transición democrática en la Argentina* (Buenos Aires: Puntosur Editores).
de Ipola, Emilio, and Liliana de Riz
  1982 "Un juego de 'Cartas Políticas': Intelectuales y discurso autoritario en la Argentina actual," 83–111, in Francisco Rojas Aravena (ed.), *América Latina: Ideología y Cultura* (San José, Costa Rica: Ediciones FLACSO).
de Riz, Liliana
  1981 *Retorno y Derrumbe: El último gobierno peronista* (México: Folios Ediciones).
  1982 "Argentina: Ni democracia estable ni régimen militar sólido," *Revista Mexicana de Sociología* (México), 44, no. 4 (October–December): 1203–23.
de Tocqueville, Alexis
  1945 *Democracy in America*, vol. 1 (New York: Vintage Books/Random House).
Decker, David R.
  1983 *The Political, Economic, and Labor Climate in Argentina* (Philadelphia: Industrial Research Unit, The Wharton School).
Deheza, José A.
  1981 *¿Quiénes derrocaron a Isabel Perón?* (Buenos Aires: Ediciones Cuenca del Plata).
Delich, Francisco
  1982a "Después del Diluvio, la Clase Obrera," 129–50, in Alain Rouquié (ed.), *Argentina, hoy* (Buenos Aires: Siglo XXI editores).
  1982b "Desmovilización social, reestructuración obrera y cambio sindical," 101–15, in Peter Waldmann and Ernesto Garzón Valdéz (eds.), *El poder militar en la Argentina, 1976–1981* (Frankfurt: Verlag Klaus Dieter Vervuert).
  1986 *Metáforas de la sociedad argentina* (Buenos Aires: Editorial Sudamericana).
Di Palma, Guiseppe
  1990 *To Craft Democracies: An Essay on Democratic Transitions* (Berkeley and Los Angeles: University of California Press).
Di Palma, Guiseppe, and Laurence Whitehead (eds.)
  1986 *The Central American Impasse* (New York: St. Martin's Press).
Di Tella, Guido
  1983 *Argentina Under Perón, 1973–1977: The Nation's Experience with a Labour-Based Government* (London: Macmillan).
  1984 "Fuerzas Armadas y Democratización en Argentina," 101–11, in Au-

gusto Varas (ed.), *Transición a la Democracia: América Latina y Chile* (Santiago: Salesianos).

Di Tella, Torcuato S.
1984 "The October 1983 Elections in Argentina," *Government and Opposition* 19, no. 2 (Spring): 188–92.

Diamandorous, P. Nikiforos
1986 "Regime Change and Prospects for Democracy in Greece, 1974–1983," 138–64, in Guillermo O'Donnell, Philippe Schmitter and Laurence Whitehead (eds.), *Transitions from Authoritarian Rule: Southern Europe* (Baltimore: Johns Hopkins University Press).

Diamond, Larry, Juan J. Linz, and Seymour Martin Lipset
1990 "Introduction: Comparing Experiences with Democracy," 1–38, in Larry Diamond, Juan J. Linz, and Seymour Martin Lipset (eds.), *Politics in Developing Countries: Comparing Experiences with Democracy* (Boulder, Colo.: Lynne Rienner Publishers).

Díaz Bessone, Ramón Genaro
1986 *Guerra revolucionaria en la Argentina, 1959–1978* (Buenos Aires: Editorial Fraterna).

Dimase, Leonardo E.
1964 "La estructura gremial argentina," 7–34, in Leonardo Dimase, Alfredo Garófano, and Gerardo Andújar, *La situación gremial en la Argentina* (Buenos Aires: Ediciones Libera).
1972 *Nucleamientos Sindicales* (Buenos Aires: Serie Documentos Documentación e Información Laboral).
1981 "La politica económica-social inaugurada en 1976 y sus efectos en los sindicatos que nuclean trabajadores de empresas estatales," *Revista CIAS* (Buenos Aires), 30, no. 301: 33–61.

Drake, Paul W.
1988 "Urban Labour Movements Under Authoritarian Capitalism in the Southern Cone and Brazil, 1964–1983," 367–98, in Josef Gugler (ed.), *The Urbanization of the Third World* (New York: Oxford University Press).
1996 *Labor Movements and Dictatorships: The Southern Cone in Comparative Perspective* (Baltimore: John Hopkins University Press).

Drake, Paul, and Iván Jaksić (eds.)
1995 *The Struggle for Democracy in Chile, 1982–1990*, rev. ed. (Lincoln: University of Nebraska Press).

Drake, Paul, and Arturo Valenzuela
1989 "The Chilean Plebiscite: A First Step Toward Redemocratization," *LASA Forum* 19, no. 4 (Winter): 18–36.

Duhalde, Eduardo Luis
1983 *El Estado terrorista Argentino* (Buenos Aires: El Caballito).

Elster, Jon
1988 "Arguments for Constitutional Choice: Reflections on the Transition to Socialism," 303–23, in Jon Elster and Rune Slagstad (eds.), *Consti-*

tutionalism and Democracy (Cambridge: Cambridge University Press).

Epstein, Edward C.
- 1987 "Inflation and Public Policy in Argentina: A Preface to Argentine Politics," *Boletín de Estudios Latinoamericanos y del Caribe*, no. 43 (December): 81–97.
- 1989 "Austerity and Trade Unions in Latin America," 169–89, in William L. Canak (ed.), *Lost Promises: Debt, Austerity, and Development in Latin America* (Boulder, Colo.: Westview Press).

Equipo Episcopal de Pastoral Social
- 1984 "Comunicado sobre Agremiación," 132–35, in Alvaro Abós, *Las organizaciones sindicales y el poder militar, 1976–1983* (Buenos Aires: Centro Editor de América Latina).

Fagen, Patricia Weiss
- 1992 "Repression and State Security," 39–71, in Juan E. Corradi, Patricia Weiss Fagen, and Manuel Antonio Garretón (eds.), *Fear at the Edge: State Terror and Resistance in Latin America* (Berkeley and Los Angeles: University of California Press).

Falabella, Gonzalo
- 1989 "¿Un 'nuevo sindicalismo'? Argentina, Brasil y Chile bajo regímenes militares," *Proposiciones* (Santiago), no. 17 (July): 58–76.

Falcón, Ricardo
- 1982 "Conflicto Social y Régimen Militar: La Resistencia Obrera en Argentina (marzo 1976–marzo 1981)," 91–140, in Bernardo Gallitelli and Andrés A. Thompson (eds.), *Sindicalismo y Regímenes Militares en Argentina y Chile* (Amsterdam: CEDLA).

Faucher, Philippe
- 1981 "The Paradise That Never Was: The Breakdown of the Brazilian Authoritarian Order," 11–39, in Thomas C. Bruneau and Philippe Faucher (eds.), *Authoritarian Capitalism: Brazil's Contemporary Economic and Political Development* (Boulder, Colo.: Westview Press).

Faúndez, Julio
- 1988 *Marxism and Democracy in Chile* (New Haven: Yale University Press.

Feldman, David Lewis
- 1985 "The U.S. Role in the Malvinas Crisis, 1982: Misguidance and Misperception in the Argentine Decision to Go to War," *Journal of Interamerican Studies and World Affairs* 27, no. 2: 1–22.

Feldman, Ernesto, and Juan Sommer
- 1986 *Crisis financiera y endeudamiento externo en la Argentina* (Buenos Aires: Centro Editor de América Latina/Centro de Economía Transacional).

Fernández, Arturo
- 1985 *Las prácticas sociales del sindicalismo, 1976–1982* (Buenos Aires: Centro Editor de América Latina).

1988   *Las prácticas sociopolíticas del sindicalismo, 1955–1985,* 2 vols. (Buenos Aires: Centro Editor de América Latina).

Fernández, Daniel C.
1982   "Las luchas obreras en la Argentina moderna," *Cuadernos Políticos* (México), no. 31 (January–March): 41–57.

Fernández, Rodolfo Peregrino
1983   *Auto-crítica policial* (Buenos Aires: El Cid Editor).

Fernández Meijide, Graciela
1988   *Las cifras de la guerra sucia* (Buenos Aires: Asamblea Permanente por los Derechos Humanos).

Fitch, J. Samuel
1988   "The Armed Forces and the Politics of Democratic Consolidation in South America," A17–A33, in Abraham F. Lowenthal (ed.), *Latin America and Caribbean Contemporary Record* 5, 1985–86 (New York: Holmes & Meier).

Foley, Michael
1989   *The Silence of Constitutions: Gaps, "Abeyances," and Political Temperament in the Maintenance of Government* (London: Routledge).

Fontana, Andrés
1984   "Fuerzas armadas, partidos políticos y transición a la democracia en Argentina," 113–29, in Augusto Varas (ed.), *Transición a la Democracia: América Latina y Chile* (Santiago: Salesianos).

1985   Fuerzas armadas e ideología neoconservadora: El redimensionamiento del estado en la Argentina, 1976–1981," 87–109, in Horacio Boneo (ed.), *Privatización del dicho al hecho* (Buenos Aires: El Cronista Comercial).

1986   "Armed Forces and Neoconservative Ideology: State Shrinking in Argentina, 1976–1981," in William Glade (ed.), *State Shrinking: A Comparative Inquiry into Privatization* (Austin: Institute of Latin American Studies, University of Texas at Austin).

1987   "Political Decision-Making by a Military Corporation: Argentina, 1976–1983," Ph. D. Dissertation, University of Texas at Austin.

Foro de Estudios Sobre la Administración de Justicia (FORES)
1985   *Definitivamente nunca más (la otra cara del informe de la CONADEP),* 2nd ed. (Buenos Aires: Foro de Estudios sobre la Administración de Justicia).

Foweraker, Joe
1993   *Popular Mobilization in Mexico: The Teachers' Movement, 1977–1987* (New York: Cambridge University Press).

1994   "Popular Political Organization and Democratization: A Comparison of Spain and Mexico," 218–31, in Ian Budge and David McKay (eds.), *Developing Democracy: Comparative Research in Honour of J. F. P. Blondel* (Thousand Oaks, Calif.: Sage Publications).

Foxley, Alejandro
1983   *Latin American Experiments in Neo-conservative Economics* (Berkeley and Los Angeles: University of California Press).

Fraga, Rosendo
  1980 "El sindicalismo en el marco del Proceso de Reorganización Nacional," manuscript, February 1980.
  1988 *Ejército: del escarnio al poder, 1973–1976* (Buenos Aires: Sudamericana/Planeta).
Freedman, Lawrence, and Virginia Gamba-Stonehouse
  1991 *Signals of War: The Falklands Conflict of 1982* (London: Faber & Faber).
Frieden, Jeffry A.
  1991 *Debt, Development, and Democracy: Modern Political Economy and Latin America, 1965–1985* (Princeton: Princeton University Press).
Fundación de Investigaciones Económicas Latinoamericanas (FIEL).
  1987 "El gasto público en la Argentina, 1960–1985," *Boletín Informativo Techint* (Buenos Aires), no. 250 (November–December): 91–113.
Gallitelli, Bernardo, and Andrés A. Thompson
  1982 "La Situación Laboral en la Argentina del "Proceso," 1976–1981," 141–90, in Bernardo Gallitelli and Andrés A. Thompson (eds.), *Sindicalismo y Regímenes Militares en Argentina y Chile* (Amsterdam: CEDLA).
García, Roberto
  1980 *Patria sindical versus Patria socialista* (Buenos Aires: Depalma).
García Delgado, Daniel, and Juan Silva
  1985 "El movimiento vecinal y la democracia: Participación y control en el Gran Buenos Aires," 67–90, in Elizabeth Jelin (ed.), *Los nuevos movimientos sociales,* vol. 2 (Buenos Aires: Centro Editor de América Latina).
García Delgado, Daniel, and Marcelo Stiletano
  1988 "La participación de los militares en los nuevos autoritarismos: La Argentina del "Proceso," 1976–1983," *Opciones* (Santiago), no. 14 (May–August): 55–88.
García Mendez, Emilio
  1987 *Autoritarismo y control social: Argentina, Uruguay, Chile* (Buenos Aires: Editorial Hammurabi).
Garretón, Manuel Antonio
  1979 "En torno a la discussión de los nuevos regímenes autoritarios en América Latina," *Working Papers* no. 52 (Washington, D.C.: Wilson Center).
  1983 *El proceso político chileno* (Santiago: FLACSO).
  1984 "Proyecto, trayectoria y fracaso de los regímenes militares del Cono Sur: Un balance," *Alternativas* (Santiago), January–April, 5–23.
  1986a "The Political Evolution of the Chilean Military Regime and Problems in the Transition to Democracy," 95–122, in Guillermo O'Donnell, Philippe C. Schmitter and Laurence Whitehead (eds.), *Transitions from Authoritarian Rule: Latin America* (Baltimore: Johns Hopkins University Press).
  1986b "Political Process in an Authoritarian Regime: The Dynamics of In-

stitutionalization and Opposition in Chile, 1973–1980," 144–83, in Arturo Valenzuela and Samuel Valenzuela (eds.), *Military Rule in Chile: Dictatorship and Oppositions* (Baltimore: Johns Hopkins University Press).
1987   *Reconstruir la Política: Transición y Consolidación en Chile* (Santiago: Editorial Andante).
1989a   *La posibilidad democrática en Chile* (Santiago: FLACSO).
1989b   "Popular Mobilization and the Military Regime in Chile: The Complexities of the Invisible Transition," in Susan Eckstein (ed.), *Power and Popular Protest: Latin American Social Movements*, 259–77 (Berkeley and Los Angeles: University of California Press).
1992   "Fear in Military Regimes: An Overview," 13–25, in Juan E. Corradi, Patricia Weiss Fagen, and Manuel Antonio Garretón (eds.), *Fear at the Edge: State Terror and Resistance in Latin America* (Berkeley and Los Angeles: University of California Press).
1995a   *Hacia una nueva era política: Estudio sobre democratizaciones* (Mexico: Fondo de Cultura Económica).
1995b   "The Political Opposition and the Party System Under the Military Regime," 211–50, in Paul Drake and Iván Jakšić (eds.), *The Struggle for Democracy in Chile, 1982–1990*, rev. ed. (Lincoln: University of Nebraska Press).
Gatto, Francisco, Graciela Gutman, and Gabriel Yoguel
   1987   *Reestructuración Industrial y sus Impactos Regionales, 1974–1984* (Buenos Aires: Programa CFI-CEPAL, Documento no. 14).
Gaudio, Ricardo, and Hector Domeniconi
   1985   "El proceso de normalización sindical bajo el gobierno radical," mimeographed.
Geddes, Barbara
   1996   "Initiation of New Democratic Institutions in Eastern Europe and Latin America," 15–41, in Arend Lijphart and Carlos Waisman (eds.), *Institutional Design in New Democracies: Eastern Europe and Latin America* (Boulder, Colo.: Westview Press).
Giddens, Anthony
   1984   *The Constitution of Society* (Berkeley and Los Angeles: University of California Press).
   1987   *The Nation State and Violence* (Berkeley and Los Angeles: University of California Press).
Gillespie, Richard
   1982   *Soldiers of Perón-Argentina's Montoneros* (Oxford: Clarendon Press).
Gilly, Adolfo
   1978   "Los consejos de fábrica: Argentina, Bolivia, Italia," *Coyoacán* (México), no. 5.
   1983   "El diciembre caliente," *Coyoacán* (México), January–June.
   1984   "Argentina después de la dictadura (Democracia, reorganización obrera, proyecto socialista)," *Coyoacán* (México), 8, no. 16 (January–March): i–xxiv.

Gómez, Jose M., and Eduardo Viola
- 1984 "Transición desde el autoritarismo y potencialidad de invención democrática en la Argentina de 1983," 29–42, in Oscar Oszlak (ed.), *"Proceso," crisis y transición democrática,* vol. 2 (Buenos Aires: Centro Editor de América Latina).

González Bombal, Inés
- 1985 "Protestan los Barrios (El murmullo suburbano de la política," 96–116, in Elizabeth Jelin (ed.), *Los nuevos movimientos sociales,* vol. 2 (Buenos Aires: Centro Editor de América Latina).
- 1988 *Los Vecinazos: Las Protestas Barriales en el Gran Buenos Aires, 1982–1983* (Buenos Aires: Ediciones del IDES no. 14).
- 1991 "El diálogo político: La transición que no fue," *Documento CEDES / 61* (Buenos Aires: CEDES).

Goodwin, Jeff, and Theda Skocpol
- 1989 "Explaining Revolutions in the Contemporary Third World," *Politics and Society* 17, no. 4 (December): 489–509.

Gould, Andrew C.
- 1994 "Conflicting Imperatives and Concept Formation," paper presented at the International Political Science Association (IPSA) 1994 World Congress, Berlin, August 21–25, 1994.

Graham-Youll, Andrew
- 1979 *The Press in Argentina, 1973–1978* (London: Whitesand Educational Scholar Trust).

Groisman, Enrique
- 1987a "El 'proceso de reorganización Nacional' y el sistema jurídico," 61–68, in Oscar Oszlak (ed.), *"Proceso," crisis y transición democrática,* vol. 1 (Buenos Aires: Centro Editor de América Latina).
- 1987b "Política y justicia durante la dictadura," *El Bimestre Político y Económico* (Buenos Aires), no. 34: 5–14.

Grondona, Mariano
- 1983 *La construcción de la democracia* (Buenos Aires: Editorial Universitaria de Buenos Aires).

Grupo de los 25/Comisión de los 25
- 1977 "Al Gobierno Nacional," *La Opinión* (Buenos Aires), January 6, 1977, 10–11.
- 1978 "Texto del discurso pronunciado en la cena organizada por la 'Comisión de los 25' en la Cuidad de Buenos Aires el día 19 de diciembre de 1978," original document.
- 1984 "Análysis de Coyuntura de Salarios," 107–9, in Santiago Senén Gonzalez, *Diez años de sindicalismo Argentino (De Perón al proceso)* (Buenos Aires: Ediciones Corregidor).

Guest, Ian
- 1990 *Behind the Disappearances: Argentina's Dirty War Against Human Rights and the United Nations* (Philadelphia: University of Pennsylvania Press).

Gunther, Richard, P. Nikiforos Diamandouros, and Hans-Jürgen Puhle (eds.)
1995 *The Politics of Democratic Consolidation: Southern Europe in Comparative Perspective* (Baltimore: Johns Hopkins University Press).

Haggard, Stephen, and Robert Kaufman
1995 *The Political Economy of Democratic Transitions* (Princeton: Princeton University Press).

Hagopian, Frances
1992 "The Compromised Consolidation: The Political Class in the Brazilian Transition," 243–93, in Scott Mainwaring, Guillermo O'Donnell, and J. Samuel Valenzuela (eds.), *Issues in Democratic Consolidation: The New South American Democracies in Comparative Perspective* (South Bend, Ind.: University of Notre Dame Press).
1993 "After Regime Change: Authoritarian Legacies, Political Representation, and the Democratic Future of South America," *World Politics* 45, no. 3 (April): 464–500.
1994 "Traditional Politics Against State Transformation in Brazil," 37–64, in Joel S. Migdal, Atul Kohli, and Vivienne Shue (eds.), *State Power and Social Forces: Domination and Transformation in the Third World* (New York: Cambridge University Press).
1996 *Traditional Politics and Regime Change in Brazil* (New York: Cambridge University Press).

Hall, John A.
1994 *Coercion and Consent: Studies on the Modern State* (Cambridge: Polity Press).

Hamrin, Carol Lee, and Suisheng Zhao
1995 "Introduction: Core Issues in Understanding the Decision Process," xxi–xlviii, in Carol Lee Hamrin and Suisheng Zhao (eds.), *Decision-Making in Deng's China: Perspectives from Insiders* (Armonk, N.Y.: M. E. Sharpe).

Hartlyn, Jonathan, and Samuel A. Morley
1986 "Bureaucratic-Authoritarian Regimes in Comparative Perspective," 38–53, in Jonathan Hartlyn and Samuel A. Morley (eds.), *Latin American Political Economy: Financial Crisis and Political Change* (Boulder, Colo.: Westview Press).

Hawes, Gary
1987 *The Philippine State and the Marcos Regime: The Politics of Export* (Ithaca, N.Y.: Cornell University Press).

Held, David (ed.)
1993 *Prospects for Democracy: North, South, East, West* (Stanford, Calif.: Stanford University Press).

Hermet, Guy, Alain Rouquié, and Juan Linz
1982 *¿Para qué sirven las elecciones?* (Mexico: Fondo de Cultura Económica).

Herreras, Casildo
1985 "Salvo su vida [Interview with Casildo Herreras]," 73–83, in Daniel

Parcero, Marcelo Helfgot and Diego Dulce, *La Argentina exiliada* (Buenos Aires: Centro Editor de América Latina).
1987 "Interview with Casildo Herreras," 199–206, in Daniel Parcero, *La CGT y el sindicalismo Latinoamericano: Historia crítica de sus relaciones, Desde el ATLAS a la CIOSL* (Buenos Aires: Editorial Fraterna).

Higley, John, and Richard Gunther (eds.)
1992 *Elites and Democratic Consolidation in Latin America and Southern Europe* (Cambridge: Cambridge University Press).

Hirschman, Albert
1970 *Exit, Voice, and Loyalty* (Cambridge, Mass.: Harvard University Press).
1992 "Exit and Voice: An Expanding Sphere of Influence," 77–101, in Albert Hirschman, *Rival Views of Market Society and Other Recent Essays* (Cambridge, Mass.: Harvard University Press).

Hobsbawm, Eric
1996 *The Age of Extremes: A History of the World, 1914–1991* (New York: Vintage Books/Random House).

Hodges, Donald C.
1991 *Argentina's "Dirty War": An Intellectual Biography* (Austin: University of Texas Press).
1993 "The Argentine Left Since Perón," 155–70, in Barry Carr and Steve Ellner (eds.), *The Latin America Left* (Boulder, Colo.: Westview Press).

Horowitz, Donald L.
1991 *A Democratic South Africa? Constitutional Engineering in a Divided Society* (Berkeley and Los Angeles: University of California Press).

Huneeus, Carlos
1986 "Autoritarismo, cuestión sucesoria y transición a la democracia: España, Brasil, Chile," *Opciones* (Santiago), no. 8 (January–April): 138–80.

Huneeus, Carlos, and Jorge Olave
1987 "La participación de los militares en los nuevos autoritarismos: Chile, en una perspectiva comparada," *Opciones* (Santiago), no. 11 (May–August): 119–62.

Huneeus, Carlos (ed.)
1987 *Para vivir la democracia* (Santiago de Chile: Centro de Estudios de la Realidad Contemporánea).

Hunter, Wendy
1994 "Contradictions of Civilian Control: Argentina, Brazil and Chile in the 1990s," *Third World Quarterly* 15, no. 4: 633–53.

Huntington, Samuel
1968 *Political Order in Changing Societies* (New Haven: Yale University Press).
1991 *The Third Wave: Democratization in the Late Twentieth Century* (Norman: University of Oklahoma Press).

Ietswaart, F. P.
1980 "The Discourse of Summary Justice and the Discourse of Popular Justice: An Analysis of Legal Rhetoric in Argentina," 149–79, in Richard L. Abel (ed.), *The Politics of Informal Justice*, vol. 2 (New York: Academic Press).

Im, Hyug Baeg
1987 "The Rise of Bureaucratic Authoritarianism in South Korea," *World Politics* 39, no. 2 (January): 231–57.

Instituto Nacional de Estadísticas y Censos (INDEC)
1989 *Censo nacional económico 1985, Industria manufacturera: Resultados definitivo, Total del país y jurisdicciones* (Buenos Aires: INDEC).

Inter-American Commission on Human Rights of the Organization of American States
1980 *Report on the Situation of Human Rights in Argentina* (Washington, D.C.: General Secretariat, Organization of American States).

James, Daniel
1976 "The Peronist Left, 1955–1975," *Journal of Latin American Studies* 8, no. 2 (November): 273–96.
1988 *Resistance and Integration: Peronism and the Argentine Working Class, 1946–1976* (Cambridge: Cambridge University Press).

Jennings, W. Ivor
1956 *The Approach to Self-Government* (Cambridge: Cambridge University Press).

Jordán, Alberto R.
1993 *El proceso, 1976/83* (Buenos Aires: Emecé Editores).

Jorrat, Jorge R.
1986 "Las elecciones de 1983: ¿'Desviación' o 'Realineamiento'?" *Desarrollo Económico* (Buenos Aires), 26, no. 101 (April–June): 89–120.

Joseph, William A.
1993 "China," 128–33, in Joel Krieger (ed.), *The Oxford Companion to the Politics of the World* (New York: Oxford University Press).

Junta Militar
1980 *Documentos básicos y bases políticas de las Fuerzas Armadas para el Proceso de Reorganización Nacional* (Buenos Aires: Imprenta del Congreso de la Nación).
1982a "Las operaciones libradas contra las bandas terroristas fueron supervisadas por los mandos orgánicos de las FF.AA.," *El Bimestre Político y Económico* (Buenos Aires), 1, no. 5 (September–October): 61.
1982b "Quince temas para concertar," *El Bimestre Político y Económico* (Buenos Aires), 1, no. 6 (November–December): 75–76.
1984 "Documento final de la Junta Militar sobre la Guerra contra la subversión y el terrorismo," 151–63, in Centro de Investigaciones sobre el Estado y la Administración (CISEA), *Argentina 1983* (Buenos Aires: CISEA/Centro Editor de América Latina).
1985 "Pautas de la Junta Militar al Poder Ejecutivo (para el ejercicio de la acción de gobierno 1981/84)," 199–203, in Enrique Vázquez, *PRN: La*

última: Origen, apogeo y caída de la dictadura militar (Buenos Aires: Editorial Universitaria de Buenos Aires).

Kandel, Pablo, and Mario Monteverde
1976 *Entorno y Caída* (Buenos Aires: Editorial Planeta).

Karl, Terry L.
1990 "Dilemmas of Democratization in Latin America," *Comparative Politics* 23, no. 1 (October): 1–21.

Karl, Terry L., and Philippe Schmitter
1991 "Modes of Transition in Latin America, Southern and Eastern Europe," *International Social Science Journal* 128 (May): 269–84.

Kaufman, Edy
1995 "Análisis de los patrones represivos en el Cono Sur: Los regímenes militares argentinos, 1976–1983," 55–78, in Leonardo Senkman and Mario Sznajder (eds.), *El Legado del autoritarismo: Derechos humanos y antisemitismo en la Argentina contemporánea* (Buenos Aires: Instituto Harry Truman/Grupo Editor Latinoamericano).

Kaufman, Robert
1977 "Mexico and Latin American Authoritarianism," 193–232, in José L. Reyna and Richard Weinhert (eds.), *Authoritarianism in Mexico* (Philadelphia: Institute for the Study of Human Issues).
1986 "Liberalization and Democratization in South America: Perspectives from the 1970s," 85–107, in Guillermo O'Donnell, Philippe Schmitter, and Laurence Whitehead (eds.), *Transitions from Authoritarian Rule: Comparative Perspectives* (Baltimore: Johns Hopkins University Press).

King, Gary, Robert O. Keohane, and Sidney Verba
1994 *Designing Social Inquiry: Scientific Inference in Qualitative Research* (Princeton: Princeton University Press).

King, Peter John
1989 "Comparative Analysis of Human Rights Violations Under Military Rule in Argentina, Brazil, Chile, and Uruguay," 1043–65, in James Wilkie and Enrique Ochoa (eds.), *Statistical Abstracts of Latin America*, vol. 27 (Los Angeles: UCLA Latin American Center Publications, University of California).

Kirchheimer, Otto
1969 "Confining Conditions and Revolutionary Breakthroughs," 385–407, in F. S. Burin and K. L. Shell (eds.), *Politics, Law, and Some Exchanges: Selected Essays of Otto Kirchheimer* (New York: Columbia University Press).

Kogan, Hilda, Alberto Bialakowsky, and Cristina Micieli
1986 "Articulaciones laborales en la crisis del sindicalismo Argentino, 1976–1981," 351–61, in Comisión de Movimientos Laborales (CLACSO), *El sindicalismo Latinoamericano en los ochenta* (Santiago: CLACSO).

Kohen, Alberto
 1981 "La multipartidaria y la salida democrática," *Comentarios* (Buenos Aires), 4, no. 10 (October): 12–14.
Kon, Daniel
 1982 *Los chicos de la guerra: Hablan los soldados que estuvieron en Malvinas* (Buenos Aires: Editorial Galerna).
Kosacoff, Bernardo
 1993 "La industria Argentina: Un proceso de reestructuración desarticulada," 11–67, in Bernardo Kosacoff et al., *El Desafío de la competitividad: La industria argentina en transformación* (Buenos Aires: Alianza Editorial).
Lakoff, George
 1987 *Women, Fire, and Dangerous Things: What Categories Reveal About the Mind* (Chicago: University of Chicago Press).
Lamounier, Bolivar
 1989 "*Authoritarian Brazil* Revisited: The Impact of Elections on the *Abertura*," 43–79, in Alfred Stepan (ed.), *Democratizing Brazil: Problems of Transition and Consolidation* (New York: Oxford University Press).
Landi, Oscar
 1988 *Reconstrucciones: Las nuevas formas de la cultura política* (Buenos Aires: Puntosur Editores).
Lijphart, Arend
 1977 *Democracy in Plural Societies* (New Haven: Yale University Press).
 1984 *Democracies* (New Haven: Yale University Press).
 1992 "Democratization and Constitutional Choices in Czechoslovakia, Hungary, and Poland, 1989–1991," *Journal of Theoretical Politics* 4, no. 2: 207–23.
 1994 *Electoral Systems and Party Systems: A Study of Twenty-Seven Democracies* (New York: Oxford University Press).
Línea
 1981a "La respuesta peronista ante la emergencia nacional," *Línea* (Buenos Aires), 2, no. 12 (July): 20–27.
 1981b "Política y sindicalismo," *Línea* (Buenos Aires), 2, no. 17 (December): 28–29.
Linz, Juan
 1964 "An Authoritarian Regime: Spain," 291–341, in Erik Allardt and Yrjö Littunen (eds.), *Cleavages, Ideologies, and Party System: Contributions to Comparative Political Sociology* (Helsinki: Westermarck Society).
 1973a "Opposition To and Under an Authoritarian Regime," 171–259, in Robert Dahl (ed.), *Regimes and Oppositions* (New Haven: Yale University Press).
 1973b "The Future of an Authoritarian Situation or the Institutionalization of an Authoritarian Regime: The Case of Brazil," 233–54, in Alfred Stepan (ed.), *Authoritarian Brazil: Origins, Policies, and Future* (Princeton: Princeton University Press).

- 1975 "Totalitarianism and Authoritarian Regimes," 175–411, in Fred Greenstein and Nelson Polsby (eds.), *Handbook of Political Science*, vol. 3: *Macropolitical Theory* (Reading, Mass.: Addison-Wesley Press).
- 1978 *The Breakdown of Democratic Regimes: Crisis, Breakdown, and Reequilibration* (Baltimore: Johns Hopkins University Press).
- 1990 "Transition to Democracy," *Washington Quarterly* 13, no. 3 (Summer): 143–64.
- 1993 "Authoritarianism," 60–64, in Joel Krieger (ed.), *The Oxford Companion to the Politics of the World* (New York: Oxford University Press).
- 1994 "Presidential or Parliamentary Democracy: Does It Make a Difference?" 3–87, in Juan J. Linz and Arturo Valenzuela (eds.), *The Failure of Presidential Democracy*, vol. 1: *Comparative Perspectives* (Baltimore: Johns Hopkins University Press).

Linz, Juan, and Alfred Stepan
- 1992 "Political Identities and Electoral Sequences: Spain, the Soviet Union, and Yugoslavia," *Daedalus* 121, no. 2 (Spring): 123–39.
- 1996 *Problems of Democratic Transition and Consolidation: Southern Europe, South America, and Post-Communist Europe* (Baltimore: Johns Hopkins University Press).

Linz, Juan, and Alfred Stepan (eds.)
- 1978 *The Breakdown of Democratic Regimes* (Baltimore: Johns Hopkins University Press).

Linz, Juan, Alfred Stepan, and Richard Gunther
- 1995 "Democratic Transition and Consolidation in Southern Europe, with Reflections on Latin America and Eastern Europe," 77–123, in Richard Gunther, P. Nikiforos Diamandouros, and Hans-Jürgen Puhle (eds.), *The Politics of Democratic Consolidation: Southern Europe in Comparative Perspective* (Baltimore: Johns Hopkins University Press).

Linz, Juan, and Arturo Valenzuela (eds.)
- 1994 *The Failure of Presidential Democracy*, vol. 1: *Comparative Perspectives* (Baltimore: Johns Hopkins University Press).

Lipset, Seymour M.
- 1960 *Political Man: The Social Bases of Politics* (New York: Doubleday/Anchor Books).
- 1983 "Radicalism or Reformism: The Sources of Working-Class Politics," *American Political Science Review* 77, no. 1: 1–18.

Lipset, Seymour M., and Stein Rokkan
- 1967 "Cleavage Structures, Party Systems, and Voter Alignments: An Introduction," 1–64, in Seymour M. Lipset and Stein Rokkan (eds.), *Party Systems and Voter Alignments: Cross-National Perspectives* (New York: Free Press).

López Saavedra, Emiliana
- 1983 *Apelación a la Democracia* (Buenos Aires: Editorial Redacción).

1984 *Testigos del "proceso" militar,* 2 vols. (Buenos Aires: Centro Editor de América Latina).
Loveman, Brian
  1991 "¿*Misión Cumplida?* Civil Military Relations and the Chilean Political Transition," *Journal of Interamerican Studies and World Affairs* 33, no. 3 (Fall): 35–74.
Lowenthal, Abraham, and J. Samuel Fitch (eds.)
  1986 *Armies and Politics in Latin America* (New York: Holmes & Meier).
Luebbert, Gregory M.
  1991 *Liberalism, Fascism, or Social Democracy: Social Classes and the Political Origins of Regimes in Interwar Europe* (New York: Oxford University Press).
Mainwaring, Scott
  1988 "Political Parties and Democratization in Brazil and the Southern Cone," *Comparative Politics* 21, no. 1 (October): 91–120.
  1991 "Politicians, Parties, and Electoral Systems: Brazil in Comparative Perspective," *Comparative Politics* 24, no. 1 (October): 21–43.
  1992 "Transitions to Democracy and Democratic Consolidation: Theoretical and Comparative Issues," 294–341, in Scott Mainwaring, Guillermo O'Donnell, and J. Samuel Valenzuela (eds.), *Issues in Democratic Consolidation: The New South American Democracies in Comparative Perspective* (South Bend, Ind.: University of Notre Dame Press).
  1995 "Brazil: Weak Parties, Feckless Democracy," 354–98, in Scott Mainwaring and Timothy Scully (eds.), *Building Democratic Institutions: Party Systems in Latin America* (Stanford, Calif.: Stanford University Press).
Mainwaring, Scott, Guillermo O'Donnell, and J. Samuel Valenzuela (eds.)
  1992a *Issues in Democratic Consolidation: The New South American Democracies in Comparative Perspective* (South Bend, Ind.: University of Notre Dame Press).
Mainwaring, Scott, Guillermo O'Donnell, and J. Samuel Valenzuela
  1992b "Introduction," 1–16, in Scott Mainwaring, Guillermo O'Donnell, and J. Samuel Valenzuela (eds.), *Issues in Democratic Consolidation: The New South American Democracies in Comparative Perspective* (South Bend, Ind.: University of Notre Dame Press).
Mainwaring, Scott, and Timothy Scully (eds.)
  1995 *Building Democratic Institutions: Party Systems in Latin America* (Stanford, Calif.: Stanford University Press).
Maira, Luis
  1986 "Authoritarianism in Central America: A Comparative Perspective," 14–29, in Guiseppe di Palma and Laurence Whitehead (eds.), *The Central American Impasse* (New York: St. Martin's Press).
Makin, Guillermo
  1985 "Argentina: The Authoritarian Impasse," 151–70, in Christopher Clapham and George Philip (eds.), *The Political Dilemmas of Military Regimes* (London: Croom Helm).

Malloy, James M. (ed.)
 1977 *Authoritarianism and Corporatism in Latin America* (Pittsburgh: University of Pittsburgh Press).
Malloy, James M., and Mitchell A. Seligson (eds.)
 1987 *Authoritarians and Democrats: Regime Transition in Latin America* (Pittsburgh: University of Pittsburgh Press).
Mann, Michael
 1986a "The Autonomous Power of the State: Its Origins, Mechanisms, and Results," 109–36, in John A. Hall (ed.), *States in History* (Oxford: Basil Blackwell).
 1986b *The Sources of Social Power,* vol. 1: *A History of Power from the Beginning to A.D. 1760* (New York: Cambridge University Press).
 1987 "Ruling Class Strategies and Citizenship," *Sociology* 21, no. 3 (August): 339–54.
 1993 *The Sources of Social Power,* vol. 2: *The Rise of Classes and Nation-States, 1760–1914* (Cambridge: Cambridge University Press).
Mantilla, Enrique S.
 1980 "Aportes de experiencias particulares a la problemática de la estrategia de desarrollo en América Latina y el modelo de relaciones industriales: El caso Argentino," paper presented at an ILO Conference in Lima, December 9–13, 1980.
Martínez, Javier
 1992 "Fear of the State, Fear of Society: On the Opposition Protests in Chile," 142–60, in Juan E. Corradi, Patricia Weiss Fagen, and Manuel Antonio Garretón (eds.), *Fear at the Edge: State Terror and Resistance in Latin America* (Berkeley and Los Angeles: University of California Press).
Maronese, Leticia, Ana Cafiero de Nazar, and Victor Waisman
 1985 *El voto Peronista '83: Perfil electoral y causas de la derrota* (Buenos Aires: El Cid Editor).
Martins, Luciano
 1986 "The 'Liberalization' of Authoritarian Rule in Brazil," 72–94, in Guillermo O'Donnell, Philippe C. Schmitter, and Laurence Whitehead (eds.), *Transitions from Authoritarian Rule: Latin America* (Baltimore: Johns Hopkins University Press).
Massera, Emilio E.
 1979 *El camino a la democracia* (Buenos Aires: El Cid Editor).
 1980 "El año de las protestas [Interview with Massera]," *Redacción* (Buenos Aires), no. 94 (December): 27–32.
McFaul, Michael
 1993 "Party Formation After Revolutionary Transition: The Russian Case," 7–28, in Alexander Dallin (ed.), *Political Parties in Russia* (Berkeley, Calif.: Research Series, University of California, Berkeley, International and Area Studies).
McGuire, James W.
 1995 "Interim Government and Democratic Consolidation: Argentina in

Comparative Perspective," 179–210, in Yossi Shain and Juan J. Linz et al., *Between States: Interim Governments and Democratic Transitions* (Cambridge: Cambridge University Press).

1997 *Peronism Without Perón: Unions, Parties, and Democracy in Argentina* (Stanford, Calif.: Stanford University Press).

Melo, Artemio Luis
1989 *La transición política Argentina, 1982–1983: Del regímen burocrático autoritario al régimen político democrático* (Rosario: Publicaciones Universidad Nacional de Rosario).

Menéndez, Luciano Benjamín
1981 *Así piensa Luciano Benjamín Menéndez* (Buenos Aires: Nemont Ediciones).

Mera, Jorge Alberto
1978 "Para una revisión del sistema de salud," *Criterio* (Buenos Aires), 51, no. 1785 (April 13): 162–71.
1979 "El Seguro Nacional de Salud y las Obras Sociales," *Criterio* (Buenos Aires), 52, no. 1821 (October 11): 592–96.

Mericle, Kenneth S.
1977 "Corporatist Control of the Working Class: Authoritarian Brazil Since 1964," 303–38, in James Malloy (ed.), *Authoritarianism and Corporatism in Latin America* (Pittsburgh: University of Pittsburgh Press).

Middlebrook, Kevin J.
1995 *The Paradox of Revolution: Labor, the State, and Authoritarianism in Mexico* (Baltimore: Johns Hopkins University Press).

Miedzir, Gustavo, Amelia Peixoto, Alberto Fernández, and Eduardo Lucita
1988 "Los agrupamientos político sindicales: Un intento de caracterización," *Cuadernos del Sur* (Buenos Aires), no. 8 (October): 147–68.

Mignone, Emilio Fermín
1988 *Witness to the Truth: The Complicity of Church and Dictatorship in Argentina, 1976–1983* (Maryknoll, New York: Orbis Books).

Ministerio de Trabajo y Seguridad Social, Dirección Nacional de Recursos Humanos y Empleo
1987 *Estructura Sindical en la Argentina* (Buenos Aires: Ministerio de Trabajo y Seguridad Social).

Misztal, Barbara
1993 "Understanding Political Change in Eastern Europe: A Sociological Perspective," *Sociology* 27, no. 3 (August): 451–70.

Mittelbach, Federico
1986 *Informe sobre desaparecedores* (Buenos Aires: Ediciones de la Urraca).

Moncalvillo, Mona
1983 *Reportajes de Humor* (Buenos Aires: Ediciones de la Urraca).

Moneta, Carlos J.
1984 "The Malvinas Conflict: Analyzing the Argentine Military Regime's Decision-Making Process," 119–32, in Heraldo Muñoz and Joseph S.

Tulchin (eds.), *Latin American Nations in World Politics* (Boulder, Colo.: Westview Press).

Montenegro, Néstor J., and Eduardo Aliverti
1982 *Los nombres de la derrota* (Buenos Aires: Nemont Ediciones).

Moore, Barrington
1966 *Social Origins of Dictatorship and Democracy: Lord and Peasant in the Making of the Modern World* (Boston: Beacon Press).

Mora y Araujo, Manuel
1979 "Sindicatos y democracia," *Carta Política* (Buenos Aires), no. 77 (November): 7–8.
1980 "Los sindicatos y los problemas políticos de la democracia moderna," *Criterio* (Buenos Aires), 53, no. 1849/50: 800–806.
1986 "The Nature of the Alfonsín Coalition," 175–88, in Paul Drake and Eduardo Silva (eds.), *Elections and Democratization in Latin America, 1980–1985* (San Diego: CILAS, Center for U.S.-Mexican Studies, IOA).

Morlino, Leonardo
1990 "Authoritarianism," 91–101, in Anton Bebler and Jim Seroka (eds.), *Contemporary Political Systems: Classifications and Typologies* (Boulder, Colo.: Lynne Rienner Publishers).
1995a "Democratic Consolidation: Definition and Models," 571–90, in Geoffrey Pridham (ed.), *Transitions to Democracy: Comparative Perspectives from Southern Europe, Latin America, and Eastern Europe* (Brookfield,Vt.: Dartmouth Publishing Company).
1995b "Parties, Groups, and Democratic Consolidation in Italy," 257–78, in H. E. Chehabi and Alfred Stepan (eds.), *Politics, Society, and Democracy: Comparative Studies* (Boulder, Colo.: Westview Press).

Mouzelis, Nicos P.
1986 *Politics in the Semi-Periphery: Early Parliamentarism and Late Industrialisation in the Balkans and Latin America* (London: Macmillan).

Movimiento Sindical Peronista (Peronist Syndical Movement)
1980 "Hablemos sobre el diálogo," *Convocatoria* (Buenos Aires), 1, no. 1 (February).

Moyano, María José
1991 "The 'Dirty War' in Argentina: Was It a War and How Dirty Was It?" 45–73, in Hans Werner Tobler and Peter Waldmann (eds.), *Staatliche und parastaatliche Gewalt in Lateinamerika* (Frankfurt am Main: Vervuert Verlag).
1995 *Argentina's Lost Patrol: Armed Struggle, 1969–1979* (New Haven: Yale University Press).

Multipartidaria
1982a *La propuesta de la Multipartidaria* (Buenos Aires: El Cid Editor).
1982b "Programa para la Reconstrucción Nacional," *El Bimestre Político y Económico* (Buenos Aires), 1, no. 3 (May–June): 130–32.

1982c "Marcha del Pueblo," *El Bimestre Político y Económico* (Buenos Aires), 1, no. 6 (November–December): 76–78.
1984 "Entrega del poder," 65–66, in Centro de Investigaciones sobre el Estado y la Administración (CISEA), *Argentina 1983* (Buenos Aires: CISEA/Centro Editor de América Latina).
Munck, Gerardo L.
1990a "Identity and Ambiguity in Democratic Struggles," 23–42, in Joe Foweraker and Ann Craig (eds.), *Popular Movements and Political Change in Mexico* (Boulder, Colo.: Lynne Rienner Publishers).
1990b "State Power and Labor Politics in the Context of Military Rule: Organized Labor, Peronism, and the Armed Forces in Argentina, 1976–1983," Ph. D. dissertation, University of California, San Diego.
1992 "Democratizing Chile: The View from Across the Andes: Transitions from Authoritarian Rule in Comparative Perspective," XVII International Congress of the Latin American Studies Association (LASA), Los Angeles, September 24–27, 1992.
1994a "Democratic Transitions in Comparative Perspective," *Comparative Politics* 26, no. 3 (April): 355–75.
1994b "Democratic Stability and Its Limits: An Analysis of Chile's 1993 Elections," *Journal of Interamerican Studies and World Affairs* 36, no. 2 (Summer): 1–38.
1994c "Authoritarianism, Modernization, and Democracy in Chile," *Latin American Research Review* 29, no. 2: 188–211.
1994d "The Critical Juncture Framework and Argentina: The Menem Revolution in Comparative Perspective," American Political Science Association (APSA) 1994 Annual meeting, New York, September 1–4, 1994.
1995 "Actor Formation, Social Coordination, and Political Strategy: Some Conceptual Problems in the Study of Social Movements," *Sociology* 29, no. 4 (November): 667–85.
1996 "Disaggregating Political Regime: Conceptual Issues in the Study of Democratization," *Working Papers* no. 228 (Notre Dame, Ind.: Helen Kellogg Institute for International Studies, University of Notre Dame).
Munck, Gerardo L., and Chetan Kumar
1995 "Civil Conflicts and the Conditions for Successful International Intervention: A Comparative Study of Cambodia and El Salvador," *Review of International Studies* 21, no. 2 (April): 159–81.
Munck, Gerardo L., and Carol S. Leff
1997 "Modes of Transition and Democratization: South America and Eastern Europe in Comparative Perspective," *Comparative Politics* 29, no. 3 (April): 343–62.
Munck, Ronaldo
1982 "Restructuración del capital y recomposición de la clase obrera en Argentina desde 1976," 191–225, in Bernardo Gallitelli and Andrés A.

Thompson (eds.), *Sindicalismo y Regímenes Militares en Argentina y Chile* (Amsterdam: CEDLA).
1984   *Politics and Dependency in the Third World: The Case of Latin America* (London: Zed Press).
1989   *Latin America: The Transition to Democracy* (London: Zed Press).
Munck, Ronaldo, with Ricardo Falcón and Bernardo Gallitelli
1987   *Argentina from Anarchism to Peronism: Workers, Unions, and Politics, 1855–1985* (London: Zed Books).
Navarro, Marysa
1989   "The Personal Is Political: Las Madres de Plaza de Mayo," 241–58, in Susan Eckstein (ed.), *Power and Popular Protest: Latin American Social Movements* (Berkeley and Los Angeles: University of California Press).
Neri, Aldo
1982   *Salud y política social* (Buenos Aires: Editorial Hachette).
Norden, Deborah L.
1996   *Military Rebellion in Argentin: Between Coups and Consolidation* (Lincoln: University of Nebraska Press).
Nun, José
1987a   "Vaivenes de un régimen social de acumulación de decadencia," 83–116, in José Nun and Juan Carlos Portantiero (eds.), *Ensayos sobre la transición democrática en la Argentina* (Buenos Aires: Puntosur Editores).
1987b   "Cambios en la estructura social de la Argentina," 117–37, in José Nun and Juan Carlos Portantiero (eds.), *Ensayos sobre la transición democrática en la Argentina* (Buenos Aires: Puntosur Editores).
O'Brien, Philip, and Paul Cammack (eds.)
1985   *Generals in Retreat: The Crisis of Military Rule in Latin America* (Manchester and Dover, N.H.: Manchester University Press).
O'Donnell, Guillermo A.
1973   *Modernization and Bureaucratic Authoritarianism: Studies in South American Politics* (Berkeley: Institute of International Studies/University of California).
1976   "Modernization and Military Coups: Theory, Comparisons, and the Argentine Case," 197–243, in Abraham Lowenthal (ed.), *Armies and Politics in Latin America* (New York: Holmes & Meier).
1978a   "Reflections on the Patterns of Change in the Bureaucratic Authoritarian State," *Latin American Research Review* 12, no. 1 (Winter): 3–38.
1978b   "State and Alliances in Argentina, 1956–1976," *Journal of Development Studies* 15, no. 1 (October): 3–33.
1979   "Tensions in the Bureaucratic-Authoritarian State and the Question of Democracy," 285–318, in David Collier (ed.), *The New Authoritarianism in Latin America* (Princeton: Princeton University Press).
1981   "Las fuerzas armadas y el estado autoritario del cono sur de América

Latina," 199–235, in Norbert Lechner (ed.), *Estado y política en América Latina* (México: Siglo XXI).
1982 "Reply to Remmer and Merkx," *Latin American Research Review* 17, no. 2: 41–50.
1983 "Democracia en la Argentina: Micro y macro," *Working Papers* no. 2 (South Bend, Ind.: Helen Kellogg Institute for International Studies).
1988 *Bureaucratic Authoritarianism: Argentina, 1966–1973, in Comparative Perspective* (Berkeley and Los Angeles: University of California Press).
1992 "Transitions, Continuities, and Paradoxes," 17–56, in Scott Mainwaring, Guillermo O'Donnell and J. Samuel Valenzuela (eds.), *Issues in Democratic Consolidation: The New South American Democracies in Comparative Perspective* (South Bend, Ind.: University of Notre Dame Press).
1993 "On the State, Democratization, and Some Conceptual Problems (A Latin American View with Glances at Some Post-Communist Countries)," *World Development* 21, no. 8 (August): 1355–70.
1994 "Delegative Democracy," *Journal of Democracy* 5, no. 1 (January): 55–69.

O'Donnell, Guillermo, and Philippe Schmitter
1986 *Transitions from Authoritarian Rule: Tentative Conclusions About Uncertain Democracies* (Baltimore: Johns Hopkins University Press).

O'Donnell, Guillermo, Philippe Schmitter, and Laurence Whitehead (eds.)
1986 *Transitions from Authoritarian Rule: Prospects for Democracy* (Baltimore: Johns Hopkins University Press).

Offe, Claus
1991 "Capitalism by Democratic Design? Democratic Theory Facing the Triple Transition in East Central Europe," *Social Research* 58, no. 4 (Winter): 865–92.

Osiel, Mark
1986 "The Making of Human Rights Policy in Argentina: The Impact of Ideas and Interests on a Legal Conflict," *Journal of Latin American Studies* 18, no. 1 (May): 135–78.

Oszlak, Oscar
1984 "Public Policies and Political Regimes in Latin America," *Working Papers* no. 139 (Washington, D.C.: The Wilson Center, Latin American Program).
1987 "Privatización autoritaria y recreación de la escena pública," 31–48, in Oscar Oszlak (ed.), *"Proceso," crisis y transición democrática*, vol. 1 (Buenos Aires: Centro Editor de América Latina).

Oxhorn, Philip
1995 *Organizing Civil Society: The Popular Sectors and the Struggle for Democracy in Chile* (University Park, Pa.: The Pennsylvania State University Press).

Palermo, Vicente
  1986 *Democracia Interna en los Partidos. Las elecciones partidarias de 1983 en la radicalismo y justicialismo porteños* (Buenos Aires: Ediciones del IDES no. 4).
Palermo, Vicente, and Marcos Novaro
  1996 *Política y poder en el gobierno de Menem* (Buenos Aires: Grupo Editorial Norma).
Palomino, Héctor
  1987 *Cambios ocupacionales y sociales en Argentina, 1947–1985* (Buenos Aires: CISEA).
  1995 "Quiebre y ruptura de la acción sindical: Un panorama desde el presente sobre la evolución del movimiento sindical en Argentina," 203–29, in Carlos H. Acuña (ed.), *La nueva matriz política Argentina* (Buenos Aires: Ediciones Nueva Visión).
Panorama Laboral
  1976–80 Weekly memorandum circulated within the ministry of labor, 1976–80.
Parcero, Daniel
  1987 *La CGT y el sindicalismo Latinoamericano: Historia crítica de sus relaciones. Desde el ATLAS a la CIOSL* (Buenos Aires: Editorial Fraterna).
Pascual, Liliana
  1980 "La salud y los Obras Sociales," *Criterio* (Buenos Aires), 53, no. 1836 (May 22): 278–83.
Payne, Leigh A.
  1994 *Brazilian Industrialists and Democratic Change* (Baltimore: Johns Hopkins University Press).
Payne, Leigh A., and Ernest Bartell
  1995 "Bringing Business Back In: Business-State Relations and Democratic Stability in Latin America," 257–90, in Ernest Bartell and Leigh A. Payne (eds.), *Business and Democracy in Latin America* (Pittsburgh: University of Pittsburgh Press).
Peralta-Ramos, Mónica
  1987 "Toward an Analysis of the Structural Basis of Coercion in Argentina: The Behavior of the Major Fractions of the Bourgeoisie, 1976–1983," 39–67, in Mónica Peralta-Ramos and Carlos Waisman (eds.), *From Military Rule to Liberal Democracy in Argentina* (Boulder, Colo.: Westview Press).
Peralta-Ramos, Mónica, and Carlos Waisman (eds.)
  1987 *From Military Rule to Liberal Democracy in Argentina* (Boulder, Colo.: Westview Press).
Perlmutter, Amos
  1981 *Modern Authoritarianism: A Comparative Institutional Analysis* (New Haven: Yale University Press).

Pérez, Ricardo
1984 "[Interview with Ricardo Pérez]," 179–88, in Osvaldo Calello and Daniel Parceco, *De Vandor a Ubaldini*, vol. 2 (Buenos Aires: Centro Editor de América Latina).
Philip, George
1985 *The Military in South American Politics* (London: Croom Helm).
Piñeiro, Armando Alonso
1992 *Historia de la guerra de Malvinas* (Buenos Aires: Planeta).
Pion-Berlin, David
1985 "The Fall of Military Rule in Argentina, 1976–1983," *Journal of Interamerican Studies and World Affairs* 27, no. 2 (Summer): 55–76.
1989 *The Ideology of State Terror: Economic Doctrine and Political Repression in Argentina and Peru* (Boulder, Colo.: Lynne Rienner Publishers).
1991 "Between Confrontation and Accommodation: Military and Government Policy in Democratic Argentina," *Journal of Latin American Studies* 23, no. 3 (October): 543–71.
1992 "Military Autonomy and Emerging Democracies in South America," *Comparative Politics* 25, no. 1 (October): 83–102.
1994 "To Prosecute or to Pardon? Human Rights Decisions in the Latin American Southern Cone," *Human Rights Quarterly* 16, no. 1: 105–30.
Plá, Alberto et al.
1984 *La década trágica: Ocho ensayos sobre la crisis argentina, 1973–1983* (Buenos Aires: Editorial Tierra de Fuego).
Polosecki, Claudio
1978 "Comisión de Gestión y Trabajo: Nuevo cuerpo gremial," *Clarín,* April 2, 5.
1979 "Nacen 'los 20': Posición disidente," *Clarín,* August 29, 5.
Portantiero, Juan Carlos
1980 "Bases políticas, ley sindical y plan del capital," *Controversia* (México), no. 4 (February): 2–3.
1987 "La transición entre la confrontación y el acuerdo," 257–93, in José Nun and Juan Carlos Portantiero (eds.), *Ensayos sobre la transición democrática en la Argentina* (Buenos Aires: Puntosur Editores).
Portes, Alejandro, and Douglas Kincaid
1985 "The Crisis of Authoritarianism: State and Civil Society in Argentina, Chile, and Uruguay," *Research in Political Sociology* 1:49–77.
Pozzi, Pablo A.
1988a *Oposición obrera a la dictadura, 1976–1982* (Buenos Aires: Editorial Contrapunto).
1988b "Argentina, 1976–1982: Labour Leadership and Military Government," *Journal of Latin American Studies* 20, no. 1 (May): 111–38.
Przeworski, Adam
1986 "Some Problems in the Study of the Transition to Democracy," 47–63, in Guillermo O'Donnell, Philippe Schmitter, and Laurence White-

head (eds.), *Transitions from Authoritarian Rule: Comparative Perspectives* (Baltimore: Johns Hopkins University Press).
1991 *Democracy and the Market: Political and Economic Reforms in Eastern Europe and Latin America* (Cambridge: Cambridge University Press).

Przeworski, Adam et al.
1995 *Sustainable Democracy* (New York: Cambridge University Press).

Quintar, Aida
1989 "La flexibilización laboral: Una nueva modalidad de fragmantación de los sectores obreros," paper presented at the Seminario Internacional sobre Revolución Tecnológica y Reestructuración Productiva, Serie IEU/ILPES, no. 25 (Santiago, August).

Redacción
1980 "Anuario 1980, los sucesos del año," *Redacción* (Buenos Aires), no. 4 (December): 63–71.
1983a "Un nuevo movimiento enfrenta al monopolio sindical," *Redacción* (Buenos Aires), no. 126 (August): 24–25.
1983b "Las trece listas que se votarán en Buenos Aires," *Redacción* (Buenos Aires), no. 128 (October): 83–90.

Reinaldo García, Cesar
1985 *Historia de los grupos y partidos políticos de la República Argentina, Desde 1810 a 1983* (Buenos Aires: Sainte Claire Editora).

Reis, Fábio Wanderley, and Guillermo O'Donnell (eds.)
1988 *A Democracia no Brasil: Dilemas e Perspectivas* (São Paulo: Edições Vértice).

Remmer, Karen
1989 *Military Rule in Latin America* (Winchester, Mass.: Unwin Hyman).

Remmer, Karen, and Gilbert Merkx
1982 "Bureaucratic Authoritarianism Revisited," *Latin American Research Review* 17, no. 2: 3–40.

Reyna, José Luis, and Richard Weinhert (eds.)
1977 *Authoritarianism in Mexico* (Philadelphia: Institute for the Study of Human Issues).

Ricci, María Susana, and J. Samuel Fitch
1990 "Military Regimes in Argentina, 1966–1973 and 1976–1983," 55–74, in Louis W. Goodman, Johanna S. R. Mendelson, and Juan Rial (eds.), *The Military and Democracy: The Future of Civil-Military Relations in Latin America* (Lexington, Mass.: Lexington Books).

Riggs, Fred W.
1990 "A Neoinstitutional Typology of Third World Politics," 205–35, in Anton Bebler and Jim Seroka (eds.), *Contemporary Political Systems: Classifications and Typologies* (Boulder, Colo.: Lynne Rienner Publishers).
1993 "Fragility of the Third World's Regimes," *International Social Science Journal,* no. 136 (May): 199–243.

Rock, David
1985 *Argentina, 1516–1982: From Spanish Colonization to the Falklands War* (Berkeley and Los Angeles: University of California Press).
Rock, David, and Suzanne E. Avellano
1986 "The Argentine Elections of 1983: Significance and Repercussions," 189–99, in Paul Drake and Eduardo Silva (eds.), *Elections and Democratization in Latin America, 1980–1985* (San Diego: CILAS, Center for U.S.-Mexican Studies, IOA).
Rodríguez, José
1983 "Reportaje a José Rodríguez," 466–79, in Mona Moncalvillo, *Reportajes de Humor* (Buenos Aires: Ediciones de la Urraca).
Rokkan, Stein
1970 *Citizens, Elections, and Parties: Approaches to the Comparative Study of the Processes of Development* (New York: David McKay).
Roldán, Iris Martha
1978 *Sindicatos y protesta social en la Argentina, 1969–1974* (Amsterdam: CEDLA).
Romero, Luis Alberto
1985 "Sectores populares, participación y democracia: El caso de Buenos Aires," 226–70, in Alain Rouquié and Jorge Schvarzer (eds.), *¿Cómo renacen las democracias?* (Buenos Aires: Emecé Editores).
Roth, Guenther
1963 *The Social Democrats in Imperial Germany: A Study of Working-Class Isolation and National Integration* (Totowa, N.J.: Bedminster Press).
Rouquié, Alain
1982a *Poder Militar y Sociedad Política en la Argentina, 1943–1973* (Buenos Aires: Emecé Editores).
1982b "Hegemonía militar, Estado y dominación social," 11–50, in Alain Rouquié (ed.), *Argentina, hoy* (Buenos Aires: Siglo XXI Editores).
1982c "El poder militar en la Argentina de hoy: Cambio y continuidad," 65–76, in Peter Waldmann and Ernesto Garzón Valdéz (eds.), *El poder militar en la Argentina, 1976–1981* (Buenos Aires: Editorial Galerna).
1986 "Demilitarization and the Institutionalization of Military-Dominated Polities in Latin America," 108–36, in Guillermo O'Donnell, Philippe C. Schmitter, and Laurence Whitehead (eds.), *Transitions from Authoritarian Rule: Comparative Perspectives* (Baltimore: Johns Hopkins University Press).
1987a *The Military and the State in Latin America* (Berkeley and Los Angeles: University of California Press).
1987b "Continuidad y cambio de los partidos en el proceso de transición a la democracia: La democracia contra los partidos, el caso argentino," 259–77, in Carlos Huneeus (ed.), *Para vivir la democracia* (Santiago de Chile: Centro de Estudios de la Realidad Contemporánea).

Rouquié, Alain, and Jorge Schvarzer (eds.)
  1985 ¿Cómo renacen las democracias? (Buenos Aires: Emecé Editores).
Rupnik, Jacques
  1995 "The Post-Totalitarian Blues," *Journal of Democracy* 6, no. 2 (April): 61–73.
Rueschemeyer, Dietrich, Evelyne Huber Stephens, and John D. Stephens
  1992 *Capitalist Development and Democracy* (Chicago: University of Chicago Press).
Sabel, Charles
  1981 "The Internal Politics of Trade Unions," 209–44, in Suzanne Berger (ed.), *Organizing Interests in Western Europe* (Cambridge: Cambridge University Press).
Sáenz Quesada, María
  1993 *El camino de la democracia: Argentina, 1972–1983* (Buenos Aires: Tiempo de Ideas).
Sánchez, Jorge Ezequiel
  1983 "La interna del Proceso," *Búsqueda de un País Moderno* (Buenos Aires), 3, no. 20 (May): 10–14.
Sánchez, Pedro
  1983 "La tormenta del pacto militar-sindical," *Redacción* (Buenos Aires), no. 123 (May): 121–25.
Santamaría, Julian (ed.)
  1982 *Transiciones a la democracia en el Sur de Europa y América Latina* (Madrid: Centro de Investigaciones Sociales).
Sartori, Giovanni
  1970 "Concept Misformation in Comparative Politics," *American Political Science Review* 64, no. 4: 1033–53.
  1984 "Guidelines for Concept Analysis," 15–85, in Giovanni Sartori (ed.), *Social Science Concepts: A Systematic Analysis* (Beverly Hills, Calif.: Sage Publications).
  1993 "Totalitarianism, Model Mania, and Learning From Error," *Journal of Theoretical Politics* 5, no. 1: 5–22.
  1994 *Comparative Constitutional Engineering: An Inquiry into Structures, Incentives, and Outcomes* (New York: New York University Press).
Schamis, Hector E.
  1991 "Reconceptualizing Latin American Authoritarianism in the 1970s: From Bureaucratic-Authoritarianism to Neoconservatism," *Comparative Politics* 23, no. 2 (January): 201–20.
Schmitter, Philippe C.
  1973 "The 'Portugalization' of Brazil?" 179–232, in Alfred Stepan (ed.), *Authoritarian Brazil: Origins, Policies, and Future* (Princeton: Princeton University Press).
  1993 "Reflections on Revolutionary and Evolutionary Transitions: The Russian Case in Perspective," 29–33, in Alexander Dallin (ed.), *Political Parties in Russia* (Berkeley: Research Series, University of California, Berkeley, International and Area Studies).

1994 "Dangers and Dilemmas of Democracy," *Journal of Democracy* 5, no. 2 (April): 57–74.
1995a "Transitology: The Sciences or the Art of Democratization?" 11–41, in Joseph Tulchin with Bernice Romero (eds.), *The Consolidation of Democracy in Latin America* (Boulder, Colo.: Lynne Reimer Publishers).
1995b "The Consolidation of Political Democracies: Processes, Rhythms, Sequences, and Types," 535–69, in Geoffrey Pridham (ed.), *Transitions to Democracy: Comparative Perspectives from Southern Europe, Latin America, and Eastern Europe* (Brookfield, Vt.: Dartmouth Publishing Company).
1995c "Organized Interests and Democratic Consolidation in Southern Europe," 284–314, in Richard Gunther, P. Nikiforos Diamandouros, and Hans-Jürgen Puhle (eds.), *The Politics of Democratic Consolidation: Southern Europe in Comparative Perspective* (Baltimore: Johns Hopkins University Press).
1996 "The Influence of the International Context upon the Choice of National Institutions and Policies in Neo-Democracies," 26–54, in Laurence Whitehead (ed.), *The International Dimensions of Democratization: Europe and the Americas* (New York: Oxford University Press).

Schmitter, Philippe, and Terry Karl
1991 "What Democracy Is . . . and What It Is Not," *Journal of Democracy* 2, no. 3 (Summer): 75–88.
1992 "The Types of Democracy Emerging in Southern and Eastern Europe and South and Central America," 55–68, in Peter M. E.Volten (ed.), *Bound to Change* (New York: Institute for East-West Studies).

Schmitter, Philippe with Terry Karl
1994 "The Conceptual Travels of Transitologists and Consolidologists: How Far to the East Should They Attempt to Go?" *Slavic Review* 53, no. 1 (Spring): 173–85.

Schneider, Cathy Lisa
1995 *Shantytown Protest in Pinochet's Chile* (Philadelphia: Temple University Press).

Schvarzer, Jorge
1983 "Cambios en el liderazgo industrial argentino en el período de Martínez de Hoz," *Desarrollo Económico* (Buenos Aires), 23, no. 91 (October–December): 395–422.
1987a *La Política Económica de Martínez de Hoz* (Buenos Aires: Hyspamérica).
1987b *Promoción industrial en Argentina: Características, evolución y resultados* (Buenos Aires: Centro de Investigaciones Sociales sobre el Estado y la Administracion).

Scully, Timothy R.
1992 *Rethinking the Center: Party Politics in Nineteenth- and Twentieth-Century Chile* (Stanford, Calif.: Stanford University Press).

Scully, Timothy, and J. Samuel Valenzuela
1993 "From Democracy to Democracy: Continuities and Changes of Elec-

toral Choices and the Party System in Chile," *Working Papers* no. 199 (Notre Dame, Ind.: Helen Kellogg Institute for International Studies, University of Notre Dame).

Senén González, Santiago
  1980 *El poder sindical* (Buenos Aires: Editorial Plus Ultra).
  1984 *Diez años de sindicalismo Argentino (De Perón al proceso)* (Buenos Aires: Ediciones Corregidor).

Shain, Yossi, and Juan J. Linz et al.
  1995 *Between States: Interim Governments and Democratic Transitions* (Cambridge: Cambridge University Press).

Sigal, Silvia, and Isabel Santi
  1985 "El discurso en el régimen autoritario: Un estudio comparativo," 145–70, in Isidoro Cheresky and Jacques Chonchol (eds.), *Crisis y transformación de los regímenes autoritarios* (Buenos Aires: Editorial Universitaria de Buenos Aires).

Silva, Eduardo
  1992/93 "Capitalist Regime Loyalties and Redemocratization in Chile," *Journal of Interamerican Studies and World Affairs* 34, no. 4 (Winter): 77–117.

Simpson, John, and Jana Bennett
  1985 *The Disappeared and the Mothers of the Plaza: The Story of the 11,000 Argentinians Who Vanished* (New York: St. Martin's Press).

Sisk, Timothy D.
  1995 *Democratization in South Africa: The Elusive Social Contract* (Princeton: Princeton University Press).

Skidmore, Thomas E.
  1973 "Politics and Economic Policy-Making in Authoritarian Brazil, 1937–1971," 3–46, in Alfred Stepan (ed.), *Authoritarian Brazil: Origins, Policies, and Future* (Princeton: Princeton University Press).
  1988 *The Politics of Military Rule in Brazil, 1964–1985* (New York: Oxford University Press).

Skocpol, Theda
  1979 *States and Social Revolution* (New York: Cambridge University Press).
  1994 *Social Revolutions in the Modern World* (New York: Cambridge University Press).

Slodky, Javier
  1987 *La negociación colectiva en la Argentina, Balance 1976–1986 y propuesta de actualización de la Ley 14.250* (Buenos Aires: Fundación Ebert).

Smith, William C.
  1989 *Authoritarianism and the Crisis of the Argentine Political Economy* (Stanford, Calif.: Stanford University Press).

Sondereguer, María
  1985 "El movimiento de derechos humanos en la Argentina," 7–32, in Elizabeth Jelin (ed.), *Los nuevos movimientos sociales*, vol. 2 (Buenos Aires: Centro Editor de América Latina).

Stepan, Alfred
1971 *The Military in Politics: Changing Patterns in Brazil* (Princeton: Princeton University Press).
1978 *The State and Society: Peru in Comparative Perspective* (Princeton: Princeton University Press).
1985 "State Power and the Strength of Civil Society in the Southern Cone of Latin America," 317–43, in Peter Evans, Dietrich Rueschemeyer and Theda Skocpol (eds.), *Bringing the State Back In* (Cambridge: Cambridge University Press).
1986 "Paths Toward Redemocratization: Theoretical and Comparative Considerations," 64–84, in Guillermo O'Donnell, Philippe Schmitter and Laurence Whitehead (eds.), *Transitions from Authoritarian Rule: Comparative Perspectives* (Baltimore: Johns Hopkins University Press).
1988 *Rethinking Military Politics: Brazil and the Southern Cone* (Princeton: Princeton University Press).
Stepan, Alfred (ed).
1973 *Authoritarian Brazil: Origins, Policies, and Future* (Princeton: Princeton University Press).
1989 *Democratizing Brazil: Problems of Transition and Consolidation* (New York: Oxford University Press).
Stephens, John D.
1989 "Democratic Transition and Breakdown in Europe, 1870–1939: A Test of the Moore Thesis," *American Journal of Sociology* 94, no. 5 (March): 1019–77.
Taccone, Juan José
1982 "Taccone: 'No creo en el pacto sindical-militar'," *Movimiento para la Revolución Nacional y Popular* (Buenos Aires), 1, no. 1 (December): 32–33.
Tarrow, Sidney
1992 "Mentalities, Political Cultures, and Collective Action Frames: Constructing Meaning Through Action," 174–202, in Aldon D. Morris and Carol Mc Clugh Mueller (eds.), *Frontiers in Social Movement Theory* (New Haven: Yale University Press).
1994 *Power in Movement: Social Movements, Collective Action, and Politics* (New York: Cambridge University Press).
1995a "Mass Mobilization and Regime Change: Pacts, Reforms, and Popular Power in Italy (1918–1922) and Spain (1975–1978)," 204–30, in Richard Gunther, P. Nikiforos Diamandouros, and Hans-Jürgen Puhle (eds.), *The Politics of Democratic Consolidation: Southern Europe in Comparative Perspective* (Baltimore: Johns Hopkins University Press).
1995b "Mass Mobilization and Elite Exchange: Democratization Episodes in Italy and Spain," *Democratization* 2, no. 3 (Autumn): 221–45.
Thompson, Andrés
1985 "Las luchas sociales en la Argentina, 1976–1983," 85–102, in Isidoro Cheresky and Jacques Chonchol (eds.), *Crisis y transformación de los*

regímenes autoritarios (Buenos Aires: Editorial Universitaria de Buenos Aires).

Thompson, Mark R.
1995 *The Anti-Marcos Struggle: Personalistic Rule and Democratic Transition in the Philippines* (New Haven: Yale University Press).

Tilly, Charles
1993/94 "Social Movements as Historically Specific Clusters of Political Performances," *Berkeley Journal of Sociology* 38:1–30.

Timerman, Jacobo
1981 *Prisoner Without a Name, Cell Without a Number* (New York: Random House).

Tironi, Eugenio
1990 *Autoritarismo, Modernización y Marginalidad: El Caso de Chile, 1973–1989* (Santiago: Ediciones Sur).

Torre, Juan Carlos
1980 "La cuestión del poder sindical y el orden político en la Argentina," *Criterio* (Buenos Aires), 53, no. 1843: 528–33.

1983a *Los sindicalistas en el gobierno, 1973–1976* (Buenos Aires: Centro Editor de América Latina).

1983b "La generosa historia de las pactos," *Extra* (Buenos Aires), 18, no. 216 (June): 21.

1990 *La vieja guardia sindical y Perón: Sobre los orígines del peronismo* (Buenos Aires: Editorial Sudamericana/Instituto Torcuato Di Tella).

Touraine, Alain
1989 *América Latina: política y sociedad* (Madrid: Espasa-Calpe).

Trabajadores y Sindicalistas Argentinos en el Exilio (TySAE)
1979 "Páginas Sindicales," mimeographed.

Troncoso, Oscar
1984 *El proceso de reorganización nacional,* vol. 1: *De marzo de 1976 a marzo de 1977* (Buenos Aires: Centro Editor de América Latina).

1985 *El proceso de reorganización nacional,* vol. 2: *De abril de 1977 a junio de 1978* (Buenos Aires: Centro Editor de América Latina).

Unamuno, Miguel
1982 "Interview with Miguel Unamuno," 77–112, in Oscar R. Cardoso and Rodolfo Audi, *Sindicalismo: El poder y la crisis* (Buenos Aires: Editorial Belgrano).

Unger, Roberto Mangabeira
1987a *False Necessity: Anti-Necessitarian Social Theory in the Service of Radical Democracy* (Cambridge: Cambridge University Press).

1987b *Plasticity into Power: Comparative-Historical Studies on the Institutional Conditions of Economic and Military Success* (Cambridge: Cambridge University Press).

1990 *A Alternative Transformadora: Como Democratizar o Brasil* (Rio de Janeiro: Editora Guanabara Koogan).

Uriarte, Claudio
1992 *Almirante Cero: Biografía no autorizada de Emilio Eduardo Massera* (Buenos Aires: Planeta).

Valenzuela, Arturo
- 1994 "Party Politics and the Crisis of Presidentialism in Chile: A Proposal for a Parliamentary Form of Government," 91–150, in Juan J. Linz and Arturo Valenzuela (eds.), *The Failure of Presidential Democracy*, vol. 2: *The Cases of Latin America* (Baltimore: Johns Hopkins University Press).
- 1995 "The Military in Power: The Consolidation of One-man Rule," 21–72, in Paul Drake and Iván Jaksić (eds.), *The Struggle for Democracy in Chile, 1982–1990*, rev. ed. (Lincoln: University of Nebraska Press).

Valenzuela, Arturo, and Samuel Valenzuela (eds.)
- 1986a *Military Rule in Chile: Dictatorship and Oppositions* (Baltimore: Johns Hopkins University Press).

Valenzuela, Arturo, and Samuel Valenzuela
- 1986b "Introduction," 1–12, in Arturo Valenzuela and Samuel Valenzuela (eds.), *Military Rule in Chile: Dictatorship and Oppositions* (Baltimore: Johns Hopkins University Press).
- 1986c "Party Opposition Under the Chilean Authoritarian Regime," 184–229, in Arturo Valenzuela and Samuel Valenzuela (eds.), *Military Rule in Chile: Dictatorship and Oppositions* (Baltimore: Johns Hopkins University Press).

Valenzuela, J. Samuel
- 1989 "Labor Movements in Transitions to Democracy," *Comparative Politics* 21, no. 4 (July): 445–72.
- 1992 "Democratic Consolidation in Post-Transitional Settings: Notion, Process, and Facilitating Conditions," 57–104, in Scott Mainwaring, Guillermo O'Donnell, and J. Samuel Valenzuela (eds.), *Issues in Democratic Consolidation: The New South American Democracies in Comparative Perspective* (South Bend, Ind.: University of Notre Dame Press).

Valle, Ramón
- 1980 "Breves consideraciones sobre las *Bases políticas de las Fuerzas Armadas*," mimeograph of document given to the minister of the interior Harguindeguy as part of the official "political dialogue" on August 27, 1980.

Vanossi, Jorge Reinaldo
- 1976 "Reflexiones sobre el nuevo régimen institucional Argentino," *Carta Política* (Buenos Aires), no. 33 (July): 41–50.

Varas, Augusto
- 1987 *Los militares en el poder: Régimen y gobierno militar en Chile, 1973–1986* (Santiago de Chile: FLACSO-Pehuén Editores).
- 1988 *La política de las armas en América Latina* (Santiago: FLACSO).

Varas, Augusto (ed.)
- 1984 *Transición a la Democracia: América Latina y Chile* (Santiago: Salesianos).

Varas, Augusto, and Felipe Agüero
- 1984 *El proyecto político militar* (Santiago: FLACSO).

Vázquez, Enrique
    1985   *PRN, La última: Origen, apogeo y caída de la dictadura militar* (Buenos Aires: Editorial Universitaria de Buenos Aires).

Veiga, Raúl
    1985   *Las organizaciones de derechos humanos* (Buenos Aires: Centro Editor de América Latina).

Velazquez, Julio
    1979a   "La Ley de Asociaciones Profesionales," *Comentarios* (Buenos Aires), 2, no. 3 (March): 24–26.
    1979b   "Por un centro amplio de coordinación sindical," *Comentarios* (Buenos Aires), 2, no. 10 (October): 20–21.

Verbitsky, Horacio
    1984   *La última batalla de la Tercera Guerra Mundial* (Buenos Aires: Editorial Legasa).
    1985a   *Ezeiza* (Buenos Aires: Editorial Contrapunto).
    1985b   *Rodolfo Walsh y la prensa clandestina, 1976–1978* (Buenos Aires: Ediciones de la Urraca, Colección el Periodista de Buenos Aires).
    1985c   *La posguerra sucia: Un análisis de la transición* (Buenos Aires: Editorial Legasa).
    1987   *Civiles y Militares: Memoria secreta de la transición* (Buenos Aires: Editorial Contrapunto).
    1996   *The Flight: Confessions of an Argentine Dirty Warrior* (New York: New Press).

Villarreal, Juan
    1987   "Changes in Argentine Society: The Heritage of the Dictatorship," 69–96, in Mónica Peralta-Ramos and Carlos Waisman (eds.), *From Military Rule to Liberal Democracy in Argentina* (Boulder, Colo.: Westview Press).

Viola, Eduardo, and Scott Mainwaring
    1985   "Transitions to Democracy: Brazil and Argentina in the 1980s," *Journal of International Affairs* 38, no. 2 (Winter): 193–219.

Waisman, Carlos
    1987   *Reversal of Development in Argentina: Postwar Counterrevolutionary Policies and Their Structural Consequences* (Princeton: Princeton University Press).

Walker, Ignacio
    1990   *Socialismo y democracia en Chile: Chile y Europa en Perspectiva Comparada* (Santiago: CIEPLAN-Hatchette).

Weffort, Francisco
    1989   "Why Democracy?" 327–50, in Alfred Stepan (ed.), *Democratizing Brazil: Problems of Transition and Consolidation* (New York: Oxford University Press).

Weiss Fagen, Patricia
    1992   "Repression and State Security," 39–71, in Juan E. Corradi, Patricia Weiss Fagen, and Manuel Antonio Garretón (eds.), *Fear at the Edge:*

State Terror and Resistance in Latin America (Berkeley and Los Angeles: University of California Press).

Whitehead, Laurence
- 1985 "Whatever Became of the 'Southern Cone Model'?" 9–30, in David E. Hojman (ed.), *Chile After 1973: Elements for the Analysis of Military Rule* (Liverpool: Center for Latin American Studies, University of Liverpool, Monograph Series no. 12).
- 1986 "International Aspects of Democratization," 3–46, in Guillermo O'Donnell, Philippe Schmitter and Laurence Whitehead (eds.), *Transitions from Authoritarian Rule: Comparative Perspectives* (Baltimore: Johns Hopkins University Press).
- 1992 "The Alternatives to 'Liberal Democracy': A Latin American Perspective," *Political Studies* 40: 146–59.
- 1994 "Prospects for a 'Transition' from Authoritarian Rule in Mexico," 327–46, in Maria Lorena Cook, Kevin Middlebrook, and Juan Molinar Horcasitas (eds.), *The Politics of Economic Restructuring in Mexico: State-Society Relations and Regime Change in Mexico* (La Jolla, Calif.: Center for U.S.-Mexican Studies/University of California, San Diego).
- 1996a "Three International Dimensions of Democratization," 3–27, in Laurence Whitehead (ed.), *The International Dimensions of Democratization: Europe and the Americas* (New York: Oxford University Press).

Whitehead, Laurence (ed.)
- 1996b *The International Dimensions of Democratization: Europe and the Americas* (New York: Oxford University Press).

Wickham-Crowley, Timothy P.
- 1992 *Guerrillas and Revolution in Latin America: A Comparative Study of Insurgents and Regimes Since 1956* (Princeton: Princeton University Press).

Woo-Cumings, Meredith
- 1994 "The 'New Authoritarianism' in East Asia," *Current History* (December): 413–16.

Zaverucha, Jorge
- 1993 "Civil-Military Relations in Spain, Argentina and Brazil," *Journal of Latin American Studies* 25, no. 2 (May): 283–99.

Zolberg, Aristide
- 1972 "Moments of Madness," *Politics and Society* 2:183–207.

Index

accommodation, strategy of, 21
actors
  contending and emerging elite, 17–18
  dominant and relevant, 16, 19, 36–37, 222 n. 28, 224 n. 41
  formation of, xxi, xxxi, 13, 15, 18–19, 190, 193, 230 n. 34, 240 n. 16. *See also* labor, reconstitution as political actor
  identity of, xxii, 18, 20
  orientation of, xxi, 14–15, 224 n. 42. *See also* opposition, types of; labor, orientation
  strategy of, xx–xxiii, 20–21. *See also* elites, strength of antichange; parties, political, strategy of
Agosti, Orlando, 55
Alemann, Roberto, 136, 261 n. 1
Alfonsín, Raúl, 155–56, 158–59, 200, 255 n. 16, 270 n. 61
Allende, Salvador, 171
allies, military's search for "responsible," 73–76, 82–83, 86, 89, 99–100, 110, 116, 148, 239 n. 6. *See also* labor, as potential ally of military
Alonso, José, 52
amnesty law, 156
Argentina. *See also under* representation, problem of; cohesion, military; threat prior to coup; opposition, strength of; institutional arrangement, interim; institutional arrangement; opposition, types of; elites, strength of antichange
  as case of bureaucratic authoritarianism, xxiv, 30–31
  and competing explanations of transition, 133, 139–46, 261 n. 3
  legacies of bureaucratic authoritarianism in, 199–203
  and phase of evolution, xix–xxx, 168–69, 192–93
  and phase of origin, xxvii–xix, 166–67, 189

and phase of transition, xxx–xxxii, 169–70, 194–95
Argentine Anti-Communist Alliance (AAA), 53
Argentine Industrial Union (UIA), 123–24
assurances, military search for, 148–59. *See also* military–trade union pact
authoritarianism, 24–25. *See also* bureaucratic authoritarianism
  defining attributes of, 27
auto workers' union (SMATA), 65, 68, 78, 80, 112, 236 n. 37, 244 n. 36, 245 n. 45
Aylwin, Patricio, 177

Balbín, Ricardo, 109, 122, 125
bank workers' union, 112, 236 n. 37, 245 n. 45
Bermeo, Nancy, 30
Bignone, Reynaldo, 138, 147
Bittel, Deolindo, 150, 153–54, 266 n. 36
Borro, Sebastián, 150
Branco, Humberto Castello, 178
Brazil. *See also under* representation, problem of; cohesion, military; threat prior to coup; opposition, strength of; institutional arrangement, interim; institutional arrangement; opposition, types of; elites, strength of antichange
  as case of bureaucratic authoritarianism, xxiv, 30–31
  and phase of evolution, 179–83, 191–92
  and phase of origin, 177–79, 189
  and phase of transition, 183–84, 194
Britain's war with Argentina. *See* Falkland/Malvinas Islands war
bureaucratic authoritarianism, xxiii–xxv, 24. *See also* military rulers under bureaucratic authoritarianism; labor under bureaucratic authoritarianism; representa-

Index 327

tion, problem of; political project, of bureaucratic authoritarian rulers cases of, xxiv, 26–27, 29–31, 225 n. 4, 227 n. 15
contrasted with democracy and totalitarianism, 27, 32–33
defining attributes of, xxiv, 26–31
historical significance of, 196–98, 203
and involvement in government of military as institution, 226 n. 11
legacies of, 198–99
paradigmatic status of, 31
as subtype of authoritarianism, 26–28, 31
synonymous terms, 227–28 n. 18
bureaucratic rings, 28, 42
business, 28, 41–43, 237–38 n. 47, 243 n. 32. See also bureaucratic rings
in Argentina, 67–68, 85, 91, 107–8, 123–25, 127, 201, 253 n. 6, 254 n. 11, 259 n. 37, 260 n. 45
impact of bureaucratic authoritarianism on, 201–3

cabinet, composition of, 61, 120, 138, 234 n. 24, 240 n. 9, 250 n. 69, 259 n. 37, 261 n. 1
Cáceres, Alberto, 54
Cafiero, Antonio, 150, 153
Canitrot, Adolfo, 69
Capellini, Jesús, 50
Cardoso, Fernando, 42
Cavalier, Armando, 86, 246 n. 48
CGT. See General Labor Confederation
change, regime. See transition
change from above and from below. See transition, modes of; elites, and non-elites in regime analysis
Chile. See also under representation, problem of; cohesion, military; threat prior to coup; opposition, strength of; institutional arrangement, interim; institutional arrangement; opposition, types of; elites, strength of antichange
as case of bureaucratic authoritarianism, xxiv, 30–31, 275 n. 12
and phase of evolution, 173–76, 190–91

and phase of origin, 171–75, 188, 273 n. 4
and phase of transition, 176–77, 194, 276 n. 20
Christian Democratic Party, 122, 126
coercion, as explanatory factor, 12–14
cohesion, military
in Argentina, xxvii–xxx, 58, 60–63, 64, 70–72, 75, 94–98, 101–2, 106–11, 114–18, 120–22, 127–29, 138, 144–45, 166–69, 192–93. See also hard-liners and soft-liners; liberalization
in Brazil, 178–82, 191
in Chile, 171, 174–75, 190, 274 n. 7
as explanation about bureaucratic authoritarianism, 185, 190
as explanatory factor, xx–xxiii, 10–16, 19, 224 n. 42
and forms of divisions under bureaucratic authoritarianism, 229 n. 26, 231 n. 42
collective bargaining, 237 n. 43, 243 n. 31
Collier, David, 27
commerce workers' union, 86, 112, 244 n. 36
conceptual framework. See political-institutional model, the
Concertation of Parties for Democracy, 177
conflicting imperatives, xxv, 25, 31, 33–37, 197. See also representation, problem of
confrontation, strategy of, 21
constitution
lack of reform of, 97
reintroduction of 1853, 148
constitutional definition, challenge of, defined, 9
construction workers' union (UOCRA), 66, 86, 112, 236 n. 37
Cordobazo, 52, 92
coup of 1976, xxvii, 50–51, 55–56
compared to 1966 coup, 58, 62, 64, 273 n. 3
preparation for, 231 n. 1
and prior sense of threat, 54, 64
coup of 1981, palace, 105, 126
consequences of, 127–28, 133–35, 144–45
crisis, political, defined, 16

Damasco, Vicente, 54
de Hoz, José Martínez, 61, 69, 94, 107, 135–36, 201, 238–39 n. 3, 243 n. 32, 254 n. 11
and conflicts with the labor ministry, 250 n. 70
position of military vis-à-vis, 249 n. 67
democracy
defining attributes of, 27
transition to. *See* transition; transition, modes of; Argentina, and phase of transition; Brazil, and phase of transition; Chile, and phase of transition
democracy, restricted, xxviii, 197
in Argentina, 98, 109–10, 115–16, 128
Democratic National Union, 179
dialogue, "political," 98, 109–10, 113, 115, 255 n. 16. *See also* Movement of National Opinion (MON)

economic elites. *See* business
election of 1983
announcement of, 148, 264 n. 25
campaign for, 154–59
as foundational election, 154–55
results of, 156, 158–59, 271 n. 66
electoral law, 148, 265 n. 26
elites. *See also* business; elites, governing; elites, strength of antichange; actors, identity of; elites, governing; elites, old governing
contending and emerging, 17–18
and non-elites in regime analysis, 12, 15, 18, 34–36, 223 n. 37
elites, governing. *See also* elites, old governing; military rulers under bureaucratic authoritarianism
elites, old governing, challenge of removing, 17–18
elites, strength of antichange
in Argentina, xxx–xxxii, 146–49, 157, 160, 170
in Brazil, 183
in Chile, 175–77, 191, 194
as explanatory factor, xxii–xxiii, 21–22

Falkland/Malvinas Islands war, 133
Argentina's decision to invade islands, 137, 139–41, 262 n. 6
as cause of transition, 139
consequences of Argentina's defeat in, 138, 142, 144
societal response to, 143, 263 n. 14, 263 n. 16
feudalization of the state, 62–64, 96
food service workers' union, 112, 244 n. 36, 245 n. 45
Framini, Andrés, 150–51
Frondizi, Arturo, 109

Galtieri, Leopoldo, 105, 107–8, 126–29, 133–38, 140–41, 143, 145, 201, 260 n. 48
Geisel, Ernesto, 181
General Labor Confederation (CGT), 240–41 n. 18. *See also* labor groupings
as arena of dialogue, 74, 79, 83–84, 239–40 n. 8
disbanding of, 98, 240 n. 9
during 1973–76 Peronist government, 52–53
intervention of, 65, 83, 242 n. 23
normalization of, 211, 240 n. 9, 268 n. 48, 269 n. 54
overseers of, 240 n. 9
reconstitution of, 114
Greece, as case of bureaucratic authoritarianism, xxiv, 30–31
guerrillas, 52–53, 64, 67, 75, 91, 166, 202. *See also* Montoneros; subversion, war against
Guillán, Julio, 68

Haggard, Stephen, 43
hard-liners and soft-liners, 94, 107, 120–23, 126–29, 135, 140, 144–46, 249–50 n. 68, 250–51 n. 71, 253 n. 4, 260 n. 49, 260–61 n. 50. *See also* cohesion, military, in Argentina; liberalization
Harguindeguy, Albano, 109, 240 n. 13, 249 n. 67, 249–50 n. 68
human rights organizations, 114, 125–26, 149, 155–56, 258 n. 33
links with labor, 271 n. 65
human rights question, 148, 155–56, 200. *See also* assurances, military search for
Huntington, Samuel, 51

Index 329

import substituting industrialization, 201–2
impossible game, 51, 202–3
institutional arrangement
 in Argentina, xix, 97, 106–7, 109–11, 115–16, 118, 168
 in Brazil, 179–81, 191–92, 194
 and bureaucratic authoritarianism, 190, 279 n. 44
 in Chile, 173–76
 as explanatory factor, xxi–xxii, 13–16
institutional arrangement, interim
 in Argentina, xxvii–xxviii, 56–64, 95–96, 101, 115, 167, 188
 in Brazil, 178, 187
 and bureaucratic authoritarianism, 187–88
 in Chile, 171, 173, 187, 274 n. 7
 as explanatory factor, xx, 10–11
institutionalization, challenge of, defined, 12, 220–21 n. 24
institutions. *See* institutional arrangement; institutional arrangement, interim
international dimension, as explanatory factor, 280 n. 46. *See also* Argentina, competing explanations of transition; Falkland/Malvinas Islands war
International Labor Organization (ILO), 83, 244 n. 37
Intransigence and Mobilization, 150
Intransigent Party, 122, 126

journalists' union (FATPREN), 66, 236 n. 37
junta, military
 composition of, 55, 95, 107, 207–10, 250 n. 69, 260 n. 48
 disbanding of junta in 1982, 138
 final dissolution of, 159
 powers of, 58–59, 127–28
 reconstitution of junta in 1982, 148
Justicialist (Peronist) Party (PJ), 54, 109, 113, 115, 121–22, 126, 137, 149, 151–59, 200. *See also* Peronism
 nomination of presidential candidate of, 153–54, 269 n. 52
 sector within, 149–50

Kaufman, Robert, 43

labor. *See also* labor groupings; labor sectors; General Labor Confederation (CGT); Law of Professional Associations; Peronism, and labor movement; individual unions by name
 categories of labor leaders, 77
 dispute over legal mandates, 91–92, 248–49 n. 64
 during 1945–73, 51–56
 and Falkland/Malvinas Islands war, 143
 impact of bureaucratic authoritarianism on, 202
 legal restrictions on union rights, 65–67, 80, 236 n. 35, 237 n. 43, 250 n. 70
 link between labor leaders and rank and file, 79–80, 82, 85, 90–93, 101, 113, 124, 248 n. 62
 links with political parties, 113–14, 124–26, 137, 149–50, 266–67 n. 37. *See also* Peronism, and labor movement
 military contacts with labor leaders, 74, 76, 78–79, 83–86, 94, 99–101, 120, 123–25, 136, 239–40 n. 8, 245–46 n. 47, 246 n. 48. *See also* military–trade union pact
 negative incorporation of, 74
 orientation, 76, 82, 86–87, 89–91, 116, 123–24, 151. *See also* labor groupings
 as participants in "political" dialogue, 109, 113
 as potential ally of military, 73–76, 86, 89–90, 93, 100, 110–11, 123, 127, 150
 reconstitution as political actor, 74–76, 77–93, 100–101. *See also* labor groupings; labor sectors
 strikes, 79–82, 84–85, 107, 243 n. 32, 253–54 n. 8; strikes, general, 88, 92, 101, 124, 150–51, 154; strikes, wildcat, 80, 84–85, 107
 as target of state terror, 67–68, 81, 237 n. 45
 union interventions, 65–66, 68, 77–79,

98, 235–36 n. 34, 236 n. 36, 236 n. 37, 236 n. 38, 236 n. 39, 242 n. 22, 248–49 n. 64; effect of union interventions, 80, 85, 90
union membership reaffiliation, 85
union membership data, 213–14
union normalization, 84, 88–89, 111–12, 136, 152–53, 256 n. 23, 256 n. 24, 268 n. 48
labor, ministry of, 61, 74, 85, 88–89, 98, 111–12, 136, 236 n. 39, 240 n. 9, 242 n. 22. *See also* de Hoz, and conflicts with labor ministry
labor code. *See* Law of Professional Associations
labor groupings. *See also* 62 Organizations
  CGT, 116, 124–26, 136–37, 143, 150, 257 n. 31
  CGT-Azopardo, 149–54
  CGT-Brasil, 150–51, 153
  CGT of Argentine Republic, 153–54, Commission of 20, 123, 255 n. 17
  division between collaborationist and oppositionist wing, 82, 85–90
  Group of 25, 83, 85–90, 92, 101, 110–14, 116, 124, 150–51, 153, 244 n. 37, 245–46 n. 47, 269 n. 50; list of unions aligned with, 244 n. 36; sectors within, 87, 245 n. 43, 246 n. 49; defections from, 87, 246 n. 51
  Intersectorial CNT–20, 123–25, 127, 136–37, 150
  Labor Action Commission (CGyT), 85–87, 245–46 n. 47; list of unions aligned with, 86, 245 n. 45
  National Labor Commission (CNT), 87–90, 99, 101, 109–13, 115–16, 123–24; sectors within the, 246 n. 52
  United Leadership of Argentine Workers (CUTA), 110–13
  unity of labor, 87, 154, 246–47 n. 53, 269 n. 54. *See also* CUTA
labor laws. *See* labor, legal restrictions on union rights; Law of Professional Associations; union social service network; collective bargaining
labor sectors, 240–41 n. 18. *See also* labor groupings, Group of 25, sectors within the; labor groupings, National Labor Commission (CNT), sectors within the
  Group of 8, 87, 240–41 n. 18
  independent, 87, 240–41 n. 18
  orthodox, 87, 240–41 n. 18
  participationist, 87, 240–41 n. 18
  Peronist Syndical Movement (MSP), 87, 90, 112–13, 246 n. 50
  verticalist, 68, 87, 150, 240–41 n. 18
labor under bureaucratic authoritarianism
  collaboration with bureaucratic authoritarian rulers, 38–39
  exclusion of, xxiv, 28–29, 33
  negative integration of, 35–36, 39–40
  opposition to bureaucratic authoritarian rulers, 33, 35–36, 39–40, 43
  reconstitution as political actor, 37–41
Laplane, Alberto, 54
Law of Professional Associations, xxviii, 52, 67, 72, 88–90, 98–100, 105–6, 115–16, 252 n. 75
  elaboration of, 252 n. 79
  responses to, 108, 110–14, 255–56 n. 17
Legislative Advisory Commission (CAL), 58–59, 63, 234 n. 21
legitimacy
  and bureaucratic authoritarianism, 34, 37
  as explanatory factor, 12–14
liberalization, 110, 113, 120, 126–27, 129, 134–37, 140, 144–45, 255 n. 15, 260–61 n. 50. *See also* hard-liners and soft-liners
Liendo, Horacio, 85, 99, 120, 125, 240 n. 9, 249 n. 67, 259 n. 37
light and power workers' federation (FATLyF), 66, 80–81, 86, 236 n. 37, 244 n. 36
Linz, Juan, 13, 16, 24, 27–28, 38, 40, 44
Luder, Italo, 153–56, 159

Malvinas war. *See* Falkland/Malvinas Islands war
mass actors. *See* elites, and non-elites in regime analysis
Massera, Eduardo, 55, 60, 139, 249 n. 67

Matera, Raúl, 109, 149
Matthei, Fernando, 176
Médici, Emílio, 179
Menem, Carlos, 201, 203, 255 n. 15
metal workers' union (UOM), 53, 65, 68, 78, 86, 111–12, 152–53, 236 n. 37, 268 n. 46. *See also* Miguel, Lorenzo
Miguel, Lorenzo, 54–55, 68, 78, 137, 150–53, 159, 240–41 n. 18, 255 n. 15, 257 n. 31, 267 n. 43, 268 n. 45
military as institution, involvement in government of, 57–63, 138. *See also* Legislative Advisory Commission
military cohesion. *See* cohesion, military
military regime. *See* bureaucratic authoritarianism
military rulers under bureaucratic authoritarianism
and doctrine of national security, 37, 75, 238–39 n. 3, 240 n. 11
and involvement in government of military as institution, 28, 36
and references to democracy, xxviii, 44; in Argentina, 97, 251 n. 73; in Chile, 274 n. 9. *See also* democracy, restricted
representation and cohesion of, xxiv–xxv, 25, 33–37, 43
military–trade union pact, 152, 155–59. *See also* assurances, military search for
Montoneros, 52, 248 n. 61
Movement of Integration and Development (MID), 109, 122
Movement of National Opinion (MON), 97, 121, 239 n. 6. *See also* Political Foundations of the Armed Forces; dialogue, "political"
Movement of Unity, Solidarity and Organization (MUSO), 150–51
Multipartidaria
actions of, 122–26, 136–37, 149
breakup of, 155, 158, 270 n. 58
formation of, 122, 258 n. 33
municipal workers' union, 112

Neves, Tancredo, 183
Nicolaides, Cristino, 138, 152

Obras Sociales. *See* union social service network
O'Donnell, Guillermo, 3, 18, 24, 26, 34, 51
Onganía, Juan, 52, 58
opposition, strength of. *See also* threat prior to coup; actors, formation of; actors, dominant and relevant; actors, contending and emerging elite
in Argentina, xxvii, xix–xxxii, 76, 82, 92–96, 100–101, 116–18, 124, 126, 128, 135–37, 144, 146, 160, 166, 168–69, 186
in Brazil, 178–83, 186, 192, 194
and bureaucratic authoritarianism, 185–87, 190, 195
in Chile, 174–76, 185–86, 190–91, 194, 275–76 n. 18
as explanatory factor, xx–xxiii, 10–11, 15–16, 19, 22
opposition, types of. *See also* actors, orientation of
in Argentina, xix, 76, 82, 85–86, 89–90, 115–18, 123, 128, 144, 168, 195. *See also* labor, orientation; labor groupings, division between collaborationist and oppositionist wing; parties, political, orientation of
in Brazil, 181, 194
and bureaucratic authoritarianism, 190
in Chile, 175, 190, 194
defined, 15
loyal opposition, 32–33
pragmatic, 15
principled, 15, 33–34, 40
semi-opposition, 40
orientation, actor. *See* actors, orientation of

pact. *See* military–trade union pact
parties, political. *See also* Multipartidaria; labor, links with political parties; Statute of Political Parties; individual parties by name
ban on, 65, 235 n. 32
during Viola government, 120–22, 125
orientation of, 110

as participants in "political" dialogue, 98, 109–10, 115
reaffiliation drive of, 148
relegalization of, 97, 133, 147
resurgence of, 109–10, 121–23, 258 n. 33
splits between, 147, 154–55, 157–58
strategy of, 122, 125
Party of the Brazilian Democratic Movement, 183
Perón, Isabel, 53–56, 255 n. 15, 266 n. 36
Perón, Juan, 50–53, 55–56, 122, 202, 232 n. 6, 232 n. 7
Peronism
and labor movement, 51, 74, 87, 99, 113, 115, 124, 149–50, 153–54, 158, 202, 231–32 n. 5, 266 n. 32. *See also* 62 Organizations
Peronist government of 1973–76, 50, 52–56, 67
survival as political force, 199–200
Peronist party. *See* Justicialist (Peronist) Party (PJ)
Pinochet, Augusto, 171, 173–77, 273–74 n. 6, 274 n. 7
plastic workers' union, 86
Political Foundations of the Armed Forces, xxviii, 72, 97–100, 105–6, 114–16, 120–21,
responses to, 108–10. *See also* political project, of Argentina's military rulers; Movement of National Opinion (MON); dialogue, "political"
political-institutional model, the. *See also* cohesion, military; opposition, strength of; institutional arrangement, interim; institutional arrangement; opposition, types of; elites, strength of antichange; Argentina; Brazil; Chile
as applied to study of bureaucratic authoritarianism, 184–96
key explanatory variables, summarized, xx–xxiii
and phase of evolution, defined, xx–xxi, 12
and phase of origin, defined, xx, 8–9;

linkage between seizure of power and constitutional definition, 8–9, 219–20 n. 17
and phase of transition, defined, xxii, 17–18
and phases in life cycle of regimes, xix, 6–7
political project
of Argentina's military rulers, xxviii, 60, 73, 75, 93–94, 96–100, 240–41 n. 13, 251 n. 74. *See also* democracy, restricted; labor, negative incorporation of; labor, as potential ally of military; allies, military search for responsible; Political Foundations of the Armed Forces, Law of Professional Associations, Movement of National Opinion (MON); dialogue, "political"
of bureaucratic authoritarian rulers, xxiv, 31, 196–98. *See also* labor under bureaucratic authoritarianism, negative integration of; democracy, restricted
political proposal. *See* political project, of Argentina's military rulers
politics
plastic nature of, xix–xx, 5
structured nature of, xix–xx, 5
Porcile, Julio, 79, 123–24, 136, 240 n. 9, 259 n. 37
post-transitional politics. *See* Argentina, legacies of bureaucratic authoritarianism in; bureaucratic authoritarianism, legacies of
president, military
nomination of, 58, 60, 63, 95, 108, 127–28, 138, 250 n. 69, 260 n. 48. *See also* presidential succession, problem of; coup of 1981, palace
powers of, 58–59,
presidential succession, problem of, 106–8, 119–20, 253 n. 1. *See also* coup of 1981, palace
Process of National Reorganization. *See* Argentina
Progressive Democratic Party, 109
project. *See* political project, of Argentina's military rulers

public administration workers' union, 112

Radical Civic Union (UCR), 109, 115, 122, 125–26, 154–56, 200
  nomination of presidential candidate of, 155, 270 n. 61
railroad workers' union (Unión Ferroviaria), 66, 236 n. 37, 244 n. 36, 245 n. 45
Reagan, Ronald, 142, 262–63 n. 12
Rega, José López, 53
regime, political, defined, xxi, 16, 27–28
regime analysis. *See also* political-institutional model, the
  and question of the state, 218 n. 9
  as research program, xvii–xix, xxiii, 3–5, 22–23, 24–25, 203–5
regime change. *See* transition
regime types. *See* authoritarianism, bureaucratic authoritarianism, democracy, totalitarianism
regimes, phases in life cycle of. *See* political-institutional model, the
Remmer, Karen, 279 n. 44
representation, problem of, xxiv, xxv, 33, 184–85, 188–90, 197–98
  in Argentina, xxvii–xxxii, 69–72, 94, 101, 129, 146, 166–70
  in Brazil, 178–80, 192
  in Chile, 171, 173–76, 191
  and labor options, 37–41
  and military cohesion, xxiv–xxv, 25, 33–37
  variable military responses to, xxiv–xxv, 25–26, 32
repression. *See* coercion; subversion, war against
return to sources, 127, 133, 135, 137, 145
Robledo, Angel, 149
Rodrigo, Celestino, 53
Rodríguez, José, 78
Romero, Leslio, 78
Rouquié, Alain, 36
Rucci, José, 52

Saadi, Vicente, 150
Saint Jean, Alfredo, 138

Salamanca, René, 52, 68
Schamis, Hector, 30
Schmitter, Philippe, 5, 18
SEGBA (state-run electrical power company), 80
Sigaut, Lorenzo, 124, 259 n. 37
situation, political, defined, xxi–xxii, 16, 222–23 n. 32
  in Argentina, xxx, 106, 114, 117–18
  62 Organizations, 55, 65, 87, 137, 150–54, 231–32 n. 5, 240–41 n. 18, 268 n. 45. *See also* Miguel, Lorenzo
Skocpol, Theda, 12
Smith, Oscar, 81
soft-liners. *See* hard-liners and soft-liners; liberalization
state apparatus, colonization of, xxviii, 62–63, 95–96
state workers' union (ATE), 112, 236 n. 36, 244 n. 36
Statute of Political Parties, 120–21, 125, 147–48, 265 n. 26
strategy. *See* actors, strategy of
strike, right to. *See* labor, legal restrictions on union rights
strikes. *See under* labor
subversion, war against, 55, 60–61, 64, 67–68, 75, 91, 95, 151, 155, 235 n. 31, 238 n. 1
supreme court, 58, 233–34 n. 19

telephone workers' union (FOETRA), 65–66, 236 n. 37, 244 n. 36, 245 n. 45
terror, state. *See* subversion, war against
textile workers' union (AOT), 65, 86, 112, 236 n. 37
Thatcher, Margaret, 142
threat, evolving sense of, 73–75
threat prior to coup
  in Argentina, 54, 166, 273 n. 3
  in Brazil, 177–78, 273 n. 3
  in Chile, 171, 173, 273 n. 3
Tosco, Agustín, 52, 68
totalitarianism, defining attributes of, 27
transition, 17–18, 218 n. 10, 223 n. 35. *See also* political-institutional model, and phase of transition;

transition, modes of; transition,
    timing of
transition, modes of
  in Argentina, xxxi, 134, 146–47, 157,
    194–95
  in Brazil, 183–84, 194
  in Chile, 176–77, 194, 276 n. 20
  defined, 20–21
transition, timing of
  in Argentina, 133, 138, 159
  in Brazil, 183–84, 277 n. 34, 278 n. 38
  in Chile, 176–77, 276 n. 20
transport workers' union, 112
Triaca, Jorge, 68, 86, 246 n. 48

Unamuno, Miguel, 55–56
unions. *See under* labor; labor groupings;
    labor sectors; labor under bureaucratic authoritarianism; union social
    service network (Obras Sociales)

union elections. *See* labor, union normalization
union social service network (Obras Sociales), 67, 88, 98, 236–37 n. 41, 252
    n. 77, 256 n. 20, 256–57 n. 25
United States, and Falkland/Malvinas
    Islands war, 142, 262–63 n. 12
Uruguay, as case of bureaucratic authoritarianism, xxiv, 30–31

Vandor, Augusto, 52, 232 n. 8
Videla, Jorge, 50, 54–55, 60, 73, 75, 86,
    94–97, 107, 109, 119–20, 246 n. 48,
    249 n. 67, 249–50 n. 68
Viola, Roberto, 54, 86, 99, 105–8, 114,
    119–29, 134–37, 140, 144–45, 246 n.
    48
  association with labor, 249 n. 67,
    249–50 n. 68, 253 n. 3